JUSTIFICATION

What's at Stake in
the Current Debates

EDITED BY
MARK HUSBANDS
AND DANIEL J. TREIER

InterVarsity Press
Downers Grove, Illinois

Apollos
Leicester, England

InterVarsity Press, USA
P.O. Box 1400, Downers Grove, IL 60515-1426, USA
World Wide Web: www.ivpress.com
E-mail: mail@ivpress.com

APOLLOS (an imprint of Inter-Varsity Press, England)
38 De Montfort Street, Leicester LE1 7GP, England
Website: www.ivpbooks.com
E-mail: ivp@uccf.org.uk

InterVarsity Press®, U.S.A., is the book-publishing division of InterVarsity Christian Fellowship/USA®, a student movement active on campus at hundreds of universities, colleges and schools of nursing in the United States of America, and a member movement of the International Fellowship of Evangelical Students. For information about local and regional activities, write Public Relations Dept., InterVarsity Christian Fellowship/USA, 6400 Schroeder Rd., P.O. Box 7895, Madison, WI 53707-7895, or visit the IVCF website at <www.intervarsity.org>.

Design: Cindy Kiple

Images: John Knill/Digital Vision

USA ISBN 0-8308-2781
UK ISBN 1-84474-027-7

Printed in the United States of America ∞

Library of Congress Cataloging-in-Publication Data

Justification: what's at stake in the current debates/edited by
Mark A. Husbands and Daniel J. Treier.
   p. cm.
Includes bibliographical references.
   ISBN 0-8308-2781-1 (pbk.: alk. paper)
   1. Justification (Christian theology) I. Husbands, Mark, 1961- II.
Treier, Daniel J., 1972-
BT764.3.J86 2004
234'.7—dc22

2003025926

British Library Cataloguing in Publication Data

A catalogue record for this book is available from the British Library.

P	18	17	16	15	14	13	12	11	10	9	8	7	6	5	4	3	2	1
Y	19	18	17	16	15	14	13	12	11	10	09	08	07	06	05	04			

CONTENTS

PART FOUR: JUSTIFICATION AND ECUMENICAL ENDEAVOR

INTRODUCTION

MARK HUSBANDS AND DANIEL J. TREIER

In what sense is the word and action of God's justification of the ungodly a genuinely concrete and present reality?

The conference on "The Gospel, Freedom and Righteousness: The Doctrine of Justification," held in April 2003 at Wheaton College Graduate School, took up the question whether imputed righteousness is fictive, forensic or transformative.

The papers in this volume consider the doctrine of justification from four corresponding points of access: (1) biblical theology; (2) dogmatics in the present Protestant crisis; (3) historical theology, with a view to Lutheran, Anglican, Reformed and Wesleyan understandings; and (4) ecumenical considerations.

Robert Gundry defends his winsomely titled "Why I Didn't Endorse 'The Gospel of Jesus Christ: An Evangelical Celebration'... even though I wasn't asked to" (*Books & Culture* 7, no. 1 [2001]) by arguing exegetically that an imputation of Christ's righteousness is not a valid theological development of biblical teaching. In his essay "The Nonimputation of Christ's Righteousness," Gundry affirms a negative imputation of our sin to Christ, as a propitiatory sacrifice, while understanding that God does not count Christ's righteousness as ours. He argues that it is *our* faith, rather than the righteousness of Christ, that is reckoned by God as the positive basis for righteousness. With a view toward giving substantial weight to the obedient life of the Christian (sanctification), Gundry hopes his views may contribute to satisfying the "legitimate concerns not only of Roman Catholics but also of pietists" (p. 45).

By contrast, "The Vindication of Imputation: On Fields of Discourse and Semantic Fields" by D. A. Carson sets forth an exegetical, semantic and methodological argument to distinguish fields of discourse that bear upon the question of the positive imputation of Christ's righteousness. Against the background of the "new perspective" on Paul and its beginning in the work of Ernst Käsemann, Carson asserts that the meaning of "justification" must be viewed within a "redemptive-historical trajectory" in which God truly acts to justify the ungodly through the death and resurrection of Christ. Carson understands Paul to be saying that Abraham's trust in the promise of God, "reckoned to him as righteousness" (Rom 4:3-5), is itself an unmerited expression of divine grace. While freely granting that no single passage *unambiguously* states such a view, Carson underscores with considerable effect a traditional Protestant commitment to the imputation of Christ's righteousness.

Bruce McCormack's essay "What's at Stake in Current Debates over Justification? The Crisis of Protestantism in the West" shifts the discussion to a sharply focused dogmatic consideration: Nothing less than the Reformation is at stake in the current debate over justification. "The doctrine of justification is *the* doctrine of the Reformation. . . . The idea of an *immediate* divine imputation renders superfluous the entire Catholic system of the priestly mediation of grace by the Church" (pp. 81, 82). McCormack undertakes an historical analysis and close reading of Thomas, Luther and Calvin to assert the initially counterintuitive proposal that to retain the Protestant insight concerning justification we must actually move beyond the Reformation. The Reformation failed to adopt a theological ontology that addressed the *analogia entis* (analogy of being) and concomitant sacramental system of grace operative within Roman Catholicism. McCormack expounds the justifying work and verdict of God within the context of an ontology of the covenant of grace. Not only is it possible, given this position, to maintain the forensicism of a belief in God's declaration as the justification of the ungodly, but a covenant ontology of grace, according to McCormack, illuminates how *as Protestants* we may maintain that justification is both judicial and transformative.

In "Justification and Justice: The Promising *Problematique* of Protestant Ethics in the work of Paul L. Lehmann," Philip Ziegler considers the moral dimension of the doctrine of justification. We find in the primary thrust of Lehmann's moral theology, according to Ziegler, an account of the radical promise of the gospel of justification. Ethics grounded in natural philosophy must be completely redefined in the quest to delineate what kind of moral reflection and action can be called for in the wake of the divine declaration. Lehmann's work is deeply influenced by the kind of moral ontology that McCormack finds so important, and it strives toward nothing less than the Reformation in America. "On Lehmann's view ... moral agency is liberated from all interest and anxiety concerning the achievement or maintenance of its own rectitude. Rather, the sole concern of Christian moral agency is gratefully to witness to the effective course of God's active righteousness in Christ" (p. 129).

Mark Seifrid's essay "Luther, Melancthon and Paul on the Question of Imputation: Recommendations on a Current Debate" turns our focus to the historical development and understanding of justification in the Lutheran, Wesleyan and Anglican traditions as a means of discerning the relative value of exegetical and dogmatic proposals. Seifrid sets Melanchthon's doctrine of justification, in which the contrition of the sinner is an indispensable cause of justification, over against Luther's claim that a person becomes righteous solely by the grace of God and not by virtue or works. The relation of good works to righteousness itself highlights Luther's emphasis upon imputation as a genuinely *effective* rather than a *mere* word of God. According to Seifrid's reading of the doctrine of justification, contemporary evangelicals such as N. T. Wright, Scott Hafemann and John Piper can be placed in the company of Melanchthon, while Seifrid displays his affection for Luther's dynamic account of justification in his affirmation that we have "the Son of God who loved us and delivered himself up for us, only in so far as we know and confess ourselves *hic et nunc* [here and now] to be sinners. All progress in the Christian life is found in returning—as sinners!—to its font and source, the crucified and risen Christ" (pp. 151-52).

Robert Kolb reflects on his participation in the August 2002 International Congress on Luther Research in Copenhagen in his essay "Contemporary Lutheran Understandings of the Doctrine of Justification: A Selective Glimpse." Presenters Simo Peura and Tuoma Mannermaa (leading theologians in the Finnish school of Luther scholarship) are set in contradistinction to the stream of Luther interpretation represented by Wilfried Härle. The first approach, represented also by the work of Robert Jenson and Carl Braaten, argues that Luther's understanding of justification in terms of union with Christ is fittingly captured in the notion of *Vergottung, theosis,* or "divinization"—an ecumenically attractive position even though the historical claim itself has received telling criticism. Härle's presentation at Copenhagen represents, according to Kolb, a distinct and ecumenically important approach to Luther in its own right and bears a family resemblance to the work of Oswald Bayer and Gerhard Forde. The set of exegetical and dogmatic interests embraced by this second stream of Luther interpretation resonates well with a number of other views in this volume. For example, Forde calls for a "radical Lutheran" proclamation of the gospel in which there is a serious engagement with Pauline material on justification *and* the distinct anthropology of Paul's gospel. Similarly, Härle concludes that the "center of Scripture is a living event. Not a doctrine or a doctrinal formulation . . . but what happens in reference to the person of Christ" (p. 166). The radical nature of the gospel means that theology exists in the service of proclamation. In a manner entirely consistent with McCormack's exhortation for evangelicals to recover the tradition of the Reformation, Kolb follows closely the example of Forde and Bayer in capturing the way justification is both "forensic" and "effective." The gospel is God's power or rule in which he gives us "a creative Word which establishes the new reality that this child of God belongs to him and is no longer a sinner because God no longer regards him or her as a sinner. God's view of things, God's Word, determines reality, God stands by his Word, his Word of forgiveness" (p. 168).

Standing in a quite different tradition, Kenneth Collins emphasizes an often neglected facet of the Reformation, namely the events surrounding Canterbury. In "The Doctrine of Justification: Historical Wesleyan and Contemporary Understandings," Collins insists that to see John Wesley as "one of the greatest champions of *sola fide* on English soil" (p. 177) requires an understanding of historical context. Effectively representing the theological significance of Cranmer's composition of the Book of Common Prayer and what eventually came down to us as the Thirty-Nine Articles of Religion, Collins contrasts Cranmer's theology of justification to the reordering of faith and works that emerged in a number of prominent seventeenth-century Caroline divines. All of this, for Collins, is essential for understanding the significance of Wesley's encounter with God under the tutelage of Peter Böhler. One of Wesley's principal emphases was that justification is a sheer unmerited gift of God, apart from human works. Nonetheless, as Collins indicates, Wesley's effective separation of the doctrines of justification and sanctification led to the belief that real, rather than "relative," change in the condition of the soul is found in sanctification rather than justification. Wesley rejects the Calvinist notion of the work of Christ as a formal cause of salvation, according to Collins, in order to account for prevenient grace (in the sense of conscience and a restoration of free will) being given "irresistibly." Collins analyzes Wesley's theological rhetoric to discern the possibility for Wesleyans to affirm both prevenient grace and justification in the Reformational terms of *sola fide*.

Anthony Lane offers a fresh translation of material from the Regensburg Colloquy and a close exposition of its ecumenical significance in "Twofold Righteousness: A Key to the Doctrine of Justification?" Lane attributes the eventual demise of the colloquy not to a specific disagreement on justification but rather to deep and irreconcilable differences on ecclesiology and sacraments; Article 5 on the doctrine of justification is the sole success in an otherwise problematic endeavor. Readers will be interested in the exposition of its guarded reception by the Vatican, Luther and Calvin. Likewise, Lane's extended consideration of a *duplex iustitia* (a twofold righteousness) as the implicit idea of Article 5 sustains his claim that Regensburg's treatment of justification ought not to be seen as a mere "patchwork of two incompatible views" (p. 209). At some distance from a reading of the Protestant tradition represented by McCormack's essay (chapter three), Lane argues that one of the most promising contributions of Regensburg is its conceptual clarity regarding the juxtaposition of inherent and imputed righteousness. In the end, Lane provocatively claims that not only is the Protestant doctrine of justification retained by an appeal to the *duplex iustitia*, but a proper understanding of Regensburg Article 5 offers us a way of more adequately bearing with the tension between contemporary affirmations of the free grace of God, on the one hand, and calls to faithful discipleship, on the other.

In "The Theology of Justification in Dogmatic Context," Paul Molnar (our sole Roman Catholic participant) effects an illuminating conversation between two of the most important theologians of the twentieth century, Karl Rahner and Karl Barth, by mining the inner logic of Rahner's *Theological Investigations* and Barth's *Church Dogmatics*. Over against the otherwise salutary observation that "one of the breakthroughs of the Joint Declaration of 1999 was the fact that the doctrine of justification was placed securely on a scriptural foundation within the context of the Trinity" (p. 225), Molnar sets forth the claim that "any agreement about justification . . . must also be an agreement about theological method, knowledge of God, the incarnation and the resurrection" (p. 227). Precisely this concern leads Molnar to assert that "differences cannot be covered over with ambiguous language" (p. 227). The Lutheran-Catholic Joint Declaration must be regarded as an exhortation for dogmatic clarity in the service of our common love for and reflection upon the gospel.

In the final essay of this volume, "The Ecclesial Scope of Justification," Geoffrey Wainwright explores the ways in which our understanding of the doctrine of justification is as much affected by, as it shapes, our understanding of the church and ecumenical dialogue. Following closely the work of Lesslie Newbigin, who was responsible for negotiating the union (in 1947) of Anglicans, Methodists, Presbyterians and Congregationalists as the united Church of South India, Wainwright elucidates a biblical and dogmatically conceived understanding of justification with potential for ecumenical reconciliation. (I) Our understanding of justification ought to be extended beyond individualist categories to include the ecclesial. (2) This would underscore that justification places the church under a concomitant life of penitence and faith to protect against its driving a wedge between its spiritual and corporeal nature.

Teasing out the main lines of ecumenical discussion on the doctrine of justification in the late twentieth century, Wainwright indicates (without quite stating the matter so) the relative merit of Roman Catholic concerns that a Lutheran understanding of justification might diminish the reality of the church. He shows little sympathy for Eberhard Jüngel's objection that Newbigin's understanding of the church as "foretaste, sign, and instrument," and hence sacrament, of God's saving work—a perspective that enjoys much ecumenical affection—sacrifices the Reformation doctrine of justification.

The essay closes by setting in relief a "free church" Wesleyan reflection on the relationship of justification and the church. By discussing justification within the context of an ecclesial focus upon ecumenical agreement, Wainwright has, among other things, demonstrated the way in which a Protestant focus upon the individual as *simul iustus et peccator* allows for a fitting recognition of the church as *simul sancta et peccatrix*. Likewise, he identifies the degree to which a Catholic focus on the church as starting point sustains appeals to the work of the Spirit and the character of divine grace as the constitutive means by which genuine repentance and renewal may indeed take place.

We hope this brief introduction, and the essays themselves, convey a sense of the stimulating conversation we enjoyed in April 2003, and the apparent need for more on the doctrine of the church. The integrity and interrelationships of our respective theological disciplines (and concomitant biblical theology and dogmatic commitments) and our respective ecclesial traditions were persistently intertwined, and led to the question how we may persist in our particular confessional insights regarding the gospel without denying the propriety (even necessity) of ecumenical endeavor. Biblical scholars Gundry and Carson differ on how to read the theological implications of New Testament texts and assess ecumenical possibilities in their light. Theologians McCormack and Lane seemingly differ in their historical assessments, whereas McCormack and Wainwright differ on assessments of ecumenical documents and the importance of a contemporary Protestant clarion call. Equally challenging is Ziegler's retrieval of Lehmann and Bonhoeffer, which poses for us the self-same question raised by McCormack: Have we in America properly encountered the Reformation? Examples of these intertwined complexities could be multiplied, yet we thank our participants for conducting such provocative conversations with a spirit of warm Christian fellowship.

Beyond them, a word of sincere acknowledgment and gratitude is due to all whose gracious support, assistance and encouragement made the twelfth annual Wheaton Theology Conference, out of which this project arises, possible. Thanks to Amanda Holm and Cindy Ingrum for particular assistance.

Many fine papers were given at the conference, only some of which could appear here in our limited space; we extend thanks to R. Scott Clark, Thomas Finger, Paul C-H. Lim and Fred Sanders for valuable contributions. Likewise, we owe thanks to Dennis Okholm, cofounder of the conference, for committing this task to us as his fourteen Wheaton years came to a close. Meanwhile, fellow theologians at Wheaton provided wise counsel and ongoing support of this work in many ways.

The conference and work of scholarship represented by this volume would simply not happen without the financial assistance of InterVarsity Press and, in particular, the friendly advice of publisher Bob Fryling and our editor, Gary Deddo.

Finally, we express our thanks to the dean of humanities and theological studies, Jill Peláez Baumgaertner, and the chair of the department of Bible, theology, archaeology and world religions, Richard Schultz, for their ongoing care and attention to fostering theological scholarship at Wheaton College.

ABBREVIATIONS

AB	Anchor Bible
BDF	F. Blass, A. Debrunner and R. W. Funk, *A Greek Grammar of the New Testament and Other Early Christian Literature*
Bijdr	*Bijdragen*
BJS	Brown Judaic Studies
BSELK	*Die Bekenntnisschriften der evangelisch-lutherischen Kirche*
CD	*Church Dogmatics*, Karl Barth
CO	*Ioannis Calvini Opera Quae Supersunt Omnia*, ed. G. Baum, E. Cunitz and E. Reuss
CR	Corpus Reformatorum
DCT	*Dictionnaire de Théologie Catholique*, ed. A. Vacant, E. Mangenot et al.
EvT	*Evangelische Theologie*
FCF	*Foundations of the Christian Faith*, Karl Rahner
ICC	International Critical Commentary
JBL	*Journal of Biblical Literature*
JETS	*Journal of the Evangelical Theological Society*
JSNT	*Journal for the Study of the New Testament*
LW	*Luther's Works*, ed. Jaroslav J. Pelikan
MSA	*Melanchthons Werke Studienausgabe*
NICNT	The New International Commentary on the New Testament
NIGTC	New International Greek Testament Commentary
NovTSup	Supplement to *Novum Testamentum*
NSBT	New Studies in Biblical Theology
SNTSMS	Society for New Testament Studies Monograph Series
SWJC	*Selected Works of John Calvin, Tracts*, ed. H. Beveridge
TDNT	*Theological Dictionary of the New Testament*, ed. G. Kittel and G. Friedrich
TI	*Theological Inquiries*
WA	Weimarer Ausgabe = D. Martin Luthers Werke
WABR	Weimarer Ausgabe: Breifwechsel
WATR	Weimarer Ausgabe: Tischreden
WTJ	*Westminster Theological Journal*
WUNT	Wissenschaftliche Untersuchungen zum Neuen Testament

JUSTIFICATION IN
BIBLICAL THEOLOGY

I

THE NONIMPUTATION
OF CHRIST'S RIGHTEOUSNESS

ROBERT H. GUNDRY

This essay grows out of some comments I made on the doctrine of imputation in *Books & Culture* 7, no. 1 (2001): 6-9, and 7, no. 2 (2001): 14-15, 39 and, to a considerable degree, responds to the book-length critique of those comments by John Piper, *Counted Righteous in Christ: Should We Abandon the Imputation of Christ's Righteousness?* (Wheaton, Ill.: Crossway Books, 2002). The response gets its impetus not only from Piper's dealing with my earlier comments but also from the wealth of exegetical argumentation in his book and from its battery of no fewer than twenty-two endorsements, the names of whose authors read almost like a Who's Who in North American evangelicalism (plus one Briton). For the Wheaton College Theology Conference my topic was both assigned and limited to the question of imputation. References below to "public dialogue" have to do with such dialogue at the conference.

The leading Protestant Reformers came to think not only that our sins were imputed to Christ but also that his righteousness is imputed to us who believe in him.[1] The symmetry of such an exchange has proved attractive in systematics; but in biblical theological quarters its second half, the imputation of Christ's righteousness to believers, is losing support—with good scriptural reasons and possibly with a good theological benefit, I will try to show, though I dissociate myself from tendencies sometimes evident in those quarters, such as the tendencies to blur a distinction between declarative righteousness and behavioral righteousness, to inter-

---

[1]See James Buchanan, *The Doctrine of Justification: An Outline of Its History in the Church and of Its Exposition from Scripture* (Edinburgh: T & T Clark, 1867), pp. 131-32, for a brief statement of this classic Protestant doctrine, but also *Diognetus* 9:1-5 for a much earlier version of the doctrine.

pret justification solely in terms of Jewish-Gentile relations in the church, and to enlarge the doctrine of justification into a doctrine of universal salvation. Naturally, my discussion will center on the letters of Paul, where an imputation of Christ's righteousness has been thought present.

The imputation—that is, charging—of our sins to Christ is not in dispute. About that imputation Paul writes explicitly, "In Christ, God was reconciling the world to himself by not counting their trespasses against them. . . . He made the one who did not know sin [to be] sin on our behalf" (2 Cor 5:19-21), and quotes Psalm 32:2 to the same effect: "Blessed is the man whose sin the Lord will not count" (Rom 4:8; cf. 1 Cor 15:3: "Christ died for our sins"). But what about the imputation—that is, crediting—of righteousness? Here are all the New Testament texts that refer explicitly to imputation in relation to righteousness.

- Galatians 3:6; Romans 4:3, 22: "it [Abraham's believing God] was counted for him as righteousness."

- Romans 4:5: "his [the believer's] faith is counted as righteousness."

- Romans 4:6: "the person for whom God counts righteousness apart from works."

- Romans 4:9: "faith was counted for Abraham as righteousness."

- Romans 4:11: "in order that he [Abraham] might be the father of all who believe without being circumcised, in order that righteousness might be counted also for them."

- Romans 4:22-24: "therefore also it [faith] was counted for him [Abraham] as righteousness; but not on account of him alone was it written, 'It was counted for him,' but also on account of us, for whom it is going to be counted, [that is, us] who believe on the one who raised Jesus our Lord from the dead."

But none of these texts says that Christ's righteousness was counted. With the exception of Romans 4:6, 11, which will come up later, they say that Abraham's faith was counted and that our faith is counted, so that righteousness comes into view not as what is counted but as what God counts faith to be. Nor does Paul ascribe this righteousness to Christ; rather, he portrays Christ as the object of faith, for example in Galatians 2:16, "even we believed in (*eis*) Jesus Christ in order that we might be declared righteous."[2]

---

[2]See also Philippians 1:29, "to believe in (*eis*) him [Christ]"; Philemon 5, "the faith that you have toward (*pros*) the Lord Jesus" (cf. Rom 10:9-14; Gal 3:26[?]; Eph 1:15; Col 1:4; 2:5; 1 Tim 3:13;

Those who understand these texts to teach an imputation of Christ's righteousness, alien to sinners, argue on the contrary that Paul's phraseology is shorthand for faith as the *instrument* by which that righteousness is received. An expansive paraphrase might read, "Faith was counted, with the result that Christ's alien righteousness was imputed."[3] To test this understanding we need to examine the way Paul and others elsewhere use the phraseology of "counting as" and "being counted as" (*logizomai eis*, Greek texts without *eis*, "as," being less relevant to our purpose).

All the Pauline texts

- Romans 2:26: "his [a Gentile law-keeper's] uncircumcision will be counted as circumcision, won't it?"

- Romans 9:8: "the children of the promise are counted as seed."

- 2 Corinthians 12:6: "lest anyone count as me more than what he sees me [to be] or [more than] anything he hears from me" (a somewhat literal translation).

All the non-Pauline texts in the New Testament

- Acts 19:27: "that the temple of the great goddess Artemis be counted as nothing."

- James 2:23: "it [Abraham's believing God] was counted for him as righteousness."

Some Greek texts outside the New Testament

- Genesis 15:6 LXX: "he [the Lord] counted it [Abraham's believing in the Lord] for him as righteousness."

- Job 41:24 LXX: "the fathomless deep was counted as a place for walking around."

---

2 Tim 1:13; 3:15). I leave aside the question whether the phrase, "by the faith of Christ" (so a literal translation of the Greek), which occurs in Romans 3:22, 26; Galatians 2:16, 20 (twice); Galatians 3:22; Ephesians 3:12; Philippians 3:9, refers to Christ's faith or faithfulness rather than to faith in him. Among others, see Moisés Silva, "Faith Versus Works of Law in Galatians," in *The Paradoxes of Paul*, vol. 2 of *Justification and Variegated Nomism*, ed. D. A. Carson, Peter T. O'Brien and Mark A. Seifrid (Grand Rapids: Baker, forthcoming), chap. 7, for what seems to me a devastating refutation of this view. But even with the understanding of Christ's faith or faithfulness, it remains that only the faith of Abraham and others like him is said to be counted as righteousness.

[3]See, for example, John Murray, *Redemption—Accomplished and Applied* (Grand Rapids: Eerdmans, 1955), pp. 155-61; Piper, *Counted Righteous in Christ*, p. 57.

- Psalm 105:31 LXX (106:31 in the Hebrew and English numbering): "it [Phinehas's zeal] was counted for him as righteousness."

- I Maccabees 2:52: "and was not it [Abraham's being found faithful when tested; cf. Genesis 22] counted for him as righteousness?"

- Philo *Quis rerum divinarum heres sit* 94: "and it is well said, 'His faith was counted as righteousness for him,' for nothing is so righteous as to put in God alone a pure and unmixed faith."

Some non-Greek texts with similar phraseology

- Genesis 31:15: "are we [Rachel and Leah] not counted by him [Laban] as foreigners?"

- Leviticus 25:31: "the houses of the villages that have no surrounding wall will be counted as open fields."

- Numbers 18:27: "your offering will be counted for you as the grain from the threshing floor or the full produce from the wine vat."

- Numbers 18:30: "when you have offered from it the best of it, then the rest of it [that is, the rest of the offering] will be counted for the Levites as the product of the threshing floor and as the product of the wine vat."

- 2 Samuel 19:19 (19:20 in the Hebrew numbering): "let not my lord count to me iniquity, nor remember what your servant did wrong" (Shimei to David).

- Job 13:24: "why . . . do you count me as your enemy?" (so also Job 19:11; 33:10).

- Job 19:15: "those who live in my house and my maids count me as a stranger."

- Job 41:27: "he counts iron as straw."

- Proverbs 27:14: "it will be counted to him as a curse."

- 4QPseudo-Jubilees[a] (= 4Q225) 2 I: "And Abraham believed God, and righteousness was counted for him."

- *Jubilees* 14:6: "and he [Abraham] believed the LORD and it was counted for him as righteousness" (cf. 31:23).

- *Jubilees* 30:17: "and it [the killing of the Shechemites by two of Jacob's sons] was a righteousness for them, and it was written down for them for righteousness."

- *Jubilees* 35:2: "This thing [the obedience of Jacob to his mother] is . . . a righteousness for me before the LORD."

- 4QMMT 117 (= 4Q398 1 II,4, and 2 II,7): "it will be counted for you as righteousness when you do what is upright and good before him."

Now it is hard. if not impossible, to think that Romans 2:26 presents a Gentile law-keeper's uncircumcision as the instrument by which an alien circumcision is received. Or that Romans 9:8 presents the children of the promise as the instrument by which an alien seed is received. Or that 2 Corinthians 12:6 presents more than what others see in Paul or hear from him as the instrument by which an alien Paul might be received. Or that Acts 19:27 presents Artemis's temple as the instrument by which an alien nothingness might be received. Or that James 2:23 presents Abraham's faith as the instrument by which an alien righteousness was received (for James emphasizes faith as needing the evidence of the believer's own behavioral righteousness[4]). Or that in its context Genesis 15:6 presents Abraham's faith as the instrument by which an alien righteousness was received.[5] Or that Psalm 105(106):31 presents Phinehas's zeal as the instrument by which an alien righteousness was received. Or that 1 Maccabees 2:52 presents Abraham's faithfulness in offering Isaac as the instrument by which an alien righteousness was received. Or that 4QMMT 117 presents upright, good behavior as the instrument by which an alien righteousness is received.

In none of these cases does an instrumental interpretation make good contextual sense. In most of them it makes absolute nonsense, as the foregoing gobbledygook shows. And in all of them the counting results in an *identification* of what is counted with what it is counted as, not in the introduction of something to be distinguished from what is counted—hence the propriety of translating the Greek preposition *eis* with "as" when used in conjunction with *logizomai*, "count."[6] Paul's parallel use of *hōs*, regularly translated "as," with *logizomai*, confirms this usage (Rom 8:36; I Cor 4:1; 2 Cor 10:2; so also Num 18:27, 30 and Job 41:24[27] in the LXX). As intimated before, "counted *to be*" would also convey the intended meaning,[7] *and this*

---

[4]"This faith-completed-by-works *is* righteousness and naturally is reckoned as such" (J. A. Ziesler, *The Meaning of Righteousness in Paul: A Linguistic and Theological Enquiry* [SNTSMS 20; Cambridge: Cambridge University Press, 1972], p. 132, italics original).

[5]Here and below, those who distinguish between context as the situation in which something is spoken or written and cotext as the language that surrounds a particular expression or passage and helps determine its meaning may substitute "cotext(ual)" for "context(ual)."

[6]As any Greek lexicon indicates, *eis* has a variety of meanings determined in part by context.

[7]Often *logizomai* occurs without an *eis*-phrase and means "consider to be," as in Romans 3:28, for example: "for we consider a person to be justified by faith apart from works of the law" (see the Greek lexicons).

counting to be occurs whether or not what is counted is intrinsically what it is counted to be.

In *Jubilees* 30:17 the killing of the Shechemites is counted to be righteousness because by the author's lights (though in disagreement with Gen 34:30; 49:5-7) it was intrinsically righteous. So also Phinehas's zeal in Psalm 105(106):31 (in agreement with Num 25:6-13). But in Romans 2:26 a Gentile law-keeper's uncircumcision will be counted as circumcision even though it is not. In Acts 19:27 the temple of Artemis is in danger of being counted as nothing even though in the opinion of the speaker it is a wonder of the world.[8] In Job 41:24 LXX the watery depths are counted as terra firma even though they are not. In Genesis 31:15 Laban counts his daughters as foreigners even though they are not foreign to him. In Leviticus 25:31 the law counts houses in unwalled villages as open fields even though they are not. In Numbers 18:27, 30 the law counts offerings as the whole of a harvest or vintage even though they are only a small part of it. And in 2 Samuel 19:19 Shimei asks David not to count him guilty even though he is in fact guilty. The lack of any reference in Galatians 3 and Romans 4 to Christ's righteousness confirms this linguistic conclusion that the counting of faith as righteousness is *not* shorthand for faith as the instrument by which an alien righteousness—Christ's—is received.[9] (Note that the counting of faith as righteousness is no less forensic than a counting of Christ's righteousness would be.)

To get around the plain and simple meaning of Paul's language, advocates of the instrumental view may argue that faith includes its object, in this instance Christ and therefore his righteousness. Faith is only as good as its object—true, so that the faith which God counts as righteousness requires Christ as its object. But the object of God's counting is faith in Christ, not Christ as the object of faith. To in-

---

[8]Cf. Antipater the epigrammist, *Greek Anthology* 9.58: "I have set eyes on the wall of lofty Babylon, on which is a road for chariots; and the statue of Zeus by the Alpheus; and the hanging gardens; and the colossus of the Sun; and the huge labor of the high pyramids; and the vast tomb of Mausolus. But when I saw the house of Artemis that mounted to the clouds, those other marvels lost their brilliance; and I said, 'Lo, apart from Olympus, the Sun never looked on anything so grand.' "
[9]On the linguistic evidence, see also Ziesler, *Meaning of Righteousness in Paul*, pp. 180-85, though he does not concern himself with the question of instrumentality. James Hervey draws an analogy between hyssop as the instrument of purgation in David's prayer, "Purge me with hyssop" (Ps 51:7), and faith as the instrument of the imputation of Christ's righteousness, but overlooks that David does not say that hyssop is counted as purgation as Paul says faith is counted as righteousness (*Aspasio Vindicated and the Scripture Doctrine of Imputed Righteousness Defended, in eleven letters from Mr. Hervey to Mr. John Wesley, in answer to that gentleman's remarks on Theron and Aspasio. With Mr. Wesley's letter prefixed. To which is annexed, A Defence of Theron and Aspasio, against the objections contained in Mr. Sandeman's letters on Theron and Aspasio. With Mr. Hervey's letters to the Author prefixed* [London: R. Aiken & Son, 1794], p. 123).

clude Christ in the faith that God counts as righteousness would be to confuse the object of faith with faith as the object of imputation or, more simply, to confuse faith with its object.

It might be asked whether an instrumental view of faith is necessary to the doctrine of an imputed righteousness of Christ. Yes, it is, because all Paul's language of imputation involves faith (even the two statements in Rom 4:6, 11 that speak of righteousness as counted occur in a passage heavily oriented to faith); and if—given an imputation of Christ's righteousness—faith too were correctly taken to be counted as righteousness rather than as instrumental toward it, the imputed righteousness that consists in faith would imply an insufficiency in the imputed righteousness of Christ. Not an attractive implication!

Paul writes that a wage is counted and since a wage is external to a person whereas faith is internal to a person, it is argued—again on the contrary—that faith must not be counted but must rather be instrumental toward the counting of something external like a wage though in other respects different from a wage, namely, the righteousness of Christ. But this argument neglects the switch away from the counting of a wage "not *according to* grace but *according to* debt"—a wage being paid to eliminate a debt and therefore not equivalent to a debt (Rom 4:4)—over to faith's being counted "*as* righteousness," that is, as equivalent to righteousness. Besides, the contrast between external and internal is being imposed on the text. Paul makes nothing of such a contrast.

But it is asked, "Would he not rather say something like, 'Now to him who works, his works are credited as (= treated as) his righteousness according to debt'" if he means that faith as the counterpart of a wage is counted as righteousness?[10] The answer is no, because in the matter of justification Paul does not want even to suggest that God credits works as righteousness. So Paul avoids the crediting of works, writes instead about the counting of a wage, and thus gains a contrast with the already mentioned and now echoed "grace" by which believers are "justified as a gift" (Rom 3:24; see also Rom 4:16; 5:2, 15-17, 20—6:1 for ongoing references to this grace). The contrast backs up Paul's immediately foregoing assertion that before God, Abraham has nothing to boast about (Rom 4:2).

Theologically it is objected that a straightforward counting of faith as righteousness not only gives righteousness an internal human origin rather than an external divine one but also makes faith a work of righteousness and thereby puts justifica-

---

[10]Piper, *Counted Righteous in Christ*, p. 56.

tion on a synergistic rather than solely gracious basis.[11] But insofar as Reformed soteriology takes faith to be a gift of God, the objection sounds hollow.[12] And this
view of faith as a gift has Pauline support: "for Christ's sake it was graciously given
you . . . to believe in him" (Phil 1:29); "faith [comes] from hearing [or 'what is
heard'] and hearing [or 'what is heard'] through the word of Christ" (Rom 10:17);
"God has allotted to each [of you] an allotment of faith" (Rom 12:3).[13]

If we were to assign to faith a human origin, or to the extent that to preserve the
element of human responsibility we were to assign to faith a human origin,[14] it
would remain that Paul emphatically puts faith and works in opposing categories:
"But to the one who works the wage is not counted according to grace, but according to debt; and to the one who does not work but believes on the one who justifies
the ungodly, his faith is counted as righteousness, just as David mentions the blessedness of the person for whom God counts righteousness apart from works" (Rom
4:4-6; see also Rom 3:27-28). In other words, Paul rejects the Jewish tradition that
God counted Abraham's faith as righteousness because it was a work (a good one,
of course).[15] Paul rejects this tradition, not by making faith the instrument by
which Christ's righteousness is received, but by saying that God counted Abraham's
faith as righteousness even though it was not a work. For "in believing [which by
its nature is trusting], Abraham did not work, but let God work."[16] Therefore the
charge of synergism does not stick. Moreover, the antithetical parallel between faith
and works militates against an instrumental view of faith, for works are not instrumental in the reception of one's own righteousness (cf. Rom 10:3, "their own
righteousness," and Phil 3:9, "my own righteousness"). That kind of righteousness

---

[11]Murray, *Redemption—Accomplished and Applied*, pp. 159-60.

[12]Piper (*Counted Righteous in Christ*, p. 125) writes that Christ "sovereignly works faith . . . in us," yet
makes the objection. So also Buchanan, *Doctrine of Justification*, p. 387.

[13]Cf. 1 Corinthians 15:10; Ephesians 2:8; Philippians 2:12-13; 3:12; 1 Thessalonians 2:13. Of
course, God does not believe for us, so that believing is a human activity even in Reformed soteriology. On the question of synergism, therefore, an imputation of Christ's righteousness on the basis
of faith offers no advantage over the counting of faith as righteousness.

[14]Cf. Han-soo Lee, "Biblical, Theological Reflections on the Tension between Divine Sovereignty and
Human Responsibility in Paul's Letters," *Chongshin Theological Journal* 6 (2001): 50-72.

[15]For references to ancient Jewish literature in this regard, see Ziesler, *Meaning of Righteousness in Paul*, pp.
43, 103-4, 109, 123, 125-26, 175, 182-83; C. E. B. Cranfield, *The Epistle to the Romans*, ICC (Edinburgh: T & T Clark, 1975, 1979), 1:229.

[16]Mark A. Seifrid, *Christ, Our Righteousness: Paul's Theology of Justification* (Downers Grove, Ill.: InterVarsity
Press, 2000), p. 68; see also the comments on Genesis 15:6 by Gerhard von Rad, "Faith Reckoned
as Righteousness," in *The Problem of the Hexateuch and Other Essays* (New York: McGraw-Hill, 1966), p.
129.

consists in works. Likewise, what God counts as righteousness consists in faith.

Does God's counting of righteousness in Romans 4:6, 11 differ from the counting of faith in the surrounding passage so as to make righteousness *rather than* faith the object of counting, and faith the instrument toward the counting of righteousness? Again no, for grammatically Paul makes faith an object of counting just as he makes righteousness its object. The conclusion to draw is that God counts both faith and righteousness because he counts them as identical to each other.

For us, then, justification is both negative and positive. Negatively, God does not count our sins against us. Jesus took them away. Positively, God counts our faith as righteousness. These complementary elements suffice to eliminate any exegetical need to import into Romans 4 an unmentioned righteousness of Christ—and also any pastoral need to do so for the healing of Christians' hurting consciences.

It is further objected, however, that since the first three chapters of Romans feature *God's* righteousness (Rom 1:17; 3:5, 21, 22, 25, 26), the righteousness in Romans 4 can hardly consist in anything so human as faith. But whatever the meaning of God's righteousness (on which see below), Romans 4 substitutes "the righteousness of faith" for "the righteousness of God" (Rom 4:11, 13; cf. 9:30; 10:6); and in view of the linguistically demonstrated fact that according to Romans 4 God counts faith as righteousness, "the righteousness of faith" in this same chapter must mean yet again the righteousness which by God's counting consists in faith. Similarly, the righteousness that comes "from" *(ek)* faith (Rom 9:30; 10:6) and from God "through" *(dia)* faith and "on the basis of" *(epi)* faith (Phil 3:9) is the faith that God counts as righteousness. Paul's language is supple: faith is the origin, the means, and the basis of righteousness in that God counts it as righteousness.[17]

Similarly once more, believing has "the result of righteousness" according to Romans 10:10 in the sense that God counts faith as righteousness. The notion that the use of *eis* to indicate a result demands an alien righteousness, that of Christ, does not pass muster. Since for Paul faith is not a work—that is, not intrinsically righteous—God's counting faith as righteousness agrees perfectly well with righteousness as the result of faith. And the argument that in the parallel clause of Romans 10:10 confession does not *consist* in salvation but only *results* in salvation fails

---

[17]Cf. Hebrews 11:7 "[Noah] became heir of the righteousness according to faith." Murray (*Redemption—Accomplished and Applied*, p. 155) argues that faith is not counted as righteousness, because Paul never says justification is "on account of" or "because of" faith; rather, "by," "through" and "upon" faith. But at least *epi*, "on the basis of," amounts to what Murray calls for.

to consider Paul's earlier use of the verb of counting with righteousness but not with salvation.[18]

So far the discussion has revolved around the technical term for counting, *logizomai*. But another term used in connection with justification may be synonymous. That is the verb *kathistēmi*, "establish," in Romans 5:19: "For just as through the disobedience of the one man [Adam] the many were established [as] sinful, in this way also through the obedience of the one [man Jesus Christ] the many will be established [as] righteous." The verb means to establish physically by way of bringing, conducting or taking, or to establish nonphysically by way of appointment, ordination or making. It is particularly the frequent use of this verb for appointing that may be synonymous with counting, because to be appointed as this or that means to be counted as such. Therefore Romans 5:19 could mean that through Adam's disobedience human beings were counted as sinful, and through Christ's obedience (that is, righteousness) human beings will be counted as righteous.

This meaning is favored by Paul's using "justify" in the sense of "declaring righteous." So let us ask, how will Christ's obedience enable sinners to be declared, counted or established as righteous? By the imputation of that obedience or by some other means? Paul did not bring Christ's obedience into the discussion of imputation in Romans 4 (or in Gal 3). But he did indicate in Romans 3:21-31 that it is the propitiatory death of Christ, represented by his blood, which enables God to be righteous even in declaring righteous those sinners who exercise faith, *which declaration Paul proceeds to explain in Romans 4 as God's counting their faith as righteousness*. So in Romans 5:19 the obedience of Christ refers again to his submission to that propitiatory death (as also in Phil 2:8: "by becoming obedient to the extent of death, even the death of a cross"), which death enables God to be righteous when he declares sinners to be righteous by counting their faith as righteousness.[19]

---

[18]Against Piper, *Counted Righteous in Christ*, p. 62.

[19]Declaring sinners righteous by counting their faith as righteousness is not to be merged with making them behaviorally righteous by the infusion of righteousness. Some think that according to Romans 3:26 God is righteous *in that* he justifies sinners who believe, rather than that justifying them does not contradict his righteousness (so Sam K. Williams, "The 'Righteousness of God' in Romans," *JBL* 99 [1980]: 277-78; cf. Cyril Blackman, "Romans 3 26b: A Question of Translation," *JBL* 87 [1968]: 203-4; Douglas A. Campbell, *The Rhetoric of Righteousness in Romans 3.21–26* [JSNTSup 65; Sheffield: Sheffield Academic Press, 1992], pp. 166-70). But this view overlooks the background of God's wrath against the unrighteousness of human beings, of Christ's propitiation, of God's passing over the sins committed earlier and, in the Old Testament, of God's not justifying the wicked (Ex 23:7; cf. Prov 17:15; Is 5:23).

To the contrary, and in support of counting Christ's righteousness as ours, appeal is made to the parallel Paul draws between Christ's obedience and Adam's disobedience. So the further question has to be asked, how did Adam's disobedience establish people as sinful? By the imputation of that disobedience or by some other means? This question moves us backward to Romans 5:12-18. The passage starts with statements that "sin entered the world" through Adam, that death entered the world "through sin," and that death spread to all human beings "in this way" (not "so" in the inferential sense of "therefore," which the underlying Greek word does not bear). "In this way" means that death spread to all human beings "through sin."

Paul then identifies more expansively the ground on which death spread to all human beings.[20] It is that "all have sinned." Does this statement mean Adam's sin counted as everybody's sin, so that we should infer God's imputing the original sin of Adam to all Adam's descendants? One might think so from I Corinthians 15:22, "For just as in Adam all are dying," by reasoning that since death is the consequence of sin, dying in Adam entails having sinned in Adam. But dying in Adam does not mean that Adam's death counted as everybody's death, for Paul does not use the past tense, "In Adam all died." He uses the present tense, "In Adam all are dying." So dying in Adam means dying one's own death as a consequence of one's own sinning, which resulted in turn from sin's having entered the world through Adam.

"All have sinned" in Romans 5:12 echoes "all have sinned" in Romans 3:23, where the statement summarizes Paul's preceding delineation of the manifold sins committed by human beings throughout history, with nary a word about Adam's original sin (Rom 1:18—3:20); and Paul refers to "our transgressions" (plural) in Romans 4:25 and to "*many* transgressions" right here in Romans 5:16. All Paul's other uses of the verb "sin" also refer to human beings' sinning for themselves.[21] But John Murray argues that Romans 5:12 cannot refer to such sinning, because infants die without having sinned for themselves.[22] Alongside

---

[20]See T. L. Carter, *Paul and the Power of Sin: Redefining "Beyond the Pale,"* SNTSMS 115 (Cambridge: Cambridge University Press, 2002), pp. 170-73, for translating *eph' hō* in Romans 5:12 with "inasmuch as."

[21]See Romans 2:12; 5:14, 16; 6:15; I Corinthians 6:18; 7:28, 36; 8:12; 15:34; Ephesians 4:26; I Timothy 5:20; Titus 3:11.

[22]John Murray, *The Imputation of Adam's Sin* (Phillipsburg, N.J.: Presbyterian and Reformed, 1959), p. 10; Murray, *The Epistle to the Romans*, NICNT (Grand Rapids: Eerdmans, 1959), 1:183.

infants other theologians add mentally deficient youth and adults. To sustain this argument it is necessary to think that "all have sinned" in Romans 3:23 at least includes a reference to the sinning of infants and the mentally deficient together with that of everybody else in Adam's original sin. Yet this inclusion so over-shoots the context of Romans 3:23—the context of manifold sins—that one may detect some embarrassment in Murray's comment on that verse: "it would not be defensible *to restrict* the reference to the sin of Adam and the involvement of posterity therein."[23] Paul's emphasis on the lack of distinction between Jews and Greeks in the matter of sin, however (see especially Rom 2:9; 3:9, 22-23 but also the whole of 1:18—3:23), shows that "all" means Jews and Gentiles alike, the question of mental capacity not in view.

Further showing that "all have sinned" in Romans 5:12 does not mean God imputed Adam's original sin to the rest of the human race is an immediately following explanation, introduced with the conjunction "for," concerning the sinning of people before the law was given, that is, during the period between Adam and Moses (Rom 5:13-14). These people's sinning "not after the like-ness of Adam's transgression" shows that Paul distinguishes their sins from Adam's original sin and attributes their sins to the presence of sin in the world due to its *entrance* through Adam. So "all have sinned" means that under the in-fluence of sin all have sinned for themselves, not that they sinned in the original sin of Adam.

The reference to people's sinning between Adam and Moses temporarily inter-rupts the comparison begun in Romans 5:12 ("On account of this, just as . . ."; see Rom 5:15 for its resumption: "But not as . . . , in this way also . . ."). Does this interruption arise from a fear that "all have sinned" in Romans 5:12 would be *mis-understood* in terms of all individuals' sinning for themselves, so that it would follow naturally but erroneously that "through Jesus Christ, righteousness and life entered the world, and life spread to all *because all individually did acts of righteousness*"?[24] Cer-tainly Paul wants to avoid self-righteousness, but because it would contradict Ro-mans 1:18—3:20 ("There is no righteous person, not even one" in Rom 3:10, for example), not because he wants Romans 5:12 to be understood differently from Romans 3:23, that is, in terms of an imputation of Adam's sin.

Sin got its start, then, in the original sin, which consisted in a transgression

---

[23]Murray, *Romans*, I:112, italics added.
[24]So Piper, *Counted Righteous in Christ*, pp. 92-93, italics original.

of God's stated command not to eat from the tree of the knowledge of good and evil. Since the law, consisting in stated commands as distinct from the compunctions of conscience (cf. Rom 2:14-15 with Rom 1:32), was not given till much later, sins committed during the intervening period were unlike Adam's sin in that they did not consist in transgressions which would have been entered as debits on an account (cf. Rom 4:15), but consisted in slavish service to sin as a dominating force.[25] Likewise death, having entered the world through Adam's transgression, ruled illegally, so to speak; death usurped power outside the law or, rather, before the law. "The many died by the transgression of one" in that through Adam's transgression death, like sin, entered the world as a force to which people fell subject in their own sinning. Then it turns out in Romans 5:18 that Adam's "transgression" in Eden contrasts not only with the sins committed between him and Moses but also with Christ's "act of righteousness." The contrast between Adam's sin and the sins committed between him and Moses has to do with a freely chosen transgression versus servitude. The contrast between Adam's sin and Christ's act of righteousness has to do with disobedience versus obedience.[26]

Romans 5:16-21 also speaks of righteousness as a gift that originated in abundant grace and came by way of Christ's act of righteousness, and of grace as

---

[25]So also Seifrid, *Christ, Our Righteousness*, p. 70 n. 91, though Seifrid follows Theodor Zahn's understanding of *eph' hō* in Romans 5:12: "under which circumstance."

[26]Because Paul excoriates Gentiles for violating what they know to be God's righteous requirement (Rom 1:32) and for doing so apparently from earliest times, not just after the law was given through Moses (see the entirety of Rom 1:18–3:20), some interpreters identify those who sinned and died between Adam and Moses as a subset of the general population, namely (as in the similar interpretation of Rom 3:23; 5:12, discussed above), infants who died too young to have known God's righteous requirement and therefore died because God imputed to them Adam's transgression—likewise in regard to mentally deficient youth and adults. Because it takes a Sherlock Holmes to detect here any reference to infants and the mentally deficient, this interpretation smacks of desperation to save the passage for an imputation of Adam's sin. The interpretation also underestimates Paul's seeing the promulgation of the Mosaic law as inaugurating a new, though now outmoded, dispensation of legal demands (Rom 4:13-15; 5:20; Gal 3:17-19, 23-25). Piper (*Counted Righteous in Christ*, pp. 100-101 n. 44) argues that "even" in the phrase "even over the ones who did not sin after the likeness of Adam's transgression" (Rom 5:14) "implies . . . a special and particular class of sinners, not all sinners before Moses." But Paul's "even" more naturally emphasizes the whole of those who sinned apart from the law between Adam and Moses, as distinguished from Adam and from those who transgressed the law after it was given. I say "more naturally" because it is very uncertain—as Piper's self-confessed wrestling shows—what subset Paul might be referring to if he is indeed referring to a subset (cf. Murray's finding it "difficult to determine" whom Rom 5:13-14 has in view [*Imputation of Adam's Sin*, p. 10]).

reigning. Since Romans 3:24; 4:4-5, 16 associated righteousness with grace and since the whole of Romans 4 defines righteousness as the faith that God graciously counts as righteousness, the gracious gift of righteousness in Romans 5:16-21 must consist in God's counting faith as righteousness rather than in Christ's act of righteousness, which made possible such a counting.[27] The language of giving and receiving a gift, though it would be compatible with imputation, neither demands nor favors it. In Acts 5:31; 10:43, for example, forgiveness of sins is given and received through Christ but not imputed; for he did not sin, was not forgiven, and therefore had no forgiveness that could be imputed to others. Paul puts in parallel Adam's transgression and Christ's act of righteousness, then, not in that both have been imputed but in that both have occasioned the entry into the world of reigning forces: sin and death on the one hand, life-giving grace on the other hand.

Later, Paul will say that the wages of sin is death in contrast with eternal life as God's gift in Christ Jesus (Rom 6:23). But neither there do we find the language of imputation. For sin is portrayed throughout Romans 6:12-23 as a slave master, so that death is not the wages you get paid *for* sinning; rather, death is the wages you get paid *by* sin. Just as God is the giver of eternal life, not its cause, so in this passage sin is the paymaster of death, not its cause. Which fact brings us back to Romans 5:12-14, where sin entered the world and death entered the

---

[27]Piper (*Counted Righteous in Christ*, pp. 105-6) argues that since the free gift results in a sentence of justification (*eis dikaiōma*—Rom 5:16), the two cannot be equated, so that the free gift consists in Christ's righteousness as the basis of that sentence. But since the free gift is admittedly "the gift of righteousness" (Rom 5:17) and, as explained above, harks back to God's counting faith as righteousness, it is this counting that constitutes the free gift and results in a sentence of justification. Besides, only a whisper of difference distinguishes "judgment" (*krima*) from its result, "condemnation" (*katakrima*, literally, "judgment against"), so that it is wrong to press the parallel difference between "the free gift" and its result, "a sentence of justification" (see Rom 5:18 as well as Rom 5:16). I reject a distinction between "righteousness" in Romans 5:17 as a gracious gift and "the righteousness of God" in Romans 3:3-8; 4:9-25 (cf. Rom 9—11) as his faithfulness to the Jews and to "all the families of the earth" in accord with the Abrahamic covenant (Gen 12:1-3). For in Romans 3:21-26 Paul explains "the righteousness of God" in terms of our "being justified as a *gift* by his *grace*" (against Williams, "The 'Righteousness of God' in Romans," p. 259). Agreed, Paul puts God's righteousness in parallel with God's faithfulness and truthfulness; but Paul defines the means by which God keeps his promise to Abraham as the counting of Abraham-like faith to be righteousness. When Paul wants to emphasize the grace of God in such counting, he portrays God's righteousness as a gift. But this emphasis does not characterize all passages dealing with the righteousness of God, so that it does not cut ice to ask, how can one submit to a gift of righteousness any more than to a gift of some other kind? (Ibid.; see Rom 10:3 for just such a submission.)

world "through sin," not "because of sin." Whatever the rest of Scripture says about death as the penalty for sinning, here the entry of sin and death to take dominion exhibits the apocalyptic language of personified forces, not of penalty or of imputation, so that the sinning and dying of people between Adam and Moses were the effects of sin and death as forces (cf. Gal 2:17, where sin functions as someone to whom service is rendered; Gal 3:22, where sin functions as a prison warden; and Rom 1:17, where Paul launches his discussion of justification with the language of apocalyptic: "for in it ['the gospel'] the righteousness of God is being revealed *[apokalyptetai]*"). This language, plus that of grace as reigning, shows that Paul does *not* delay such personifications till Romans 6, where they are generally recognized. In fact, sin appeared as a personified force as early as Romans 3:9, where the statement that "all are under sin" means in context that sin dominates them in that God has given them over to it.[28] With the giving of the law, of course, the legal framework of transgression and penalty comes in alongside the framework of personified forces, so that Paul's question in Romans 6:1 whether we should sin in order that grace may abound implies a false legalistic argument just as by common consent the further part of Romans 6, particularly verses 12-23, and Romans 7, particularly verses 7-25, reprise the language of personified forces.[29]

Those who advocate an imputation of Christ's righteousness usually regard the crucifixion as "the *climax* of his atoning sufferings" and "the *climax* of a perfect life of righteousness."[30] Thus the righteousness of Christ includes his law-abiding obe-

---

[28]See especially Romans 1:24, 26, 28; against Piper, *Counted Righteous in Christ*, pp. 100-101 n. 44. Douglas J. Moo (*The Epistle to the Romans*, NICNT [Grand Rapids: Eerdmans, 1996], p. 319) details the active role of sin as a dominating force in Romans 5–7: sin not only enters the world (Rom 5:12) but also reigns (Rom 5:21; cf. 6:13-14), gains obedience (Rom 6:16-17), pays wages (Rom 6:23), seizes opportunity (Rom 7:8, 11), and deceives and kills (Rom 7:11, 13). See also Chris Forbes, "Paul's Principalities and Powers: Demythologizing Apocalyptic?" *JSNT* 82 (2001): 61-88, esp. pp. 72-74, with further bibliography; J. Louis Martyn, *Galatians: A New Translation and Commentary*, AB 33A (New York: Doubleday, 1997), pp. 272-73, 308-9, 317, 388-89, 536-37, for similar personifications in Galatians; and Revelation 20:14 for an example of personifications in apocalyptic ("Death and Hades were cast into the lake of fire").

[29]On the tension in one and the same document between sin as a personified force and sin as a responsible act of the human will, see John K. Riches, "Conflicting Mythologies: Mythical Narration in the Gospel of Mark," *JSNT* 84 (2001): 29-50.

[30]Piper, *Counted Righteous in Christ*, pp. 41-42, italics added. Much more fully, see Albrecht Ritschl, *A Critical History of the Christian Doctrine of Justification and Reconciliation* (Edinburgh: Edmonston and Douglas, 1872), pp. 213-14, 248-67 et passim. But Ritschl surveys the doctrine from a systematic theological rather than biblical exegetical standpoint.

dience prior to and in addition to his obedient submission to crucifixion.[31] But a number of data show not only that Christ's "act of righteousness" (Rom 5:18) equates with his "obedience" (Rom 5:19) but also that the act of righteousness consisted in obeying God the Father to the extent of dying on a cross and did not include the totality of Christ's earthly life:

- the parallel with Philippians 2:8, where the obedience of Christ is tied specifically to his death on a cross, not to his preceding life on earth or even to his incarnation[32]

- the references earlier in Romans 5 to Christ's dying for the ungodly, dying for us while we were still sinners, shedding his blood for our justification and reconciling us to God through his death (Rom 5:6-11)

- the absence of any contextual indication that Christ's obedience included a previous life of obedience to the law

- the failure of Paul, despite his extensive discussions of the law and writing that Christ was born "under the law" (Gal 4:4), ever to make a point of Christ's keeping the law perfectly or on our behalf (not even his sinlessness in 2 Cor 5:21 being put in relation to law-keeping)

---

[31] The technical terms are "active obedience" and "passive obedience," respectively; but these are not meant to be distinguished chronologically, for the active obedience is thought to run through the crucifixion, and the passive obedience to start at the incarnation. A systematic theological objection is lodged that to exclude an imputation of Christ's active obedience leaves the door open for the introduction of believers' own obedience as the only ground for hope after obtaining the remission of past sins (Buchanan, *Doctrine of Justification*, p. 189, in reference to the teaching of Piscator). But whether or not the active obedience of Christ is imputed, why should his death suffice only for past sins, those committed prior to conversion?

[32] In Phil 2:5-11 Christ's emptying himself by taking the form of a slave implies obedience, but refers solely to his death in that "he emptied himself" is a Greek way of echoing what Isaiah 53:12 says about the suffering Servant—that is, Slave—of the LORD: "he poured out his soul unto death." "He emptied" echoes "he poured out." "Himself" echoes "his soul," which is the Semitic equivalent of a reflexive pronoun (cf. 1 Tim 2:6 with Is 53:10; Mk 10:45 par. Mt 20:28). Paul delays Isaiah's "unto death" for incorporation in the statement, "he humbled himself by becoming obedient unto death, even the death of a cross," crucifixion being called in the Roman world "a slave's death." So the incarnation is expressed, not in the self-emptying phrase but in the phrases "having come to be in the likeness of human beings" and "having been found in fashion as a human being"; and these phrases simply represent the precondition of obedience unto death (cf. Heb 2:10, 14-18, esp. v. 14: "Therefore, since the children have shared in blood and flesh, in the same way he himself also partook of the same that through death he might render impotent him who had the power of death, that is, the devil"; see Robert H. Gundry, "Style and Substance in 'The Myth of God Incarnate' According to Philippians 2:6-11," in *Crossing the Boundaries: Essays in Honour of Michael D. Goulder*, ed. D. E. Orton and S. E. Porter [Leiden: E. J. Brill, 1994], pp. 273-93, and Wesley's letter to Hervey, dated October 15, 1756, as quoted in Hervey, *Aspasio Vindicated*, pp. xiv-xv).

- the extremely scant attention that Paul pays elsewhere to Christ's previous life in any respect

- the extremely heavy emphasis that Paul does lay elsewhere on the death of Christ

- the present antithetical parallel with Adam's transgression, which hardly refers to a whole life of sinning but refers instead to the original sin in Eden, the only sin of Adam mentioned in Scripture

- the probable singularizing of both Adam's transgression and Christ's act of righteousness by the modifier "one"

This last datum requires elaboration, because a number of commentators translate the relevant phrases in Romans 5:18 "through one's [Adam's] transgression" and "through one's [Christ's] act of righteousness" rather than "through one transgression" and "through one act of righteousness." In favor of "one's" it is argued that the whole passage deals with a comparison between the two individuals Adam and Christ, that "one" refers to Adam and Christ a number of times in Romans 5:12, 15-17, 19, and that in Romans 5:18 "one's" would strengthen the contrast with "all people" (twice) in the same verse and in Romans 5:12, and with "the many" in Romans 5:15 (twice) and 19 (twice). In Romans 5:18, on the other hand, "one" lacks the definite article that it has when referring to Adam and Christ in Romans 5:15, 17, 19 and does not modify "man" as it does in Romans 5:12, 15, 19. Moreover, when in Romans 5:15, 17, 19 "one" refers to Adam in connection with his "transgression" or "disobedience," and to Christ in connection with his "grace" or "obedience," "one" always has the definite article.[33] The absence of definite articles with "one" in Romans 5:18 therefore favors that "one" modifies "transgression" and "act of righteousness," and this construal makes for an expansion of "one transgression" to the "many transgressions" in Romans 5:16 and to the multiplication of sin in Romans 5:20, and for a contrastive expansion of "one act of righteousness" to "abundance" of grace in Romans 5:15 and to the "superabundance" of grace in Romans 5:20. All in all, then, this datum and the other data belie the notion that God imputes to believers a righteousness of Christ that he built up over a lifetime of obedience to God and the law; and it would be odd for the righteousness that believers do gain to be described as "*of*" God if it consists of Christ's obedience *to* God.

---

[33]"One" lacks the definite article in Romans 5:12 because there is no previous reference to the man Adam. Romans 5:16 is only a partial exception, if an exception at all, because as a participle "having sinned" modifies "one" directly rather than governing a genitive, as in "the transgression *of* the one," "the grace *of* the one man," and so on.

According to a counter argument, Paul makes no distinction between Christ's prior life of obedience and his propitiatory death. But Paul's putting Christ's act of righteousness in parallel with Adam's single act of disobedience and probably limiting the act of obedience to "one" make precisely that distinction. It is then argued that there were "many acts of obedience in Jesus' final days and hours," such as "the obedience of Gethsemane, or the obedience when the mob took him away, or the obedience when he was interrogated, [and so forth]."[34] But we are dealing with Paul, not with the Gospels; and he writes about one act of obedience, not about many acts of obedience during the passion, much less about prior acts of obedience. Moreover, "a unified act involving many acts of obedience"[35] would make a poor parallel with Adam's initial, solitary act of disobedience.[36]

To be sure, *dikaiōma*, translated "act of righteousness" in Romans 5:18 and "righteous requirement" in Romans 8:4 (also in Rom 1:32), may be collective in Romans 8:4 for all the requirements of the law. But that collective meaning is unsure, even unlikely, for Paul writes in Galatians 5:14 that "the whole law is fulfilled in *one* command, 'You shall love your neighbor as yourself.' "[37] Even if *dikaiōma* is collective in Romans 8:4, there it is not modified by "one" as it probably is in Romans 5:18; and in Romans 5:18 the word lacks the qualifying phrase "of the law" that it has in Romans 8:4, and refers in Romans 5:18 to an act, not to a set of requirements.

To be sure again, whereas Adam's act of disobedience brought the entrance of sin and death, an act of disobedience by Jesus would have disqualified him from dying for our sins. But this fact does not imply that his whole life of obedience is imputed to believers. It implies only that his obedience prior to crucifixion—what Matthew

---

[34]Piper, *Counted Righteous in Christ*, p. 112.

[35]Ibid.

[36]One and the same person may commit many acts, including acts of different and even diametrically opposed sorts; so the singularity of the person, whether Adam or Christ, does not explain the singularity of each one's act (against Murray, *Romans*, 1:201-2). The statement in 2 Corinthians 8:9 that though Christ was rich he became poor is sometimes used to encompass the whole of his life in one act of obedience. But his becoming poor is put in terms of "grace," not of obedience; and it is an open question whether the becoming poor has to do with his incarnation, with his itinerant ministry or alone with his crucifixion.

[37]See the full discussion by H. W. M. van de Sandt, "Research into Rom. 8,4a: The Legal Claim of the Law," *Bijdr* 37 (1976): 252-69, and cf. Romans 13:8-10. The love commandment does not include all the commandments in the law, as though it were collective for them. Rather, it provides their point of convergence (*anakephalaioutai*), so that fulfilling it results in fulfilling them too (cf. Christ as the point of convergence for "all things in heaven and on earth" in Eph 1:10, where he is hardly collective for everything in the universe—Paul was no christopantheist).

3:15 calls the "fulfilling of all righteousness"—qualified him to die for our sins.[38] It is Christ's act of righteousness, then, the obedient dying of a propitiatory death that assuaged the wrath of God so as to make God's declaration of believing sinners to be righteous both right in the upholding of his moral character and right in the exercise of his saving grace.[39] The resurrection of Christ demonstrates God's acceptance of that death as the basis of this declaration (Rom 4:25). Thus the talk of a legal fiction, or of "justifiction" according to an unfortunate typographical error in *Right with God: Justification in the Bible and the World*, is off the mark.[40]

---

[38]In public dialogue Donald A. Carson argued that inasmuch as John's baptism had to do with repentance, the submission of Jesus to that baptism despite his sinlessness marked his fulfillment of all righteousness on our behalf (Mt 3:15). But "on our behalf" does not tally with Matthew's emphasis on Jesus' righteousness as exemplary. Matthew is the only evangelist to say that Jesus went to John "for the purpose of being baptized by him" (Mt 3:13), so that Jesus sets the example to be followed in the Great Commission (Mt 28:19-20, unique to Matthew in respect to baptism). Only Matthew's Jesus says, "Take my yoke upon you and learn from me, because I am meek and lowly in heart" (Mt 11:29). To make Jesus an example of obeying his own prohibition of oaths (Mt 5:33-37, again unique to Matthew among the Gospels, though see Jas 5:12), Matthew alone has Caiaphas put Jesus under oath ("I adjure you") and Jesus answer, "*You* said [it]" instead of "I am," to the high priest's question whether he (Jesus) is "the Christ, the Son of God" (Mt 26:63-64; contrast Mk 14:61-62; Lk 22:62-63). And so on. Therefore Jesus' fulfilling all righteousness in baptism at Matthew 3:15 looks exemplary rather than vicarious. Matthew's transferring "for the remission of sins" from "the baptism of repentance" (Mk 1:4; Lk 3:3) to the Word of Institution over the cup (Mt 26:28) adds to this impression.

[39]"There can be no justification of the sinner which is not simultaneously a justification of God in his wrath against the sinner" (Seifrid, *Christ, Our Righteousness*, p. 171).

[40]D. A. Carson, ed., *Right with God: Justification in the Bible and the World* (Grand Rapids: Baker, 1992), p. 49. The death of Christ as a propitiation in Romans 3:25 implies that sin requires the penalty of death. But this implication does not negate Paul's switching in Romans 5:12-21; 6:12-23 to sin and death as dominating forces. It is popular nowadays to interpret biblical righteousness not as behavior according to a moral norm but as behavior according to the terms of a covenant. This view is correct in what it affirms but wrong in what it denies; for at least where God is concerned, the terms of a covenant are rooted in his moral character (N.B.: not in a moral norm external to him). Take, for example, Leviticus 11:45; 19:2; 20:26: "You shall be holy, for I am holy" (Gottlob Schrenk, " δίκη, δίκαιος, κτλ.," *TDNT* 2:195; Moo, *Romans*, pp. 83-84). If righteousness were covenantal apart from God's moral character, no need would arise for Christ to be made sin for us, to become a curse for us, to shed his blood as a propitiation of God's wrath against our unrighteousness—a wrath that derives from the righteousness of God as a moral attribute. What saves justification from the realm of fiction is Christ's propitiation, not an amorally covenantal character of righteousness. Nor does a covenantal setting dispossess justification of its legal, juridical connotation, for in the biblical world covenants were legally binding treaties. See further Mark A. Seifrid, "Righteousness Language in the Hebrew Scriptures and Early Judaism," in *The Complexities of Second Temple Judaism*, vol. I of *Justification and Variegated Nomism*, ed. D. A. Carson, Peter T. O'Brien and Mark A. Seifrid (Grand Rapids: Baker, 2001), pp. 416-42; Moo, *Romans*, pp. 241-42.

Earlier I noted that in Romans 4 Paul shifts to "the righteousness of faith" from "the righteousness of God" in Romans 1—3. Do these two expressions refer to different kinds of righteousness? Yes, but they are intertwined, because in Romans 3:21-26 "the righteousness of God" comes "to all who exercise faith." His righteousness, which is never said to *be* counted or imputed (passive voice), consists in his counting (active voice) of our faith as righteousness while at the same time maintaining his moral character. The righteousness of faith is the moral accomplishment that God counts faith to be even though it is not intrinsically such an accomplishment.[41] The active element in God's righteousness should not surprise us, for overwhelming evidence exists that in Paul and his Jewish heritage the righteousness of God is not a merely static moral attribute. Rather, his righteousness takes the form of justificatory action. Sometimes this action consists in meting out justice by way of punishment. Usually it consists in meting out justice by way of salvation, though the salvation of some may entail the punishment of others—and does entail Christ's suffering punishment for our sins that we might be saved. Often God's righteousness and salvation appear in juxtaposition.

- Psalm 24:6: "He will receive . . . *righteousness* from the God of his *salvation.*"

- Psalm 51:14: "Deliver me from bloodguiltiness, O God, the God of my *salvation*; [then] my tongue will joyfully sing of your *righteousness.*"

- Psalm 71:15-16: "My mouth will tell of your *righteousness*, of your *salvation* all day long. I will come with the mighty deeds of the Lord GOD; I will make mention of your *righteousness*, yours alone."

- Psalm 98:1-3: "His right hand and his holy arm have accomplished *salvation* for him. The LORD has made known his *salvation*; he has revealed his *righteousness* in the sight of the nations. . . . All the ends of the earth have seen the *salvation* of our God."

- Isaiah 45:8: "Let the clouds pour down *righteousness*; let the earth open up and *salvation* bear fruit, and *righteousness* spring up with it."

---

[41]According to Seifrid (*Christ, Our Righteousness*, pp. 136-37), God's word of promise effected Abraham's faith (Rom 4:16-22), so that faith was counted as righteousness because it really was righteousness, a work of God. But the passage seems to emphasize Abraham's not succumbing to doubt rather than the faith-producing effectiveness of God's promissory word. Even on Seifrid's reading, why does Paul take care at the beginning of Romans 4 to oppose faith and works instead of saying from the start that faith is God's work and omitting the opposition between faith and works, especially since the law was not yet given in Abraham's time?

- Isaiah 45:21-25: "And there is no other God besides me, a *righteous* God and a *Savior*. . . . Turn to me and be *saved*. . . . The word has gone forth from my mouth in *righteousness*. . . . Only in the LORD are *righteousness* and strength. . . . In the LORD all the offspring of Israel will be *declared righteous*."

- Isaiah 46:13: "I bring near my *righteousness*, it is not far off. And my *salvation* will not delay, and I will grant *salvation* in Zion."

- Isaiah 51:5-6, 8: "My *righteousness* is near; my *salvation* has gone forth. . . . But my *salvation* will be forever, and my *righteousness* will not be broken. . . . But my *righteousness* will be forever, and my *salvation* to all generations."

- Isaiah 56:1: "For my *salvation* is about to come, and my *righteousness* to be revealed."

- Isaiah 59:17: "He [the LORD] put on *righteousness* like a breastplate and a helmet of *salvation* on his head."

- Isaiah 61:10: "He has clothed me with garments of *salvation*; he has wrapped me with a robe of *righteousness*."

- Isaiah 62:1: "For Jerusalem's sake I will not keep quiet, until her *righteousness* goes forth like brightness, and her *salvation* like a torch that is burning."

- Isaiah 63:1: "Who is this . . . marching in the greatness of his strength? It is I who speak in *righteousness*, mighty to *save*."

- Jeremiah 23:5-6: " 'Behold, the days are coming,' declares the LORD, 'when I will raise up for David a *righteous* branch; and he will . . . do justice and *righteousness* in the land. In his days Judah will be *saved*. . . . And this is his name by which he will be called: "The LORD [is] our *righteousness*." ' "

- *4 Ezra* 8:36, 39-40: " 'For in this, O Lord, your *righteousness* and goodness will be declared, when you are merciful to those who have no store of good works.' . . . He answered me and said, . . . 'I will rejoice over the creation of the righteous . . . and their *salvation*.' "

- CD 20:20: "*Salvation* and *righteousness* will be revealed to those who fear God."

- 1QS 11:11-15: "As for me, if I stumble, God's mercies will always be my *salvation*; and if I fall in the sin of the flesh, in the *righteousness* of God, which endures eternally, will my judgment be. . . . [H]e judges me in the *righteousness* of his truth, and in his great goodness he always atones for all my sins; in his *righteousness* he will cleanse me from the uncleanness of human being and from the sin of the sons of Adam, in order [that I might] praise God for his *righteousness*."

- IQM 18:7-8: "Many times you have opened for us the gates of *salvations* [plural].
  . . . You, O God of *righteousness*, have acted for the sake of your name."

- *1 Enoch* 99:10: "They will walk in the path of his [the Most High's] *righteousness*
  . . . and they will be *saved*."

See also Psalms 31:1; 35:23-24; 71:2; 89:17; 96:13; 98:9; 111:3; 143:11; Isaiah
1:27; 51:6, 8; 53:11; IQS 11:2-3(?); IQH^a 12:37.[42]

So oriented is this usage to action that "righteousness" occurs in the plural for
righteous acts.

- Judges 5:11: "There they will recount the *righteousnesses* [that is, righteous acts] of
  the LORD, the *righteousnesses* for his warriors in Israel."

- 1 Samuel 12:7: "concerning all the *righteousnesses* of the LORD that he did for you
  and your fathers."

- Psalm 103:6: "The LORD performs *righteousnesses* and judgments for all who are
  oppressed."

- Daniel 9:16, 18: "O Lord, in accordance with all your *righteousnesses*, let now your
  anger and your wrath turn away. . . . For we are not presenting our supplications
  before you on account of our *righteousnesses*, but on account of your great compas-
  sion."

- Micah 6:5: "to know the *righteousnesses* of the LORD [referring to his saving Israel
  from King Balak of Moab]."[43]

Clearly, Paul too uses "righteousness" in this salvifically active way, as to be expected from his writing that God's righteousness is "being witnessed by the Law
and the Prophets" (Rom 3:21) and as shown almost immediately in Romans by
his juxtaposing "salvation" with "the righteousness of God": "For I am not
ashamed of the gospel, for it is God's power resulting in *salvation* to everyone who
believes. . . . For in it the *righteousness* of God is being revealed from faith to faith, as
it is written, 'But the righteous person by faith will live' " (Rom 1:16-17; note the
echo of Ps 98:1-3, quoted above, in the universal revelation of God's righteous-

---

[42]Seifrid ("Righteousness Language," pp. 415-16, 429-30, 435-38) figures that in the Old Testament
divine righteousness appears as salvific four times more often than it appears as punitive, and he
mounts an impressive argument against a reference to divine righteousness in IQS 11:2-3.

[43]For a general survey of righteousness as an action, human as well as divine, behavioral as well as declarative, see Ziesler, *Meaning of Righteousness in Paul*, pp. 22-34. Paul portrays righteousness as so active
that it wields weapons and speaks in Romans 6:13; 10:6-10; 2 Corinthians 6:7.

ness).[44] And Romans 3:26 defines the righteousness of God ("his righteousness") in terms of an action as well as an attribute: "for the demonstration of his righteousness at the present time, in order that he might be righteous [an attribute; cf. Rom 3:5] and declaring righteous [an action] the person of faith in Jesus." The righteousness is God's, not Christ's, because God, not Christ, is the one who according to the next chapter counts faith as righteousness. As already noted, Christ enters the picture as the object of faith, whose obediently righteous act of propitiation made it right for God to count faith as righteousness. In that God set forth Christ as a propitiatory sacrifice, the righteousness of God is a punitive action. But in that as a result he counts faith as righteousness, his righteousness is a salvific action. If we correlate Jewish usage starting in the Old Testament with its distinctively Pauline, christologically based elaboration in Romans 1—4, we have excellent reason to intertwine the righteousness of faith and the righteousness of God.

Similarly, in Romans 9:30—10:4, Paul says that "righteousness" derives "from faith" and again calls it "the righteousness of God" in that according to his earlier explanation God is the one who counts faith as righteousness. Furthermore, "Christ is the end of the law for righteousness to everyone who believes" in that he is the object of their believing. Piper gives what he calls "the most literal, straightforward translation of Romans 10:4"—that is, "The goal (or end) of the law is *Christ for righteousness* for everyone who believes"—and interprets the italicized phrase as meaning that Christ *is* their righteousness.[45] But Paul's earlier explanation requires Christ to be the object of the faith that God counts as righteousness rather than that Christ be the righteousness of believers. Besides, the word order in Piper's literal translation misleadingly makes "end" the subject of the sentence, makes "Christ" the predicate nominative, and ties "Christ" closely with "for righteous-

---

[44]The fact that the gospel rather than the righteousness of God is his power resulting in salvation does not undermine the meaning of righteousness as salvific action. Nor is it absurd for Paul to say that in the gospel God's salvifically active righteousness is being revealed (along with his righteous character). For the gospel is powerful *as proclaimed* (1 Cor 1:18, 23-25); and the proclamation of it is revealing God's salvifically active righteousness just as in the parallelistically constructed statement of Romans 1:18 the wrath of God is being revealed through his action of giving sinners over to their own depravity (Rom 1:24, 26, 28; cf. the revelation of each person's "work" [an action] in 1 Cor 3:13 and of "faith" [an action] in Gal 3:23; against Williams, "The 'Righteousness of God' in Romans," pp. 259-62, though Williams admits that "God's righteousness" at Rom 1:17 "would likely bring to mind ideas of deliverance or salvation," and also recognizes that the gospel is powerful as proclaimed [pp. 255-57]).

[45]Piper, *Counted Righteous in Christ*, pp. 87-89 (italics original). For the present purpose it is unnecessary to decide whether "end" indicates a goal, a termination or both.

ness." Apparently Paul's advancing the predicate nominative, "the end of the law,"
to the head of the sentence for emphasis has deceived Piper into thinking the
phrase is the subject, whereas "Christ" is the subject, so that "for righteousness"
relates to "the end of the law" (see the standard translations).[46] And even Piper's
misleading translation leaves open the question, Christ for *whose* righteousness, or
for *what* righteousness? In view of Paul's earlier writing in Romans, we should answer, Not the righteousness of Christ, but either God's righteousness or the righteousness that faith is counted to be—probably the latter, since Paul immediately
goes on to mention "the righteousness of *(ek)* faith" as opposed to "the righteousness of *(ek)* the law" (Rom 10:5-6).

Since the righteousness of God stands opposite righteousness that derives
"from the law," it is also "righteousness *from* God," that is, from the God who
counts faith rather than works of the law (see Phil 3:6-9 with Rom 4:1-6).[47] Similarly, according to 1 Corinthians 1:30 Christ became "wisdom for us" who by
faith are in him. Since this wisdom is made up of "both righteousness and sanctification and redemption," Christ became those too. But this wisdom, unlike the
wisdom of the world, comes "from God," so that the righteousness which helps
make it up also comes from God, just as in Philippians 3:9. Earlier in 1 Corinthians
1 Paul referenced "the word of the cross" and told his addressees, "God was
pleased through the foolishness of the proclamation to save those who exercise
faith. . . . But we proclaim Christ crucified . . . Christ the power of God and the
wisdom of God. . . . For look at your calling, brothers and sisters. . . . God has
elected the foolish things of the world . . . in order that no flesh should boast in
God's presence" (1 Cor 1:18-29, excerpts).

So the crucified Christ became for us wisdom from God in that believing in
Christ makes us the objects of God's electively, salvifically active wisdom. He became for us sanctification from God in that believing in Christ makes us the objects
of God's electively, salvifically active sanctification. He became for us redemption

---

[46]Cf. John 1:1, where the Greek text puts the predicate nominative "God" first for emphasis in the
statement that "the Word was God." See Williams, "The 'Righteousness of God' in Romans," p.
284. The two foregoing paragraphs oppose also Cranfield, *Romans*, 1:97-98; 2:515.

[47]For "righteousness from God," see also Psalm 24:6; Isaiah 54:17; Baruch 5:2, 9. The Greek genitive that underlies "the righteousness *of* God" may convey the meaning "from." In fact, the loose-
ness of the relation between a Greek noun in the genitive (most often introduced by "of" in English translation) and the noun on which it depends allows a wide variety of meanings to be
determined by context: possession, separation, origin, description, apposition, comparison, content, agency, etc.

from God in that believing in Christ makes us the objects of God's electively, salvifically active redemption. Parallelistically, then, he became for us righteousness from God in that believing in Christ makes us the objects of God's electively, salvifically active righteousness.

And Paul's linking the cross with our exercise of faith meshes with the explanation in Romans 3—4 that the propitiatory death of Christ enables God to count our faith as righteousness and to be righteous in doing so. The death is Christ's; but the righteousness is God's. It comes from God, not from Christ, and does not consist in an imputed righteousness of Christ any more than God imputes to believers a wisdom of Christ, a sanctification of Christ or a redemption of Christ. Nowhere, for example, does Paul say that Christ was redeemed, so that Christ's redemption could be counted as ours. Hence, the righteousness from God that Christ became for us is God's elective, salvific action of counting our faith in Christ to be righteousness.

With a view toward making the righteousness Christ's in I Corinthians 1:30, Donald A. Carson stressed in public dialogue the word *Christ*. But is Christ's righteousness from God in respect to having his own righteous conduct counted as ours, or in respect to him as the object of the faith that God in *his* righteousness counts as equivalent to righteousness? Stressing "Christ" does not answer this question, but the latter answer—Christ as the object of faith-counted-as-righteousness—has the advantage of Paul's other statements.

In 2 Corinthians 5:21 the making of him who did not know sin to be sin on our behalf refers again to the propitiatory death of Christ, for which his sinlessness qualified him (cf. I Pet 3:18); and our becoming the righteousness of God in him refers to the attained purpose of that death, namely, God's counting as righteousness the faith that united us to the Christ who died for us.[48] We do not become the sinlessness of Christ, much less his righteousness, by having it imputed to us as a moral accomplishment on his part and our behalf. We become *God's* righteousness, but not God's righteousness as a moral quality. Just as in Galatians 3:13 Christ "became" a curse in the sense that he became the object of God's curse (see Deut 21:23 for God as the curser in the passage Paul quotes), so also in 2 Corinthians 5:21 we "become" the righteousness of God in the sense that we become the objects of his salvifically active righteousness, of his declaring

---

[48]Since elsewhere Paul uses the phrase "in Christ" predominantly for the location of believers, 2 Corinthians 5:21 is best taken as indicating the location of believers where they become God's righteousness, not the location of that righteousness.

us righteous because we have believed in his Son, whose death as the sinless-one-made-sin propitiated God's wrath against our sins (cf. Rom 10:3, which speaks of subjection to the righteousness of God and therefore implies being an object of its action; also Isaiah 53:11, which says that the Servant of the LORD "will justify the many, as he will bear their iniquities," but says nothing about imputing to them his righteousness as a moral quality).

If Paul had meant that the righteousness of Christ replaces our sins, we would expect him to have said so. How easy it would have been for him to write in 2 Corinthians 5:21, "in order that we might become the righteousness *of Christ*." But he did not. Or to write in Philippians 3:8-9, "in order that I might gain Christ and be found in him, not having my righteousness [derived] from the law but [having] *his* righteousness [based] on faith." But Paul did not. Instead, he writes about the righteousness of or from God (eleven times), almost always in passages where God and Christ are distinguished from each other (nine times).[49] It is perfectly astounding that time after time after time those who advocate an imputation of Christ's righteousness—my former self included and, for that matter, those who advocate its infusion and others who advocate participation in it through union with Christ—quote Pauline passages that speak of God's righteousness only to substitute the righteousness of Christ in their expositions of those passages. This shift in gears seems to occur by automatic transmission.

The only New Testament passage, non-Pauline, that mentions the righteousness of Christ does not deal in imputation, infusion or union with him, but attributes our faith to his righteousness: "to those who have received a faith of equal value to ours through the righteousness of our God and Savior Jesus Christ" (2 Pet 1:1).[50] One could note Peter's linking the righteousness and deity of Christ and, moving over to Paul, argue that he presents the righteousness of God as worked out in the obedient life and death of his divine Son. To make this argument, in fact, appeal is regularly made to the unity of Father and Son in the Trin-

---

[49]Romans 1:17; 3:5, 21, 22, 25, 26; 10:3 (twice); 1 Corinthians 1:30; 2 Corinthians 5:21; Philippians 3:9. Only Romans 1:17 and Romans 3:5 lack a nearby distinction between God and Christ, but neither do they associate God and Christ. To paper over the inconvenient fact that Paul never speaks of Christ's righteousness but does speak of the righteousness of God as distinct from Christ, Piper (*Counted Righteous in Christ*) repeatedly refers to "divine righteousness," as though "divine" would include Christ as well as God the Father.

[50]This translation interprets the Greek preposition *en* as instrumental: "through." Alternatively, the phrase locates our faith "in" Christ's righteousness. Tied as it is to the designation of him as "our God and Savior," his righteousness carries the usual meaning of divine salvific action (see above).

ity, as though that unity demands that God's righteousness be Christ's too.[51]

I wonder why on this basis a righteousness of the Holy Spirit is not added to the mix, and whether God the Father along with the Holy Spirit lived and died obediently in union with God the Son. Not everything said about one person of the Trinity applies to the other persons. The Father does not obey the Son, for example, as the Son is said to obey the Father.[52] Moreover, there are explicit scriptural affirmations of the deity, differentiation and unity of God the Father, Son and Holy Spirit on which the development of trinitarian doctrine rests, but no similar affirmations on which the doctrine of an imputation of Christ's righteousness can validly be developed. And the trinitarian appeal fails to account for this absence despite repeated mentions of God's righteousness in passages that distinguish God and Christ from each other. So it would be specious to say that the denial of an imputed righteousness of Christ robs him of glory that belongs to him.[53] We are not dealing with a question of Christ's glory, but with the questions of what the Bible does and does not teach and of whether the doctrine of an imputation of Christ's righteousness represents a valid development of biblical teaching. *Of course* theologians are not limited to repeating what the Bible says, but what they develop in and for their own circumstances should at least arise out of what the Bible says. So long as the Bible does not provide such statements, and in the present case says much that points in a contrary direction, an appeal to the difference between an exegetical field of discourse and a systematic theological field of discourse does no good for the putative doctrine.[54]

In summary, where can sinners find righteousness? In Christ. Whose righteousness can they find there? God's. What does it consist in? God's counting faith as righteousness. How does he do so without contravening his wrath against our unrighteousness? By setting forth Christ as a propitiatory sacrifice.[55]

Finally, what practical difference does it make whether we affirm or deny an im-

---

[51]Cf. Piper, *Counted Righteous in Christ*, p. 181 n. 26: "the absence of doctrinal explicitness and systematization in Paul may be no more problematic for the doctrine of the imputation of Christ's righteousness than it is for the doctrine of the Trinity."

[52]Matthew 26:39, 42, 44; Mark 14:36, 39; Luke 22:42; John 5:30; 6:38; 10:18; 12:49-50; 17:4; Hebrews 5:8.

[53]Contrast Piper, *Counted Righteous in Christ*, p. 51.

[54]Against Carson in this volume.

[55]Cf. the extrabiblical use of *protithēmi*, "set forth," used in Romans 3:25, and its nominal cognate *prothesis* for the laying out of a dead body. The substitution of "expiatory" and "expiation" for "propitiatory" and "propitiation" would affect the basic arguments of this essay very little.

putation of Christ's righteousness? Well, Mark A. Seifrid observes that "in reducing 'justification' to a present possession of 'Christ's imputed righteousness', Protestant divines inadvertently bruised the nerve which runs between justification and obedience."[56] I therefore suggest that *Paul does not match the imputation of our sins to Christ with an imputation of Christ's righteousness to us believers because he (Paul) wants to emphasize the obedient life of righteousness that we are supposed to live—and indeed will live if we are true believers—apart from the Old Testament law, under which Christ was born, and to emphasize the judgment of our works at the end.* This suggestion does not imply that an imputed righteousness of Christ would contradict the need of believers to live a life of righteousness apart from the Old Testament law and in view of the final judgment. But it *is* to say that the absence from Paul of an imputed righteousness of Christ, especially one that includes a lifetime of obedience to the law, leaves more theological and rhetorical space for emphasizing that need and therefore helps Paul resist antinomianism with the doctrines of union with Christ in death to sin and coming alive to righteousness (that is, behavioral righteousness) and of the gift of the Holy Spirit as a sanctifying influence (see, for example, Rom 6:1—7:6; I Cor 6:9-11, 17-20; Gal 5:13-26). This emphasis may go a long way toward evacuating the longstanding complaint that despite protestations to the contrary, the classic Protestant doctrine of double imputation tends to shortchange sanctification[57] and thus may also go a long way toward satisfying the legitimate concerns not only of Roman Catholics

---

[56]Seifrid, *Christ, Our Righteousness*, p. 175; cf. John Wesley's early (but later abandoned) rejection of an imputation of Christ's active obedience: "It is not scriptural; it is not necessary. . . . But it has done immediate hurt. I have abundant proof, that the frequent use of this phrase ['the imputed righteousness of Christ'], instead of 'furthering men's progress in vital holiness,' has made them satisfied without any holiness at all; yea, and encouraged them to work all uncleanness with greediness" (letter to Hervey as quoted in Hervey, *Aspasio Vindicated*, p. vii; cf. p. ix, "But the *nice, metaphysical* doctrine of *imputed righteousness*, leads not to repentance, but to licentiousness" [italics original], and p. xxiv, "We swarm with Antinomians on every side. Why are you at such pains to increase their number?"). Hervey's response that God's goodness prompts thankful obedience (pp. 70, 79, 245-46, and "Assertion IX" on p. 407) contains an important point but neglects the equally important point that Paul threatens professing Christians with damnation if they do "the works of the flesh" (Gal 5:19-21; for Wesley's change of mind, see "The Lord Our Righteousness" [a sermon preached November 24, 1765], in *The Works of John Wesley*, vol. I, *Sermons* I,1-33, ed. Albert C. Outler [Nashville: Abingdon, 1984], pp. 447-65). Seifrid believes in an imputation of Christ's righteousness but wants to balance its present imputation with final justification at the Last Judgment.

[57]I use *sanctification* here in the popular sense of godly living. The biblical usage is richer, of course. See Ziesler, *Meaning of Righteousness in Paul*, pp. 5-7, for a survey of different ways in which Protestants have dealt with the criticism that "there is no road from it [forensic justification] to ethics" and Albert Schweitzer, *The Mysticism of Paul the Apostle* (New York: Seabury, 1968), p. 225, for the most famous statement of this criticism.

but also of pietists in the Lutheran tradition, in the Anabaptist and Baptist traditions, in the Keswick movement, in the Holiness movement and in Pentecostalism.
That most of these pietists hold to double imputation means only that they should
consider dropping the doctrine of an imputation of Christ's righteousness, a doctrine which at least at the subconscious level may prompt them—wrongly, in my
view—to portray sanctification, perfect love, life on the highest plain[58] or baptism
in the Holy Spirit as a second blessing normally delayed till after conversion inasmuch as Christ's righteousness is supposedly imputed at conversion (cf. the concerns of those who emphasize the lordship of Christ as part of salvation from its
very start[59]).

---

[58]An allusion to Ruth Paxson's book, *Life on the Highest Plain: A Study of the Spiritual Nature and Needs of Man*
(Chicago: Moody Press, 1928); cf. Dr. and Mrs. Howard Taylor, *Hudson Taylor's Spiritual Secret* (London: China Inland Mission, 1935). For details on the theology of a second blessing, see James
D. G. Dunn, *The Christ and the Spirit*, vol. 2: *Pneumatology* (Grand Rapids: Eerdmans, 1998), pp. 81-85,
222-42, with criticism and bibliography.

[59]See, e.g., John F. MacArthur Jr., *The Gospel According to Jesus: What Does Jesus Mean When He Says "Follow
Me"?* (Grand Rapids: Zondervan, 1988). In public dialogue Bruce McCormack claimed that to reject an imputation of Christ's righteousness leaves no basis for distinguishing sanctification from
justification and therefore leads to an understanding of justification as transformative rather than
forensic, as infusive rather than declarative. But in the absence of an imputation of Christ's righteousness, why should not sanctification be ascribed to a distinct though not delayed work of the
Holy Spirit instead of being drawn under the umbrella of justification in terms of infusion?

2

THE VINDICATION OF IMPUTATION

On Fields of Discourse and Semantic Fields

D. A. CARSON

For many Protestants today, the doctrine of imputation has become the crucial touchstone for orthodoxy with respect to justification.[1] For others, imputation is to be abandoned as an outdated relic of a system that focuses far too much attention on substitutionary penal atonement and far too little attention on alternative "models" of what the cross achieved.[2] For still others, including N. T. Wright, imputation should be abandoned, even though (he maintains) everything that Reformed theologians want to preserve under that rubric he thinks he preserves under his much larger categories.[3] And for still others, such as Robert

---

[1]The latest, but neither the first nor the last, is John Piper, *Counted Righteous in Christ: Should We Abandon the Imputation of Christ's Righteousness?* (Wheaton, Ill.: Crossway, 2002). Perhaps I should add that informed Protestants would not want to say that the Reformation invented their understanding of justification. Besides claiming that they are faithfully expounding texts of the New Testament, they would say that the Reformers are in line with a substantial patristic stream (though they would aver that the Reformers clarified aspects of the doctrine): see Thomas C. Oden, *The Justification Reader* (Grand Rapids: Eerdmans, 2002).

[2]Joel B. Green and Mark D. Baker, *Recovering the Scandal of the Cross: Atonement in the New Testament and Contemporary Contexts* (Downers Grove, Ill.: InterVarsity Press, 2000). In recent years, a handful of scholars from various traditions have either recognized the violent language of the atonement and then sought to dismiss it, or in some way or other marginalized related biblical themes dealing with God's wrath and judgment. See, *inter alios*, Anthony W. Bartlett, *Cross Purposes: The Violent Grammar of Christian Atonement* (Harrisburg: Trinity Press International, 2001); J. Denny Weaver, *The Nonviolent Atonement* (Grand Rapids: Eerdmans, 2001); C. D. Marshall, *Beyond Retribution: A New Testament Vision for Justice, Crime and Punishment* (Grand Rapids: Eerdmans, 2001). For a more traditional exposition from the same period, see David Peterson, ed., *Where Wrath and Mercy Meet: Proclaiming the Atonement Today* (Carlisle: Paternoster, 2001).

[3]His literature is so well known it need not be listed here. Some specific points and their sources will be introduced later.

Gundry, what is to be rejected is certainly not every aspect of imputation, but affirmations of the imputed righteousness of Christ.[4]

What I propose to do in this short paper is peck away at various aspects of the
debate, in the hope, somewhat forlorn and certainly modest, that by keeping in mind
some of the larger parameters of the debate while simultaneously focusing on a handful of biblical texts, I may be able to help some students, and (who knows?) perhaps
a few others, to take on board some elements that are sometimes overlooked.

(1) In both exegesis and theology, imputation has been tied not only to discussions of what Christ accomplished on the cross, but also to the relation between Adam's sin and our sin. With respect to the latter subject, commonly five
distinguishable positions have been maintained, three of them bound up with
distinctive understandings of imputation.[5] Exploring these matters would take
us immediately to Romans 5:12 and related passages, but I am not going to explore them in this paper, as important as they are. For the sake of brevity I will
largely focus on the currently most disputed element, namely, the imputation of
Christ's righteousness to us.

(2) For clarity of thought and expression, it is important to distinguish between two domains of discourse, viz. exegesis and theology.[6] Of course, for

---

[4]Robert H. Gundry, "Why I Didn't Endorse 'The Gospel of Jesus Christ: An Evangelical Celebration'
. . . even though I wasn't asked to," *Books & Culture* 7, no. 1 (2001): 6-9; and his response to the criticism
of Thomas C. Oden, "On Oden's 'Answer,'" *Books & Culture* 7, no. 2 (2001): 14-15, 39. See also Gundry's stimulating contribution to this volume, which of course I have not seen as this essay is being revised, but merely heard as it was presented at the Wheaton Theology Conference, April 10-12, 2003.
[5](a) Immediate imputation, by which, in virtue of the federal and natural union between Adam and
his posterity, the sin of Adam is imputed to his posterity, even though the sin is not their act, and
that this imputed sin is the judicial ground of the penalty pronounced on them. (b) Mediate imputation, by which it is affirmed that Adam's corrupt nature comes to all his posterity, so that all that
is really imputed to them is their own inherent, though inherited, depravity. (c) Under the "realistic"
theory, all of humankind was generically in the persons of Adam and Eve, so that their sin was, in
reality, the sin of the entire race. In this instance, what is imputed to Adam's posterity is in fact their
own sin, and nothing more. The other two most common positions deny any notion of imputation.
(d) The hereditary corruption is no more than an instance of "like producing like," and imputation
is left out of the equation. (e) Some have argued that Adam sinned, and all others sin, but that there
is no causal or natural connection between the two. This summary is a somewhat modified version
of that offered by Charles Hodge, *Systematic Theology*, 3 vols. (New York: Scribners, Armstrong, 1872),
2:192-93.
[6]I am here using "theology" in the American sense, rather than the British sense. On the U.K. side of
the Atlantic, "theology" is the umbrella discipline that includes exegesis, dogmatics, historical theology, and much more. In North America, "theology," whether systematic, biblical, philosophical,
historical, or something else, is a more synthetic discipline, and is regularly set over against exegesis.

those who want the "norming norm" of their theology to be Scripture, the links between the two disciplines must be much more than casual. Nevertheless, not only their respective methods, but even their respective vocabularies, can be very different.

Two examples might help. If one were to study sanctification, especially in the light of Reformation debates, one would immediately be caught up in the time-honored distinction between justification and sanctification. The former, it is argued, marks entrance into salvation, into the Christian way, and is forensic and unrepeatable; the latter is characterized by growth, development, and growing conformity to Christ across time. Of course, the heirs of the Reformation have often noted that some passages where the ἅγιος word-group appears cannot be understood within this framework, and so they have acknowledged the existence of what they variously called "positional sanctification" or "definitional sanctification."[7] In such passages, Christians are set aside for God, possessed by God, in exactly the same way that, say, a certain shovel was set aside for God under the Mosaic code for the exclusive purpose of taking out the ash from the prescribed burnt offerings.[8] Thus the Corinthians are said to be "sanctified" (I Cor I:3), even though by the standards of customary theological discourse they are a singularly unsanctified lot. Indeed, Paul says that they are "sanctified" and thus "called to be holy" (I Cor I:3). The common New Testament ethical appeal is here very strong: be what you are. Some contemporary scholars go much farther, and argue that all or at least almost all Pauline references to holiness/sanctification belong to this "positional" or "definitional" category.[9] Assuming for the moment that they are exegetically right, does this mean that the Reformation and post-Reformation doctrine of sanctification is sadly mistaken?

Of course not. There are plenty of New Testament passages—indeed, Pauline passages—where the apostle can write movingly of spiritual growth, of growing conformity to Christ, without using the holiness/sanctification word-group. In Philippians 3, for instance, Paul does not think that he has already obtained all that he is aiming for, but he presses on to take hold of that for which Christ Jesus took hold of him. He cheerfully "forgets" what is behind, and presses on toward the goal to win the prize for which God has called him heavenward in Christ

---

[7]E.g., Anthony A. Hoekema, *Saved by Grace* (Grand Rapids: Eerdmans, 1989), esp. pp. 202-9.

[8]E.g., Numbers 4:14-15.

[9]So David Peterson, *Possessed by God: A New Testament Theology of Sanctification and Holiness*, NSBT (Leicester, U.K.: Inter-Varsity Press, 1995).

Jesus.[10] In other words, he is talking about sanctification without deploying the ἅγιος or קָדוֹשׁ word groups.

So the scholar deeply committed to exegetical rigor might well insist that Paul never, or only rarely, talks about sanctification in a progressive sense; the systematician, by contrast, might lecture for a long time, and very faithfully, about Pauline teaching on sanctification. Of course, if the latter has not done his or her philological homework, he or she might erroneously connect the theme of sanctification to the wrong texts, by hunting out occurrences of ἅγιος and cognates. If the former scholar has not been careful, it will not be long before he or she is calling into question the entire structure of the doctrine of sanctification in its Protestant heritage. But if each is aware of the other's field of discourse, the claims that each will make will be more modest than will otherwise be the case.

Or consider what Paul says about reconciliation. At the philological level, the recent work by Porter is very helpful;[11] at the exegetical level, especially in its treatment of 2 Corinthians 5, the most recent work of Seyoon Kim will surely command wide assent.[12] But one of the things that all Pauline scholars note is that the apostle speaks exclusively of *us* being reconciled to *God*; the apostle never speaks of *God* being reconciled to *us*. Nevertheless a long and honorable heritage within theological discourse does not hesitate to speak of God being reconciled to us. It is bound up with biblical treatments of God's wrath, and of the nature of the peculiarly Christian (as opposed to pagan) understanding of propitiation. When properly done, I find such discourse convincingly Pauline, and faithful to other biblical documents, even though the καταλάσσω word-group is never used to convey the idea. So I remain happy to sing, in the words of Charles Wesley's immortal hymn "Arise, My Soul, Arise," the lines "My God is reconciled, /His pardoning voice I hear; /He owns me for his child, /I can no longer fear."

The biblical scholar who is narrowly constrained by the exegetical field of discourse may be in danger of denying that it is proper to speak of God being reconciled to us; the theologian who is not exegetically careful may be in danger of trying

---

[10]Cf. further 1 Corinthians 14:1; 2 Corinthians 7:1; 1 Thessalonians 5:15; 2 Thessalonians 1:3; 1 Timothy 6:11; Hebrews 12:14; 1 Peter 1:15; 2 Peter 3:18; and G. C. Berkouwer, *Faith and Sanctification* (Grand Rapids: Eerdmans, 1952), pp. 101ff.

[11]Stanley E. Porter, *Καταλάσσω in Ancient Greek Literature, with Reference to the Pauline Writings*, Estudios de Filología Neotestamentaria 5 (Córdoba: Ediciones El Almendro, 1994).

[12]Seyoon Kim, *Paul and the New Perspective: Second Thoughts on the Origin of Paul's Gospel* (Grand Rapids: Eerdmans, 2002).

to tie the notion that God is reconciled to us to the wrong passages.

The bearing of these reflections is obvious. Even if we agree that there is no Pauline passage that *explicitly* says, in so many words, that the righteousness of Christ is imputed to his people, is there biblical evidence to substantiate the view that the substance of this thought is conveyed? And if such a case can be made, should the exegete be encouraged to look at the matter through a wider aperture than that provided by philology and formulae? And should we ask the theologian to be a tad more careful with texts called up to support the doctrine?

(3) For many in the traditional Protestant confessional camp, imputation has become one of the crucial criteria deployed to distinguish between a faithful understanding of justification and a suspect understanding of justification—the latter usually associated with one voice or another in the so-called new perspective on Paul.[13]

The issues are extraordinarily complex. At the risk of oversimplifying matters, we might say that the influence of Ernst Käsemann, mediated through E. P. Sanders and others, has convinced many that "justification" primarily has to do with God's covenantal faithfulness.[14] In the further step taken by N. T. Wright, if people are "justified" they are declared to belong to God's covenantal community. In this understanding, there are at least two significant divergences from the traditional view: (a) justification is no longer thought of as the entry-point of the believer's experience with God, but is now bound up with the believer's ongoing status with respect to the covenant community; and (b) justification is no longer immediately tied to justice/righteousness. It is this latter point that is important for our discussion. As I read the trends, the mistakes fuelled by Käsemann's work are now, gradually, being rolled back—and none too soon.

I cannot resist an anecdote. A few years ago I found myself in prolonged conversation with a retired classicist and expert on the Septuagint. He had heard, vaguely, of the new perspective, and wanted me to explain it to him. I took a half-hour or so

---

[13]On the whole, this is how John Piper, *Counted Righteous*, casts his work. Incidentally, Piper seems to take his list of who falls into this camp from Gundry's list of people who do not wholeheartedly embrace the imputation of Christ's righteousness to the believer, and as a result ends up lumping, for instance, Mark Seifrid and N. T. Wright in the same camp. No one who has read their works closely could make that mistake: Seifrid has been one of the most perceptive critics of the new perspective.

[14]This is not to say that Käsemann, Sanders and later "new perspective" writers are all saying the same thing when they assert that "justification" primarily has to do with covenantal righteousness. In particular, Käsemann holds that Paul critically expands the term to include "creation-faithfulness," and unlike later writers in this stream, does not disassociate justification from judgment. Doubtless Käsemann has been influenced by Adolf Schlatter.

to give him a potted history of some of the stances that fall within that rubric, including the view that "justification," for some, has come to mean something like "God's declaration that certain people truly belong to the covenant community." He asked a simple question: "Do those who hold this view know any Greek at all?" As far as this Greek expert was concerned, all the δικ-words—δικαιοσύνη, δίκαιος, ἀδικία, δίκος, δικαιόω, and so forth—have to do with justice, with righteousness. He was, of course, perfectly aware that one cannot assume that etymology necessarily provides any word's true meaning. But from his own reading and re-reading of Greek texts from Homer through to the Byzantine period, he found it frankly incredible that anyone could think that the δικ- words could be fairly understood in categories that left out justice/righteousness. I think that insight, though naively put perhaps, is fundamentally sound, and a rising number of studies are combining to overthrow Käsemann's heritage.[15] Moreover, there is a stinger in the tail to the view that δικαιοσύνη refers to God's declaration that one is in the covenant, and not to righteousness: it means that δικαιοσύνη is one big step removed from the cross. I hasten

---

[15]The most important of these is the essay by Mark A. Seifrid, "Righteousness Language in the Hebrew Scriptures and Early Judaism," in *Justification and Variegated Nomism, Volume 1: The Complexities of Second Temple Judaism*, ed. D. A. Carson, Peter T. O'Brien and Mark A. Seifrid (Tübingen: Mohr-Siebeck, 2001), pp. 415-42. See further his continuing linguistic discussion in volume 2 (forthcoming). In addition, see Douglas J. Moo, *The Epistle to the Romans*, NICNT (Grand Rapids: Eerdmans, 1996), pp. 70-90; and, more briefly, Peter Stuhlmacher, *Paul's Letter to the Romans: A Commentary*, trans. Scott J. Hafemann (Louisville: Westminster John Knox, 1994), pp. 61-65. The writers just cited are not in perfect agreement, of course, but they all insist on tying δικ- terms explicitly to righteousness. Among the many observations that Seifrid offers is the fact that in the Hebrew Bible the terms בְּרִית ("covenant") and צדק ("righteousness"), despite their very high frequency, almost never occur in close proximity. In general, "one does not 'act righteously or unrighteously' with respect to a covenant. Rather, one 'keeps,' 'remembers,' 'establishes' a covenant or the like. Or, conversely, one 'breaks,' 'transgresses,' 'forsakes,' 'despises,' forgets' or 'profanes' it" (p. 424). Righteousness language is commonly found in parallel with terms for rightness or rectitude over against evil. Moreover, the attempt to link "being righteous" with "being in the covenant" or with Israel's "covenant status" does not fare much better in Qumran and rabbinic literature. Pace N. T. Wright, "Romans and the Theology of Paul," in *Pauline Theology, Volume III: Romans*, ed. David M. Hay and E. Elizabeth Johnson (Minneapolis: Fortress Press, 1995), pp. 38-39, who claims that "righteousness" means covenant faithfulness, and therefore that this "righteousness" is "not a quality of substance that can be passed or transferred from the judge to the defendant" (p. 39). Cf. further D. A. Carson, "Why Trust a Cross? Reflections on Romans 3:21-26," in the forthcoming festschrift for Roger Nicole, *The Glory of the Atonement*, ed. Charles E. Hill and Frank A. James III (Downers Grove, Ill.: InterVarsity Press, 2004). It is no answer to insist that God's saving act of righteousness, by which we are declared righteous before him, fulfills his covenantal promises. Doubtless that is true, but it entirely misses the point. The question is whether the term δικαιοσύνη refers to the fulfillment of or faithfulness of God's covenantal promises, or refers to God's vindication of both himself and his people.

to add that Tom Wright does not wish to minimize the importance of the cross, and has written insightfully and movingly on this theme. That is not quite the issue. The issue is how the cross and δικαιοσύνη are linked. And one of the tests, for the traditional confessional camp, to preserve the view that justification refers to God's declaration that his people are *righteous* in his eyes, and that this is not some legal fiction but grounded on Christ's substitutionary death, is imputation.

In terms of the response to the so-called new perspective, this is a telling argument. But Robert Gundry, as far as I can tell, does not see himself as one of the voices within the new perspective: he has always been more of a free spirit than to belong too whole-heartedly to any one preserve! One may argue that his stance is inconsistent, or flawed in exegetical or other ways, and enter into debate with him, but one should not forget that he is as deeply confessional as most of his opponents when it comes to his affirmation of penal substitutionary atonement.

(4) The issue should now be ratcheted up a notch in terms of its theological complexity. For many, the imputation of the righteousness of Christ is bound up not only with a proper understanding of justification, but with discussions of Christ's active and passive obedience. The matter received classic expression in the much-quoted words of W. G. T. Shedd:

> First, I would explain what we mean by the imputation of Christ's righteousness. Sometimes the expression is taken by our divines in a larger sense, for the imputation of all that Christ did and suffered for our redemption, whereby we are free from guilt, and stand righteous in the sight of God; and so implies the imputation both of Christ's satisfaction and obedience. But here I intend it in a stricter sense, for the imputation of that righteousness or moral goodness that consists in the obedience of Christ. And by that righteousness being imputed to us, is meant no other than this, that that righteousness of Christ is accepted for us, and admitted instead of that perfect inherent righteousness that ought to be in ourselves: Christ's perfect obedience shall be reckoned to our account so that we shall have the benefit of it, as though we had performed it ourselves: and so we suppose that a title to eternal life is given us as the reward of this righteousness. . . .
>
> A second difference between the Anselmic and the Protestant soteriology is seen in the formal distinction of Christ's work into his active and his passive righteousness. By his passive righteousness is meant his expiatory sufferings, by which He satisfied the claims of justice, and by his active righteousness is meant his obedience to the law as a rule of life and conduct. It was contended by those who made this distinction, that the purpose of Christ as the vicarious substitute was to meet the entire demands of the law for the sinner. But the law requires present and perfect obedi-

ence, as well as satisfaction for past disobedience. The law is not completely fulfilled by the endurance of penalty only. It must also be obeyed. Christ both endured the penalty due to man for disobedience, and perfectly obeyed the law for him; so that He was a vicarious substitute in reference to both the precept and the penalty of the law. By his active obedience He obeyed the law, and by his passive obedience He endured the penalty. In this way his vicarious work is complete.[16]

I wish to say four things about this exposition.

First, Shedd presupposes that what God requires is perfect righteousness. I entirely agree with this, although I would track the matter rather differently, as we shall see. Nevertheless it has to be admitted that there are some today, such as Don Garlington, who argue that the old covenant did not make such an absolute demand.[17] The topic at hand, imputation, is only marginally tied to that debate, so I cannot probe it in detail here. For the moment, it is enough to say that they seem to base a great deal of their argument on a certain understanding of "perfection" and on a rather disputed reading of Romans 2, which all sides admit is a complex and difficult passage. And for reasons I shall articulate far too briefly toward the end of this paper, I remain unpersuaded by either argument.

Second, the response of Tom Oden to Gundry, though well-intentioned, rather misses the mark. "Does the active obedience of Christ prior to his death form any part of the righteousness of Christ?" Oden asks. "The critic [i.e., Gundry] appears to answer no. But consider the alternative: Suppose Jesus is a bum, a philanderer, a punk. Would he be qualified to become our Mediator?"[18] In his response, Gundry points out, fairly enough, that this is a straw man. In his earlier essay, Gundry had written, "Certainly evangelicals affirm that Jesus had to live a life of perfect righteousness if he was to qualify as the bearer of sins."[19] In other words, the disputed issue is

---

[16]William G. T. Shedd, *A History of Christian Doctrine,* 2 vols. (Edinburgh: T & T Clark, 1888 [1865]), 2:341; cited also in Hodge, *Systematic Theology,* 3:148-49. Cf. also William G. T. Shedd, *Dogmatic Theology,* 3 vols. (New York: Charles Scribner's Sons, 1889) 2:546-549.

[17]Don Garlington, *Faith, Obedience, and Perseverance: Aspects of Paul's Letter to the Romans,* WUNT 79 (Tübingen: Mohr-Siebeck, 1994), passim. This is a fairly common stance among the various strands of the "new perspective." Cf. the verdict of Jacob Neusner on E. P. Sanders's defense of that position, in Neusner's *Ancient Judaism: Debates and Disputes* (BJS 64; Chico, Calif.: Scholars Press, 1984), p. 198: "[N]ow exactly what Sanders means when he says that it would be 'un-Pharisaic' [of Paul] to exact perfect obedience to the law I do not know." See also Timo Laato, "Paul's Anthropological Considerations: Two Problems," in *Justification and Variegated Nomism, Vol. 2: The Paradoxes of Paul,* ed. D. A. Carson, Mark A. Seifrid and Peter T. O'Brien (Tübingen: Mohr-Siebeck, forthcoming).

[18]Thomas C. Oden, "A Calm Answer," *Books & Culture* 7, no. 2 (2001): 13.

[19]Robert H. Gundry, "Why I Didn't Endorse," 6; referred to in Gundry, "On Oden's 'Answer,'" p. 14.

not Jesus' righteousness. Gundry goes on to say, "A forensic declaration does not equal or demand that kind of imputation. All that is needed to make forensic sense of Paul's statement is for Christ's obedient submission to death for our sins to result in God's declaring righteous us whose sins have been imputed to Christ."[20]

So now the question may be put more sharply. For our pardon, is nothing more required than that the sins of sinners be imputed to Christ and that he bear them away? Or is there some sense in which sinners must be *reckoned* righteous, as well as ultimately *becoming* righteous? Are sinners reckoned righteous on no other ground than that their sins have been expiated? Is that sufficient—or, better put, does that exhaust the biblical descriptions of what must take place? This is precisely the position of Johannes Piscator, who represents, I suspect, a distortion of Melanchthon.[21] If I read him aright, Gundry would say yes to these questions. Certainly this stance is reflected in his treatment of Romans 5:12-21. Moreover, when he also points out Paul's pretty consistent preference for expressions referring to "the righteousness *of God*" rather than to "the righteousness *of Christ*," Gundry still does not want to say that "the righteousness *of God*" is imputed to us, but that this righteousness is nothing other than the result of God counting (imputing) our *faith* to us. In his view, there is no positive imputation *of righteousness* to us (whether labeled God's or Christ's), but a positive imputation of our faith to us as righteousness.

Third, to make matters more interesting yet, a few scholars in the Protestant tradition who avoid speaking of the imputation of Christ's righteousness because they cannot find that exact form of speech in the New Testament, nevertheless eagerly teach the substance of the matter. One might call this a biblicist position. I am thinking, for instance, of the late Broughton Knox, long-time Principal of Moore College. Though he scrupulously avoids the term imputation, nevertheless he writes such things as these:[22]

> Thus it comes about that what Christ did during His life on earth, He did not for Himself alone but as the representative and corporate Head of all those who are "in Him." His work for man may be looked at from two points of view. He lived the perfect life. Alone of all mankind His life was flawless, a life of perfect obedience, trust, and love. Moment by moment, as God's eye rested on that perfect life, it evoked the judgment, "My beloved Son, in whom I am well pleased." Christ is justified by

---

[20] "On Oden's 'Answer,' " p. 15.

[21] I am indebted for this observation to Mark A. Seifrid, in a paper so far unpublished, "The Justification of the Ungodly: Promise and Peril in the Current Discussion of Justification," p. 23.

[22] I am indebted to Graham Cole for isolating these passages for me.

the perfection of His life. God gives to Him the verdict of whole-hearted approval. Alone of mankind He stands in heaven by right, having fulfilled the conditions to which God had attached the reward of life. Christ stands before God, approved, crowned, exalted. We who are Christ's stand in God's presence covered with the robe of Christ's merits. We have put on Christ, says the Apostle (Gal 3:27). We are "in Christ." As God has raised Christ from the dead and exalted Him to the highest throne of heaven, crowning His perfect righteousness, so we who are in Him are made to sit with Him in the heavenly places (Eph 2:6), for He is our righteousness, the sole means of our justification (1 Cor 1:30; 2 Cor 5:21).[23]

Thus He [Christ] fulfilled every man's obligation to be completely obedient to the will of God. . . . Secondly, Jesus bore every man's penalty.[24]

That "Secondly" of the last line is significant, for it shows that Knox is closer to Shedd than he thinks he is, even though he avoids Shedd's terminology. But note in passing that Knox also appeals to corporate categories of Christology to deal with this issue. To this point I shall return at the end of the essay.

Fourth, however sympathetic one wishes to be with Shedd, however much one wishes to defend the view that the imputed righteousness of Christ is worth defending, however much one acknowledges that the perfection of Christ is something more in Scripture than the set-up that qualifies him for his expiatory death, however heuristically useful the distinction between the active and passive righteousness of Christ, one is left with a slightly uneasy feeling that the analytic categories of Shedd have somehow gone beyond the New Testament by the absolute bifurcation they introduce. A passage like the so-called Christ-hymn in Philippians 2 seems to depict Christ's obedience as all of a piece, including his willingness to become a human being and his progressive self-humiliation, climaxing in his obedience on the cross itself. By virtue of all of this obedience, Christ was vindicated, and his people are saved. Perhaps it is not that Shedd's categories have so much gone beyond the sweep of New Testament categories, as that they have not quite come up to them. To this, too, I shall return.

(5) It is time, past time perhaps, to devote some attention to the most crucial passage where Paul says that something was indeed imputed to a certain person as righteousness—even though Paul does not unambiguously say that what was imputed was Christ's righteousness. No, he says that faith was imputed—cred-

---

[23]David Broughton Knox, *Justification by Faith* (London: Church Book Room, 1959), p. 6.

[24]David Broughton Knox, *The Everlasting God: A Character Study of God in the Old and New Testaments* (Hertfordshire: Evangelical Press, 1982).

ited, reckoned—to Abraham as righteousness, and the same is true today (Rom 4:3-5). The passage is notoriously complex. I shall restrict myself to the following observations.

(a) In Jewish exegesis, Genesis 15:6 was not quoted to prove that Abraham was justified by faith and not by works. Rather, the passage was commonly read in the light of Genesis 22 (the *aqedah*), and was taken as explicit evidence of Abraham's merit. In I Maccabees 2:52, Abraham was found to be πιστος, faithful (not simply "believing," ἐπίστευσεν, as in the LXX), faithful ἐν πειρασμῷ (which surely refers to Gen 22), and the previous verse explicitly sees this in the category of work (μνήσθητε τῶν πατέρων ἡμῶν τὰ ἔργα ἃ ἐποίησεν, 2:51). About 50 B.C., Rabbi Shemaiah has God saying, "The faith with which your father Abraham believed in Me merits that I should divide the sea for you, as it is written: 'And he believed in the LORD, and He counted it to him for righteousness'" (*Mekhilta* on Ex 14:15 [35*b*]). Similarly, *Mekhilta* 40*b* speaks of "the merit of the faith with which [Abraham] believed in the LORD"—and then Genesis 15:6 is quoted.[25] What this means, for our purposes, is that Paul, who certainly knew of these traditions, was explicitly interpreting Genesis 15:6 in a way quite different from that found in his own tradition, and he was convinced that this new way was the correct way to understand the text. In the words of Cranfield, "It was clearly essential to the credibility of his argument that he should not by-pass a text which would seem to many of his fellow Jews the conclusive disproof of the point he was trying to establish and which was on any showing a text of cardinal importance in the biblical account of Abraham, but should show that, rightly interpreted, it confirmed his contention."[26] Paul's

---

[25] Cf. discussion in H. Moxnes, *Theology in Conflict: Studies in Paul's Understanding of God in Romans,* NovTSup 53 (Leiden: Brill, 1980), pp. 155-63.

[26] C. E. B. Cranfield, *The Epistle to the Romans,* 2 vols., ICC (Edinburgh: T & T Clark, 1975-1979), I:229-30. In a lengthy essay that circulated for a while on the web (at <www.angelfire.com/m.2/paulpage/Imputation.pdf>), but which has subsequently been withdrawn, Don Garlington, "Imputation or Union with Christ? A Response to John Piper," cites some of the same Jewish sources to argue, rather, that what Paul means is precisely what they mean: that is, Abraham's faith is imputed to him as righteousness precisely because his faith showed him to be faithful to the covenant and thus endowed with covenant righteousness (e.g., pp. 3-4 on my printout). But not only does this reading domesticate Paul by ascribing to him the meaning found in the texts of Jewish "background" (cf. the perennially *à propos* warnings of Samuel Sandmel, "Parallelomania," *JBL* 81 [1962]: 2-13), it fails to take seriously the profoundly *polemical* context of Romans 3—4. I am grateful to Peter T. O'Brien for initially drawing my attention to this essay by Garlington. Apparently it is scheduled to appear in print in *Reformation & Revival Journal,* along with a response from John Piper, who kindly sent me a copy. Piper similarly draws attention to Garlington's false dichotomy.

justification of his exegesis follows in the ensuing verses.

(b) Romans 4:4-5 has been understood in various ways. Barrett holds that the key lies in the verb λογίζομαι, which he thinks links nicely with πιστεύω and χάρις, but not with ἐργάζομαι and ὀφείλημα, that is, "since Abraham had righteousness *counted* to him, he cannot have done works, but must have been the recipient of grace."[27] But this argument founders on the fact that in Romans 4 Paul uses λογίζομαι with both κατὰ ὀφείλημα and κατὰ χάριν. H. W. Heidland offers a still more subtle linguistic distinction that I shall not probe here.[28] Because Paul says that faith is counted as righteousness, Gundry says that, in effect, Abraham's righteousness "consists of faith even though faith is not itself a work."[29] Faith becomes the equivalent of righteousness that is the way God "counts" faith, though of course faith and righteousness in themselves are not to be confused. Merely to assert, however, that faith of such equivalent value is not itself a work would not have impressed readers familiar with the Jewish background, where the precise counter-claim was standard fare. Moreover, although it is true that one important Old Testament text with the same grammatical construction (in the LXX) establishes a similar sort of equivalence (Ps 106:28), the equivalence in that case is not between *faith* and righteousness, but between *a righteous deed* and righteousness (the righteous deed in question is the zealous execution of public sinners by Phinehas, Num 25:7-13). In other words, in this instance "God's 'reckoning' Phinehas as righteous (see Num 25) is a declarative act, not an equivalent compensation or reward

---

[27]C. K. Barrett, *A Commentary on the Epistle to the Romans* (London: Adam & Charles Black, 1971), p. 88.
[28]H. W. Heidland, "λογίζομαι κτλ," *TDNT* 4:290-92, argues that Paul is playing off the Hebrew meaning of λογίζομαι (viz. חָשַׁב) with respect to κατὰ χάριν, over against the Greek meaning of the verb with respect to κατὰ ὀφείλημα. In the LXX, λογίζομαι renders חָשַׁב in all but five of its occurrences, and the Hebrew verb has little to do with "counting" or "reckoning" in a commercial sense, and much more to do with the notion of "plan," "invent," "devise," or, alternatively, to denote a kind of thinking in which will and emotion are involved, or to denote "count (as)" or "count [something or someone](as)," often as a subjective judgment (e.g., Gen 31:15; I Sam 1:13; Job 41:27, 29 [MT 41:21, 24]; Is 5:28). But this presupposes not only that Paul made this subtle distinction in his interpretation of Genesis 15:6, but that he expected his readers to, which is highly unlikely (or that he was incompetent if he did *not* expect them to, which is scarcely more attractive). More importantly, not only here in Romans 4 but even more so in Galatians 3:6-7 (where Paul again quotes Gen 15:6), the apostle fastens not on the verb λογίζομαι but on the verb πιστεύω: note (1) the contrast between τῷ . . . ἐργαζομένῳ and τῷ . . . μὴ ἐργαζομένῳ, πιστεύοντι δέ and, further (2) after πιστεύοντι the addition of ἐπὶ τὸν δικαιοῦντα τὸν ἀσεβῆ (on which see further comment below).
[29]Gundry, "Why I Didn't Endorse," p. 8.

for merit (cf. also Gen 31:15; Ps 32:2)."[30]

Of greater interest, because they are conceptually closer to Genesis 15:6, are those passages where the same construction is used to say that *something* is imputed or reckoned to another *as something else*. Thus Leah and Rachel assert that their father "reckons" them as "strangers" (though obviously they are not, Gen 31:15). The Levite's tithe is "reckoned" as the corn of the threshing-floor and as the fullness of the winepress, though transparently it is neither (Num 18:27, 30). If a certain sacrifice is not eaten by the third day, its value is lost, and it is not "reckoned" to the benefit of the sinner (Lev 7:18): clearly the passage "envisions a situation in which righteousness could be 'reckoned' to a person, even though the individual concerned admittedly is a sinner."[31] The relevant expression, לְ...חָשַׁב is used in other passages to refer to the offering of sacrifices that are "reckoned" to a person's benefit (e.g., Num 18:27, 30).

In other words, neither the verb nor the grammatical form will allow us to decide whether this "faith" that Abraham exercises was originally viewed as a righteous act which God himself then declared to be righteous (as the act of Phinehas was declared to be righteous, Ps 106:28, above), or, alternatively, that this "faith" that Abraham exercises is to be viewed as belonging to a different species than "righteous act," with the result that when it is "reckoned" or "imputed" to Abraham "as righteousness" it provides an instance in which, although God himself "reckons" it as righteousness, this is an instance in which *something* is imputed to another *as something else*.[32] How then shall we decide? We clearly see, of course, that the Jewish heritage in which Paul stood before his conversion opts for the former. The polemical context of Romans 3—4 argues rather emphatically that Paul now

---

[30]Moo, *The Epistle to the Romans*, p. 262 n. 35. This distinction perfectly reflects the fact that sometimes λογίζομαι conceives of the "counting" or the "imputing" as a reckoning up of what is in fact there, and sometimes conceives of the "counting" or the "imputing" as a reckoning up of one thing *as* another thing. See further below.

[31]O. Palmer Robertson, "Genesis 15:6: New Covenant Expositions of an Old Covenant Text," *WTJ* 42 (1980): 266. The other examples just mentioned are drawn from pp. 265-66. On this issue, cf. further H. H. Schmid, "Gerechtigkeit und Glaube: Genesis 15,1-6 und sein biblisch-theologischer Kontext," *EvT* 40 (1980): 408; and many commentaries on Genesis.

[32]Strangely, Don Garlington, "Imputation or Union with Christ?" n. 4, refers to the sorts of passages in which there is *not* strict equivalence as supporting a "non-imputational" reading of λογίζομαι. It is true that λογίζομαι has a semantic range large enough to include non-imputational readings: see, for instance, Romans 3:28, briefly discussed below. But these passages are not among them. In each instance, something that is not-X is *reckoned* to be X. To label them "non-imputational" in order to enforce the conclusion that the faith of Romans 4:3 demonstrates that Abraham was thus rightly reckoned to be righteous is to pre-judge the linguistic matters and, as I shall argue above, distort the flow of Paul's argument.

opts for the latter. Whose interpretation of Genesis 15 is justified?

Part of the hermeneutical distinction between the two positions is this: when dealing with the patriarchs, Paul the Christian is especially careful to observe the salvation-historical sequence, whereas his theological opponents tend to lump texts together thematically rather than salvation-historically. For instance, later in this chapter Paul carefully draws inferences from whether God's declaration that Abraham's faith is counted to him as righteousness precedes or succeeds circumcision. So also here. Paul is saying in effect that this faith must not be read in connection with the *aqedah*, found seven chapters later, but in the light of its own context. In the immediate context, God made gracious promises to Abraham, completely unmerited—and Abraham believed God. Thus Abraham's response of faith is simply trust in the God who graciously made the promise—that is, in Cranfield's words, "his faith was counted to him for righteousness can only be a matter of χάρις, that is, if his faith is understood (in accordance with the context of this verse in Genesis) as his reliance upon God's promise (cf. Gen 15:1, 4)."[33] Detached from Genesis 22 and firmly attached to the context, it is hard to see how this faith is in any sense a work. Indeed, as Paul makes clear a little later in the same chapter, the specific promise of God that Abraham believed was God's promise that through Abraham's seed the blessing would come (cf. Rom 4:13).

(c) That is why Paul can draw the analogy he does in Romans 4:4: where wages are earned, they are credited to a person κατὰ ὀφείλημα, but where (implicitly) something is *not* earned, it is credited κατὰ χάριν. By implication, then, because the faith of Romans 4:3 is not in any sense something earned, if it is credited to Abraham it must be κατὰ χάριν. Unpacking this further in Romans 4:5, Paul says that in the case of the person who does not work but who trusts God who justifies the wicked (as Abraham trusted God who graciously gave the promise), that trust, that faith, is credited as righteousness.

One of the reasons this may be formally confusing is that some translations do not adequately distinguish rather different expressions in Greek. Consider the NIV:

Romans 4:3: Abraham believed God, and it [presumably the faith] was credited to him *as righteousness.*

Romans 4:4: when a man works, his wages are not credited to him *as a gift,* but *as an obligation.*

Romans 4:5: his faith is credited *as righteousness.*

---

[33]Cranfield, *Epistle to the Romans,* 1:231.

But the first and third expressions (εἰς δικαιοσύνην) tell us what something is credited to a person *as* (if I may end a clause this way), what this crediting terminates in (εἰς). By contrast, the analogy of Romans 4:4 does *not* tell us what the wages are credited *as*, that is, what they terminate in, but simply specifies whether they are credited "according to obligation" or "according to grace." In other words, the structure of the crediting or imputing language is not consistent through these verses, so it becomes easy to force the wrong kind of parallelism and miss the train of thought. Romans 4:4 establishes that there is a crediting, an imputing, that is nothing more than getting your dessert; there is also a crediting, an imputing, that means something is credited to your account that you do *not* deserve. But Paul does *not* make this analogy from the field of wages walk on all fours and try to specify what this wage is credited *as*. It is sufficient for his argument, at this juncture, that the distinction between merited imputation and unmerited imputation be preserved. Romans 4:3, then, is clarified by Romans 4:4: when faith is imputed to Abraham as righteousness, it is *unmerited*, it is all of grace, because it is nothing more than believing God and his gracious promise. That same approach is then applied in Romans 4:5 to Paul's discussion of justification, and the inevitable conclusion is drawn: "to anyone who does not work but trusts God who justifies the ungodly, their faith is credited as righteousness" (TNIV).

(d) Of course, if this is applied to Abraham, it is tantamount to calling him ungodly, wicked, ἀσεβής. In other words, it is not enough to say that for Paul, Abraham's faith is not a righteous "act" or "deed" but it *is* a genuinely righteous stance, a covenant faithfulness, which God then *rightly* or *justly* counts to Abraham as righteousness. That does not make sense of the "meriting"/"not meriting" contrast implicit in the wages analogy. More importantly, it does not bear in mind Paul's own powerful conclusion: it is the *wicked* person to whom the Lord imputes righteousness. In the context, that label is applied to Abraham no less than to anyone else. In Paul's understanding, then, God's imputation of Abraham's faith to Abraham as righteousness *cannot* be grounded in the assumption that that faith is itself intrinsically righteous, so that God's "imputing" of it to Abraham is no more than a recognition of what it intrinsically is. If God is counting faith to Abraham *as* righteousness, *he is counting him righteous*—not because Abraham *is* righteous in some inherent way (How can he be? He is ἀσεβής!), but simply because Abraham trusts God and his gracious promise. In that sense, then, we are dealing with what systematicians call an alien righteousness.

This entire argument flows out of Paul's discussion of justification in Romans 3:21-26, where Paul argues that God simultaneously vindicates himself and justifies *the ungodly* by setting forth Christ to be the ἱλαστήριον. In short, the flow of the argument is not affirming that God credits something intrinsic to us or properly earned by us or reflective of us to be our righteousness, but it is arguing that God counts us righteous, even though we are ungodly, by crediting faith as such righteousness—that is, faith in the justifying God who justifies the ungodly by setting forth Christ as the propitiation for our sins. Thus God credits us with a righteousness we do not have.

In other words, "faith" in Romans 4:3 depends on how "faith" has been used in the preceding verses. It is not faith in some purely psychological sense that is credited as righteousness, but faith with a certain object: in Genesis 15:3, faith in God's gracious promise, and in Romans 3—4, faith in God who justifies the ungodly by setting forth Christ as the propitiation for our sins. It is *such* faith that is counted for righteousness. The significance of this observation will become clearer after the next two subsections.

(e) In Romans 4:6-8, Paul advances his argument by providing an Old Testament instance that shows what it means to say that God justifies the ungodly.[34] David, we are told, "speaks of the blessedness of the man to whom God credits [imputes] righteousness apart from works" (Romans 4:6)—and then the Old Testament text, Psalm 32:1-2, is cited. Observe the parallelism:

| 4:5 | God | justifies | the ungodly |
| 4:6 | God | credits righteousness | apart from works |

In other words, "justifies" is parallel to "credits righteousness"; or, to put the matter in nominal terms, justification is parallel to the imputation of righteousness. Observe two further points. *First*, if one asks whether this imputation, this crediting, is merely an accurate counting of the righteousness that is in fact intrinsically there, or, alternatively, an imputation of an alien righteousness (for as we have seen, λογίζομαι can be used in both contexts), we must decisively opt for the latter. For the parallelism shows that God justifies *the ungodly* (Rom 4:5); he credits righteousness *apart from works* (Rom 4:6)—and this latter phrase is further elucidated in the quotation itself (Rom 4:7-8) as the works of those who

---

[34]The Greek καθάπερ, "just as," or, in the NIV, "David says *the same thing*," invites the reader to discern just what comparison Paul is constructing.

have committed transgressions and sins. *Second*, both elements of the parallelism establish God as the One who is acting: it is *God* who justifies the ungodly (Rom 4:5), it is *God* who imputes righteousness apart from works. The words are striking, because formally they contradict what God says he will do in the Old Testament. God says, "I will not acquit the guilty" (Ex 23:7).[35] Again, Scripture says, "Acquitting the guilty and condemning the innocent—the Lord detests them both" (Prov 17:15). C. K. Barrett goes so far as to say that, by contrast, Paul's words, "God justifies the ungodly," actually "describe God as doing what the Old Testament forbids."[36] That is true only at the formal level. The Old Testament context shows that God is passionately committed to *justice*, and therefore Israel's magistrates must never pervert justice by acquitting the guilty or condemning the innocent (cf. also Is 5:23). At very least one must conclude that in these passages, "to justify" is a forensic term; it cannot mean "to make (personally and ethically) righteous." But more important, Hofius has shown that even in the Old Testament there is ample evidence in God's dealings with Israel that on occasion God *does* justify the ungodly (even though that terminology is not used): witness Hosea, Jeremiah, Isaiah 40.[37] Paul's assertions in Romans 4 presuppose his detailed account of Christ's cross-work in Romans 3:21-26. There he explains how God presented Christ as the propitiation for our sins, "so as to be just and the one who justifies those who have faith in Jesus" (Rom 3:26).[38] In other words, "God's forgiveness is no cheap forgiveness that condones wickedness, but the costly, just and truly merciful forgiveness διὰ τῆς ἀπολυτρώσεως τῆς ἐν Χριστῷ Ἰησοῦ, which does not violate the truth which the Exodus verse attests."[39]

(f) The same argument can be extended a little farther into Romans 4 by observing the structural parallels that tie together Romans 3:27-31 and Romans 4. In other words, Romans 4 appears to be an enlarged meditation on the themes that are briefly summarized in Romans 3:27-31:

---

[35]The LXX puts this into the second person.

[36]Barrett, *Romans*, p. 88.

[37]Otfried Hofius, " 'Rechtfertigung des gottlosen' als Thema biblisher Theologie," *Jahrbuch für biblische Theologie* 2 (1987): 79-105. I am grateful to Mark Seifrid for drawing my attention to this essay.

[38]Thus I accept the more traditional rendering of Romans 3:25-26, which understands the lines to give us the "internal" explanation of the cross. See especially the commentary by Moo, *Romans*, pp. 218-43; and Carson, "Why Trust a Cross?"

[39]Cranfield, 1:232 n. 1.

faith excludes boasting   3:27   4:1-2

faith is necessary to preserve grace   3:28   4:3-8

faith is necessary if Jews & Gentiles alike are to be saved   3:29-30   4:9-17

Christian faith, then, far from overturning the OT, fulfills   3:31   4:18-25
the OT anticipation

If this parallelism holds up, then Romans 3:28 is parallel to Romans 4:3-8, and we have something to add to the parallelism we detected in the last subsection between Romans 4:5 and Romans 4:6. To put the three passages together:

4:5	God	justifies	the ungodly
4:6	God	credits righteousness	apart from works
3:28	[a person]	is justified	apart from the works of the law

Apart from the switch to the passive voice, then, once again we perceive that justification of the ungodly *means* the imputation of righteousness. Intriguingly, the same "imputation of righteousness" theme crops up in Romans 4:9-11, along with the "imputation of faith as righteousness" theme. Abraham, we are told, becomes the father of *all* who believe, because his faith was credited to him as righteousness *before* he was circumcised. Thus he is the archetypical model not only for the circumcised, but for *all*. Nor is Abraham at this juncture a model of faithfulness to the covenant, since he had not yet received the covenant sign! Paul concludes, "So then, [Abraham] is the father of *all* who believe but have not been circumcised, in order that *righteousness might be credited to them*" (Rom 4:11). In this text, the passive voice triumphs (as in Rom 3:28), but it is righteousness that is being imputed to these Gentile believers, not faith imputed to them *as* righteousness.

(g) Thus within the space of a few verses the apostle Paul can say two *formally* different things:

4:3, 9   [God] credits faith to Abraham as righteousness
4:6, 11   [God] credits righteousness apart from works [i.e., to the ungodly]

Robert Gundry wants these two utterances to be saying the same thing. More precisely, he holds that the righteousness that is imputed (in Rom 4:6, 11) is not God's, and still less Christ's, but is simply "the righteousness of faith" (Rom 4:11)—"i.e., the righteousness which by God's counting consists in faith even though the exercise of faith is not intrinsically (a work of human) righteousness. 'The righteousness of God,' which is not said to be counted/imputed, is his salvific action of counting faith as righteousness, an action made [probable]—given God's righteous character—by Christ's propitiatory death."[40] In other words, for Gundry the controlling expression is the one Paul draws from Genesis 15:6: God counts [imputes] faith to Abraham—and, in principle, to us—as righteousness. If the apostle then speaks of God imputing righteousness to us, this is merely his short-hand way of saying the same thing: the "righteousness" which, Paul says, God imputes to us is in reality the faith that God imputes to us as righteousness. Thus Gundry not only is denying that Paul speaks of Christ's righteousness being imputed to us, but he is denying that Paul speaks of God's righteousness being imputed to us. The only imputation he sees is the imputation of faith as righteousness.[41] But too many textual factors stand against this reductionism.

First, it is not transparent that the two expressions, "[God] imputes faith to X as righteousness" and "[God] imputes righteousness to X" mean exactly the same thing. In the one case, the thing that is imputed or counted is faith; in the other, the thing that is imputed or counted is righteousness. It does not help to say that in God's eyes, since he "counts" the faith to be righteousness, therefore from this perspective they *are* the same thing, for it does not solve the problem of the language. If God has counted or imputed our faith to us as righteousness, then, once he has so counted or imputed it, does he then count or impute the righteousness to us, a kind of second imputation? The awkwardness of conjoining the expressions in any obvious way makes us suspect that they are not saying exactly the same thing.

Second, the language of "God imputing righteousness to us" is powerfully and repeatedly placed in the immediate context of human ungodliness and wickedness, with the result that it reads as God imputing an (alien) righteousness to us precisely when we are unrighteous. It does not read as God imputing faith to us as righteousness. That is a slightly adjacent thought, as we shall see.

Third, the variations in language are somewhat clarified by the further explana-

---

[40] This is from a private e-mail, dated April 16, 2003, in which Dr. Gundry graciously unpacked his views for me a little more, thus lessening any potential I might have had for misrepresenting him. I am grateful for his patience.

[41] That is why, in the essay that provoked some of these debates ("Why I Didn't Endorse," p. 9), Gundry concludes his piece with a postscript in which he suggests that there might be a more fruitful dialogue between evangelicals and Roman Catholics "if both sides were to give up their respective notions of imputation and infusion."

tion that Paul offers toward the end of Romans 4. There Paul speaks of Abraham being fully persuaded that God had the power to do what he had promised, and would in fact keep his promise. "This is why 'it was credited to him as righteousness' "—and thus the words of Genesis 15:6 are repeated again. But these words, Paul avers, "were written not for him alone, but also for us, to whom God will credit righteousness—for us who believe in him who raised Jesus our Lord from the dead" (Rom 4:23-24). One might almost think, at first blush, that Gundry has it right, that is, that the notion "faith imputed to Abraham as righteousness" is written for us, and this is immediately linked with the notion that God will credit us with righteousness. But immediately one is forced to wonder if that is right, for the "us" of whom this is said are those "who believe (τοῖς πιστεύουσιν) in him who raised Jesus our Lord from the dead." In other words, the believing is now portrayed as *the means or the condition or the instrument*[42] of the imputation of righteousness, not as that which is imputed as righteousness.

Fourth, this is entirely in line with the fact that in the verses immediately preceding Romans 4, Paul is at pains to stress the instrumental nature of faith. If in Romans 3:21-26 the controlling expression is ἡ δικαιοσύνη τοῦ θεοῦ, the controlling expression in Romans 3:27-31 is πίστις. We are justified "by faith" (πίστει, ἐκ πίστεως, διὰ τῆς πίστεως —all of which presuppose faith as the means of appropriating the gift, not that which is reckoned as the gift). That point is summarized in the very next verse, the opening verse of Romans 5: "Therefore, since we have been justified through faith (ἐκ πίστεως), we have peace with God through our Lord Jesus Christ." The instrumentality of faith is commonplace in the New Testament: see, for instance, Philippians 3:8-9 (on which more below), or Hebrews 11, to go no farther. The reader of the text of Romans has thought his or her way through the object of the Christian's faith and the ground of the Christian's justification (Rom 3:21-26), as well as the importance of faith and of nothing else as the means for appropriating the grace, whether one is Jew or Gentile (Rom 3:27-31), before reading the statement about Abraham's faith at the beginning of Romans 4.

Fifth, although Gundry asserts, doubtless fairly, that he can find no unambiguous instance in the LXX, the New Testament, or in pagan literature, of λογίζομαι

---

[42]Even if one holds (as I do) that the delivering up and the raising of Jesus is the means of our believing (cf. also Eph 2:8-9, where faith is the gift of God), and thus the fruit of grace, this does not in the slightest vitiate Pauline insistence, in the appropriate context, that faith is the means or instrument by which grace is appropriated.

being used to refer to something being imputed *in an instrumental sense*, one must also aver that the verb is not a *terminus technicus*. It has an astonishingly wide range of meaning. Note, for instance, Romans 3:28: "we reckon (λογιζόμεθα) that a man is justified by faith (πίστει)": here (i) the "reckoning" is certainly not imputation in any technical sense, (ii) the justification (in the light of the preceding paragraph) is grounded in Christ's cross-work, and (iii) the *means* of benefitting from Christ's propitiatory death is unambiguously faith. In the light of such linguistic realities, it seems a bit doctrinaire to read the Genesis 15:6 citation in Romans 4 in the controlling way that Gundry advocates. The primary point of the quotation, in Paul's argument, is that Abraham's faith in the sheer gratuity of God's promise is what was counted to him as righteousness. That point is correlated with the fact that righteousness is imputed to the ungodly, but the expressions make slightly different points.

In the light of these contextual considerations, then, Herman Ridderbos speaks, not incorrectly, of this crediting of faith as righteousness as an instrumental usage.[43] In the flow of the argument from Romans 3 to Romans 4, I think that is conceptually correct, though not syntactically perspicuous.

This may be unpacked a little further. At the end of Romans 3, the object of the faith that is transparently instrumental in Romans 3:27-31 is transparently Jesus (Rom 3:26) in function of his propitiatory death, set forth by God himself (Rom 3:21-26). As Simon Gathercole observes, in Romans 4 Paul identifies three specific "objects" to the faith that is approved:

. . . πιστεύοντι δὲ ἐπὶ τὸν δικαιοῦντα τὸν ἀσεβῆ (Rom 4:5)

. . . ἐπίστευσεν θεοῦ τοῦ ζῳοποιοῦντος τοὺς νεκροὺς καὶ καλοῦντος τὰ μὴ ὄντα ὡς ὄντα (Rom 4:17)

. . . τοῖς πιστεύουσιν ἐπὶ τὸν ἐγείραντα Ἰησοῦν τὸν κύριον ἡμῶν ἐκ νεκρῶν (Rom 4:24)[44]

Thus, although in broad terms it is true to say that the object of both the Christian believer at the end of Romans 3, and of Abraham in Romans 4, is the God who graciously promises, one can specify a little more detail. The God who is the object of faith is the One who justifies the ungodly (Rom 4:5), the One who

---

[43]Herman Ridderbos, *Paul: An Outline of His Theology* (Grand Rapids: Eerdmans, 1975), pp. 176-78.

[44]Cf. Simon J. Gathercole, "Justified by Faith, Justified by his Blood: The Evidence of Romans 3:21— 4:5," in *Justification and Variegated Nomism, Vol. 2: The Paradoxes of Paul*, ed. D. A. Carson, Peter T. O'Brien and Mark A. Seifrid (Tübingen: Mohr-Siebeck, forthcoming).

brings to life what is dead and calls into existence what is not (Rom 4:17, whether this life-giving power brings a son to Abraham and Sarah or calls the dead into life, whether Jesus or those who are spiritually dead), the One who raises Jesus from the dead (Rom 4:24; cf. also Rom 10). Faith is not faith which merely trusts a God who justifies the godly; faith is not faith "which believes in a God who leaves the dead as dead and leaves non-existent things as non-existent";[45] faith is not faith which reposes in a God who does *not* raise Jesus from the dead. In other words, Paul detects a pattern of God doing the unthinkable, the transforming, the reversing. What this says about God's justification of the ungodly *as an event bound up with the resurrection of Jesus* I shall probe a little below. For the moment, it is sufficient to observe that faith, *because of its object*, is imputed to the believer as righteousness. It was because Abraham was "fully persuaded that God had power to do what he had promised" (Rom 4:21) that this faith "was credited to him as righteousness" (Rom 4:22). These words, Paul immediately adds, were written no less for us, to whom the Lord will impute righteousness (Rom 4:24)—"for us who believe in him who raised Jesus our Lord from the dead. He was delivered over to death for our sins and was raised to life *for our justification*" (Rom 4:24-25). In short, righteousness is imputed when men and women *believe* in this sense: we are fully persuaded that God will do what he has promised. *What* God has promised, this side of the "But now" of Romans 3:21, is the atoning death and resurrection of Jesus. That is why there is no tension between believing the God who raised Jesus from the dead (Rom 4:24) and believing in Jesus (Rom 3:26) whose death and resurrection vindicate God.

In the light of these thematic lines running through Romans 3—4, then, the righteousness that God imputes to the ungodly is bound up with his promises concerning the seed, and thus ultimately with his word concerning Christ's death and resurrection. Faith in such a God is faith that is imputed as righteousness, not because the faith is itself meritorious but because it focuses absolutely on the God who justifies the ungodly by the means he has promised. In such a redemptive-historical trajectory, the expression "his faith was imputed to him as righteousness" is necessarily a kind of shorthand for the larger exposition. To interpret it in a minimalist fashion and then to squeeze under this minimalism the rest of the imputation utterances of the chapter is precisely to invert the priorities of the argument. It is in this sense, then, that it is not unjust to conclude, with Ridderbos, that this

---

[45]Ibid.

crediting of faith as righteousness is an instrumental usage.[46]

(6) I must now step back and draw in a number of other texts that shed light on this discussion. Ideally space should be reserved for detailed consideration of Romans 5:12-21, but under the present restraints I restrict myself to brief comments on one or two other passages.

Several Pauline texts contrast, in one way or another, righteousness that comes through the law with righteousness that comes through faith in Christ.[47] For instance:

> What is more, I consider everything a loss compared to the surpassing greatness of knowing Christ Jesus my Lord, for whose sake I have lost all things. I consider them

---

[46]Here, it appears, Don Garlington wants to have his cake and eat it: "It is just such an appraisal of the reckoning of righteousness that opens up the intention of Romans 6:4: *because of its object*, faith, and faith alone, is accepted in the place of allegiance to the law of Moses, including most prominently the various boundary markers of Jewish identity. In strict terms, faith is *reckoned as* righteousness: our faith in Christ is looked upon as tantamount to righteousness in its quintessential meaning—conformity to the will of God—because *in Christ* we have become God's very righteousness (2 Corinthians 5:21)" ("Imputation or Union with Christ," p. 5 on my printout [emphasis his]). Apart from the gratuitous reference to boundary markers, which are scarcely central to Paul's concerns in the opening chapters of Romans, Garlington is entirely right to emphasize that it is faith's *object* that is crucial in Paul's argument. That is what makes faith, intrinsically in Paul's argument, a means. On the other hand: (a) It is far from clear that Paul accepts faith "in place of allegiance to the law of Moses": faith shuts out the law, which condemns. (b) While by stressing faith's object Garlington implicitly recognizes faith as means, by then defining faith's "quintessential meaning" as "conformity to the will of God" he surreptitiously makes this faith essentially the righteousness which is then *rightly* imputed to believers as righteousness. The language is notoriously slippery. In some broad sense, of course, God-commanded faith is in "conformity to the will of God," but in the context this faith justifies *the ungodly*, that is, those who are *not* in conformity to the will of God. Like most who take this line, Garlington has not come to terms with Paul's insistence that the faith he has in view is not in any sense *properly* seen as something intrinsically the believer's and so "good" that it earns this imputation as righteousness. Rather, it is categorized as a "gift" (Rom 4:4), which is given to *the ungodly*. (c) Garlington is entirely right to show that it is *in Christ* that we have become God's very righteousness. But the antithetical nature of the way he casts this union in Christ is troubling: see further below.

[47]Inevitably something must be said about the heated debate between those who take the subjective genitive ("the faith[fulness] of Christ") and those who take the objective genitive ("faith in Christ"). Despite the claims of Richard B. Hays, *The Faith of Jesus Christ: The Narrative Substructure of Galatians 3:1-4:11*, 2nd ed. (Grand Rapids: Eerdmans, 2002), which is doubtless the premier defense of the former option, linguistically much more can be said for the objective genitive. From the voluminous literature, see especially Moisés Silva, "Faith Versus Works of the Law in Galatians," in *Justification and Variegated Nomism. Volume 2: The Paradoxes of Paul*, ed. D. A. Carson, Mark Seifrid and Peter T. O'Brien (Tübingen: Mohr-Siebeck, forthcoming). In most of the relevant passages, there is a sense in which at one level the decision one forms on this issue does not *necessarily* control too much of the ensuing discussion. For instance, even if one were to adopt the subjective genitive in the expression in Romans 3:21-26 (i.e., reading "the faithfulness of Jesus Christ"), there is still a major emphasis on faith (e.g., Rom 3:22, 25, 26).

rubbish, that I may gain Christ, and be found in him, *not having a righteousness of my own that comes from the law, but that which is by faith in Christ*—the righteousness that comes *from God* and is *through faith.* (Phil 3:8-9, emphasis added)

Here, transparently, the righteousness that Paul seeks is not inherent, that is, it is not his own. Nor does it consist in faith; rather, it comes *through* faith (διὰ πίστεως) or is "based on faith" (ἐπὶ τῇ πίστει). This righteousness is explicitly said to be God's: that is, it is alien to Paul. Although the language of imputation is not used, we find ourselves in the same conceptual world as in Romans 3—4.

The language of 2 Corinthians 5:19-21 is also instructive. "God was reconciling the world to himself in Christ [or: God was in Christ, reconciling the world to himself], not counting [imputing] men's sins against them. . . . God made him [Christ] who had no sin to be sin for us, so that in him we might become the righteousness of God." Explicitly, then, Paul speaks of the non-imputation of our sins to ourselves—that is, God refuses to count up to our account what is in fact there—on the ground that God made Christ, himself sinless, to be sin for us. True, the text does not explicitly *say* that God imputes our sins to Christ, but as long as we perceive that Jesus dies in our place, and bears our curse, and was made "sin" for us, it is extraordinarily difficult to avoid the notion of the imputation of our sins to him.

To this thought, Paul then adds the words, "so that in him we might become the righteousness of God." If there were no other passage treating these themes, it would be possible, just barely, to read this as follows: "Our sins are imputed to Christ, who by his death expiates them, so that we might *become righteous.*" In other words, there would be no hint of the imputation of righteousness to believers. But three things stand against such a reading.

First, Paul's treatment of these themes elsewhere (though we have merely glanced at Rom 3—4 and Phil 3:8-9) affirms that God credits righteousness to the ungodly. It is entirely natural to take the last clause of 2 Corinthians 5:21 the same way. It would be entirely unnatural in the context of 2 Corinthians 5 to say that this "righteousness" which we "become" is in reality faith that is imputed to us as righteousness; Genesis 15:6 is not in play.

Second, within 2 Corinthians 5:19-21, the thought that our sins are imputed to Christ commends itself as a parallel to the notion that righteousness is in turn imputed to us. What might be thought by some to stand against such a view is that this righteousness is explicitly said to be *God's* righteousness, not *Christ's* righteousness. I shall return to this in a moment, but even so the opening clause of verse 19 must not be overlooked: *God was in Christ* reconciling the world to himself, or "*God* was reconciling the world to himself *in Christ*." All sides recognize that what "God" and "Christ" do in the New Testament can sometimes be distinguished. It is commonplace to observe that the Father commands and the Son obeys, never the reverse; the Son dies on the cross, the Father does not (we disown patripassianism). Before we retreat too quickly into such distinctions, however, the distinctions themselves must be distinguished. The first—that the Father commands and the Son obeys—pertains to their roles relative to each other. Similarly, in certain acts the Son may be shown to be the Father's agent, not the reverse: New Testament writers can speak of God creating all things (e.g., Acts 14:15; Rev 4:11), or of Christ creating all things (e.g., Col 1:15-20), but sometimes of Christ or the Son or the Word being God's agent in creation (e.g., Jn 1:2-3), never of the Father being the Son's agent in creation. These sorts of distinctions, then, pertain to the respective roles that the Father and the Son enjoy *relative to each other*. But the second—the Son dies on the cross, and the Father does not—is rather different. In this distinction, the Son does something that the Father does *not* do, precisely because what the Son is doing is made possible by his humiliation and incarnation. In this regard, there are numerous things that the Son does that the Father does not do; there are no texts that tell us that everything the Son does, the Father also does. But the New Testament writers take some pains to affirm the reverse: all that the Father does, the Son also does. The *locus classicus* of this theme, of course, is John 5:16-30, but the same theme is implicit, for instance, in the ease with which New Testament writers take Old Testament texts that refer to Yahweh and make them refer without hesitation to Jesus Christ. It is understandable, of course, that New Testament writers should take pains to say that Jesus does all that God does, and refrain from saying that the Father does all that Jesus does. Yet once the point is observed, one cannot leap from our careful avoidance of patripassianism to the conclusion that although *God* imputes [his] righteousness to us, Christ does *not* impute [his] righteousness to us. For in the case of patripassianism, we are denying that the Father does everything the Son does, if what the Son does is conditioned by the incarnation, while in the case of imputation the action is fundamentally God's, and everything the Father does the Son also does.[48] This is all the more important, then, when we recall the opening words of this passage. Whether we understand the word order to support "God was in Christ, reconciling the world to himself," or "God was reconciling the world to himself in

---

[48]This form of words, of course, is Johannine, not Pauline, but I have briefly argued that the thought is not peculiar to either of them but common to both.

Christ," what God was doing is then fleshed out in a particular way. On the one hand, God made Christ who had no sin to be a curse for us: here the distinction between God and Christ turns absolutely on the peculiar role of Christ in his death, though even here it is *God* who "made Christ" be a curse for us (as it is God, in Rom 3:25, who "presents" Christ as a propitiation). On the other hand, all this takes place so that "in him [i.e., Christ] we might become the righteousness of God." The "in him" phrase doubtless reflects the "union with Christ" theme about which I'll say more in a moment. What should be clear, however, is that on the basis of the parallels just advanced, it is difficult to imagine why this righteousness should be understood to be "the righteousness of God" and *not* the righteousness of Christ.

Third, the text does not say that, owing to the non-imputation of our sins to us, or owing to the imputation of our sins to Christ, we become *righteous* (i.e., the adjective), but that in Christ we become *the righteousness of God* (i.e., the noun). On first glance, this is an astonishingly awkward locution. I shall return to it in a moment.

(7) In this final heading, I want to broaden the aperture again, draw together some Pauline considerations not yet explored and respond to one or two objections.

First, Paul does not think of sin and evil *primarily* in legal terms. The origin of evil is bound up with rebellion, with idolatry, with the de-godding of God (cf. Rom 1:18—3:20). What draws down God's wrath, above all things, is the obscenity of competition—for there is no God but God. That is why in Paul's thought sin and death reign from Adam to Moses. The law makes sin transgression; it does not create an evil that was not already there by virtue of our rebellion, by virtue of our idolatry. It is vital to understand this if we are to grasp the sweep and power of salvation in Christ Jesus. That is why Seifrid, in an unpublished letter, is not too strong when he comments on Garlington's insistence that the Old Testament does not demand utter righteousness, utter holiness:

> I shall not here pursue his [Garlington's] dilution of the demands of the mosaic covenant by appeal to a certain understanding of "perfection" except to note that he stands at odds with Paul, James, the author of Hebrews, Jesus, the prophets of Israel and Moses himself. Other than that, he is in perfect agreement with Scripture. He doesn't understand that our acts of sin are expressions of unbelief and the desire to annihilate God. This desire resides in all our hearts. If it were not there, we would sin no more. The Law merely exposes us for what we are. He should let it do its work, because apart from it Christ's work means nothing.

Sin is more than the breaking of rules (though the "rules" clarify and help to quantify the horrendous breach of idolatry). If the first commandment is to love God with heart and soul and mind and strength (Mk 12:28-34; cf. Deut 6), the first sin is the failure to love God with heart and soul and mind and strength. The first sin is therefore not a matter of doing something, so much as of not doing something. It is not only a positive evil; it is the failure to do a positive good. As a rule, the less clear we are on the horrendous odium and multi-faceted comprehensiveness of human idolatry, the less clear we will be on what the cross achieved and on our desperate need for a Redeemer.

Second, I cannot too strongly emphasize how often Paul's justification language is tied to "in Christ" or "in him" language—yet this brute fact, far from clarifying matters, has sometimes merely muddied the waters.

On the one hand, justification is, in Paul, irrefragably tied to our incorporation into Christ, to our union with Christ. Thus, as we have seen, in Philippians 3:8-9 Paul wants to be found *in him*, not having a *righteousness* of his own. In 2 Corinthians 5:19-21, we are told that God made Christ who had no sin to be sin for us, so that *in him* we might become the *righteousness* of God. It is because of God that we are *in Christ Jesus*, who has become for us *righteousness* (and other things: 1 Cor 1:30). Passage after passage in Paul runs down the same track. If we speak of justification or of imputation (whether of our sins to Christ or of δικαιοσύνη being credited to us) *apart* from a grasp of this incorporation into Christ, we will constantly be in danger of contemplating some sort of transfer *apart* from being included in Christ, *apart* from union with Christ.

On the other hand, the theme of union with Christ has been distorted in various complex ways. Many have pointed out that in the Joint Declaration of Lutherans and Catholics, the shocking element was not simply that both sides indulged in slippery language to mask substantial differences, but that when the Lutherans articulated their *own* position they managed to avoid all reference to imputation, preferring instead "union with Christ" language. But how is such language to be understood? Those with an inside track to the discussions assert that it was tacitly understood in *theosis* categories—which of course ends up sacrificing the Reformation understanding of justification altogether.[49] Some think of imputation and union with Christ in frankly antithetical terms,[50] instead of seeing the latter as the grounding of the former. Still others adopt so vitalistic or even mystical an understanding of "union

---

[49]At the Wheaton Theology Conference at which this paper was read, Dr. Anthony Lane made this point most forcefully.
[50]Hence the title of Don Garlington's paper to which I have already referred, "Imputation or Union with Christ? A Response to John Piper."

with Christ" that its usage with respect to justification is misconstrued.

It is important to see that the "in Christ" language in the Pauline writings is fundamentally metaphorical, and sufficiently flexible that the dictates of the immediate context can shape the notion in various ways.[51] In other words, imputation is crucial, but it is itself grounded in something more comprehensive. Christians are so incorporated into Christ, "in him," that their sins are expiated when he dies. That is why we can say, with Paul, "I am crucified with Christ"; that is how God sees it. I am so incorporated into Christ that Christ's death is my death, and Christ's life is my life: "For you died," Paul writes, "and your life is now hidden with Christ in God. When Christ, who is your life, appears, then you also will appear with him in glory" (Col 3:3-4). In other words, the language of incorporation or of identification is precisely what grounds "the great exchange": when Christ died, he died my death, so I can truly say I died in him; now that Christ lives, his life is mine, so I can truly say I live in him.

But in the case of Galatians 2:20-21 there may be additional precision. The "Christ in me" and "I in him" language always needs unpacking, with close attention to the immediate context. When Paul writes, "I no longer live, but Christ lives *in me*" (Gal 2:20), we must ask what ἐν + dative of personal pronoun means in this context, and commonly in Paul. The phrase "Christ lives in me" is often understood in a vitalistic sense, or in a real sense by means of the Spirit, or the like—and certainly Paul and other New Testament writers can think in those terms. But the fact that the Greek preposition has been glossed by the English word "in" does not qualify as an argument. At the end of Galatians 1, Paul says this of the believers in Judea who heard of his conversion: "they glorified God ἐν ἐμοί"—and despite exegetical efforts to the contrary, the prepositional expression should probably not be rendered by "in me." In fact, in as many as 30 percent of the instances of ἐν + dative of personal pronoun in the Pauline corpus, the expression is somewhat akin to a dative of reference: "they glorified God *with respect to me*."[52] In the context of Galatians 2:20-21, there is nothing in the immediate context that suggests vitalism; there is plenty that bespeaks Paul's concern to explain justification (Gal 2:14-18). Thus in Galatians 2:20, Paul is not saying that he is literally dead. He has been crucified with Christ (Gal 2:19), because Christ has died in his place: as the apostle goes on to explain, Christ bore the curse for him (Gal 3:13). Because of this sub-

---

[51]The literature on this subject is of course extensive and complex. In this collection, see the essay by Bruce McCormack, "What's at Stake in Current Debates Over Justification? The Crisis of Protestantism in the West."

[52]Hence the NIV's paraphrastic but certainly idiomatic and faithful "because of me."

stitution, Paul is so identified with Christ that he can say that he was crucified with Christ. But so also with respect to Paul's life. "I no longer live," he writes, not because there is no sense in which he is living, but because "Christ lives *with respect to me* (ἐν ἐμοί)." So great is his identity with Christ that, as he has been crucified with Christ, so also Christ's life is his. But as this does not mean that Paul is literally[53] dead, so it does not mean that there is no sense in which he can speak of himself living. That is why he immediately goes on to say, "And the life I live in the flesh, I live by faith [note the instrumental force of ἐν πίστει] in the Son of God who loved me and gave himself for me"—which brings us back to Christ's substitutionary death. The remarkable thing about this passage, however, is that not only is Christ's death the Christian's death, but Christ's life is the Christian's life.[54]

That insight sheds light on I Corinthians 1:30: "It is because of [God] that you are *in Christ Jesus,* who has become for us wisdom from God—that is, our *righteous-*

[53]The terminology is admittedly tricky. As one scholar remonstrated me in private, "Surely Paul is 'literally' dead—crucified with Christ. 'Literally' depends on whether reality is defined by what we see or by what we hear in the Gospel." What lies behind this riposte, I think, is that if the alternative to "literally" is "metaphorically," then the latter seems too weak, too unreal. But one might equally fear that "literally" in its strongest sense leads inexorably to the well-known errors of Watchman Nee (e.g., *The Normal Christian Life,* 3rd ed. [London: Victory, 1961]). But one may put something other than "metaphorical" over against "literal": for example, juridical. And in any case, "metaphorical" does not signify "unreal." In ordinary parlance, one does not speak of being "dead to something" the way Paul can speak of being "dead to sin": one is either dead, or one is not. The fact that someone can be "dead to something" shows that what one means by "dead" is not the customary meaning: the "literal" meaning has been extended to something more specialized. Luther's affirmation of Scripture as a *litera spiritualis,* grounded on the observation that Scripture speaks not of everyday things but of eternal things, not of the fallen creation but of God and the gospel, though I sympathize with what he is trying to preserve, is in danger of sanctioning, however unwittingly, a kind of gnostic approach. Provided one does not import into the notion of "not literal" the assumption of the unreal, but tries instead to sort out as humbly as possible just what Paul means, I do not see a safer way of insisting that in Galatians 2:20 Paul does not mean that he is "literally" dead.

[54]The main thrust of my argument is, I think, pretty convincing, even if this proposal for the exegesis of Galatians 2:20 is rejected. Certainly the secondary literature on Galatians 2:20 reveals exegetical landmines and debates, only a few of which can be mentioned here. One must reckon not only with Galatians 1:24 but with Galatians 1:16: it pleased God "to reveal his Son ἐν ἐμοί." F. F. Bruce (*Commentary on Galatians,* NIGTC [Grand Rapids: Eerdmans, 1982], p. 93) comments, "The prepositional phrase ἐν ἐμοι could be a substitute for the simple dative (cf. φανερόν ἐστιν ἐν αὐτοῖς, Rom 1:19; ἐν τοῖς ἀπολλυμένοις ἐστὶν κεκαλυμμένον, 2 Cor. 4:3), but here it probably points to the inwardness of the experience. For Paul the outward vision and the inward illumination coincided: Jesus, whom he persecuted, was revealed as the Son of God, and the revelation was the act of God himself." On this basis, many (e.g., Hans Dieter Betz, *Galatians,* Hermeneia [Philadelphia: Fortress, 1979], p. 71) link Galatians 1:16; 2:20 and 4:6 on the (reasonable) assumption

ness, holiness, and redemption."[55] Gundry says, "That the wisdom comes from God favors that righteousness, sanctification, and redemption—which make up or parallel wisdom—likewise come from God. Thus, the righteousness that Christ be-

---

that Paul makes little distinction between saying that God or Christ or the Spirit is "in" the believer. Some go further and apply this "in" language even to Galatians 1:24: "they glorified God [who is] in me." After all, it is God who is being glorified, not Paul. Nevertheless: (1) It is God who is being glorified in Galatians 1:24 even on the (now standard) reading: "and they glorified *God* on account of me." Thus the object of the verb "to glorify" is not in dispute. (2) Betz's work does not inspire confidence. He does not so much as comment on the ἐν ἐμοί in Galatians 1:24. When he raises the question of the meaning of the phrase in Galatians 1:16, he begins with a footnote: "See on the philological question BDF, §220,1." Apparently Betz obtained this reference to BDF from the BDF index, which turns out to be a typo. In fact, BDF §220(1) mentions Colossians 1:16, not Galatians 1:16, and the discussion treats ἐν + dative of a personal instrument, not dative of reference. (3) Probably the commentary with the most detailed justification for taking ἐν ἐμοί in Galatians 2:20 to mean "within me" is that of Ernest de Witt Burton, *The Epistle to the Galatians*, ICC (Edinburgh: T & T Clark, 1921), pp. 50-51, 137-38. But his entire argument is based on the assumption that the only alternative to "within me" is "by means of me to others," which he has no trouble dispatching to oblivion, with the assumption that his only alternative must therefore be right. The errors in method are palpable. (4) Most commentaries that reflect on ἐν ἐμοι in Galatians 1:24 rightly perceive that at least in this instance the prepositional expression must mean "on my account" or the like. Indeed, many cite the parallel to which J. B. Lightfoot (*Saint Paul's Epistle to the Galatians* [London: Macmillan, 1896], p. 86) first drew attention, namely, Is 49:3 LXX: "You are my servant, Israel, ἐν σοὶ δοξασθήσομαι." (5) Some grammarians hold that even in Galatians 1:16 the phrase should be taken to mean something like "in the case of": e.g., A. T. Robertson, *A Grammar of the Greek New Testament in the Light of Historical Research* (Nashville: Broadman, 1934), p. 587. In this light, cf. again the parallels adduced by Bruce, above. (6) Even if in 2:20 the prepositional phrase ἐν ἐμοι is rendered by "in me," we should not too quickly leap to the conclusion of F. F. Bruce (p. 144): "[I]t is by the Spirit that the risen life of Christ is communicated to his people and maintained within them. It makes little practical difference whether he speaks of Christ living in them or the Spirit dwelling in them (cf. Rom 8:10a, 11a), although the latter expression is commoner (contrariwise, although it makes little practical difference whether he speaks of them as being 'in Christ' or 'in the Spirit', it is the former expression that is commoner)." In general terms, that is true, but precisely because the "in Christ" language takes on different hues in different contexts, one cannot fail to observe that in the context of Galatians 2:20, "living" terminology is parallel to the "crucified" terminology: I am crucified with Christ, and Christ lives ἐν ἐμοι and the Spirit *cannot* replace Christ in both sides of the parallel. Add to this the strong context of justification (Gal 2:15ff.), the parallel of ἐν ἐμοί as a dative of reference at least in Galatians 1:24 and perhaps in Galatians 1:16, and the very least that must be said about the force of the prepositional phrase in Galatians 2:20 is that the dative of reference reading should not be ruled out of court too quickly. Or to put the matter another way, even if some sort of "incorporation" idea lurks behind the expression in Galatians 2:20, the idea in this context is tied much less to any sort of vitalism than it is to the kind of deep identification of the believer with Christ that stands behind "the great exchange."

[55]It is disputed whether the four items—wisdom, righteousness, holiness, redemption—are all parallel, or wisdom is the controlling element with the latter three elucidating it. The use of τε plus the context in which the dominant theme is "wisdom" argue persuasively for the latter, though little in my argument depends on the point.

comes for us who are in him is not his own righteousness, but God's. Nor does Paul use the language of imputation."[56] But observe:

(a) Gundry's antithesis is perplexing: the wisdom is God's, he says, *not* Christ's, even though the text says "Christ has become for us wisdom" and "Christ has become for us . . . righteousness," and so forth. Again, this is bound up with the language of union in Christ: "you are *in Christ Jesus.*" Nevertheless, the next word is a relative pronoun whose referent is Christ, who is *explicitly* said to have become our righteousness. Why, then, the complete antithesis ("God's, *not* Christ's")? This is not far removed from the ideas found in 2 Corinthians 5:19-21: God was in Christ, reconciling the world to himself. So yes, this righteousness is God's; and yes, this righteousness is Christ's. The text says so.

(b) True, there is no explicit mention of imputation. But to argue that the language of imputation *could not* be used here because it would not fit other elements in the list (e.g., redemption) is to presuppose that Christ necessarily becomes our righteousness, sanctification and redemption—whether these constitute wisdom or must be added to wisdom as parallels—in exactly the same way. But that is precisely why the "in Christ" language, the language of union with Christ, is more comprehensive than the categories tied more immediately to righteousness/justification. Compare rather similarly 1 Corinthians 6:11: "But you were washed, you were sanctified, you were justified in the name of the Lord Jesus Christ and by the Spirit of our God." Thiselton has it right when he paraphrases along these lines: you were "sanctified," set apart as holy; you were justified, that is, put right in your standing, in the name of the Lord Jesus, that is, precisely because you are united with Christ Jesus, by the Spirit of our God.[57] The point of 1 Corinthians 1:30 is that for Paul, the real "wisdom" is bound up not with the arrogance he finds in Greek pretensions, but with salvation, and thus with categories like sanctification, righteousness, redemption. That is precisely why Christ has become for us the true wisdom. Those who are in Christ find that Christ has become for them everything needed for salvation. The precise way in which Christ "becomes" these various elements can only be unpacked by what is said elsewhere. Granted such parallels as 2 Corinthians 5:19-21, Galatians 2:20-21, Philippians 3:8-9 and Romans 4, however, it is surely a brave scholar who insists that "Christ has become . . . our righteousness" has nothing to do with Christ's righteousness being imputed to us.

---

[56]Gundry, "Why I Didn't Endorse," p. 7.

[57]Anthony C. Thiselton, *The First Epistle to the Corinthians,* NIGTC (Carlisle, U.K.: Paternoster, 2000), p. 454.

(c) Very often Paul's language of justification/sanctification/redemption points back to the saving event itself, rather than *directly* to their impact on us. Recall the objects of faith noticed by Gathercole in Romans 4:

... πιστεύοντι δὲ ἐπὶ τὸν δικαιοῦντα τὸν ἀσεβῆ (Rom 4:5)

... ἐπίστευσεν θεοῦ τοῦ ζῳοποιοῦντος τοὺς νεκροὺς καὶ καλοῦντος τὰ μὴ ὄντα ὡς ὄντα (Rom 4:17)

... τοῖς πιστεύουσιν ἐπὶ τὸν ἐγείραντα Ἰησοῦν τὸν κύριον ἡμῶν ἐκ νεκρῶν (Rom 4:24)[58]

The God who justifies the ungodly is the same God who raised Jesus from the dead: the two participial verbs in Romans 4:5 and Romans 4:24 respectively portray the same saving event. To think of the justification of the ungodly as *mere* declaration with respect to the believer, *based upon* the redemptive event but distinct from it, rather than seeing justification as the great event itself in which God simultaneously is vindicated while justifying the ungodly, thereby *incorporating* the declaration *into* the saving event, is a painful reductionism that fails to see *how* our being "in Christ" ties us to the justifying event itself. This is commonplace in Paul's use of "justification" terminology.[59]

In short, although the "union with Christ" theme has often been abused, rightly handled it is a comprehensive and complex way of portraying the various ways in which we are identified with Christ and he with us. In its connections with justification, "union with Christ" terminology, especially when it is tied to the great redemptive event, suggests that although justification cannot be reduced to imputation, justification in Paul's thought cannot long be faithfully maintained without it.

Finally, I must directly address the question, "If all of your exposition is right, or merely largely right, why does not Paul at some point or other come right out and simply say, unambiguously, 'Christ's righteousness has been imputed to us'?"[60] Per-

---

[58]Cf. Simon J. Gathercole, "Justified by Faith, Justified by his Blood: The Evidence of Romans 3:21—4:5," in *Justification and Variegated Nomism, Vol. 2: The Paradoxes of Paul*, ed. D. A. Carson, Peter T. O'Brien and Mark A. Seifrid (Tübingen: Mohr-Siebeck, forthcoming).

[59]This is greatly stressed in the varied writings of Mark A. Seifrid. See especially his essay, "Paul's Use of Righteousness Language Against Its Hellenistic Background," in *Justification and Variegated Nomism, Vol. 2: The Paradoxes of Paul*, ed. D. A. Carson, Mark A. Seifrid and Peter T. O'Brien (Tübingen: Mohr-Siebeck, forthcoming), passim. Seifrid himself unpacks union with Christ language in close allegiance to Luther, but, in a slightly different structure, Calvin likewise sees union with Christ as the fundamental issue that separates him from Trent on the matter of justification: see Craig B. Carpenter, "A Question of Union with Christ? Calvin and Trent on Justification," *WTJ* 64 (2002): 363-86.

[60]The question was explicitly raised by Robert Gundry at the Wheaton Theology Conference.

haps a useful answer emerges in two points, the second more important than the first.

(a) Although the question is worth raising, one must always be careful of reading too much into silence, not least when one is dealing with occasional documents. Robert Gundry is a firm defender of the view that several New Testament
writers hold to some (distinctively Christian) notion of propitiation, and I concur.
But that does not alter the fact that the ἱλαστήριον / ἱλασμος word-group is rather
rare in the New Testament; nor does the notion of propitiation depend on one
word-group alone.

(b) Strictly speaking, there is no passage in the New Testament that says that
our sins are imputed to Christ, though most confessional Christians, including
Robert Gundry, would insist on the point. True, we are told that Christ was made
a curse for us (Gal 3:13), and was made sin for us while our own sins were not imputed to us (2 Cor 5:19-21). We are told that he died in our place, and gave his
life a ransom for many, and much more of the same. He is depicted as a lamb whose
death expiates sin. Still, the fact of the matter is that there is no passage that explicitly asserts that our sins are imputed to Christ, even though most of us, I think, are
prepared to defend the proposition that this point is taught in Scripture, even if
the λογίζομαι terminology is not deployed in its support. So why should a scholar
who accepts that Paul teaches that our sins are imputed to Christ, even though no
text explicitly says so, find it so strange that many Christians have held that Paul
teaches that Christ's righteousness is imputed to us, even though no text explicitly
says so?

This is part and parcel of the "great exchange"; on the face of it, this reading
makes most sense of most passages. And if our terminology in our theological expression does not perfectly align with Paul's terminology, that is not unprecedented
either, as we have already observed in the domains of sanctification and reconciliation.

JUSTIFICATION
AND THE CRISIS
OF PROTESTANTISM

3

WHAT'S AT STAKE IN CURRENT DEBATES OVER JUSTIFICATION?

The Crisis of Protestantism in the West

BRUCE L. McCORMACK

The doctrine of justification is *the* doctrine of the Reformation, that doctrine which—more than any other—gave to sixteenth-century Protestantism its character as Protestant. To put it this way is not to claim for the doctrine of justification the status of "central dogma" in the sense which that phrase acquired in the course of nineteenth-century debates over fundamental differences between the Lutheran and Reformed theological "systems." Indeed, that entire discussion was misguided from the outset. For it presupposed that one doctrine could and did act as the "material principle" of each of the two dogmatic systems, that is, a doctrine from which the contents of all other doctrines could be deduced more or less analytically. There was no "central dogma" for any of the Reformers in this sense. The Reformers did not attempt to construct analytically deduced *systems* of doctrine, but contented themselves instead with the elaboration of *loci communes*—a collection of theological topics drawn together from Scripture and ordered by means of the progress of salvation history, from creation to eschatology. But to acknowledge that the Reformers did not pursue systems in the analytical sense takes nothing away from the fact that they were indeed systematic. They understood that Christian doctrines are organically related to one another. For that reason, they also understood that the decisions made in one area need to be consistent with the decisions made in other areas. If it could be shown that they were not, a strong presumption would then have existed that a mistake had occurred somewhere. Moreover, it was possible for the Reformers to honor the rejection of deductive systems resident in the option for *loci communes* without surrendering the belief that some doctrines had a more basic character than others, influencing and coloring and shaping the way in which others were articulated to an extent that was not true of all doctrines. My contention would be that the Reformers' *forensic* understanding of justification had precisely that kind of wide-reaching influence. For the idea of an *immediate* divine imputation renders superfluous the entire Catholic system of the priestly mediation of grace by the Church. To speak of a positive imputation of Christ's righteousness to the believer is to affirm the priesthood of all believers, the communion of the saints with its necessary protest against clericalism, the primacy of the preached word in worship, etc.

The great Reformers themselves confirm this understanding of the centrality of justification. Luther understood the doctrine of justification to be the doctrine by which the church stands or falls; the doctrine, in other words, by the understanding and lived appropriation of which it is decided whether a community of faith is a Christian church. So he could say in his 1537 Smalcald Articles, "On this article rests all that we teach and practice against the pope, the devil, and the world. Therefore we must be quite certain and have no doubts about it. Otherwise all is lost."[1] For Calvin, too, a rightly ordered understanding of justification was basic to the whole of the Christian life. He called it "the main hinge on which religion turns," and he added, "For unless you first of all grasp what your relationship to God is, and the nature of His judgment concerning you, you have neither a foundation on which to establish your salvation nor one on which to build piety toward God."[2] Lutheran and Reformed theologians disagreed on a number of things, but the one thing on which there was no disagreement was the central importance of justification by grace through faith, for it was that, above all, which defined Protestantism and gave to each of its member churches its character as Protestant. What is at stake in this doctrine is nothing less than the Reformation itself.

In putting it this way, I have already provided you with a succinct and clear answer to the question posed by my title. What is at stake in current debates over justification? My answer is: nothing less than the Reformation. This is not to suggest that the crisis of Protestantism, which we are experiencing today in the West, has its sole source in a relative incomprehension of the Reformers' teachings on the subject of justification. The current crisis has many sources, many of them less than theological (having to do with the ongoing impact upon the churches of our in-

---

[1] Martin Luther, "Smalcald Articles," Part II, art. I in *The Book of Concord: The Confessions of the Evangelical Lutheran Church*, ed. and trans. Theodore Tappert (Philadelphia: Fortress, 1959), p. 292.
[2] John Calvin *Institutes of the Christian Religion* 3.2.1.

creasingly secularized culture). So even if the Protestant doctrine of justification were suddenly to be believed, taught and confessed on a churchwide basis, there is no guarantee that such a turn of events would save Protestantism. But this much seems clear: the absence of clarity about this doctrine and the inability of its would-be defenders to offer an adequate response to the challenges which are currently being brought against it are contributing mightily to the theological confusion which reigns in the churches of the Reformation and, in all likelihood, hastening the demise of Protestantism in the West.

This is not, I assure you, the hysterical response of an ultra-conservative Protestant who feels threatened by any and every change. To the contrary, it is my belief that the great Reformers themselves deserve at least some of the blame for the current crisis with regard to their chief article of faith. There were too many questions relevant to a comprehensive understanding of justification that remained suppressed as a consequence of the Reformers' lack of interest in questions they perceived to be "philosophical" rather than theological. We are paying a high price for that lack of interest today. So what I have written will not take the form of a plea that we simply return to the Reformation. We will need to move beyond the Reformation in order to save it. But moving "beyond," for me, means going "through" the Reformation and not doing an end-run around it—as do those who today give every sign of wanting a Protestantism without the Reformation.

At the heart of the Reformation understanding of justification lay the notion of a positive imputation of Christ's righteousness. That was the truly distinctive element in the Reformation understanding, and given the centrality of the doctrine for defining Protestantism, its abandonment can only mean the transformation of the Reformation into something qualitatively different.

Such a claim does not, of course, guarantee the truthfulness of the Reformation view. Only Holy Scripture can guarantee the truth of any set of doctrinal affirmations. But it is not my intention here to take on the truth-question. I intend instead to address a question that I regard as belonging to the prolegomena to any genuinely ecclesial exegesis of the Bible. As a baptized member of a Protestant church, I am to do my exegesis under the guidance of the confession of my church—until such time as the exegesis done in this way is made impossible by the demonstration of a fundamental conflict between Scripture and confession. But before that point is ever reached, before a truly ecclesial exegesis can even get off the ground, I need to be instructed in and by my confessional tradition. I need to know and understand both the presuppositions and implications of the theologies that came to expression in the confessions of my church. I need to understand the Reformation doctrine in its strengths and in its weaknesses. Above all, I need to understand the ways in which the Reformers' other theological commitments may have contributed unwittingly to the current demise of their "central" doctrine. And I need to think through the question of how their other commitments might be brought into line with their "central" doctrine—in such a way as to make it less vulnerable to criticism. Only where all this is done, will I be fair to the Reformation view when the time comes to test it in the light of Holy Scripture.[3]

Let me put all my cards on the table. Where the doctrine of justification in particular is concerned, my own conviction is that the Reformers had it basically right with their emphasis upon a positive imputation of Christ's righteousness. But, unfortunately, they were not in a position to explore the *theological ontology* that was implied in their understanding of justification. And this left their articulation of the doctrine vulnerable to criticism. In an age like our own, in which men and women are crying for real change, for real transformation of the fundamental conditions of life, this can all too easily appear to be a decisive weakness. And it can also make the Protestant tradition appear weak and emaciated in comparison with those traditions, like the Catholic and the Orthodox, which have always given explicit attention to matters ontological.

In what follows, I will engage in a close reading of Thomas Aquinas, Martin Luther and John Calvin on the doctrine of justification and its relation to the theme of regeneration. What I hope to demonstrate is that the break with Medieval Catholicism which we might have expected to be complete if we paid attention only to the Reformers' doctrine of justification was actually less than complete due to a residual commitment to Medieval Catholic understandings of regeneration and a shaky grasp of the relation of justification and regeneration. I hope to show, secondly, that the reason for all of this is that the Reformers' refusal to engage directly issues of theological ontology made them blind to the extent to which they continued to subscribe to ontological assumptions which could, logically, *only fund a Catholic ordering of regeneration and justification* (to the detriment of their own definition of justification). Finally, I will suggest that there is an alternative understanding of theological ontology embedded in

---

[3]Whatever the merits and demerits of Albrecht Ritschl's massive three-volume study of soteriology in its material details, it seems to me that his strategy for doing dogmatic theology is the right one; first, the history of the doctrine, then a consideration of biblical material, and only then a turn to dogmatic reconstruction. See Ritschl, *Die christliche Lehre von der Rechtfertigung und Versöhnung*, 3 vols. (New York: Olms, 1978).

the forensic frame of reference which would have overcome the residual problems contained in the Reformers' ongoing attachment to a theologically outmoded ontology—an alternative which I will seek briefly to describe.

THE TEACHING OF THOMAS AQUINAS ON JUSTIFICATION

To understand Thomas Aquinas's teaching on justification, we must place it in the context in which he himself placed it, viz. a consideration of the nature of grace, its divisions and causes. For Thomas, considered on the most general level of reflection, grace is two things: it is the action of God upon the soul and the effect of that action.

Considered as the effect of God's work in the soul, grace is a remaking of the soul or, as Thomas also speaks of it, a "healing."[4] This "healing" is said to take place in the essence of the soul, not in the soul's powers (or faculties) only. This distinction between the "essence" of the soul and its powers is an extremely important one for an understanding of the nature of grace and how it works. So it would reward us to examine it more closely. In back of this distinction lies Thomas's theological ontology of the human.

For Thomas, the soul is an incorporeal—which is to say, "spiritual"—substance. As such, however, it is also the "form" which makes the matter of which the body is composed to be a *human* body and, indeed, this *particular* human body. Thomas rejected every Platonist understanding of the soul which would see it as something that is complete in and for itself apart from the body. Thomas held that soul and body belong together in a unity. You do not find one without the other "in nature"—which is to say, in this world. Either is an "incomplete substance" in the absence of the other. It is true that the soul is able to survive the death of the body, which also means that it can exist in separation from the body. But this is "unnatural" or, as Thomas preferred to say, "beyond nature."[5] To claim this much is also to suggest that the "form" that is the soul is unique in kind. It alone, out of all the "forms" found in nature, is capable of continuing to exist in the absence of matter. Once created, it is immortal.

Now "form," generally considered, is the "whatness" of a thing; that which makes it to be what it is. In living things, however, the "form" is that whereby the thing in question *acts*. But the human is not just any living thing. In brute animals, that whereby a thing acts is what Thomas (following Aristotle) called the "sensitive

---

[4]Thomas Aquinas, *Summa Theologica* Ia2ae, Q.111, art. 2; Ia2ae, Q.111, art. 3.
[5]F. C. Copleston, *Aquinas* (Harmondsworth, U.K.: Penguin, 1955), p. 167.

soul." Animals are capable of more than providing nourishment for themselves and reproducing; they can also experience sensation. But the human soul transcends this "sensitive soul" in that the human soul has the intellectual powers of mind and will which allow it to know and to will spiritual realities, to make universal judgments, to enter into fields of study like pure mathematics (which have no known applications), etc. For this reason, Thomas (again following Aristotle) denominates the soul in the human an "intellectual soul." So the "form" that the human soul is turns out to be unique in kind from a second direction, as well. Not only is it immortal, it is also intellectual in character.

The final step is to see how the soul subsists; that is, how it receives and has its being and existence. Thomas says, "nothing acts except so far as it is *in act*; and so, a thing acts by that whereby it is *in act*."[6] "Form," it turns out, is *the act* in which a thing has its being and existence. Thomas equates "form" with the "first principle of life" in living things, and since this principle in humans is intellectual in character, "form" is also the "principle" of intellectual activity. Now the act from which the human individual lives may be viewed from two angles. Viewed from the side of its origin in divine action, the act from which the human lives is a divine act of "creation out of nothing." Thomas held that every individual soul is created by a special act of God. The soul is not "generated" through the reproductive process; it is joined to the body in the moment of conception. Viewed from the side of the terminus of this divine act in the human, the language of "the act from which the human lives" is descriptive of the ground in humans from which all other acts proceed. Viewed from the first angle, the soul *subsists* on the basis of a special act of God. Viewed from the second angle, as the terminus of the divine action in the human, the soul *subsists* through an existence proper to itself. This sets it apart from all other forms found in nature, in that all other forms are generated and, as a consequence, are never found in the absence of matter (as was previously suggested).[7] The soul, then, we might say by way of summary, is a spiritual substance which is incomplete in the absence of the body. It is intellectual in nature and has its subsistence in itself (as a consequence of the divine will).

I hope that this much is reasonably clear. But there is a problem in it that comes clearly into focus when we inquire more closely into the distinction between the "essence" of the soul and its powers. Grace, we said at the outset, finds its "seat"

---

[6]Thomas Aquinas, *Summa Theologica* Ia, Q.76, art. I (emphasis added).
[7]James A. Weisheipl, *Friar Thomas D'Aquino* (Washington, D.C.: Catholic University of America Press, 1974), pp. 208-9.

in the "essence" of the soul and *not* in the powers (not even in the highest powers of mind and will). It is clear what Thomas hopes to achieve with this distinction. For Thomas, the distinction between the "essence" of the soul and its powers is the distinction between the "subject" (a word which he will use on occasion) and the powers or faculties possessed by that subject. In Thomas's hands, however, the distinction has the feel of something more nearly ideal than real—and this for two reasons. First and most important, when we turn to the question of the *nature* of that "grace" which is infused into the "essence" of the soul in justification, the only word Thomas has at his command for speaking of it is "light." Now the metaphor light is most commonly employed in theology (and philosophy as well) to suggest something like intellectual illumination. But such a conclusion would appear to betray Thomas's intention to locate infused grace in the "essence" of the soul rather than in its intellectual powers of mind and will. This conceptual confusion is only further heightened by the fact that Thomas can make "intellect" to be descriptive of *both* the "essence" of the soul and one of its highest powers.

Second, to speak of that whereby a human acts in terms of an *act* is to render the distinction between the "essence" of the soul and the powers of the soul *in action* in terms that *appear* to place them on the same plane of reality. Both are acts; the difference is that the "essence" of the soul is *the act* that founds all other, subsequent acts. The first act, then, is an utterly inward act which grounds all actions directed outwards ("outside of myself"). But this means that the distinction is largely a logical one, the result of an attempt to posit the existence of a ground of activity.

To be sure, Thomas wants this distinction to be understood as something real and not merely ideal. The distinction between the subject and the powers possessed by that subject is in complete conformity with the ontological presupposition which governs Thomas's reflections throughout the *Summa Theologica*, namely, that "essence" precedes and grounds existence in all things finite. Only in God are the two identical. But however clearly realistic Thomas may be on the level of intention, his execution of these distinctions leaves us with nagging questions about conceptual clarity. And if I were asked to put my finger on the source of this conceptual fuzziness, I would say that it has much less to do with the Aristotelian distinctions with which he works than it does with the constitutive role that infant baptism is playing on the whole of his thinking about grace. The reasons for this claim will be clear in a moment. It is now time that we return to the subject of grace.

Grace, we have said, is infused into the soul. The infusion of grace results in a "healing," a remaking of the soul after the image of God. Now how does this come about? To enter into this question is to come up against the doctrine of justification.

In a human nature properly ordered after the image of God—the mind (which Thomas regarded as the highest part of human nature) is in subjection to God and the lower (appetitive) powers of the soul are in subjection to the mind. It is this right ordering of human nature which Thomas defined as "justice."[8] The effect of sin on human nature is to introduce a disordering into the individual's very being. No longer is the individual in subjection to God. Her relationship with God is broken. No longer does the mind rule the appetites, but the appetites rule the mind. It is this essential derangement of nature that is addressed in divine justification. For Thomas, justification is the process by which God makes us to *be* just.[9] It is the process by means of which our nature is re-created and re-ordered after the divine image. It is the process by which God actually makes human beings to *be* righteous. That is the most basic definition; now let's look at it a bit more closely to see precisely how justification comes about.

"Justification" is a movement from a state of injustice to a state of justice. Any movement, Thomas said, involves a mover who sets things in motion, the movement itself and the object of the movement.[10] The mover in this case is God, who infuses grace into the sinner. To explain the nature of the movement itself, Thomas says that God moves all things according to the mode proper to each. Men and women are also moved in accordance with the characteristics of human nature. But men and women are, by nature, beings endowed with free choice. And so God moves the sinner toward justice by moving his/her free will. "He infuses the gift of justifying grace in such a way that, at the same time, He also moves the free choice to accept the gift of grace."[11] Grace is here depicted as exercising an influence on free will, whereby it is turned toward God. To be turned towards God is, at the same time, to be turned away from sin. Thus, the immediate result of the infusion of justifying grace is a "double movement" of the will.[12] And, finally, the object of the movement is the forgiveness of sins. The infusion of justifying grace has as its final goal the forgiveness of sins. There are, therefore, four elements in justification for Thomas. There is: (1) the infusion of justifying grace; (2) a movement of free choice directed toward God by faith; (3) a movement of free choice

---

[8] Thomas Aquinas *Summa Theologica* Ia2ae, Q.113, art. 1.

[9] Ibid.

[10] Thomas Aquinas *Summa Theologica* Ia2ae, Q.113, art. 6.

[11] Thomas Aquinas *Summa Theologica* Ia2ae, Q.113, art. 3.

[12] Thomas Aquinas *Summa Theologica* Ia2ae, Q.113, art. 5.

against sin; and (4) the forgiveness of sins. It should be noted that the four elements required for justification are simultaneous in time; they do not succeed one
another. Justification is complete in an instant.[13] Thomas has arranged these elements here in a logical, rather than a chronological, order. Thomas held that justification occurs in an instant, but it has to be remembered that he did not think that
anyone is perfected in an instant. When we fall away and commit sin, we require to
be forgiven anew and for this the infusion of grace through the sacramental system
has been established. Therefore justification, or the making just of human nature,
is something that is repeated throughout the Christian life as we make use of the
means of grace—especially the grace given through the sacrament of penance.

Now Thomas's explanation of how justification comes about does have something curious about it. You will have noticed that he lays a great deal of emphasis
upon the thought that God moves all things according to the mode proper to
each and that this means that God moves men and women through the exercise
of a spiritual influence on their free choice. But Thomas does know of a grand
exception. "Infants are not capable of movements of free choice and so they are
moved by God towards justice only by reception of a form in their souls. This
does not take place without a sacramental act; for just as original sin, from which
they are justified [or moved to a state of "justice"], reaches them not by their own
will but by fleshly origination, so too grace has its source in them by spiritual
rebirth."[14] But precisely here is the curious element. Thomas speaks here as
though the case of the infant is simply an *exception* to the rule of what normally
happens in justification. For the entire presentation of the doctrine of justification as he has described it presupposes that the recipient of God's justifying
grace is an adult. The "infusion of grace," as we saw, is understood by Thomas
to consist in a spiritual movement of free choice in the human. But, of course,
grace so construed would seem most naturally to find its "point of entry" on the
level of the intellectual powers of the soul. *In other words: there would be no need to
locate the infusion of grace in the essence of the soul if it were not for the fact that the Church's
accepted practice was to baptize infants. And that also means that Thomas's tendency to understand
justification as rooted in an "ontological healing" of the soul, rather than in a more personal understanding of the operations of grace, is a function of the fact that the regeneration of the infant is
the truly paradigmatic case where that infusion of grace which initiates justification is concerned.*

---

[13]Thomas Aquinas *Summa Theologica* Ia2ae, Q.113, art. 7, 8.
[14]Thomas Aquinas *Summa Theologica* Ia2ae, Q.113, art. 3, ad. I.

This does not mean that Thomas has been inconsistent—far from it. The justification from original sin, which is made ours in infant baptism, is repeated thereafter with respect to *acts* of sin through the sacrament of penance throughout our lives. But it is very likely that the conceptual difficulties we encountered earlier do find their source precisely at this point.

Thomas created problems for himself by speaking of the nature of infused grace in terms of light. That metaphor, suggesting as it does an illumination of the mind, works well enough in the case of adults (though it does render problematic the effort to locate infused grace in the essence of the soul rather than in the intellectual powers). But in the case of the regeneration of the infant in baptism, grace needs to be understood in terms of something other than light. The soul, we have seen, is a spiritual "substance." And that which would "heal" this substance substantially ought itself to be something substantial, perhaps even quasi-physical. Healing, after all, is a metaphor drawn from the world of medicine where the object requiring help is a physical body.

But I hasten to add that such problems as I have identified in Thomas's conception are only, so to speak, "around the edges." In comparison with most other accounts of "ontological healing" which are being advocated today, it is tremendously coherent. And it is coherent because Thomas was able to appeal to a highly developed theological ontology to make clear what he meant by "ontological healing." "Ontological healing" was not, in his hands, a theological rhetoric left hanging in the air by a refusal to engage ontological questions—which is often the case with many of our contemporaries.

It should be added that Thomas did have a place in his doctrine of justification for the Pauline language of "imputation." In that the infusion of grace brings about the forgiveness of sins, it is right to say that the "non-imputation of sin" is the effect of an infusion of justifying grace. As the Pauline idea of imputation would play a sizable role in Reformation theologies, it is important to point out here that Thomas limits "imputation" to its negative side, the non-imputation of sin. Of what would later be thought of as a positive imputation of Christ's righteousness, Thomas knew nothing. In its place is the infusion of grace into the soul (i.e., regeneration). But this also means that *the work of God "in us" was being made the basis of God's forgiveness*. And that was precisely the point at which the Reformation would finally have to raise the necessary objection. Whether the Reformation was finally able to raise the question in the most decisive way possible is a question we will have to consider.

THE REFORMATION REACTION

Everything Thomas said about justification focused finally upon a single point the Protestant churches (both Reformed and Lutheran) would reject with increasing clarity and force. Thomas saw justification as a process by which we are actually made to *be* righteous. The Protestants, too, held that there is a process by which we are actually made to be righteous, but they referred to this as sanctification or "repentance," not justification. But Medieval theologians like Thomas made no distinction between justification and sanctification. The Protestants had a problem with this because it made God's forgiveness of our sins conditional upon the current state of our actual righteousness. And even if one took great care, as Thomas most certainly did, to insist that the state of our actual righteousness is not ultimately conditioned upon what *we do* (since the infusion of grace is the operative element which produces righteousness in the soul), the Protestants would still have seen a danger in this Medieval soteriology. The problem with Thomas, they would have said, lies in the fact that he makes the root of our justification to lie in what God does *in us*. But to the extent that we see our salvation as in any way contingent upon what we are or have become at a particular point in time, we shift the locus of our attention from what Luther called the "alien righteousness of Christ" (which is complete in itself) to a work of God in us which is radically incomplete. And to just that extent, we make personal assurance of salvation to rest on a work which, as incomplete, can never bring adequate comfort. Those with sensitive consciences are thrown back on their own experience of grace, in an effort to discern whether God has really been at work "in them."

What, then, was the Protestant alternative? In its fully developed form, the alternative was to understand justification in terms of a twofold imputation. Calvin's definition sets forth the fully developed view in a clear and succinct form: "we explain justification simply as the acceptance with which God receives us into his favor as righteous men [and women]. And we say that it consists in the remission of sins and the imputation of Christ's righteousness."[15] To the most decisive question treated under the heading of "justification"—namely, how do those of us separated from Jesus Christ in space and time come to participate in Christ's righteousness—the answer which Calvin gives is "by imputation." Christ's righteousness is "imputed" to us and, on that basis, we are forgiven (i.e., the negative nonimputation of sin is contained in the positive imputation of Christ's righteousness). It should

---

[15]Calvin *Institutes* 3.2.2.

be noted that it is the role played by the imputation of Christ's righteousness in justification, and that alone, which makes possible the Protestant distinction between justification and sanctification. Indeed, there is no other sufficient basis for making a distinction. If, for example, we make regeneration to be the basis of the non-imputation of sin—as Thomas had it—there remains no reason to distinguish between the two. Regeneration, after all, is sanctification viewed from the angle of an initiating moment rather than as part of a larger process. Hence, Calvin insists on the imputation of Christ's righteousness.

Now I have deliberately styled this form of the Protestant doctrine of justification as the "fully developed form." I do so in order to indicate that it is the product of a development in thought. It did not suddenly appear, as if overnight, in the early years of the Reformation but was the result of a good bit of refinement. In this development, the decisive role was played—for both the Reformed and the Lutherans—by Calvin's response to the challenge of a one-time Lutheran by the name of Andreas Osiander. In what follows in this section, I want to begin with a brief sketch of Luther. I will then turn to a much closer examination of Calvin.

Martin Luther (1483-1546). It has long been recognized that Luther's thinking on the subject of justification did not achieve the degree of systematic coherence and consistency of the later Lutheran "Formula of Concord." As Paul Althaus acknowledged:

> Luther uses the terms "to justify" [*justificare*] and "justification" [*justificatio*] in more than one sense. From the beginning, justification most often means the judgment of God with which he declares man to be righteous [*justum reputare* or *computare*]. In other places, however, this word stands for the entire event through which a man is essentially made righteous (a usage which Luther also finds in Romans 5), that is, for both the imputation of righteousness to man as well as man's actually becoming righteous. Justification in this sense remains incomplete on earth and is first completed on the Last Day. Complete righteousness in this sense is an eschatological reality.[16]

Now, on Althaus's view, both of these possibilities result in a forensic view of justification. Both entail a positive imputation of Christ's righteousness. And there is much to be said in favor of this interpretation—on the basis of Luther's 1535 commentary on Galatians especially:

> These two things make Christian righteousness perfect: The first is faith in the heart, which is a divinely granted gift and which formally believes in Christ; the second is

---

[16]Althaus, *The Theology of Martin Luther,* p. 226.

that God reckons this imperfect faith as perfect righteousness for the sake of Christ, His Son, who suffered for the sins of the world and in whom I begin to believe. On account of this faith in Christ God does not see the sin that still remains in me. For so long as I go on living in the flesh, there is certainly sin in me. But meanwhile Christ protects me under the shadow of His wings and spreads over me the wide heaven of the forgiveness of sins, under which I live in safety. This prevents God from seeing the sins that still cling to my flesh. My flesh distrusts God, is angry with Him, does not rejoice in Him, etc. But God overlooks these sins, and in His sight they are as though they were not sins. This is accomplished by imputation on account of the faith by which I begin to take hold of Christ; and on His account God reckons imperfect righteousness as perfect righteousness and sins as not sin, even though it really is sin.[17]

And again,

Therefore this is a marvelous definition of Christian righteousness: it is a divine imputation or reckoning as righteousness or to righteousness, for the sake of our faith in Christ or for the sake of Christ. When the sophists [by which he means the "scholastics"] hear this definition, they laugh; for they suppose that righteousness is a certain quality that is first infused into the soul and then distributed through all the members. They cannot strip off the thoughts of reason, which declares that righteousness is a right judgment and a right will. Therefore this inestimable gift excels all reason, that without any works God reckons and acknowledges as righteous the man who takes hold by faith of His Son. . . . [R]ighteousness is not in us in a formal sense, as Aristotle maintains, *but is outside us*, solely in the grace of God and in His imputation.[18]

Two things are abundantly clear in these passages. First, Luther was well aware of positions like that of Thomas and set out to overcome them. Righteousness is not to be understood as an "accidental form of the soul" as *per* Thomas but is "outside of us" and made ours through divine imputation. Second, there can be little question but that Luther had in view a positive imputation of Christ's righteousness and not simply a negative, non-imputation of sin.

What is less than clear, though, is the role played by faith. So enamored was Luther with the thought that we are justified by faith, rather than by our works, that he was inclined in many contexts to give faith a priority over the act of divine

---

[17]Martin Luther, *Luther's Works*, vol. 26, ed. Jaroslav Pelikan (St. Louis: Concordia 1963), pp. 231-32.
[18]Ibid., pp. 233-34. Emphasis added.

imputation. At times, Luther even goes so far as to suggest that our faith, considered from the human standpoint as something we do, can take us a good ways where justification is concerned. But faith is imperfect and at the point at which it becomes inadequate—losing its hold on Christ, perhaps?—the divine imputation of Christ's righteousness enters in to make up for what is still lacking. "For because faith is weak . . . therefore God's imputation has to be added."[19] Indeed, "faith begins righteousness but imputation perfects it until the day of Christ." Now it might appear as though this would make faith a "work," something that we do as a precondition to what God does. Luther was very aware of that possibility and strove to eliminate it. "Faith," he says, is a divinely granted gift. Moreover, it is formal in character, though not in the sense advocated by Aristotle. Like the metal clasp of a ring, which holds a precious jewel, faith lays hold of Christ.[20] Faith is the "form" of righteousness, that which grasps righteousness. But the righteousness in question is Christ's alone. Luther's problem with Aristotelian conceptions seems to lie in the thought that a "re-forming" of the form that is the soul would require far too great a reordering of the human in the moment in which faith first takes its rise than is experientially verifiable. Luther is painfully aware of the ongoing presence of sin in the Christian life and so he prefers to think of the dawning of faith in the individual as the presence of a "little spark,"[21] which—precisely as weak or small— must be accounted righteous by God for Christ's sake.

The residual problem created by Luther's analysis (and one he bequeathed to later generations of Protestant theologians) lies in the fact that the priority of the giving of faith over the act of divine imputation would seem clearly to require a certain logical priority of regeneration (a work of God "in us") over justification. And to the extent that that were so, the "break" with Catholic understandings of justification like Thomas's would be less than complete.

The foregoing account of Luther's views also leaves some other important questions unresolved. What does it mean to say that faith "lays hold" of Christ? What, precisely, is it that is imputed to us by God? It is the righteousness of Christ, to be sure. But how are we to understand this? What are we speaking of when we speak of Christ's "righteousness"? Is it that righteousness which is proper to him as deity, the very righteousness of God, which the Logos brought with him, so to speak, into his incarnate mode of existence? Or is it a "righteousness" which is his by vir-

---

[19]Ibid., p. 232.
[20]Ibid., pp. 89, 132, 134, 229, 231.
[21]Ibid., p. 230.

tue of the life of obedience he lived in his divine-human unity, as the already incarnate One, the God made flesh? And, secondly, having answered this first series of questions, we would then still need to ask: what is the manner or mode of our "participation" in the righteousness of Christ so defined? Imputation may give us an initial clue. But can we say more than this?

My own conviction is that Luther's answers to such questions are far from clear. Recently, however, a new school of Luther interpretation has suggested that answers to such questions are available when Luther is seen in the right light. The "Finnish" school which has formed around Professor Tuomo Mannermaa of the University of Helsinki would like to understand Luther's doctrine of justification as closely related to Eastern Orthodox notions of *theosis* or "divinization." It should be noted that this line of interpretation is carried out in studied opposition to a thoroughgoing attachment to the more traditional forensic reading. The result is a view of salvation that is—as the blurb on the back of a recent book introducing the Finnish school to readers in the West has it—"more ontological and mystical than ethical and juridical."[22] The interpretive issues raised by the Finnish school are complex and cannot be addressed here. Suffice it to say that, although Luther's tendency to prioritize regeneration over justification does open a door to the Finnish interpretation, it is my view that this new reading brings as much to Luther as it reads out of him. The note of a positive imputation of Christ's righteousness, which was clear in the passages we considered, is suppressed. In its place, an ontology of grace is advanced which, in my judgment, finds a tenuous basis in Luther's writings at best. Luther was not, so far as I have been able to discover, inclined to understand grace as something substantial that is infused into the very "essence" of the soul; he was far more inclined to see it as the personal favor of God.[23] But more than that I cannot say here. I should note, however, before proceeding, that the new Finnish reading of Luther has found a warm reception in the "evangelical Catholic" wing of the Evangelical Lutheran Church in America, a movement whose views are having a profound impact on the American theological scene through the journal *Pro Ecclesia*. The Finnish theologians also contributed appreciably to the final received text of the Joint Declaration on the Doctrine of Justification signed by representatives of the Lutheran World Federation and the Roman Catholic Church at

---

[22]Carl E. Braaten and Robert W. Jenson, *Union with Christ: The New Finnish Interpretation of Luther* (Grand Rapids: Eerdmans, 1998).

[23]See on this point Jaroslav Pelikan, *The Christian Tradition*, vol. 4 (Chicago: University of Chicago, 1983), pp. 152-53.

a great celebration in Augsburg, Germany, on Reformation Day, 1999.

John Calvin (1509-1564). In the history of the development of the Protestant doctrine of justification in the sixteenth century, the role played by Andreas Osiander in forcing further clarification of Luther's view can scarcely be overestimated. Osiander started his career as a close confidant of Luther. He was a participant in the Marburg Colloquy in 1529 and the Diet of Augsburg the following year. Already at Augsburg, however, Osiander showed himself to be unhappy with Melanchthon's defense of a forensic understanding of justification. In 1549, he was granted the first chair in theology at the University of Königsberg by his long-time benefactor and protector, Archduke Albrecht of Prussia—this over the objections of the faculty and in spite of the fact that he lacked an academic degree. The "Osiandrian controversy" began with a disputation on justification held in Königsberg on October 24, 1550. The outcry, which the publication of Osiander's views produced locally, forced the Archduke to appeal for an opinion to church authorities in other principalities. For this purpose, he asked for and received from Osiander a personal confession which was entitled *Von dem einigen Mittler Jesu Christo und rechtfertigung des glaubens bekanntnus*, published on September 8, 1551. Evaluations quickly poured in and were almost universally negative. Indeed, Osiander deserves credit for accomplishing something many at the time would have thought impossible— uniting the Philippists and the Gnesio-Lutherans (who were otherwise bitter opponents) in opposition to him. The only exception was the cautious attempt of Johannes Brenz to mediate between Osiander and his opponents.[24] The Formula of Concord condemned Osiander's views on the basis of the very forensic theory that he had sought to overcome.[25]

A thorough treatment of Osiander's views has no real relevance to our subject here. Suffice it to say that Osiander made much of the ideas of mystical union with Christ and an essential indwelling of Christ in the believer. What is of greater interest is Calvin's critique of Osiander and the light it sheds on Calvin's doctrine of justification.

Calvin's mature doctrine of justification is set forth in the definitive 1559 edition of his *Institutes of the Christian Religion* 3.2. The chapter begins with a consideration of the place of the doctrine of justification in Christian soteriology and an attempt to provide a complete definition of the basic terms. In sections 5-12, he

---

[24]For more on the Osiandrian Controversy, see Gottfried Seebass, "Osiander," *Theologische Realenzyklopädie* 25 (Berlin: Walter de Gruyter, 1995), pp. 507-15.
[25]See *Solid Declaration* 3 in *The Book of Concord*, pp. 539-51.

then addresses Osiander's doctrine of "essential righteousness." All of this material is new in the 1559 edition. He then turns to a consideration of Roman Catholic teaching. The order of presentation strongly suggests that, by this point in time, Osiander's doctrine had superseded even the Roman teaching as Calvin's primary target. The chapter concludes with a renewed emphasis on the thought that we are justified before God on the basis of a righteousness that is "not in us but in Christ."[26]

I will return momentarily to questions surrounding the place of the doctrine of justification in Calvin's soteriology. We may most usefully begin with a consideration of basic definitions. The basic meaning of *justification*, as Calvin employs the term, is "acquittal." " 'To justify' means nothing else than to acquit of guilt him who was accused, as if his innocence were confirmed."[27] The situation presupposed is that of a legal proceeding. A person stands in a judgment box, accused of wrongdoing. The question being deliberated is the question of guilt. The sentence rendered, however, is that of acquittal. Acquittal differs from clemency in that the latter does not expunge a conviction of wrongdoing from the record of the accused. Clemency merely means that an individual has been granted some sort of release from the debt he owed to society as a consequence of his guilt. But the guilt remains. Acquittal, on the other hand, is a declaration of innocence. No reason for condemnation remains.

The question is: how can this happen? How can the sinner be seen as innocent before the judgment seat of God when, in himself, he is nothing of the sort? Calvin's answer is: by means of the imputation of Christ's perfect righteousness. "Therefore, since God justifies us by the intercession of Christ, he absolves us not by the confirmation of our own innocence but by the imputation of righteousness, so that we who are not righteous in ourselves may be reckoned as such in Christ."[28] Calvin means nothing else but this when he says, "justified by faith is he who, excluded from the righteousness of works, grasps the righteousness of Christ through faith, and clothed in it, appears in God's sight not as a sinner but as a righteous man."[29] It might be tempting to try to press the image of being "clothed" in Christ's righteousness in the direction of an actual righteousness, a *being* righteous, but the context clearly forbids this:

---

[26]Calvin *Institutes* 3.2.23.

[27]Calvin *Institutes* 3.2.3.

[28]Calvin *Institutes* 3.2.4.

[29]Calvin *Institutes* 3.2.2.

As iniquity is abominable to God, so no sinner can find favor in his eyes in so far as he is a sinner and so long as he is reckoned as such. Accordingly, wherever there is sin, there also the wrath and vengeance of God show themselves. Now he is justified who is reckoned in the condition not of a sinner, but of a righteous man; and for that reason, he stands firm before God's judgment seat while all sinners fall. If an innocent accused person be summoned before the judgment seat of a fair judge, where he will be judged according to his innocence, he is said to be "justified" before the judge. Thus, justified before God is the man who, freed from the company of sinners, has God to witness and affirm his righteousness.[30]

Innocence? Here, again, this is not true of the individual in and for him/herself. No matter how advanced we may be in comparison with our fellow sinners in the way of sanctification, we can never undo the unrighteousness which we have done. We can never stand before God as those who are innocent. And the making of us to be actually righteous through sanctification could not accomplish the "innocence" of which Calvin speaks. If this nevertheless happens, if God regards us as innocent, there can only be one explanation for it. "Therefore, we explain justification simply as the acceptance with which God receives us into his favor as righteous men. And we say that it consists in the remission of sins and the imputation of Christ's righteousness."[31]

Given his repeated insistence that Christ's righteousness is made to be ours by imputation, it was with complete consistency that Calvin also made the transfer of our guilt to Christ to be accomplished by the same means: "This is our acquittal: the guilt that held us liable for punishment has been transferred to the head of the Son of God."[32] And, commenting upon 2 Corinthians 5:21, Calvin says, "The Son of God, utterly clean of all fault, nevertheless took upon himself the shame and reproach of our iniquities, and in return clothed us with his purity." How? "He who was about to cleanse the filth of those iniquities was covered with them by transferred imputation."[33] A wondrous exchange has occurred. Christ clothed himself with the guilt that accrues to our sins and, as a consequence, clothes us with his righteousness resulting in our acquittal. And the mechanism by means of which this wondrous exchange takes place is imputation.

With these basic definitions in place, Calvin turns to his critique of Osiander.

---

[30] Ibid.
[31] Ibid.
[32] Calvin *Institutes* 2.16.5.
[33] Calvin *Institutes* 2.16.6.

The root of his criticism is to be found not simply in the account of the wondrous exchange, which we have just set forth, but also in certain basic commitments which are registered in his Christology. Obviously, we cannot enter fully into the subject of Christology here. Suffice it to say that Calvin would not allow for any "mixing" of Christ's divine nature with his human nature. And that is the point he hammers home in his criticism of Osiander's teaching.

Osiander's view, as Calvin understands it, is that justification is a term descriptive of a process by means of which the believer is united to God in such a way that he/she is made a participant in God's "essence." Put another way, the "essential righteousness" of Christ is infused into the believer. Such a view, Calvin concedes, might appear plausible on the surface. Osiander begins with the observation that "we are one with Christ." With this assertion, Calvin can scarcely disagree. But how are we "one?" How is "union" with Christ effected? And with what, specifically, are we united? Calvin says that Osiander's fundamental error lies in his failure to understand rightly the nature of the "bond of this unity."[34] Osiander treats the fact that union comes about through the Holy Spirit as a matter of little importance if it does not result in a mingling of Christ's essence with our own.[35] Worse still, in speaking of "Christ's essence," what Osiander has in view is the very essence of God. The "essential righteousness" of Christ is the righteousness that is his by virtue of being God, the divine righteousness he—so to speak—brought with him into the hypostatic union with human flesh. So Calvin numbers among Osiander's "deceptions" the following ideas: "that Christ is our righteousness because He is God eternal, the source of righteousness, and the very righteousness of God Himself." Osiander "has expressed himself as not content with that righteousness which has been acquired for us by Christ's obedience and sacrificial death, but pretends that we are substantially righteous in God by the infusion both of his essence and of his quality." Osiander's view, thus, entails a "mixture of substances by which God—transfusing Himself into us, as it were—makes us part of Himself."[36] Whatever else is meant by Calvin's talk of the Holy Spirit as the bond which joins us to Christ, it is clearly intended to exclude this possibility.

Because Osiander has made himself guilty of such a mixing of substances, he has also confused two things that must be kept separate: justification and regeneration. Osiander holds that God "justifies not only by pardon but by regenerating." Against

---

[34]Calvin *Institutes* 3.2.5.
[35]Ibid.
[36]Ibid.

this, Calvin says that although the two things (justification and regeneration) cannot be torn apart in reality, they must be carefully distinguished on the level of sound teaching. It is quite true that "as Christ cannot be torn into parts, so these two which we perceive in him together and conjointly are inseparable—namely, righteousness and sanctification. Whomever, therefore, God receives into grace, on them he *at the same time* bestows the spirit of adoption [Rom 8:15], by whose power he remakes them to his own image."[37] Justification is, thus, never without regeneration and vice versa. Still, "to be justified means something different from being made new creatures."[38] To be justified is to be received, to be accepted as one who is innocent. "There . . . the question is simply one of guilt and acquittal."[39]

Through his critique of Osiander, Calvin's own positive interpretation of justification has been considerably deepened. Earlier, I noted that we would eventually have to pose the question "what, precisely, is that righteousness of Christ's which is made ours in justification?" and the answer has now been made abundantly clear. The righteousness of Christ that Calvin has in mind is his "acquired righteousness," the righteousness that is created by his work—which is to say, through his life of perfect obedience and his sacrificial death. In making this distinction between "essential righteousness" and "acquired righteousness," Calvin made a significant contribution not only to the Reformed understanding of justification but also to Protestantism in general. The Lutheran Formula of Concord expressed itself this way: "Christ is our righteousness not according to the divine nature alone or according to the human nature alone but according to both natures; as God and man, he has by his perfect obedience redeemed us from our sins, justified and saved us."[40] *By his perfect obedience:* the emphasis here, too, lies on what Calvin called the "acquired righteousness" of Christ.

Calvin has also, it should be noted, given expression to a careful ordering of the relation of justification to regeneration. In saying, "Whomever, therefore, God receives into grace, on them he *at the same time* bestows the spirit of adoption [Rom 8:15], by whose power he remakes them to his own image," Calvin makes justification to be logically prior to—and the foundation of—that bestowal of the Spirit of adoption by means of which the believer is regenerated. On this view, regeneration would have to be seen as the logical consequence of the divine verdict registered in justification.

---

[37]Calvin *Institutes* 3.2.6 (emphasis added).
[38]Ibid.
[39]Ibid.
[40]*The Book of Concord*, pp. 539-40.

In sum, Calvin's understanding of justification is strictly forensic or judicial in character. It is a matter of a divine judgment, a verdict of acquittal. And the means by which it is accomplished is imputation. I hope that this much has been made clear. For now I am going to have to muddy the waters a bit.

As clear and self-consistent as Calvin's doctrine of justification is when taken in isolation, a real question can be raised as to its fit with the rest of his soteriology. Calvin begins Book III with a chapter devoted to a theme which he would subsequently touch upon in his debate with Osiander, viz. that of "union with Christ." If we were to ask, after a rapid reading of this chapter, how we come to participate in the acquired righteousness of Christ, the answer that might easily be drawn is "through our union with Christ."

> As long as Christ remains outside of us, and we are separated from him, all that he
> has suffered and done for the salvation of the human race remains useless and of no
> value for us. Therefore, to share with us what he has received from the Father, he had
> to become ours and to dwell within us.

Calvin goes on to say that it is the Holy Spirit who is "the bond by [which] Christ effectually unites us to Himself."[41] Now the reason this answer is problematic is that the answer which Calvin gives to the same question within the context of his treatment of justification is "by a divine act of divine imputation." Whether these two answers are compatible and, if so, how they are compatible are only the most obvious parts of our problem. But there is more.

At several points in the *Institutes*, Calvin appears to make "union with Christ" to be logically, if not chronologically, prior to both justification and regeneration. To the extent that this is so, "union with Christ" is made to appear as a third, independent aspect of the Holy Spirit's work, to be ranged alongside of both justification and regeneration as their common root. Most famously, Calvin appears to do this in a passage with which he opens his discussion of the place of justification in Christian soteriology. There he says, "By partaking of him, we principally receive a double grace: namely, that being reconciled to God through Christ's blamelessness, we may have in heaven instead of a Judge a gracious Father; and secondly that sanctified by Christ's spirit we may cultivate blamelessness and purity of life."[42] The effect of such a statement would seem to make justification and regeneration the effects of a logically prior "participation" in Christ that has been effected by the uniting action of

---

[41]Calvin *Institutes* 3.1.1.
[42]Calvin *Institutes* 3.2.1.

the Holy Spirit. "Therefore, that joining together of Head and members, that indwelling of Christ in our hearts—in short, that mystical union—are accorded by us
the highest degree of importance, so that Christ, having been made ours, makes us
sharers with him in the gifts with which he has been endowed."[43]

Now the problem with such statements—and it is a problem of sizeable pro-
portions—is that one of the "gifts" he speaks of—viz. regeneration—is very difficult to distinguish conceptually from that "union" which is supposed to give rise
to both justification *and regeneration*. For surely the establishment of the intimate relation of head and members, the indwelling of Christ in our hearts, is what Calvin
also means by "regeneration." Moreover, the apparent contradiction that would
arise here gives rise to a further problem. If Calvin were indeed intending to make
"union with Christ" the root of justification, he would be breaking with the ordering of justification above regeneration which he at least implied in the context of
his debate with Osiander, thereby guaranteeing that his "break" with Medieval
Catholic views was not as clean and complete as he himself obviously thought and
hoped. For where regeneration is made—even if only logically—to be the root of
justification, there the work of God "in us" is, once again (and now on the soil of
the Reformation!) made to be the ground of the divine forgiveness of sins. Such a
conclusion is softened to some extent by the element of simultaneity, by the fact
that the priority here spoken of is strictly logical. If it were not so, then what Wil-
helm Niesel has described as the burden of Calvin's response to Osiander would be
something of which he, too, was still guilty. "If God were only to justify us in view
of a new life previously begun in us, we should never be certain of salvation but
would constantly have to ask whether the new life begun in us really qualified for
God's verdict of justification."[44] What distinguishes Calvin from Osiander, according to Niesel, is the latter's commitment to the note of "previously begun." What
Niesel does not seem to appreciate, however, is that the expedient of rejecting a
chronological priority of regeneration over justification and an insistence on their
simultaneity are scarcely adequate by themselves to prevent simultaneity from slid-
ing gradually into the relation of "previously begun." Only the strict emphasis
upon imputation is capable of closing the door with finality upon the Medieval
Catholic view.

Now there is much more that could be said here on the subject of "union with

---

[43]Calvin *Institutes* 3.2.10.
[44]Wilhelm Niesel, *The Gospel and the Churches: A Comparison of Catholicism, Orthodoxy and Protestantism* (Philadelphia: Westminster Press, 1962), p. 195.

Christ" in Calvin's theology which might narrow the distance between imputation and "union with Christ" as possible answers to the question of how we come to share in Christ's acquired righteousness. But that will have to remain a subject for another day. My goal here has been simply to identify a conceptual problem accentuated by the order of teaching with which Calvin opens book three of his *Institutes* (first, union with Christ, then regeneration and only then justification). It is quite true, as Niesel argued long ago, that Calvin's motive in organizing book three in this way was to take the ground out from beneath Catholic polemic against the Protestant doctrine of justification on the grounds that it constituted a "legal fiction." But one has to ask: did Calvin really maintain the kind of conceptual clarity which would have allowed him, in a different set of historical circumstances, to reverse the treatment and to take up justification before regeneration? Or was the treatment of regeneration prior to justification not necessitated by the foregrounding of "union with Christ"?

What I have tried to show here is that Calvin's definition of *justification*, and the view of the relation of justification and regeneration that definition required, collided sharply with possible implications of his chosen order of teaching.

WHAT WENT WRONG?

In 1992 I presented a paper on the subject of incarnation and atonement in the Reformed tradition in Kappel, Switzerland, at an officially sponsored dialogue between the churches belonging to the World Alliance of Reformed Churches (WARC) and the Orthodox Churches. I will never forget the question-and-answer session that followed my presentation. As soon as I had finished reading, my good friend T. F. Torrance leaped to his feet to say something very close to the following:

> I just want to assure our Orthodox brethren that Professor McCormack's way of reading the Reformed tradition is not the only way to read it; in fact, it is the wrong way to read it. If you really want to understand what Calvin believed about the atoning work of Christ, you can't start with *Institutes* 2.15-17. You have to start with the view of atonement which is implied in his treatment of eucharistic feeding in 4.17 and and only then turn to 2.15-17.

My initial reaction to this intervention was to think there was something hermeneutically odd, to say the least, about looking away from the one section of the *Institutes* in which Calvin treats Christ's atoning work directly (i.e., 2.15-17) in order to generate a doctrine of the atonement on the basis of passages dealing with other doctrines. It was also clear to me what Torrance hoped to accomplish with this strategy. He saw his own soteriology of "ontological healing" (a variant on the Eastern idea of *theosis*) as required by Calvin's understanding of eucharistic feeding. If he could show that much, then he could return to the teaching on the subject of atonement in 2.15-17 and subordinate its judicial elements to the ontological elements of his own theory in such a way that the element of penal substitution, while not simply being dismissed, drifts into the background.

But as I got some distance from this experience and subjected Calvin to renewed scrutiny, I came to the conclusion that the problem was not just the result of Torrance's dogmatic commitments and his strange hermeneutic. Calvin himself bears at least some of the responsibility. You see, there is a structural tension that runs right through the heart of the *Institutes* between the forensicism of his doctrines of atonement and justification, and the more nearly patristic understanding of those themes which are suggested by a good bit of the rhetoric that Calvin employs in speaking of the eucharist. The tension is made quite clear in *Institutes* 4.17.9 (to give just one example), where Calvin says (in dependence on Cyril of Alexandria) that "the flesh of Christ is like a rich and inexhaustible fountain that pours into us the life springing forth from the Godhead into itself. Now who does not see that communion of [*sic*] Christ's flesh and blood is necessary for all who aspire to heavenly life."[45] Now, at the very least, it has to be said that it is hard to understand how a theologian who rejects all mixture of the divine and human natures in Christ, who everywhere in his Christology laid emphasis on the thought of "two natures unimpaired after the union"[46] and who, on that basis, rejected the doctrine of a communication of attributes from the divine nature to the human nature as taught by the Lutherans (not to mention Osiander's confusion of Christ's "essential" divine righteousness with his "acquired righteousness"!) can now speak of the life flowing forth from the Godhead into Christ's human nature. Surely, the life flowing forth from the Godhead cannot be infused into the human nature of Christ in the absence of all the divine attributes? If there is a "communication of [divine] life" into the human nature of Christ, it would seem logical to affirm a communication of other attributes as well.

Now I would suggest that the cause of the confusion created by Calvin's love for Cyril's rhetoric in the area of eucharistic teaching lay in his unwillingess to address ontological questions directly. Had he done so, he might have realized that he

---

[45]Calvin *Institutes* 4.17.9.
[46]Calvin *Institutes* 2.14.1: "For we affirm his divinity so joined and united with his humanity that each retains its distinctive nature unimpaired, and yet these two natures constitute one Christ."

could not reasonably affirm Cyril's rhetoric on the life-giving character of Christ's "body" without accepting Cyril's soteriology of divinization, as well as the (largely) Platonic ontology of "participation" which made that soteriology possible in the first place. He might also have seen that he was creating serious problems for his doctrine of justification. For Calvin was committed to a judicial theory of the atonement and an equally judicial answer to the question of how believers come to participate "in Christ" which could not be easily squared (if at all) with the understandings of divinization and "participation" advocated by Cyril.

The problem with refusing to engage ontological questions as an essential part of the dogmatic task is that we all too easily make ourselves the unwitting servants of the ontology that is embedded in the older theological rhetoric that we borrow—and so it was with Calvin. I don't mean to imply that there are not resources in Calvin's theology for resolving the confusion; there are. I simply want to highlight the problem.

The importance of these observations for a more adequate defense of Calvin's understanding of justification in the face of the Roman Catholic charge of a "legal fiction" (a charge which is now becoming fashionable even among Protestants!) is not far to seek. Calvin contented himself, when attempting to counter this charge, with asserting the temporal simultaneity of justification with sanctification. That's not a bad answer as far as it goes and it is not surprising that it might have satisfied Protestants for a very long time. To assert the temporal simultaneity of justification and sanctification is to suggest that God doesn't lie in pronouncing a sinner just for Christ's sake because God is *also*—at the same time—making him/her to be righteous. But today's Protestants no longer seem to be as impressed with that answer as their forebears were. Today's Protestants give every indication of wanting to understand justification as being itself transformative. The tragedy is that Calvin had the resources at his disposal to meet this demand *without abandoning his judicial framework*. But he did not realize it.

We live in a time in which the churches of the Reformation are in doctrinal chaos. Many there are who, appalled by the gnosticism and even paganism of a good bit of the theology to be found on the left wing of their churches, have turned longing eyes towards Rome and Constantinople. And clearly there is much to be admired there. The Roman Church and the Eastern Orthodox churches have been able, for various reasons, to sustain a theological existence in their churches which, for us Protestants, exists only in memory. But even more, the Roman and Eastern Orthodox churches are the institutional bearers of soteriologies of transformation that exercise a fascination among many. I think it is accurate to say that there are no hotter topics in Protestant theology today than the themes of *theosis*, union with Christ, the de Lubacian axiom "the Eucharist makes the church," etc. Efforts to find what look like Roman and Eastern soteriologies in the Reformers themselves are rapidly becoming something of a cottage industry.

In the process, the churches are slowly coming under the influence of a concept of "participation" in Christ that owes a great deal to the ancient Greek ontologies of pure being. To appropriate this doctrine intelligently would require that we submit ourselves to the ancient ontologies embedded in them. But, like Calvin, we rarely stop to consider that. We do not raise the question whether or not there might be a theological ontology less inimical to our received doctrine of justification. In truth, forensicism (rightly understood!) provides the basis for an alternative theological ontology to the one presupposed in Roman and Eastern soteriology. Where this is not seen, the result has almost always been the abandonment of the Reformation doctrine of justification on the mistaken assumption that the charge of a "legal fiction" has a weight, which in truth, it does not.

In concluding this lecture, I want to engage in a thought experiment. My thought experiment will suggest to you a way of ordering the central concepts of Christian soteriology that will not bring the content of those concepts into a relation of contradiction to the Reformation understanding of justification. In the process, I will try to at least give you a glimpse of a theological ontology which is more commensurate with the Reformation understanding of justification than the ancient Greek ontology which the Reformers themselves inherited—more commensurate, precisely because of its capacity to render intelligible the ordering of concepts which I will suggest. I am not going to try here to defend all the moves I will make by reference to Scripture. But I hope that you will be able to form some impression of their usefulness in understanding a person like Paul.

A THOUGHT EXPERIMENT

I am going to carry out my thought experiment in three movements. First, a defense of the Protestant understanding of justification in view of current revivals of the charge of a "legal fiction"; second, some reflections on the concept of "union with Christ"; and, third, a brief sketch of the theological ontology embedded in the doctrinal material treated in the first two steps.

The charge of a "legal fiction." Earlier I noted that an understanding of the relation of justification to regeneration is implied by what Calvin says concretely about justification. This is seen clearly in a passage to which I have already directed your attention. "Whomever, therefore, God receives into grace, on them he at the same time bestows the spirit of adoption [Rom 8:15], by whose power he remakes them in his own image." I want to take this passage as providing me with my clue for a proper ordering of the relation of justification and regeneration. Justification is clearly seen in this passage as logically prior to regeneration. Indeed, justification brings regeneration in its wake. The only interpretive question needing to be clarified is whether Calvin intended us to understand the relation as causal in nature. Are these two distinct (albeit simultaneous) acts of God or are they two "moments" in a single act of God? It is not clear to me that Calvin ever posed the question to himself in quite this form; hence it is also not clear to me that he answered it as clearly as I might like.

My own answer would be that justification and regeneration are conceptually distinguishable "moments" in a single act of God. The term "justification" has its home in the judicial sphere. In justification, God pronounces a judicial verdict upon the sinner. But God's verdict and the divine word pronounced in it are not at all that of a human judge. The human judge can only *describe* what he hopes to be the real state of affairs. The human judge's judgment is in no sense effective; it does not create the reality it depicts. It seeks only to conform to an already given reality. God's verdict differs in that it creates the reality it declares. God's declaration, in other words, is itself constitutive of that which is declared.[47] God's word is always effective. When it goes forth, it never returns to Him void. So a judicial act for God is never merely judicial; it is itself transformative.

To put it this way is to suggest that the faith that receives the divine verdict is itself produced by that verdict. Imputation is itself regenerative. Now this may seem counter-intuitive, given the fact that in Romans 4 Paul appeals to Abraham as an analogy. Genesis 15:6, to which Paul makes appeal in Romans 4:3, says, "Abraham believed God, and it was reckoned to him as righteousness." We might understandably think, *Surely you must first have a subject capable of believing if his faith is*

---

[47]John Murray says something quite similar, though with a different result than the one I am aiming at here. He says that, "the declarative act of God in the justification of the ungodly is constitutive. In this consists its incomparable character." Murray, *Redemption Accomplished and Applied* (Grand Rapids: Eerdmans, 1955), p. 123. But Murray makes the divine declaration to be constitutive not of regeneration but only of "the righteous state or relation which is declared to be." Regeneration he treats prior to justification and, curiously enough, as distinct from "effectual calling"—which is a move that even the Westminster Confession did not make.

then to be reckoned to him as righteousness. Surely the logic of the statement is, first, a believing subject and then the divine verdict. And if it were Paul's intention in this context to specify the order of these things, it would pose an insuperable obstacle to the view I am arguing for here. But seen in context, Paul's concern is to contrast justification by faith with justification by works. It would be strange if, given this intention, he were to turn around and treat faith as a "work"—that is, as a human possibility, as a condition which we humans must first provide before divine imputation can occur. So Paul's intention in citing Genesis 15:6 cannot be to negotiate the logical relation between justification and regeneration. To understand that relation, we would have to look to Paul's teachings everywhere on the nature of faith. Paul understands faith to be a gift of God wrought by his grace in the human heart. Faith is a divine possibility and never at any point a human possibility. God does not do our believing for us; it is we who believe. But believing is not something we can muster up on our own steam.

In sum, the judicial metaphor of justification and the corollary term *imputation* describe the objective turning of God toward us. The same thing is true of another judicial metaphor, namely that of adoption. Adoption is a legal term. It refers to the bestowal on one not naturally born to a parent or parents all the rights and privileges proper to a naturally born son or daughter. That Paul employs the metaphor of adoption at all shows that men and women are not children of God merely by virtue of having been created by him. The comparison implied here is to the one natural born Son of God, Jesus Christ. To be adopted as children of God is to be granted all the rights and privileges which belong to the God-human—the first of which is the bestowal of the Spirit of adoption (Rom 8:15) who enables us to call with confidence upon God as our Father. But if the gift of the Holy Spirit is itself a consequence of adoption and not the condition of its occurrence, then here too, in the case of adoption, a legal metaphor is being employed to describe the objective side of the act in which God turns towards the individual in his grace without respect for the subjective consequences of that turning *in us*. For the latter, other terms are needed—terms like regeneration.

But is this understanding of the relation of justification and regeneration sufficient to deliver the Protestant conception of justification from the charge of a "legal" fiction? Up to now, I have spoken only of imputation as itself regenerative. That by itself helps to get the ordering of our concepts right but that only makes possible a complete answer to the traditional Catholic criticism; it does not yet provide it.

A complete answer to the charge must begin with the recognition that imputation is regenerative, but it is also more than that. The heart of the Reformation understanding of imputation had to do with the positive imputation of Christ's righteousness. The point was to secure the claim that Christ's righteousness is made to be *wholly* ours, so that we might appear before God as not merely forgiven sinners but as those who are already regarded by God as innocent, in advance of the completion of God's work in us. That Christ's "alien" righteousness is "imputed" to us means that we are covered by it, much as the blood of the sacrificial lamb covered the children of Israel at the Feast of Unleavened Bread. Christ is our Passover sacrifice (I Cor 5:7)—an idea closely connected in Paul's mind with justification. But how are these two aspects of imputation related? That is, how are the aspect of being clothed in Christ's righteousness and the aspect of regeneration, which is the immediate consequence of divine imputation, related? The attempt to answer that question necessitates that we take a step back and try to locate the place of divine imputation in a larger frame of reference.

The divine imputation is a verdict whose final meaning can only be grasped when it is seen in the framework of a teleologically-oriented covenant of grace. It is a verdict that looks backward and forward simultaneously. It looks back on the eternal divine decision to enter into a gracious covenant with the human race—a covenant in which what God demands of his covenant partners is something God himself provides in Christ. Thus, the decision registered in the divine imputation is not a novum, but the manifestation of the eternal decision of the triune God to redeem God's people on the basis of Christ's work. The eschatological dimension is even more important for my purposes here. The regeneration, which flows from justification as its consequence, is the initiation of a work that is completed only in the eschaton, only in the glorification of the saints. Hence, God's pronouncement of a sinner as innocent takes place with a view towards the final purification of the sinner in the eschaton. And that has to mean that God does not simply clothe us in Christ's righteousness in advance of the completion of his work but does so with a view towards that consummation.

Now the eschatological convergence which all of this implies for the divine verdict and the human reality spoken of in that verdict will not mean an end of Christ's work of intercession—and this leads us to one final observation. To be "clothed with Christ's righteousness" in time, means to be clothed with the saving efficacy of his death (which addresses the problem of guilt) and the saving efficacy of his life of obedience (in which the new humanity is inaugurated). In the eschaton, however, the consummation of God's work in us will mean that we no longer need to be clothed with Christ's righteousness on the side of the saving efficacy of his life of obedience. For in being purified, our lives will have been brought so completely into conformity to his life of obedience that there will remain no difference between his humanity and ours. We will be "like him" (I Jn 3:2) without remainder. The new humanity inaugurated in and by him will be ours as well. Still, with respect to the guilt that accrues to sins previously committed, we will need to be "covered." It is for this reason that Hebrews says that Christ's priesthood is permanent (Heb 7:24) and that he ever lives to make intercession for those who draw near to God through him (Heb 7:25).

In sum, the divine imputation by means of which God regards us as innocent in time is two-sided. It entails being clothed with the saving efficacy of Christ's death and the saving efficacy of Christ's life with a view towards the eschatological consummation. In the eschaton, imputation is one-sided in that we will be clothed then only with the saving efficacy of Christ's death. It will be one-sided because at that point, God will not simply regard us as righteous—we will actually *be* righteous.

Now if I am right up to this point in my reflections, then the ground has been taken out from beneath the charge of a "legal fiction" without recourse to the vexed problem of our union with Christ. Imputation, understood as a judicial act with transformative consequences, is adequate to handle the problem. With that move in place, let me return to the concept of our "union with Christ." I would like to suggest that there is a way of thinking about "union with Christ" which is completely compatible with the position I have outlined to this point.

Union with Christ. The being of the Christian "in Christ" is to be construed along the lines of the conformity of my life to his life of obedience, which brings about his likeness in me. Union with Christ, biblically considered, refers to a union of wills, the uniting of my will with his by virtue of which my life is conformed to his. I do not participate in the historical humanity of Christ (a thought which would require a unity on the level of "substance" if it is really to move beyond the thought of a unity of wills); rather I participate in the *kind* of humanity which Jesus instantiated and embodied through his life of obedience. That, I would take it, is why the first epistle of John says that when we see him as he is, in his eschatological return, we shall be *like* him (I Jn 3:2). Now notice: this "union" is a unity-in-differentiation. The individuation of Christ's humanity and my own could be thought to be transcended in a higher unity in an age which thought in terms of a Platonic realism which held that universals are more real than particulars or in terms of the

Aristotelian distinction of substance and accidents. But I think that most philosophers in the West today would agree that the ancient Greek ontologies have lost their power to compel belief. I also think that the uncritical expansion of the concept of perichoresis today on the part of a good many theologians provides a kind of ironic evidence that that is indeed the case. Perichoresis, I would argue, is rightly employed in trinitarian discourse for describing that which is *dissimilar* in the analogy between intra-trinitarian relations among the divine "persons" on the one hand and human to human relations on the other. Nowadays, we are suffering from "creeping perichoresis," that is, the overly expansive use of terms which have their home in purely spiritual relations to describe relations between human beings who do not participate in a common "substance" and who, therefore, remain distinct individuals even in the most intimate of their relations. This surely has to be true of the relation of the human believer to the human Jesus as well.

What has prevented us from seeing this, I think, is the degree of residual Catholic content in the Reformation understanding of eucharistic feeding. It is no accident that it is in the context of his treatment of eucharistic feeding that Calvin borrows rhetoric from the early church that brings him into conflict with his own doctrine of justification. For too long, sacramentology has been the tail wagging the dog of Christian theology when other topics—Trinity, Christology, election and so on ought to have been seen as more basic.

Be that as it may, the horticultural/organic images employed in the New Testament to describe the relation of Christ to the believer should be understood, I think, as metaphors that successfully bear witness to the intimacy of that relation but mislead if taken more literally. That these metaphors are employed for speaking of a relation that is quite unlike themselves in essential respects becomes quite clear when considering the image of the vine and the branches employed by Jesus in John 15. At first glance, the image might easily be seen to connote an organic connectedness between Christ and the believer. So it is easy to understand how the early church might find in such an image a proof of its conviction that the union of the believer with Christ is an ontological union of a "person" in whom being is mixed with non-being (that's us) with a "person" in whom being is pure and unalloyed with non-being (Jesus). Where that occurs, the life communicated from the vine to the branches flows organically from the source. To be sure, it would be difficult to understand, on this view, why the Holy Spirit would be needed as the bond joining us to Christ. At most, the Spirit's activity might be seen as necessary in the first, initiating moment. But once the Spirit has joined our humanity to Christ's, the life that is in Christ would flow into us directly, much as nourishment arises from the vine into the branches. It would be difficult on this view as well to know why the Spirit would be called "the Lord and Giver of Life." But there are good reasons to believe that all of this is only an analogy for describing what is, in the first instance at least, an ethical relation—an ethical relation with ontological overtones to be sure, but an ethical relation. The difference between the relation between a vine and a branch and the relation between Christ and the believer is that the first relation is impersonal and the second is personal. The flow of life-giving nutrients from the vine to the branches takes place naturally, automatically; it does not require an act of will on the side of either vine or branch. But in the case of the relation of Christ and the believer, we are dealing with a *willed relation*. That, already, marks the dissimilarity in the analogy being constructed here. The similarity lies on the side of the intimacy connoted by the image; that is the point of contact in the analogy. Moreover, the context in which this organic image is employed makes it clear that the subject is "bearing fruit"—that is, the performing of works of love which correspond to Christ's own. And this ethical relation of lived—which is to say, willed—existence to Christ's takes place on the foundation of justification. John 15:3 says, "You are already clean because of the word I have spoken to you."

Paul's use of the language of "engrafting" has much the same result. The term is drawn from the horticultural sphere, but it is used in Romans 9—11 to speak of inclusion in the covenant of grace, an inclusion that results in a share in all the gifts and privileges that belong to the covenant. That Paul would preface his use of the horticultural image with the affirmation that the adoption as sons and daughters of God belonged to the Israelites long before us Gentiles suggests strongly that the image of "engrafting" is employed as a synonym for adoption—which would clearly mean that the horticultural image is subordinated to the legal. If that is correct, it would also have ramifications for how we understand the "engrafting" spoken of in relation to baptism in Romans 6.

In conclusion, "union with Christ" is most certainly a New Testament concept. But we make a mistake, I think, if we jump to the conclusion that it can only refer in Greek fashion to a substantial participation in the being of Christ. The Greek ontology of pure being is far removed from Paul's mind especially. Paul's thought is shot through with eschatology—which leads him to be very concerned that his disciples should live in such a way that they will have no reason to be ashamed on the Day of Christ. This does not mean that an ontology is not implied by his thought. But the key to teasing it out lies in attending carefully to his eschatology and his overwhelming preoccupation with ethics. Where this is done, it will be seen that *the ethical is itself ontological.* The being of the human is constituted, in large measure, by what she does. To explain what I mean, I turn finally to the subject of covenant ontology.

Covenant ontology. For all its faults, the one virtue of postmodernism in the philosophical realm has been its protest against a certain metaphysical understanding of the human. This is not to suggest that all metaphysics are equally misguided. It is simply to acknowledge frankly just how difficult it is to demonstrate philosophically the existence of a "unified subject"—a "self" which would ground and unify all the random states of consciousness that make up the "empirical self." Is there something that underlies these random states of psychological experience? Is there something that secures for the individual a "personal identity" which remains unchanged throughout the many changes she undergoes as a consequence of experiencing these random states? Our common sense reaction is to say, "Yes, of course." I am "I"—whether I am awake or asleep, present to myself (introspectively) or absent from myself (with my attention absorbed by other matters), whether I am in my childhood or my maturity. But again, demonstrating the truth of this common sense observation is far more difficult than one might think.

In spite of the difficulties, there is nothing wrong with speaking of an "essence" of the human. To speak of an "essence" of the human is to speak of a self-identical element that perdures through all growth and change on the level of conscious existence. One could, of course, seek to define this "essence" *metaphysically*—and much of the classical Christian tradition did so, following the Platonists in thinking of "essences" as universal ideas or the Aristotelians with their doctrine of "substances." But it is not necessary to define the "essence" of the human in this metaphysical way, and it is most certainly not the preferable way to go about things. To tie the fortunes of Christian theology so strictly to philosophical metaphysics—whether ancient or modern—is to make theology vulnerable to the critiques of the adopted metaphysic being brought against it by more recent philosophical criticism. What so often happens in such circumstances is that theology presents to the world the unedifying spectacle of constantly following philosophical trends that have already lost their power to convince philosophers even as theologians finally make adjustments to them. It is not a pretty picture. It is far better to approach a question like that of the "essence" of the human on strictly theological grounds and only then ask whether there might not be "parables" of such a theological account in the philosophical world. It is precisely such a theological account that I would like to advance under the heading of "covenant ontology."

What is the unchanging "essence" of the human? The "essence," I would argue, is not to be found in some kind of metaphysical substratum, something "beneath" the empirical, psychological self. Indeed, the "essence" of the human is not to be "in us" at all. The "essence" of the human—the "essence" of every individual human—lies in the divine act of relating to that individual in the covenant of grace.

I have long been fascinated by the fact that the names of God's elect are written in his "book of life" (Rev 20:15). It has to be one of the most special evidences of the dignity that God bestows upon human beings that the names which we give to our children are the names he himself has inscribed into his "book." The role God gives to parents is that significant. But even more significantly for our purposes here, these are the names by which God knew us and called us from eternity. Before any of us were, God called us by name. In so doing, God was granting us an identity that was fixed and unassailable when none of us existed yet. That God does this at all is indicative of the fact that it is he who holds our "personal identity" in his hands, who makes us to be who we are—both as a "race" of human beings and as individual members of it.

What we are "essentially" is that which God has chosen us to be in entering into covenant with us: "He chose us in Christ before the foundation of the world to be holy and blameless before him in love" (Eph 1:4). In this is our true humanity: to live in such a way that we conform to the purpose of God in electing, creating and redeeming us. That Christians do not always live up to this ideal is obvious. Only in Christ do we see the perfect conjoining of human "essence" (defined as that which we were chosen to be) and human existence. Or we might say: only in him is his "nature" (that which he makes of himself as a self-determining agent) in complete conformity to his "essence" (that which God called him to be as mediator of the covenant). Of Jesus Christ alone, then, can we say that he is what he does—without further qualification. In us, "essence" and existence (or "nature") tend to fall apart and will continue to do so until the final consummation. But in those moments in which we respond to God's call in faith and obedience, in those moments in which our lived existence is brought into conformity to Christ's—our existence conforms to "essence." But that is, obviously, not a continuous relation. Of all other humans than Jesus, we have to say that they are what they do on the level of their existence (their "natures" are the product of their self-determining activities through time)—but that, in an even more important and basic sense, they are not what they do (to the extent that their existence does not conform to their essence). Now notice in this depiction, "essence" is not treated along the lines of either a metaphysical "substance" (with the ancients) or an abstract metaphysical subject (with the moderns). What we are essentially is a divine act which establishes a covenantal relation—a relation which perdures and makes us to be what we are even when, in our perversity, we choose to live on the basis of a lie rather than the truth. I am I, I am identical with myself in all the random and unrelated moments of my existence, because God has chosen to make me his covenant-partner in Jesus Christ. That is my true identity.

It is of the utmost importance to see that the covenant ontology, which I have here described, is fully commensurate with the understanding of union with Christ that I set forth earlier. Covenant ontology is an ontology of correspondence. We are what we truly are (and what we will be in the eschaton) in those moments when our humanity is conformed on the level of lived existence to the humanity inaugurated in time by Christ's life of obedience. We are what we will be through correspondence. To put it this way is to tease out the ontology embedded in my earlier contention that union with Christ takes its rise through a unity of wills, not through a unity of substances. Human *being* is the product of decision, of willed action—both on the side of God's act of relating to us and on the side of our act of relating (or choosing not to relate) to him. But if human being is the product of decision, of willed action and there is no deeper-lying "substance" of the human, then the thought of a quasi-perichoretic indwelling of the historical humanity of Christ is shown to be an ontological impossibility.

Finally, covenant theology is fully compatible with and indeed, embedded in, the understanding of justification I outlined above. Justification, I suggested earlier, is itself regenerative. The faith and obedience by means of which my humanity conforms to the humanity of Jesus Christ is the effect of the divine declaration given in the justification of the ungodly. Nothing could make clearer the fact that, at its heart, forensicism is deeply ontological. At the very root of forensic thinking lies the recognition that human being is the function of a decision which gives rise to a willed relation. Human being is the function of a decision God *made* in eternity past in his electing grace. And it is a function of a decision God *makes* in time in justifying the ungodly. The former is the ground of the latter; the latter actualizes the content of the former in time.

With respect to the modality of the Holy Spirit's work, one final observation. Justification is rightly understood as a trinitarian act. The Father pronounces the verdict registered in justification on the basis of the Son's righteousness in the power of the Holy Spirit. Thus, the Holy Spirit is the power of the divine declaration which gives rise to faith and obedience. The only question remaining is that of how the Spirit works. The question is an important one if we are to close the circle, so to speak, coming to as full an understanding as possible of the covenant ontology embedded in a Protestant understanding of justification.

For much of Christian theological history, the work of the Spirit has been thought of along the lines of a kind of divine surgery. The will, on this view, is thought of as something quasi-substantial, a "thing" that can be operated upon by God so as to effect a "healing." The problem with this is that the will is not something substantial. What we call "will" is, in truth, the mind—but the mind seen as directed toward an object or end, accompanied by either desire or a sense of duty/ obligation. It is not something special "in us" to be ranged alongside of the mind as a distinct power or "faculty." Given that this is so, it is a real question what there might be "in us" upon which God might operate. We would be better off, I suspect, thinking of the work of the Holy Spirit in terms of an existential encounter of divine person with human person whose point of entry, if you will, is the mind.[48] It is no accident that Paul speaks in Romans 12:2 of a transformation which takes place through a renewal of the mind or that he would speak of the restoration of the divine image in Ephesians 4:22-24 and Colossians 3:10 once again in terms of a renewal of the mind with the result that the image itself is seen to consist in true knowledge of God. For Paul, of course, knowledge of God is not merely cognitive; it is not localized in the mind alone—though we make a huge mistake if we think the knowledge of God is so special in nature that it bears nothing in common with what everywhere else passes for cognitive knowledge. Paul is very concerned with what his disciples think, the ideas with which they stock their minds (see especially Phil 4:8 and Col 3:2). In accordance with this emphasis on the mind in the process of renewal, we would do well to conceive of the modality of the Spirit's working primarily in terms of "illumination." The power of the Father's declarative word is the Holy Spirit's illumination of the human mind. As Calvin put it in the very same chapter in which he treated the theme of union with Christ, "faith is the principal work of the Holy Spirit. . . . Paul shows the Spirit to be that inner teacher by whose effort the promise of salvation penetrates into our minds, a promise that would otherwise only strike the air or beat upon our ears." Calvin goes on to appeal to the

---

[48]The difference between this form of Christian existentialism and the non-Christian, philosophical versions has to do with the fact that the former refers to an encounter that is full of content. It is not characterized by a leap into the void but rests on real knowledge.

writings of the apostle John who saw the "proper office of the Spirit" to consist in "bringing to mind" what Christ had taught by his mouth.[49] God's declaration in justification is revelation, and revelation transforms the whole person. What happens in revelation is that the word of God breaks into the circle of self-enclosedness in which the sinner finds himself/herself with the power of a reality that is inescapable and indubitable. Where this occurs, the whole person undergoes a fundamental reorientation. He/she is brought into a sphere where conformity of existence to essence becomes possible for the first time. With this brief explanation of the Spirit's work, my attempt to sketch the relation of justification to covenant ontology is now complete.

CONCLUSION

In this essay, I have not tried to demonstrate the truthfulness of the view I have been describing. To do that would require a tremendous amount of biblical work to test the various parts of the picture. What I have done, though, is to put an alternative before you that can only be adequately tested in the light of Scripture once it has been recognized as a possibility. I have done so in the conviction that, all too often, what exegetes think of as the spectrum of possible interpretations of New Testament teachings is unduly limited by their own lack of imagination where possible interconnections and implications are concerned.

It could be, however, that after all the testing that needs to be done is completed, it will have been shown that the Reformation was in many respects a mistake. I don't believe that, but it is at least a theoretical possibility. My hope in the meantime is that the Reformation will not be brought to a premature conclusion by those whose power to affect the outcome is equaled only by their ignorance of the unexploited potential of their own tradition.

May God have mercy upon the churches of our day, and upon each of us as we seek to work our way through the welter of conflicting opinions that now increasingly divide even the evangelical denominations. Amen.

---

[49]Calvin *Institutes* 3.1.4.

4

JUSTIFICATION AND JUSTICE

The Promising Problematique of Protestant Ethics in the Work of Paul L. Lehmann

PHILIP G. ZIEGLER

Dietrich Bonhoeffer made two sojourns to America: the first as a visiting fellow at Union Theological Seminary in New York City during the academic year 1930-1931; the second, lasting just over a month, in the summer of 1939. No other figure was more humanly prominent in Bonhoeffer's American experience than Paul L. Lehmann.[1] Neither did Bonhoeffer encounter anyone else in America with whom he shared such invigorating theological rapport.[2] Lehmann in return coveted Bonhoeffer's theological companionship for both himself and the American church; indeed, throughout the 1930s it was Lehmann's hope that Bonhoeffer would attain a professorship in the United States and contribute to "the shaking up of the American 'theistic scenery' as it was at the time."[3]

In the wake of his final trans-Atlantic visit, Bonhoeffer composed an essay in which he reflected upon Protestant Christianity in America. The essay, significantly titled "Protestantism without Reformation," lay on his desk to be discovered at the

---

[1] Cf. Eberhard Bethge, *Dietrich Bonhoeffer: Theologian, Christian, Contemporary,* trans. Edwin Robertson (London: Collins, 1970), pp. 114-15: "[Lehmann] was Bonhoeffer's companion and loyal helper at the most important turning-point of his life."

[2] "With Lehmann he could talk and argue; Lehmann understood the nuances of European culture and theology. . . . He was working on a thesis at Union Theological Seminary, where he also had a position as assistant in systematic theology. He could understand why theological statements by both professors and students at the seminary were capable of making Bonhoeffer's hair stand on end" (Bethge, *Dietrich Bonhoeffer,* p. 144).

[3] Ibid., p. 115.

end of the war.[4] Amidst various acute and provocative observations, Bonhoeffer identifies the field of theology as a point at which "there opens up an almost incalculably deep opposition" between American Protestantism and the churches of the Reformation.[5] In explanation, he writes:

> God has granted American Christianity no Reformation. He has given it strong revivalist preachers, churchmen and theologians, but no Reformation of the church of Jesus Christ by the Word of God. . . . American theology and the American church as a whole have never been able to understand the meaning of 'criticism' by the Word of God and all that signifies. Right to the last they do not understand that God's 'criticism' touches even religion, the Christianity of the church and the sanctification of Christians, and that God has founded his church beyond religion and beyond ethics. . . . In American theology, Christianity is still essentially religion and ethics.[6]

His conclusion is trenchant: "Because of this the person and work of Jesus Christ must, for theology, sink into the background and in the long run remain misunderstood, because it is not recognized as the sole ground of radical judgment and radical forgiveness."[7]

Such was Bonhoeffer's view of the "theistic scenery" that a young Paul Lehmann hoped his German friend and colleague would join him in upsetting. It was scenery whose contours, in their shared view, had become largely inhospitable to properly evangelical Christianity as a result of the grinding glacial forces of "Protestantism without Reformation" in America. And though all hopes for such theological collaboration with Bonhoeffer ended abruptly on gallows during the murderous fury of the final days of the Third Reich, Lehmann himself subsequently worked to make good on the promise of this early vision. He endeavored to alter the "theistic scenery" of American Protestant theology by a fresh avowal of that radical judgment and radical forgiveness effectively enacted in Jesus Christ that lies at the heart of the gospel of justification. In this way, it may be said that Lehmann lived out his theological existence for the sake of "getting the Reformation in America."

Remarks from a lecture Lehmann delivered at Eden Theological Seminary in

---

[4]Dietrich Bonhoeffer, *No Rusty Swords: Letters, Lectures and Notes, 1928-1936*, ed. Edwin H. Robertson, trans. Edwin H. Robertson and John Bowden (London: Collins, 1965), pp. 92-118 [*Gesammelte Schriften* I: 323-54]. For recent reflection on the abiding significance of Bonhoeffer's observations in this essay see Christopher Morse, "The Need for Dogmatic Theology. Bonhoeffer's Challenge to the US in the 1930s and the 1990s," *Ecumenical Review* 47 (1995): 263-67.

[5]Bonhoeffer, *No Rusty Swords*, p. 114.

[6]Ibid., p. 117.

[7]Ibid., pp. 117-18.

1939 titled "The Predicament of Protestant Thought" show his deep agreement with Bonhoeffer's critical assessment.[8] There is, he says, a clash in the Protestant church between two figures, namely the "pious person" and the "good person." Confronted by pressing questions concerning Christian responsibility for the world, the competing visions of these two figures generate "unhappy suspicions which divide the contemporary household of faith between those who believe that the social impact of the gospel cannot wait upon individual conversion, and those who believe that if individuals are won over to the Lord Jesus Christ the social problem will take care of itself." Both views trade upon common assumptions that, at its heart, Christian faith is either a matter of *religion* (piety) or of *morality* (virtue). To Lehmann's mind, that each view claims the support of the law and the prophets only further "confounds the confusion," and shows a lack of sensitivity to the *critical* relation between the Word of God and the church. The truth of the matter is that "the law and prophets are both against both" and acknowledgment of this divine judgment is the first and decisive step toward advancing the church "beyond religion and morality." In terms evocative of Bonhoeffer's own, he concludes:

> The common interests and concerns which bind us together as contemporary Protestants are as nothing, compared with the fact that we are separated from the central insights of the Reformers into the relations of God and man. It is not a socio-historical problem we are facing, for there is no criterion in sociology or in history, sociologically considered, by which our actual unity and our actual division could be distinguished from their spurious counterparts. It is a *theological* problem in which we are involved.[9]

Engagement with *this* theological problem, Lehmann was convinced, held the promise of a fresh turning of the churches to that Word of God which the Reformers identified with God's righteous judgment and justifying grace in the person of Christ. It is by force of its devastatingly salutary encounter with *this* Word that the identity of the Christian community, *and therefore* its responsibility and relevance to the struggle for a better justice in the world, can be discerned and enacted. From the first, Lehmann identifies this as the decisive point of departure for any and all specifically Christian exposition of relations not only between God and the human, but also between human beings.[10] Lehmann's theological ethic is thus an exercise in

---

[8] Paul L. Lehmann, "The Predicament of Protestant Thought: The Theological Lectures at the Fifth Annual Convocation of Eden Theological Seminary," *PLL Papers*, box 6, file 23. Subsequent citations are all drawn from pages 6 and 7 of the typescript.
[9] Ibid.
[10] Paul L. Lehmann, *Forgiveness: Decisive Issue in Protestant Thought* (New York: Harper & Row, 1940), p. 6.

what Oliver O'Donovan characterizes as "moral reflection," that is, a "necessary taking-stock of the world" and "discrimination prior to any decision we may subsequently make to influence the world."[11] What Lehmann would keep before us is the crucial fact that for Christian ethics, the world is unavoidably a *different* place because of the determinative encounter with the Word that justifies the ungodly.[12] It is for this reason that the doctrine of justification is a—perhaps even *the*—decisive element of the theological description of the moral field, or reality, within which a properly Protestant ethic will live, move and take its being.

In what follows, I aim to trace out something of the main lines of Paul Lehmann's early account of the relation between the radical judgment and radical forgiveness of the gospel of justification and the ethical orientation of the Christian community in the broad human struggle for social justice. Lehmann taught a variety of theological disciplines at a range of institutions between the 1930s and 1980s, and the corpus of his writings, both published and unpublished, is significant in both scope and scale.[13] My engagement with his work here must, of necessity, be selective, though I trust not arbitrary. Two of Lehmann's earlier programmatic essays in particular will concern us: the first, entitled "Toward a Protestant Analysis of the Ethical Problem," was written in 1944 during Lehmann's tenure as professor of biblical history at Wellesley College; the second, "The Dynamics of Reformation Ethics," is the text of his 1950 inaugural lecture as Stephen Colwell Professor of Applied Christianity at Princeton Theological Seminary. What I hope to elucidate on the basis of these two texts is the substance of Lehmann's claim that, for Christian theology, the beginning of all social and political criticism as well as endeavor is the salutary critique of morality and religion which takes place in the

---

[11]Oliver O'Donovan, *Common Objects of Love: Moral Reflection and the Shaping of Community* (Grand Rapids: Eerdmans, 2002), p. 13.

[12]Cf. John Webster, *Barth's Ethics of Reconciliation* (Cambridge: Cambridge University Press, 1995), p. 100.

[13]During his early decades, Lehmann was a member of the teaching faculties of Elmhurst College, Eden Theological Seminary, Wellesley College, Princeton Theological Seminary and the Harvard Divinity School. He would later serve on the staff of Union Theological Seminary in New York and Union Seminary, Richmond, Virginia. In addition to the already cited *Forgiveness: Decisive Issue in Protestant Thought*, the texts for which Lehmann is best known include *Ethics in a Christian Context* (New York: Harper & Row, 1963), *The Transfiguration of Politics: The Presence and Power of Jesus Christ in and over Human Affairs* (New York: Harper & Row, 1975) and the posthumously published *The Decalogue and a Human Future: The Meaning of the Commandments for Making & Keeping Human Life Human* (Grand Rapids: Eerdmans, 1995). For a study of Lehmann's ethics, see Nancy J. Duff, *Humanization and the Politics of God: The Koinonia Ethics of Paul Lehmann* (Grand Rapids: Eerdmans, 1992).

advent of the justification of the ungodly in the person and work of Jesus Christ. As a first step toward this end, brief consideration of a key text from the corpus of Lehmann's great teacher and mentor, Reinhold Niebuhr, will usefully set the stage.

THE VOLATILIZATION OF JUSTIFICATION IN NIEBUHR'S *INTERPRETATION OF CHRISTIAN ETHICS*

If Lehmann's close association with trajectories emerging from the theologies of Bonhoeffer, Barth, Calvin and Luther manifests his commitment to "getting the Reformation," his lifelong engagement with Niebuhr's theology reminds us that the aim was to "get the Reformation *in America.*" In Niebuhr, Lehmann believed he discerned signs that the defenses of "Protestantism without Reformation" had perhaps been breached. Here was an American theology which was "revelational," "theocentric" and "confessional"—as Niebuhr himself styled it—a theology that eschewed philosophical or experimental grounding, was in no sense scholastic, but nevertheless allowed classical Christian doctrines to serve as "the quiet frames of reference for theological thinking but . . . not its stereotypes."[14] Lehmann was a sympathetic and generous reader of Niebuhr's theology, often finding dogmatic substance and promise when others came away far less satisfied.[15] It is thus valuable to recall Niebuhr's widely regarded account of the Christian orientation to the struggle for justice, since Lehmann's critique of it will quickly and sharply bring into relief the prominence and function of the doctrine of justification in Lehmann's own approach to this question.

In the concluding chapter of *An Interpretation of Christian Ethics* (1935) Niebuhr describes what he considers the distinctive Christian contribution to the struggle for human justice. Foregoing despair in face of the confusion of the moment, Christians are to bring the resources of their religion to bear upon the social situation in order to seek "to coerce its anarchy into some new order without the fury of self-righteousness."[16] The tendency toward self-righteousness in this endeavor, that is, toward "the religious sanctification of partial values, is so powerful that no religion, no matter how potent its presuppositions, escapes." And yet, Niebuhr continues, "whatever the delinquencies of historic Christianity in this matter, there is no question but that the essential genius of the Christian faith is

---

[14]Paul L. Lehmann, "The Promise of Theology in America," *The Student Word* 35, no. I (1942): 74-75.

[15]Cf., for example, Lehmann's highly appreciative treatment of Niebuhr's christology in "The Christology of Reinhold Niebuhr," in *Reinhold Niebuhr: His Religious, Social, and Political Thought*, ed. Charles W. Kegley and Robert W. Bretall (New York: Macmillan, 1956), pp. 252-80.

[16]Reinhold Niebuhr, *An Interpretation of Christian Ethics* (New York: Harper & Brothers, 1935), p. 145.

set against the religious sanctification of partial and relative values."[17]

When Niebuhr elucidates the "essential genius of Christian faith," he speaks of "prophetic religion," that impulse within the later Hebrew prophets, and at work in the proclamation of Jesus, to call down absolute religious claims and "to oppose the self-righteousness of the righteous."[18] Prophetic religion announces that there is "a transcendent perspective from which 'all our righteousness are as filthy rags,'" and it invokes an idea of divine goodness that "not only fulfils, but may negate, the highest human goodness."[19] By directing the gaze of the faithful toward a "supramoral pinnacle," such "genuine theism," as Niebuhr characterizes it, severely chastens the inflated and all-too-human claims to right at play in any given social struggle.[20] Embrace of the transcendent perspective of prophetic religion thus cultivates what Niebuhr styles "a religious reservation in which lie the roots of the spirit of forgiveness"[21] and which undermines all pretense to self-righteousness. In sum, "when life is lived in this dimension, the chasms which divide [persons] are bridged, not directly, not by resolving the conflicts on the historical level, but by the sense of an ultimate unity in, and common dependence upon, the realm of transcendence."[22] Christian ethics then, on Niebuhr's account, orient themselves in the socio-historical sphere by reference to a moral field constituted by the dialectical dynamic between divine transcendence and all-too-human justice.

Given the presence of terms like righteousness, forgiveness and reconciliation in Niebuhr's discourse, there is no doubt that he here intends with all of this to invoke that moral reality carved out for Christian faith by the gospel of justification. This is made all the more certain when we read Niebuhr observing that

> forgiving love is a possibility only for those who know that they are not good, who feel themselves in need of divine mercy, who live in a dimension deeper and higher than that of moral idealism, feel themselves as well as their fellow men convicted by sin by holy God and know that the differences between the good man and the bad man are insignificant in his sight.[23]

And yet, the principal organizing categories of Niebuhr's analysis—transcendence,

---

[17]Ibid., p. 143.
[18]Ibid., p. 138.
[19]Ibid., p. 141.
[20]Ibid., p. 142.
[21]Ibid., p. 141.
[22]Ibid., p. 139.
[23]Ibid.

theism, reserve—seem to draw their breath from somewhere else. They seem, finally, to inhabit a markedly different landscape from that constituted by the reality of the gospel of justification. It is as though Niebuhr were offering an extended gloss upon the ethical significance of divine impartiality attested by a text like, "God makes the rain to fall on the just and unjust alike" (Mt 5:45), rather than upon the evangelical *kerygma* at whose heart is the witness that "in Christ, God was reconciling the world to himself. . . . [F]or our sake he made him to be sin who knew no sin, so that in him we might become the righteousness of God" (2 Cor 5:19, 21). The logic of Niebuhr's account seems finally to trade upon the sheer formality of his most decisive categories: the capacity of words like *theos* and transcendence to chasten all human pretense in matters of justice depends precisely upon their distance from *any* determinative content that might be ascribed to them. Is this because Niebuhr fears that a God whose identity were *too* determinate and a salvation whose content were *too* positive would inevitably fuel the "self-righteous fury" of the parochially Christian in human affairs?

In short, although Niebuhr's remarks concerning the Christian relation to the struggle for justice intimate that they take as their context the reality of the gospel of justification, the logic of these same remarks betrays that they inhabit another, finally more decisive home. Certain critical questions follow from this. To put the matter perhaps too sharply: How is it possible for a recognizably Christian ethic to emerge when the gospel of the radical judgment and gratuitous justification of the ungodly is volatilized into talk of *sheer transcendence*? When the enacted identity of the God of gospel is abstracted into talk of *theism*? And when the self-giving freedom of *agape* capacitated by the gospel of God is translated without remainder into a prudential *religious reservation*? Niebuhr's endeavor to describe the ethical orientation of Christian faith breaks off far too soon then; though it aims to draw faith's thinking beyond religion and morality, it instead achieves at best a highly moral form of religiosity. Niebuhr would set Protestant ethics down in a landscape whose discernible contours are so spare, and whose surfaces so frictionless, that purchase is impossible and paralysis inevitable.

Lehmann is acutely aware of this rather severe shortcoming in Niebuhr's proposal. In a manner akin to the text we have been considering, Niebuhr's Gifford Lectures, published as *The Nature and Destiny of Man*,[24] also claim that "the Chris-

---

[24]Reinhold Niebuhr, *The Nature and Destiny of Man: A Christian Interpretation*, 2 vols. (New York: Scribner's Sons, 1964).

tian answer to the problem of life" lies at the base of the entire undertaking, and is "assumed in the discussion of the problem."[25] But, there as here in Lehmann's view, "Niebuhr's argument proceeds rather more *as though* this answer were assumed than *on the basis of* this assumption."[26] In other words, acknowledgment of the reality of the gospel of the free grace of God in Christ fails effectively to govern Niebuhr's treatments of grace, forgiveness or, indeed, the identity and agency of God.[27] Lehmann wonders aloud why, "If christology is the clue to meaningful history" as Niebuhr avers, do his reflections on the Christian contribution to the struggle of human justice proceed "as though this revelation had not occurred?"[28] The answer to this question would seem to be that the chastening utility of empty transcendence is, in Niebuhr's assessment, too valuable to allow it to be filled out with the concreteness which talk of the divine identity rooted in a robust account of the person and work of Christ would entail. This, even though Niebuhr is left with

> no explicit position in terms of which . . . relativities are to be integrated and decisions are to be made. Faith in the revelation of God in Christ is implicitly such a position; but only *implicitly*. Professor Niebuhr has abundant evidence to show that the dangers of being *explicit* are great. But is so tenuous a commitment to Christian faith and duty adequate particularly for a time in which men [and women] need . . . solid ground on which to stand either inside the Church or out of it?[29]

Here, Lehmann lays his finger upon the problematic consequences of what Stanley Hauerwas in his own recent Gifford Lectures describes as the "thinness" of Niebuhr's theology, that is, its failure sufficiently to suffer the specification of the identity of the God of the gospel, and so also therefore of the content of salvation itself.[30] The price of settling for a highly moral religiosity humbled by a strictly formal commitment to transcendence would seem, on Lehmann's reading, to require "the abandonment of the attempt to explore and to explain the

---

[25]Ibid., I:6.

[26]Paul L. Lehmann, "Human Destiny—Reinhold Niebuhr: A Symposium," *The Union Review* 4, no. 2 (1943): 19.

[27]Paul L. Lehmann, "The Christian Faith and Contemporary Culture," *The Student World* 36, no. 4 (1945): 330.

[28]Lehmann, "Human Destiny," p. 19.

[29]Ibid., pp. 19–20.

[30]Stanley Hauerwas, *With the Grain of the Universe: The Church's Witness and Natural Theology* (Grand Rapids: Brazos, 2001), p. 138.

relation between revelation and the concrete issues of life in the world *from the side of revelation*."[31]

Lehmann considers Niebuhr's work to be symptomatic of the fact that Protestant ethics has "never really come into its own" on precisely this score. Schooled in Troeltsch's historical investigations, Lehmann takes it to be a matter of record that—no less than its patristic and Medieval antecedents—Protestant ethics has failed to make good on the revolutionary ethical promise of the gospel of justification; by virtue of its relentless recourse to a christianized account of *natural law* worked out as a species of the doctrines of creation and providence, it has traded away its birthright for a mess of pottage.[32] "Almost immediately after the Reformers had made their attempt at a theology adequate for a gospel of forgiveness," Lehmann contends, "the focus of the theological [and ethical] problem was returned to the point from which they had deflected it."[33] Niebuhr's own recourse to the discourse of "transcendence," "genuine theism" and "religious reserve" in his attempt to orient the Christian in the struggle for human justice reflects the persistence of this legacy, even where, in Lehmann's view at least, American theology was beginning to show signs of "getting the Reformation."

So, while perhaps faintly echoing the effective pressure of the radical judgment and forgiveness that are the heart of the gospel of justification, the chastening dialectic of Niebuhr's proposal—that is, the dialectic between the formally transcendent demand of revelation and a rationally determined norm of human justice—cannot, finally, be identified as the ethical dialectic of the gospel. The latter in fact consists, Lehmann tells us, in the dialectic "between a God whose act of self-revelation has disclosed Him both as Lord *and Saviour* and [human beings] whose acts are never acts of obedience and justice yet who never disavow the demand to obey and to do justly."[34] For theology, this means that the question of our orientation in the struggle for social justice must be asked and answered explicitly at the creative intersection of *soteriology* and ethics. The transcendence which is left abstract by Niebuhr becomes concrete in Lehmann's analysis by a clear identification of the

---

[31]Paul L. Lehmann, "Obedience and Justice," *Christianity and Society* 8, no. 3 (1942): 37. Emphasis added.

[32]On this issue see Paul L. Lehmann, "Towards a Protestant Analysis of the Ethical Problem," *The Journal of Religion* 24, no. 1 (1944): 1-3. Cf. also Ernst Troeltsch, *The Social Teaching of the Christian Churches*, 2 vols., trans. Olive Wyon (reprint, Louisville: Westminster John Knox, 1992), esp. 2:494, 528, 602, 673, 999.

[33]Lehmann, *Forgiveness*, p. 10.

[34]Lehmann, "Obedience and Justice," p. 37, emphasis added.

God of the gospel as the Savior, the One who "is rich in mercy" and who "out of the great love with which he loved us, even when we were dead through our trespasses, made us alive together with Christ" (Eph 2:4-5). Lehmann's wager is that the free and salutarily devastating mercy that constitutes the transcendence of the God of the gospel is better able to capacitate and direct the Christian contribution to coercing "anarchy into some new order without the fury of self-righteousness" without sacrificing or obfuscating the integrity of faith in the reality of reconciliation *en route.*

THE CONCRETENESS OF TRANSCENDENCE:
PAUL LEHMANN ON JUSTIFICATION AND JUSTICE

> There is a Protestant analysis of the ethical problem. It is the attempt to deal with the question of the nature and application of the good in terms of the Pauline and Reformation conception of justification by faith. . . . Suppose [someone] is justified by faith! What does that mean in itself, and what kind of ethical thinking does the conception of justification require?[35]

So begins Lehmann's early programmatic essay "Towards a Protestant Analysis of the Ethical Problem." Staying close to the Reformers, Lehmann speaks of justification itself as "the forensic judgment of God whereby [the human] is predicated with both sin and righteousness"; it is the creative and paradoxical declaration *simul justus et peccator* by means of which God makes it possible for the human "to know and to conform to the conditions proper to his [or her] life in the world."[36] The effective reality of this judgment is the "specific *given* which defines the relations between God and [the human] in the world"; it is the sum and substance of the "prior and purposeful activity of God . . . which marks out what is central to the gospel," and—note well—also "what is central to the *relevance* of the gospel in the world."[37] For this reason, Lehmann considers that "a theologian is competent or incompetent as a theologian according as he [or she] is zealous for and jealous of the activity of God, irrespective of the human and subjective correlations."[38]

The decisive context of Christian existence in and for the world is, hence, that which is brought into being by the effective promise of Christ. The Reformers themselves gave voice to this when they conceived of justification as God's way of

---

[35]Lehmann, "Protestant Analysis of the Ethical Problem," p. 1.
[36]Ibid., p. 3.
[37]Paul L. Lehmann, "Grace and Power," *Christianity and Society* 10, no. 1 (1944): 27, emphasis added.
[38]Lehmann, *Forgiveness*, p. 116.

dealing with men and women in the world, not as they are, but as they are *in Christ*. The upshot of this is that justification also denotes, for Lehmann, the way in which human persons live "before God in the world, not as they are, but as they are in Christ."[39] When the promise of Christ at the heart of justification is taken to determine the relation between God and the human in the time between creation and redemption, this relation is clearly not grounded in any correlation between divine and human reason, or will, or desire, but rather solely in "the correspondence of grace and faith."[40]

An ethic of justification will be one that "takes seriously the activity of the God who acts," since the advent of justification establishes the reality—the moral field—within which the question of ethics is to be firmly set.[41] Justification, says Lehmann following Calvin closely at this point, is that act of God by which our "true position in the world—as a pilgrim between creation and redemption—is put within the orbit of [human] knowledge and behaviour in the world."[42] It is the task of Christian ethics therefore to raise the question of the good and the right in light of the "disconcerting consequences" of God's gracious action for the human creature in Jesus Christ.[43]

Owing to the radicality of the divine judgment and forgiveness that are its mainsprings, an ethic of justification demands that ethical categories and relations held in common with rationalistic or naturalistic ethics be *thoroughly* redefined.[44] If the "nature and possibility of right action" are not intrinsically open to us, but rather must come to us from the initiative and activity of God, and more particularly, from the "redemptive act of the creator God," then it is the self-communication of the divine will enacted in the event of our justification which "furnishes their decisive content."[45] Set within the ambit of justification, the ethical question becomes how to live out of the righteousness of God, which not only judges every righteousness, but also creatively "overcomes every unrighteousness." What is right and good is thus not principle but *act*. Nothing is good in itself; that alone is good which corresponds *in act* to God's own elected act, namely his world-dissolving judgment on

---

[39]Lehmann, "Protestant Analysis of the Ethical Problem," p. 3.

[40]Ibid., p. 4.

[41]Ibid., p. 7.

[42]Ibid., p. 3. Cf. Calvin *Institutes* 3.6.7.

[43]Cf. Lehmann, *Forgiveness*, p. 121.

[44]Lehmann, "Protestant Analysis of the Ethical Problem," p. 1.

[45]Ibid., pp. 4-5.

sin and world-constituting forgiveness of the sinner in Christ. On Lehmann's view, the promise of such a christologically centered, actualist moral ontology is the overcoming of the "unhappy divorce between soteriology and ethics." To cite Lehmann:

> When justice is understood as the setting right of what is not right in man's relationship to man, both private and public, then, the struggle for justice becomes the concrete expression, in behaviour, of man's response to what God has done and is doing to set things right between man and himself. The faith by which man is justified becomes what Luther called a "busy, living, active thing" by which men learn in the struggle for justice, what is means concretely to forgive and to be forgiven.[46]

The result of this is that, for faith, human moral agency is liberated from all interest and anxiety concerning the achievement or maintenance of its own rectitude. Rather, the sole concern of Christian moral agency is gratefully to witness to the effective course of God's active righteousness in Christ. In the wake of God's justifying act, moralism is shown to be an absurd compound of unbelief and embarrassment at the gospel, an impatient attempt to compensate for the fragility of the good report of the reality of our justification in the face of the seemingly still vigorous world of sin. The repentance that flows from faith in this regard, transforms worry about *virtue* into desire for *obedience*, the strictures of *duty* into the gift of *vocation*. Obedience and vocation emerge as key categories in Lehmann's ethics as a consequence of its roots in the reality of justification: the former names free and joyful human agency in its discrete correspondence to God's own act; the latter denotes the pattern of this correspondence over time in relation to actual situations, relations and gifts.

Lehmann revisited these themes in another key some years later. At the heart of the "Dynamics of Reformation Ethics," to which Lehmann addressed himself in a lecture at Princeton Theological Seminary in 1950, is the δύναμις of the triune God. The "moving strength" of the divine constitutes the "overtones and undertow of biblical experience" formative for Christian imagination and fixes the eyes of the people of God "upon the future for God's next move."[47] Lehmann here provides an account of the context of Christian ethical life recast in terms of *temporality*. "The unique disclosure and vitality of Christian faith," Lehmann declares, is that "respon-

---

[46]Paul L. Lehmann, "Forgiveness," in *The Dictionary of Christian Ethics*, ed. John Macquarrie (Philadelphia: Westminster Press, 1967), p. 131.

[47]Paul L. Lehmann, "The Dynamics of Reformation Ethics," *Princeton Seminary Bulletin* 43, no. 4 (1950): 18.

sibility for and towards the future is determined by the frontiers of the present."[48] The revolutionary insight of the Reformers was to see that it is God's act of gracious justification of the sinner that makes the present a frontier laden with promise— that is, a present afforded a genuine future—rather than the mere terminus of past occurrence. The reality of reconciliation, that is, makes the present into a time in which God can be known and obeyed anew because "the presence and power of God in Christ" renders it a moment "where the new possibilities of life . . . cut across the outworn patterns of the past."[49] As Lehmann says elsewhere, to reckon with one's justification is "to move into a new order and a new sovereignty which are not yet triumphant but which are nevertheless real and effective."[50]

The Christian church tenses forward in this way because, for faith, God's salu- tary activity anticipates all our experience and reasoning as their *pre-supposition* and *initiation*, rather than being an inference therefrom. Consequently, attention falls upon "the shape of things to come in dedicated expectation of fresh and purpose- ful manifestations of God's moving strength."[51] The frontiers of the present are themselves a function, finally, of the "moving strength of God which anchored it- self in Jesus Christ in the perpetual present wherein the future meets and fulfills the past by transforming it."[52]

How is a difficult remark like this last one to be understood? Recall that Lehmann is attempting to articulate the Reformers' emphasis upon the concreteness of the divine identity and divine prevenience in decidedly temporal categories: the divine δύναμις is not sheer caprice, because its identity is "anchored" in the enactment of an existence in time, namely that salutary existence of Jesus Christ; but neither is this δύναμις trapped in the past because the event of its temporal "anchoring" makes it- self contemporary to every present as the promise of forgiveness, thus constituting its frontier and giving point to the future.[53] Yet, to what end does Lehmann here trans- pose this emphasis into language of temporality? It is, I think, in order to make clear that to be justified by the grace of God is not simply to have arrived but rather to have been set in motion in a particular way. As Lehmann writes, to be judged and forgiven

[48]Ibid., p. 18.
[49]Ibid., p. 22.
[50]Paul L. Lehmann, "The Standpoint of the Reformation," in *Christianity and Property*, ed. Joseph Fletcher (Philadelphia: Westminster Press, 1947), p. 102.
[51]Lehmann, "Dynamics of Reformation Ethics," p. 19.
[52]Ibid., p. 18.
[53]Ibid., p. 19. Traditional doctrines of incarnation, resurrection and ascension underwrite notions such as these.

is "to discern and to move across the line between the possibilities which are played out and those which are full of promise."[54] The concrete identity and consequence of the δύναμις of the God of the gospel at work in the world means simply, but significantly, then that a properly Protestant account of the theological concept of the "order of things" will never be conservative in its entailments.[55] The eschatological character of such an "order" precludes any and all such *stasis*. Said differently, as a consequence of the identity and activity of God the order of redemption is itself ever a *dandum* and never a simple *datum*—ever a *giving* and never simply something given into our possession. For this reason, its consequences in the world are forever and properly destabilizing. It is because the event of justification is a revolutionary effect of incarnation and atonement, and not a mere tinkering with the self-unfolding of creation, that its consequences are similarly revolutionary, so that "the believer in the God who acts and who calls, who creates and who redeems, always begins by moving against the focus of power in the existing situation."[56]

It is Lehmann's contention that an adequate account of the ethos of Christian faith will be "an analysis of theological order according to which the moving strength of God is on the side of social change—social change, [i.e., as a] herald of 'things which are not, to bring to nought things that are' (1 Cor 1:28)."[57] The Christian community will thus discern the fitting ontic effect of theological order of redemption in the world in

> the integration of the premises and the institutions of social life so that responsibility for what is going on is continually exercised in the direction of self-criticism. Whenever in human affairs, responsibility for what is going on is identified with self-justification, then, disorder has become the order of the day.[58]

Along with this work of self-critical discernment also comes the task of reflecting

---

[54]Ibid., p. 18.

[55]"It is in open-ness and change—not in the status quo—that men are to discern the moving strength of God" (p. 20). Significantly in this essay, as elsewhere, Lehmann sees that the Reformers themselves "drew back from the dynamics of their own ethical foundations" and instead "barricaded the dynamics of the community of the justified behind the familiar but cracking bulwarks of an order that the moving strength of God had set aside. They fell back upon the ancient tradition of natural law" (ibid., p. 22).

[56]Lehmann, "Protestant Analysis of the Ethical Problem," p. 16. Development of the consequences of this insight would particularly preoccupy Lehmann in later years, and culminated in his "theological hermeneutics of revolutionary politics," *The Transfiguration of Politics.*

[57]Lehmann, "Dynamics of Reformation Ethics," p. 22.

[58]Ibid., p. 20.

upon, advocating for and applying "the presuppositions, the character, and the responsibilities of theological order."[59] The execution of this variegated task is intrinsic to the life of the church as a "community of experiment" as Lehmann could
refer to it.[60]

What is most important to observe for our present purpose is that the orientation of the Christian congregation in and toward the world is won by calling to mind
and directing the will toward the "world of the Word of God." Hence, theological
description of *this* context within which the intersection and interaction of church
and world occurs is of immense practical importance. The faithfulness and effectiveness of efforts to engage any situation *Christianly* are, in Lehmann's view, a function
of the degree to which the community is able to discern and keep abreast of the dynamic and determinant reality of the salutary Word of God always *already* at work in
the world to "make all things new." Integral to such a view is constant anticipation
of "criticism by the Word of God." In fact, it is precisely the humble freedom effected by such salutary criticism—concretely, by the judgment and forgiveness in-
gredient in the event of justification—that drives the Christian community forward
without "the fury of self-righteousness" toward the frontier of social change.

SOME CONCLUDING REMARKS

In lieu of an extended recapitulation, allow me merely to set out in short compass
a concluding restatement of what I take to be the challenge and provocation of
Lehmann's position.

The reality of justification transfigures the nature of the boundary between the
Christian community and the world. Lehmann was adamant that because God was
in Christ reconciling the world—and not the church!—to himself, this boundary
does not mark the point at which the effectiveness of God's justifying grace breaks
off, so much as the point at which the summons to Christian responsibility—that
is, the call to bear faithful witness as a member of the company of disciples set
apart for the service of this grace—is particularly pressed and may in fact be humanly answered. Here, on this same boundary, it is the persistent, present and prior

---

[59]Ibid., p. 22.
[60]"The *koinonia* is a kind of laboratory of humanization in the world. Here, an experiment is contin-
    ually going on in bringing the concrete stuff of action into dynamic and concrete relation to a per-
    spective upon action. The perspective is God's action in the world to make men free to be the selves
    who God intended them to be, through the humanizing results of the way men behave." Lehmann,
    "Contextual Ethics," p. 73.

agency of the God of the gospel, which rules out any religious valorization of parochially Christian correctness, and banishes the "fury of self-righteousness" that threatens to beset all moral engagement. It is God's vital and fierce mercy—and not purported "supramoral transcendence" as in Niebuhr's view—that chastens Christian moral action precisely as it both capacitates and orients it. Here, on this boundary, Christians ever stand as beggars before the Lord of mercy together with other sinners who have not yet been claimed in baptism for free and responsible witnesses to their shared moral poverty and the wealth of God's grace.

The reality of justification in Christ altogether excludes any thought of a righteousness of which we are possessed or out of which to assert ourselves. As those who knowingly suffer the devastatingly salutary event of God's justifying grace, Christians are ethical actors who ever and only "bear a righteousness not their own" (Phil 3:9) such that any thought of a righteousness of our own whatsoever is decisively ruled out, precisely because Christ is "at once the *end* of all religion, including any sort of *Christian* religion."[61] And Christians stand confronted by neighbors who also and always bear a similarly alien righteousness. It is in this encounter that Christian freedom comes into its own, in this encounter that Christian obedience is concretely enjoined; and it is upon this encounter that the divine promise that we might enact truly human parables of the kingdom of God rests with effect. It is in this encounter that Christians may ask and risk a discerning answer to the decisive ethical question, namely (as Lehmann would characteristically phrase it), "What is the God of the gospel doing here and now in the world to make and to keep human life human to which we have been freed actively to correspond as Christ's grateful witnesses?"

And so, Lehmann once observed, for evangelical Christians—that is, for Christians who by grace have received the good report that the world-destroying and world-constituting event of justification constitutes the all-encompassing and determinative context of life—all human struggles, including the struggle for a better human justice, "derive their significance from the struggle of God." For this reason, while "obedience and justice belong to the world of the creation they are genuinely relevant in a world of sin only in so far as Christians think and act in the light of the fact that this world has been redeemed."[62] This affirmation, far from fanning the flames of self-righteous fury, ever wins from a grateful and vital creature the free, happy and humble cry, "we are beggars, this is true."

---

[61]Karl Barth, *The Epistle to the Philippians*, trans. J. W. Leitch (London: SCM Press, 1962), pp. 99-100.
[62]Lehmann, "Obedience and Justice," pp. 38-39.

PART
THREE

JUSTIFICATION IN
PROTESTANT TRADITIONS

5

LUTHER, MELANCHTHON AND PAUL ON THE QUESTION OF IMPUTATION

Recommendations on a Current Debate

MARK A. SEIFRID

It is more than a little dangerous for someone who is neither a historian nor a Lutheran to venture observations and reflections in the area of Reformation studies. The few attempts of this sort by biblical scholars I have read are sufficiently embarrassing that it is best not even to name them. I am quite aware, therefore, of the dangers of dilletantism. Nevertheless, the greater danger, it seems to me, is that biblical scholars dealing with central theological concerns should remain ignorant of historical considerations, particularly those having to do with the Reformation. I therefore intend to follow Luther's advice: *esto peccator et pecca fortiter.*[1] It is to be freely conceded from the outset that the seemingly unending variety of questions spawned by exegetical debate cannot be swept aside by a simple appeal to the past. Yet it is equally obvious that there are recurrent issues which former debates illumine and may even set aside. Conservative theologians in particular, it seems to me, have an obligation to discern clearly where the boundaries lie of that which must be defended, and where adaptation and diversity of opinion are to have free reign. For a variety of reasons, this exercise of discernment is especially important at the moment in relation to the doctrine of justification. In the first place, directly or indirectly, ecumenical discussions have prompted current debate. Biblical scholarship itself in the last generation has produced a fresh series of questions about Paul's understanding of justification in its relation to Second Temple Judaism. Equally significant,

---

[1] *"Sed fortius fide et gaude in Christo, qui victor est peccati, mortis et mundi"* (WABR 2; p. 372, Nr 424, 84-85).

I think, although not yet fully appreciated, has been the "discovery" of Adolf Schlatter by American evangelicals. Despite his disagreements with Luther, Schlatter reappropriates significant elements of the Reformer's understanding of justification, which (as we shall see shortly) are quite different from the usual Protestant understanding mediated to us by Melanchthon and Calvin. The same may be said for the work of Peter Stuhlmacher, whose work is well known among at least some American evangelicals. For a number of reasons, therefore, questions on the essential features of a biblical understanding of justification are not likely to disappear for quite some time.

In what follows I intend to outline something of the contour of Luther's understanding of justification by comparing it with that of Melanchthon. I shall not break any new ground here—or at least I hope that I don't! Virtually everything I have to say will be regarded as commonplace not only by Reformation scholars, but by European theologians in general, and undoubtedly also by many Lutherans here in America.[2] Yet for one reason or another, the matters we are about to discuss have remained relatively unknown among American evangelicals. In a very small way, I want to do my best here to remedy this situation. It quickly will become apparent that I am not an impartial observer. I want, in fact, to commend something of Luther's understanding of justification. To that end, I shall not only compare it with that of Melanchthon, but also, very briefly, with Paul's argument in Romans 4. In conclusion, I shall venture some recommendations on how we ought to speak about justification.

The most appropriate and useful point at which to examine the thinking of Luther and Melanchthon on the question of justification is in their debate on the topic, conducted privately in the home of Johannes Bugenhagen in late 1536.[3] The immediate cause of their encounter was the controversy stirred up by Conrad Cordatus, who had been incited to complain to various authorities, including Luther, by a lecture delivered by one of Melanchthon's students, Caspar Cruciger. Cruciger, working from Melanchthon's notes, had claimed that the contrition of the sinner

---

[2]The basic ideas have long been available in the English translations of two of the standard presentations of Luther's thought: Paul Althaus, *The Theology of Martin Luther*, trans. Robert C. Schulz (Philadelphia: Fortress, 1966); Gerhard Ebeling, *Luther: An Introduction to His Thought*, trans. R. A. Wilson (Philadelphia: Fortress, 1970).

[3]The text appears in H. E. Bindseil, *Philippi Melanchthonis Epistolae, Iudicia, Consilia, Testimonia Aliorumque ad eum Epistolae quae in Corpore Reformatorum Desiderantur* (Halle: Gustav Schwetschke, 1874), pp. 344-48. Johannes Aurifaber's sixteenth-century German version, which varies slightly from the former, is printed in WATR 6:148-53.

is a *causa sine qua non* of justification.[4] I will comment briefly the development and significance of Melanchthon's views shortly. My first concern is the debate between Luther and Melanchthon which Cordatus's complaint precipitated, and the way in which it illumines their differing conceptions of justification.

The form of the debate, which was preserved by Melanchthon, is of interest itself, since Melanchthon appears in it not, as one might have thought, in the role of the accused, but as the accuser.[5] In fact, as Martin Greschat suggests, the debate in part seems to reflect Melanchthon's concern that at times Luther's statements on justification seemed to reflect an Augustinian position, according to which justification was understood in terms of the inward renewal of the human being.[6] At the same time, the transcript of the debate shows equally clearly that Luther himself is concerned to rein in Melanchthon with respect to the role of works in justification. There were, then, suspicions on both sides that essential matters of Reformation teaching were being compromised.

Melanchthon begins by pressing Luther on his views of Augustine: "Does justification take place through the renewal of the human being, or gratuitously through imputation, which is *extra nos* and by faith?"[7] Luther immediately opts for the latter, but formulates the issue in his own terms: "we are righteous before God gratuitously, solely by the pure mercy of God, by which, and for the sake of which, in Christ, he reckons righteousness to us."[8] Melanchthon then responds by setting forth his own position, and pressing Luther to accept it:

> I do not maintain that a human being is righteous through mercy alone. The reason: our righteousness, that is a good conscience on account of works (Latin: *bona conscientia in operibus*), is necessary. Or don't you want to allow that one may say that the human being is primarily righteous through faith, and in a lesser way through works? It is thus: faith is confidence, and in order that this confidence remains certain, it should be understood that the perfection of the Law is not demanded, but that faith

---

[4]As both Martin Greschat, *Melanchthon neben Luther*, pp. 217-30 and Timothy J. Wengert, *Law and Gospel: Philip Melanchthon's Debate with John Agricola of Eisleben over Poenitentia* (Texts and Studies in Reformation and Post-Reformation Thought; Grand Rapids: Baker, 1997), pp. 206-10 show, Cruciger's claim that he was only representing Melanchthon's views was entirely valid.

[5]Melanchthon is likewise quite confident of his position in his letter of response to Cordatus's charges, November 1, 1536.

[6]Greschat, *Melanchthon neben Luther*, pp. 230-42.

[7]WATR 6:149, 7-10; Bindseil, *Melanchthonis Epistolae*, p. 344.

[8]WATR 6:149, 13-15, "*daß wir um sonst, allein aus lauter Barmherzigkeit Gottes, damit und um welcher Willen in Christo er uns die Gerechtigkeit zurechnet, für (= vor) ihm gerecht werden.*" Bindseil, *Melanchthonis Epistolae*, p. 344: "*quod sola imputatione gratuita sumus iusti apud Deum.*"

supplements what is lacking with respect to the Law. You yourself allow that two kinds of righteousness are necessary before God, namely that of faith and that of a good conscience. . . . How is that different from saying that the human being is not righteous through faith alone? For you do not understand justification to be the beginning of regeneration as Augustine does.[9]

Melanchthon's concern here appears to be two-fold. In the first place, as we have noted, he is defending the legitimacy of his position, in part by appealing to Luther's own formulations. Secondly, as Greschat has argued, Melanchthon wants to bring Luther to further define the difference between his understanding of justification and that of Augustine.[10] Indeed, Melanchthon's confidence here suggests that he supposes that Luther will have to come over to his view.

In fact, however, Luther not only does not budge, but directly challenges Melanchthon's position:

I maintain that the human being, becomes, is and remains righteous (Latin: *fieri, esse, et manere iustam*), or that the person is righteous, solely by mercy. For this (mercy) is complete righteousness, which is set over against God's wrath, sin, and death, etc. and swallows up all things, and makes human beings entirely holy and guiltless, as if in fact they were without sin. For in that God reckons righteousness to the human being gratuitously, it leaves no sin remaining, as John says, "whoever is born of God, does not commit sin," for to be born of God and to be a sinner contradict one another. The human being is righteous on account of this righteousness of faith, not on account of works or fruit, which God commands and repays or rewards. I call this (latter righteousness) an outward righteousness and one of works, which in this flesh and life is not able to make pure or holy (Latin: *simpliciter sancta*).[11]

Luther here directly addresses the issue, which provoked Cordatus and precipitated the debate, rejecting even the minor and circumscribed role of works in justification,

---

[9]WATR 6:149, 16-34; Bindseil, *Melanchthonis Epistolae*, pp. 344-45. Greschat, *Melanchthon neben Luther*, p. 237, understands this objection to reflect Melanchthon's concern with the possibility that Luther bases justification on the renovation of the human being. This reading might be possible if one relies solely on the Latin form of the debate edited by Bindseil: here Melanchthon's objection begins with a question: "*An homo sola illa misericordia iustus est?*" But Aurifaber's wording is different. Here Melanchthon asserts: "*Daß der Mensch durch die Barmherzigkeit allein gerecht werde, halte ich nicht.*" Most significantly, Melanchthon's correspondence in this period, especially his letter of response to the charges against him, suggests that it is Melanchthon's newly formed understanding of justification and works which is being tested here: see Wengert, *Law and Gospel*, pp. 208-9.
[10]Greschat, *Melanchthon neben Luther*, pp. 236-42.
[11]WATR 6:149-50; Bindseil, *Melanchthonis Epistolae*, p. 345.

which Melanchthon had at least temporarily adopted.[12] Moreover, as is apparent from Luther's response, his approach to this question is entirely different from that of Melanchthon. The mercy of God effects a "perfect righteousness" which "swallows up wrath, sin and death." The imputation of righteousness effects a new reality. Luther's further elaborations make this perspective quite clear. It is not that virtues or works make a person righteous, but just the opposite: works are good because of the righteousness of the person who performs them.[13] One may speak of the "necessity" of good works, but not as a necessity derived from the Law. It is rather a necessity of the liberated will, that is, a necessity of nature itself. The righteousness of faith alone therefore does not belong only to the beginning of the Christian life, to be supplemented by a righteousness of works. The righteousness of faith is beginning, middle and end.[14] Even when Melanchthon confronts Luther with Paul's statement in 1 Corinthians 9:16 ("woe to me if I do not preach the Gospel"), Luther refuses to allow that any partial cause figures into justification. "Faith," he says, "is always present, unceasing, and powerful, otherwise it is not faith." Faith is the sun, whose brilliance and radiance is unchangeable.[15] It is not a work, as Sadoletus supposes, but a work of the divine promise, a gift of the Holy Spirit.[16] This gift makes the person new continually. "In summary," says Luther:

> believers are a new creation, a new tree. Therefore all the language which is customary in the Law does not belong here. . . . For the sun is not supposed to shine, it does so, by nature, unbidden, for it is created for this purpose; therefore a good tree brings forth fruit without command; three and seven are already ten, they are not supposed to become it. Therefore here (in the Gospel, *MAS*) it is not said what ought to take place or what must be, it is rather said what already takes place and now is.[17]

Even Martin Greschat, who is concerned to demonstrate the proximity of Melanchthon to Luther and the influence of the former on the latter, observes that Luther remains unmoved by Melanchthon's argument.[18]

In fact, as is well known, it was Melanchthon's understanding of justification

---

[12]Wengert, *Law and Gospel*, pp. 205-6, observes that already in the 1534 Scholia on Colossians Melanchthon learned to speak of the necessity of works without speaking of their necessity in justification.

[13]WATR 6:150, 21-26, and 151, 21-33; Bindseil, *Melanchthonis Epistolae*, pp. 346-47.

[14]WATR 6:150, 12, continuing to 151, 33; Bindseil, *Melanchthonis Epistolae*, pp. 345-47.

[15]WATR 6:151, 39 continuing to 152, 2; Bindseil, *Melanchthonis Epistolae*, p. 347.

[16]WATR 6:152, 22-30; Bindseil, *Melanchthonis Epistolae*, p. 347.

[17]WATR 6:153, 4-12; Bindseil, *Melanchthonis Epistolae*, p. 348.

[18]Greschat, *Melanchthon neben Luther*, pp. 238-41.

which had undergone significant development in the period between 1530 and 1534.[19] In the *Apology* to the Augsburg Confession, Melanchthon was somewhat confusingly able to describe justification as a "being made righteous" as well as a "being pronounced righteous."[20] A significant shift takes place already in the 1532 commentary on Romans, where Melanchthon interprets "justification" to mean to "repute as righteous or accepted" and appeals to the example of Scipio's acquittal by the people of Rome to illustrate his point.[21] The same example appears in the 1533 printing of the *Loci*.[22] Timothy Wengert points in particular to the 1534 *Scholia* on Colossians, which reveal Melanchthon's consolidation of his understanding of justification in purely forensic terms over against his earlier writings, especially earlier editions of these *Scholia*.[23]

I am not going to venture a detailed discussion of the causes of the shift in Melanchthon's thinking on the topic of justification. That is for the experts.[24] But several observations are in order in any case. It is first of all worth noting the connection which Wengert has pointed out between Melanchthon's narrowing of the concept of justification to a mere pronouncement and his coming to insist on the necessity of good works. Since "justification" no longer had an effective dimension, the Law (in its "third use") moved in to fill the vacuum left behind.[25] The debate with Luther seems to show that Melanchthon is still learning that if he wishes to speak of the necessity of good works, he must make it clear that they are excluded from justification. From another direction, Stephen Strehle has offered a rather negative assessment of Melanchthon's understanding of imputation, suggesting that it lands him in a contradictory position between Anselm's doctrine of the

---

[19]See the penetrating discussion in Wengert, *Law and Gospel*, pp. 177-210, further Robert Stupperich, "Die Rechtfertigungslehre bei Luther und Melanchthon 1530-1536," in *Luther and Melanchthon in the History and Theology of the Reformation*, ed. Vilmos Vatja (Philadelphia: Muhlenberg, 1961), 73-88 = *Luther und Melanchthon: Referate und Berichte des Zweiten Internationalen Kongresses für Lutherforschung, Münster 8.-13. August 1960* (Göttingen: Vandenhoeck & Ruprecht, 1961).

[20]See, e.g., *BSELK* 175, pp. 37-39.

[21]*MSA* 5:39, pp. 7-16.

[22]*CR* 21, 421.

[23]Wengert, *Law and Gospel*, pp. 177-85.

[24]Stupperich, "Die Rechtfertigungslehre," p. 80, argues quite plausibly that the less that Melanchthon needed to respond to arguments from the Roman side, the more he distanced himself from Luther's way of speaking.

[25]Wengert, *Law and Gospel*, pp. 185-206, esp. p. 196, where Wengert points out the significant shift in Melanchthon's 1534 *Scholia* on Colossians: the "subject" who uses the Law is no longer God but rather the righteous person.

atonement and Ockham's voluntarist doctrine of justification. That is, Melanchthon inconsistently affirms both the necessary demands of divine justice in the cross and, at the same time, a legal fiction by which God accepts faith as righteousness.[26] Even if we cannot pursue the validity of this charge here, it is worth pondering further. In any case, it is clear that Melanchthon and Luther differ dramatically from one another on the question of justification because they proceed from radically different perspectives. For this reason they appropriate Augustine quite differently from one another. As the debate itself shows, Melanchthon takes the human being as his starting-point, and thinks of justification in terms of human qualities and response. It is surely for this reason that he has such great difficulty in understanding Luther, who views justification first and foremost in terms of the work of the Gospel, the word of God, which, apart from any contribution from the fallen human being, brings the new creature into existence, in whom faith and all its works are present.

It is worth pausing briefly to consider further Luther's distinctive understanding of justification, especially in view of current debate among American evangelicals. A sample from his 1535 Galatians commentary will suffice for our purposes. Paul's statement in Galatians 2:16, that a person is not justified by works of the Law, but by faith in Christ, elicits from Luther a lengthy discussion of the deficiencies of the scholastic understanding of justification and a positive expression of his own views. Taking up the topic of imputation, he expresses himself as follows:

> Here it is to be noted that these three things are joined together: faith, Christ, and acceptance or imputation. Faith takes hold of Christ and has him present, enclosing him as the ring encloses the gem. And whoever is found having this faith in the Christ who is grasped in the heart, him God accounts as righteous. This is the means and the merit by which we obtain the forgiveness of sins and righteousness. "Because you believe in me," God says, "and your faith takes hold of Christ, whom I have freely given to you as your Justifier and Savior, therefore be righteous." Thus God accepts you or accounts you righteous only on account of Christ, in whom you believe.[27]

The distinctions between Luther's framework and that of Melanchthon are again immediately apparent. Luther happily alternates between speaking of righteousness imputed because of the Christ who is present and because of faith. He understands faith simply as the work of God through the Gospel. It is the new creation, the present

---

[26]Stephen Strehle, *The Catholic Roots of the Protestant Gospel: Encounter Between the Middle Ages and Reformation*, Studies in the History of Christian Thought 60 (Leiden: Brill, 1995), p. 72.
[27]LW 26, p. 132 = WA 40:233, 16-24.

Christ, and not a quality or virtue in the human being.[28] Luther does not define faith simply as a "means and instrument" as do the later Formula of Concord and Westminster Confession. He is thus free to develop his powerful reading of the first commandment as a call to faith.[29] Christ's role in justification is likewise different for Luther. While Luther thinks in terms of union with the crucified and risen Lord, Melanchthon thinks primarily of the cross, and that as a past transaction, the benefits of which are mediated to the present by faith. The later Protestant formulaic description of justification as the "imputation of Christ's righteousness" was a development of the Melanchthonian view. Although this sort of language appears occasionally with both Luther and Melanchthon, it appears to come into prominence only after Luther's death, in the Osiandrian controversy (1550-1551), when it served as a means of Protestant self-definition over against Osiander's claim that only the indwelling, divine presence of Christ justifies.[30] It was apparently also Osiander, the "heterodox father of Protestant orthodoxy" who first assigned Christ's active obedience and passive obedience differing roles in justification.[31] None of these developments, although they had their legitimate ends, can be made to fit into Luther's understanding of justification. As the text cited makes clear, he speaks of the imputation of righteousness. In many other contexts he speaks of the non-imputation of sin. But he does not speak of the imputation of *Christ's* righteousness—or does so only rarely—because he regards Christ himself as present in faith. "Imputation" functions somewhat differently in Luther's thought from the way it does in Melanchthon's. For the latter, "imputation" is necessary in order to mediate Christ's cross-work to the believer. But for Luther, Christ's saving benefits are already mediated in the union of

---

[28]Because Luther's framework for justification embraces the event of the cross and resurrection, mediated by the Word, he does not run into the problems of later Protestant *ordines salutis* which were centered on the individual, and thus had trouble accounting for the gift of faith prior to justification.

[29]See "Der grosse Katechismus," in *Luthers Werke: Studienausgabe* 6/4, ed. Otto Clemen (1912; reprint, Berlin: de Gruyter, 1967), pp. 4-5:

Therefore the sense of this commandment is this: that it demands true faith and confidence of the heart, which grasps the one true God and cleaves to him alone. And it says as much as this: Take care that I alone am your God, and never seek another. That is, whatever good you might lack, obtain for yourself and seek from me. And where you suffer sorrow and distress, creep and hold fast to me. I, I shall supply your need, and deliver you from all distress. Only let not your heart cleave to or nor depart to another. (My translation)

[30]The formula is lacking in the *Confessio Augustana* (1530) and in the First Helvetic Confession (1536), and even in Melanchthon's 1543 *Loci*, but it appears in the 1555 *Loci*, Calvin's 1559 *Institutes*, the Second Helvetic Confession (1566) and the Formula of Concord (1576).

[31]Albrecht Ritschl, *Die christliche Lehre von der Rechtfertigung und Versöhnung*, 3 vols., 3rd ed. (Bonn: Adolf Marcus, 1889), 1:247-49.

faith, the "blessed exchange" between the sinner and the justifying Savior.[32] "Impu-tation" therefore appears in Luther's usage as the divine approbation of the crucified and risen Christ, and of the faith that grasps him (and in which he is present). As we shall see in a moment, for Luther "imputation" remains "exceedingly necessary," since our own righteousness is only incipient, and sin remains with us. Yet for him it is not merely the initial act by which God imparts salvation, but rather the continuing way in which God governs and purifies the life of the justified. As again our citation from the Galatians commentary shows, Luther thinks of "imputation" as a forensic and declaratory act. Yet it is no mere declaration, but rather an effective word of God: "Because you believe in me ... and your faith takes hold of Christ, therefore be right-eous!" We may recall that the same idea appears prominently in the disputation be-tween Melanchthon and Luther, where the latter argues, "in that God reckons right-eousness to the human being gratuitously, it leaves no sin remaining, as John says, 'whoever is born of God, does not commit sin.'" From this perspective, it is fully comprehensible that Luther quickly moves to a sanative interpretation of imputation in the immediate context of the Galatians text we have cited: "Now acceptance or im-putation is extremely necessary, first, because we are not yet purely righteous, ... God cleanses this remnant of sin in our flesh."[33]

In a debate on justification from the same period, Luther is able to say:

> The imputation of God is more than simply justification. Now, justification is before all else. It does not impute the sin remaining in nature, (treating it) as if it does not exist, but rather proclaims righteous because of Christ. ... The mercy of God thus makes nothing out of all sin, just as from nothing [the mercy of God has made] all things. ... Daily we sin, daily we continue to be justified, just as daily the Physician knows to heal the sickness, until it is healed.[34]

We shall draw some lessons from the debate between Melanchthon and Luther, and the differences in their understanding justification shortly. First, however, I want to turn our attention briefly to Paul's argument in Romans 4, which contains the most

---

[32] See the 1520 tractate on *The Freedom of a Christian*.

[33] LW 26, pp. 132-33 = WA 40:233, 25-27.

[34] *"Imputatio Dei maior est, quam pura iustificatio. Nam maxima est iustificatio, quod peccatum remanens in natura non imputat, tanquam non sit, sed potius indicat esse iusticiam propter Christum. Fides agnoscit: Dilectio Dei dissimulat pec-cata. Misericordia Dei ex omni sic peccato facit nihil, sicut ex nihilo omnia. Cogimur ex ratione seu cognitione philosophie pervenire ad cognitionem Evangelii. Quotidie peccamus, quotidie iustificamur continenter, sicut morbum quotidie cogitur sanare medicus, donec sanatur"* (WA 39.I:122, 8-15). Stupperich, "Die Rechtfertigungslehre," p. 87, suggests that Luther's language here reflects both an attempt to accommodate Melanchthon's lan-guage and to assert his own position.

extensive and prominent use of the language of imputation in all his letters.

We may begin by making the simple observation that Paul speaks of faith itself being reckoned as righteousness.[35] For the apostle, the "reckoning of faith as righteousness"does not signify an acceptance of faith for something it is not ("as if it were righteousness"), but a recognition of faith for what it is. Not only do linguistic parallels support this interpretation (here I agree with Robert Gundry's argument and extensive examples),[36] but also Paul's dramatic depiction of Abraham's faith in Romans 4:18-22: against all hope, in the face of his moribund condition (τὸ ἑαυτοῦ σῶμα νενεκρωμένον), and Sarah's equally lifeless womb (τὴν νέκρωσιν τῆς μήτρας Σάρρας; Rom 4:19), Abraham was made strong in faith, "giving glory to God . . . *therefore* it was reckoned to him as righteousness" (Rom 4:22).[37] Of course, if faith *is* righteousness, the question immediately arises as to why the divine "pronouncement" upon it is not to be regarded as a form of compensation. Why doesn't Abraham have a cause for boasting (καύχημα; Rom 4:2)? In what sense is "faith" different from "works"?

In answering this question from the text, we find ourselves, *nolens volens*, on the same path as Luther, since it is quite clear that for Paul God's word of promise to Abraham does not merely define Abraham's faith: it creates it. This understanding is especially apparent in the three characterizations of the promising God that appear in Paul's argument (Rom 4:5, 17, 24-25). According to the first characterization, Abraham's justifying faith was not a general belief, but concretely a "believing on" the God who "justifies the ungodly" and who promised him that his "seed would be heir of the world" (Rom 4:5, 13).[38]

---

[35]His discussion of the justification of Abraham in Romans 4 is obviously guided by Genesis 15:6, "Abraham believed God and it was reckoned to him as righteousness." Paul expressly cites this text at the opening and closing of the chapter (Rom 4:3, 23), and makes repeated reference to it in the course of his argument (Rom 4:5, 9, 22).

[36]See especially the references to "reckoning as righteousness" in the account of Phinehas's intercession for Israel in LXX Psalm 105:30-31 (MT 106:30-31), and in I Maccabees 2:52, which interprets Genesis 15:6 in terms of Abraham's faithfulness; Romans 2:26 (οὐχὶ ἡ ἀκροβυστία οὐτοῦ εἰς περιτομὴν λογισθήσεται) is debatable, but probably should be interpreted realistically given the following context; also Romans 9:8 (τὰ τέκνα τῆς ἐπαγγελίας λογίζεται εἰς σπέρμα); further: LXX I Kingdoms 1:13; 2 Chronicles 9:20; Lamentations 4:2; Isaiah 29:17; 32:15; 40:17; Wisdom 2:16; 3:17; 9:6.

[37]We here leave aside the difficult question as to the originality of the καί.

[38]Paul obviously understands the promise of "seed" in Genesis 15:6 to embrace the other forms of the divine promise to Abraham (the blessing of the nations, the possession of the land) and interprets the promise of the land as possession of the "age to come."

It is Paul's second characterization of God in Romans 4:17 that is most significant for our concerns. Here Abraham's faith recedes into the background. The sole actor now is "the God whom (Abraham) believed," who "makes alive the dead and calls that which is not into being." In God's presence (κατέναντι οὗ ἐπίστευσεν θεοῦ), the word of promise was not merely a future event, it was a *reality* (Rom 4:17-19). The "call" of the Creator is ultimate. Necessary though it was to the promise in the course of its fulfillment, Abraham's faith was only the effect of the divine promise performing its work. It sprang from the word of the one who creates ex nihilo, beyond and apart from any human calculation or contribution. Paul's description of Abraham's faith in Romans 4:18-22 provides further indications that he thinks in these terms. The citations of Genesis 15:5-6 in Romans 4:18, 22 are a reprise of the opening citation in Romans 4:3, and thus bracket the entire discussion. The verses decisively reveal that Paul's description of Abraham remains rooted in this locus.[39] Yet here in his dramatic narration of Abraham's faith, Paul speaks of a later stage in Abraham's story, immediately prior to Isaac's birth: Abraham is almost 100 years old (Rom 4:19; Gen 17:17), and Sarah's womb is dead (Rom 4:19; Gen 18:11; cf. Gen 17:18). Paul rather obviously overlooks Sarah's inducement of Abraham to beget at child with Hagar (Gen 16), the unbelieving laughter of Abraham and Sarah (Gen 17:17-19; Gen 18:12-15), and Abraham's inexcusable yielding of Sarah to Abimelech (Gen 20). This metalepsis heightens Paul's prior description of the promissory word of the Creator given to Abraham. He presents Abraham not merely as one who acted, but more fundamentally as one acted upon by the promise of God: "he was made strong in faith" (Rom 4:20).

In his third and final characterization of God in this passage, Paul equates the faith of Abraham with that of those who "believe on the one who raised Jesus our Lord from the dead" (Rom 4:24). In fact, he underscores the identity their faith and its object ("the justifier of the ungodly" and "the one who raised Jesus") with diction which otherwise is unusual for him: πιστεύειν ἐπί.[40] The material link with the previous characterization is likewise obvious. In both cases, faith grasps God as the Creator who makes the dead alive—a reversal of the rejection of the Creator which Paul describes in Romans 1. "Justification" here again is based upon faith: as with Abraham, righteousness is reckoned to us who believe (Rom 4:24). In that sense Abraham is our father (Rom 4:16; cf. Rom 4:18). But the connection

---

[39]Romans 4:18 (κατὰ τὸ εἰρημένον, Οὕτως ἔσται τὸ σπέρμα σου); Romans 4:22 (ἐλογίσθη αὐτῷ εἰς δικαιοσύνην).

[40]It appears elsewhere in Paul only in the citation of Is 28:16 in Rom 9:33; 10:11.

with Abraham's faith, grounded as it is in the word of promise, is deeper yet. Subtly, but definitely, Paul presents Jesus as the "seed" in whom the promise has come to fulfillment. He breaks off his vivid depiction of Abraham's faith at its most dramatic point, suddenly speaking not of Isaac, but of Jesus, "our Lord," whom God raised from the dead. This one is the "heir of the world" according to the promise to Abraham (Rom 4:13). The "seed" which consists of Jews and Gentiles (Rom 4:16-17) exists in union with the crucified and risen Lord, who was delivered up and raised for "us," a union between the one and the many which Paul goes on to elaborate in Romans 5:12-21. The justification of the ungodly Abraham through the word of promise had its end in the cross and resurrection where the promise was fulfilled. The work of the promise in creating Abraham's faith had its necessary counterpart in the outworking of the promise in God's delivering up Jesus and raising him from the dead. Given the current debate on imputation, it is crucial to see that the crucified and risen Lord appears explicitly in Paul's argument only in Romans 4:24. Only at the point of fulfillment of promise in the resurrection of the crucified Jesus does Paul gather together the loose threads that have pointed to God's saving work in him. The justification of the ungodly, the blessing of the forgiveness of sins and the removal from divine wrath of which Paul speaks in the earlier part of the chapter point forward to the hour of fulfillment in Jesus Christ. Paul does not feel compelled to formulate justification along the way in terms of Christ (much less in terms of the "imputation of Christ's righteousness"), because he understands that faith itself is created by that promise of God fulfilled in the resurrection of Jesus. Only a Melanchthonian nervousness requires that one read every step of Paul's argument in Romans 4 as explicitly referring to Christ.[41]

We may now turn our attention to the current debate over the "imputation of Christ's righteousness." It is striking, although not surprising, how closely the argument in John Piper's recent book parallels Melanchthon's thought.[42] One can almost predict his positions, if one is aware of the Melanchthonian framework. To insist that faith is only the means of receiving righteousness, and not the extrinsic

---

[41]In fact, while "faith" appears in Romans 3:21-26 as the instrument by which the justifying work of God in Christ is mediated to us, here God's "giving up" Jesus and his raising him from the dead appear as the instrument by which he creates justifying faith: our justification is said to depend on our believing "on" God, who raised Jesus from the dead. Paul continues his argument in Romans 5:1 precisely in this way: "Therefore, being justified by faith, we have peace with God through our Lord, Jesus Christ."

[42]John Piper, *Counted Righteous in Christ: Should We Abandon the Imputation of Christ's Righteousness?* (Wheaton, Ill.: Crossway, 2002).

righteousness of God itself presupposes that, along with Melanchthon, one understands faith—a divine gift, to be sure!—as a human quality or virtue, and not the new creation effected by the Gospel.[43] To insist that justification is not "liberation from sin's mastery" but a bare divine declaration is, again with Melanchthon, to relegate justification solely to the role of quieting the conscience.[44] And, naturally, to insist that one define justification in terms of "the imputation of Christ's righteousness," is to adopt a late-Reformational, Protestant understanding. As we have seen, it is impossible to force Luther into this paradigm. Melanchthon himself tried and failed. Shall we then declare Luther outside the Reformation? Shall we say that the great Reformational insight came in the 1535 *Loci* and not in the summer of 1518? I don't think that it is merely my predilection for Luther that leads me to regard this thought as entirely untenable.

At the same time, I want to say that just as Melanchthon's concern to avoid an Augustinian understanding of justification in terms of the inward renewal of the human being was quite valid, I share Piper's concern about certain developments within evangelical theology. Where it is argued that there is no distinction between Law and Gospel, where it is claimed that there are no unconditioned promises of God, or where justification is construed as a pronouncement upon a human quality, there is certainly cause to be concerned, for precisely the same reasons that Melanchthon once was.[45] It is here, and not in Gundry's mild, and basically legitimate, protest that the real danger lies.

We may also recall that the *disputatio cum Luthero* was not occasioned by Melanchthon's suspicions about Luther's teaching, but by suspicions that Melanchthon had provoked. Given the way in which Piper's thought parallels that of Melanchthon, it should come as no surprise that some of his own statements appear to stand outside a Reformational framework in much the same way as the problematic statements of Melanchthon do. He is able to argue, for example, that within the justified God produces an "experiential righteousness" of "habitual obedience and faith," which is *not* as "filthy rags" (Is 64:6), but truly pleases God. Although he regards this "experiential righteousness" as mere evidence of justification, he understands justification at the final judgment to be contingent on an inherent righteousness:

---

[43]Ibid., pp. 53-64. It is the nature of the gift that is at stake, of course.

[44]Ibid., pp. 75-80.

[45]So, respectively, Scott J. Hafemann, *The God of Promise and the Life of Faith: Understanding the Heart of the Bible* (Wheaton, Ill.: Crossway, 2001) and N. T. Wright, *What Saint Paul Really Said: Was Saul of Tarsus the Real Founder of Christianity?* (Grand Rapids: Eerdmans, 1997).

good works are a *conditio sine qua non* for justification![46] Here, he appears to me to be
not only remarkably close to the untamed Melanchthon, but, in fact, nearly Tridentine in his understanding of justification. In the end, I suspect that he would be
perfectly happy to accept Melanchthon's mature view, that one may speak of good
works as necessary so long as one does not speak of them as necessary to justification. This configuration is unstable, in my view, but it is perfectly acceptable. Perhaps, on the question of our righteousness, he might even be induced to read
Luther's *Against Latomus.*[47]

Be that as it may, my point at the moment is that, as was the case with Luther
and Melanchthon, both sides have reason to harbor suspicions about the Reformational status of the other's views. Surely the outcome of their debate is instructive
for us. Although they maintained their differences, Luther and Melanchthon accepted one another's teaching on justification. That is not at all to say, of course, that
there were no boundaries. It became quite clear that Luther was not representing an
unmodified Augustinianism. And although the debate over the place of good works
in justification was to break out again after Luther's death, Melanchthon seems to
have learned to speak more circumspectly about the matter. Don't the Reformers,
therefore, set a precedent for us to follow? Isn't it sufficient to agree that God's justifying work in Christ is a forensic act, by which in the Word and faith we are granted
an alien, extrinsic righteousness, which is final and unconditioned? On this point, I
would very much like to woo all the parties to the various disputes on justification.

Finally, I have made no attempt to hide my preference for Luther's way of understanding justification. Before all else, my own study has persuaded me that this
way of thinking about justification is the most faithful to the biblical text. In closing, I would like to convey at least something of the richness of this understanding
of the justifying work of God in Christ, even if a brief sketch cannot do it justice.
In the first place, one of the benefits of this dynamic and comprehensive understanding of justification is that it is accompanied by the recognition that "sanctification" is not a second stage, but simply another perspective on God's work in
Christ. Growth is merely grasping more firmly and fully that which has been accomplished and given to us in Christ. That is to say that growth is growth in faith
and in the repentance inherent to faith. Numerous biblical passages, which do not

---

[46]John Piper, *The Purifying Power of Living by Faith in Future Grace* (Sisters, Ore.: Multnomah, 1995), pp.
150-53, 362-67.
[47]See LW 32:135-260, especially pp. 161-80, Luther's defense of the thesis, "every good work is sin,"
and his exposition of Isaiah 64:5-12 (v. 6 "all our righteous deeds are as filthy rags").

fit into the usual Protestant scheme, thereby become comprehensible. How else are we to understand that we have been justified by the Spirit (1 Cor 6:11), and justified from sin (Rom 6:7), and that the Corinthian church is made up of "sanctified ones" (1 Cor 1:2)? The list could go on. The Protestant definition of justification in terms of imputation is no mere description of biblical teaching for which terminology is lacking in Scripture, as is the case, for example, with the doctrine of the Trinity. Here we are dealing in some measure with the replacement of the biblical categories with other ways of speaking. This development need not be regarded as deleterious, and certainly has to be appreciated in his historical significance, but it is not without its dangers and shortcomings.

The implications are not merely theoretical. Melanchthon's relegation of justification to the role of quieting the conscience attenuated its connection to Christian ethics, and thus later helped to engender various pietistic protests against the "arid" formulations of Protestant orthodoxy. Hans Emil Weber has observed acutely that this transposition of justification to the conscience prepared the way for the subjectivism of nineteenth-century theology.[48]

Luther's dynamic conception of justification much more effectively conveys the way in which God's mercy is granted only in judgment. The justification of the sinner takes place only in and through the justification of God in the event of the cross and resurrection of Jesus Christ. "Justification" is no mere transaction to be applied to my account. God's "yes" is given only in and with his "no," a "no" and "yes" which are mine only in so far as faith echoes them in my heart.[49] Both in the foolishness of pride and sin and in the despair of misery, suffering and failure, this Gospel of the justifying work of God in Christ both conquers and carries us sinners. The path of the Christian life thereby becomes clear in a way that it could never do with Melanchthon's approach. All growth in the Christian life, both individually and corporately, is found not in the triumph of progress and ascent (as one might suppose from the usual scheme of "sanctification"), but in that daily repentance and self-judgment by which God "makes out of unhappy and proud gods, true human beings, that is, wretches and sinners."[50] We have the Son of God who

---

[48]Hans Emil Weber, *Reformation, Orthodoxie und Rationalismus*, 2 vols., 2nd ed. (reprint, Gütersloh: Gerd Mohn 1937, 1940), 1:104.

[49]See Rudolf Hermann, "Das Verhältnis von Rechtfertigung und Gebet nach Luthers Auslegung von Röm. 3 in der Römerbriefvorlesung," in *Gesammelte Studien zur Theologie Luthers und der Reformation* (Göttingen: Vandenhoeck & Ruprecht, 1960), pp. 11-43.

[50]WA 5:128, 38-129, 1.

loved us and delivered himself up for us, only in so far as we know and confess our-selves *hic et nunc* to be sinners. All progress in the Christian life is found in returning to its font and source, the crucified and risen Christ. Of course, in so "grasping" him there is real growth and progress in life and in the knowledge of him! In so far as we recognize this truth, we are freed from the temptation of becoming techni-cians of grace, who suppose to find resources for growth in our practices, programs or persons. In a broader theological sense, there is a gain to be made here as well. In that God's saving righteousness includes his wrath and his love, simultaneously and without diminution of either, this understanding of justification guards us from playing off one against the other. God's ultimate wrath is found nowhere but in his ultimate love, and vice versa. By construing divine justice within the frame-work of bare legal conceptions, Protestant thought separated love from justice and, quite contrary to its own intent, arguably prepared the way for the totalization of love in modern theology.

There is obviously much more to be said on these matters, which we cannot pur-sue now. If I have conveyed at least something of the value of Luther's understand-ing of justification, and of the reasons for a certain tolerance for divergent opinions in this matter, I shall be quite content.

6

CONTEMPORARY LUTHERAN UNDERSTANDINGS OF THE DOCTRINE OF JUSTIFICATION

A Selective Glimpse

ROBERT. KOLB

In the concluding plenary session of the tenth International Congress on Luther Research in Copenhagen in August 2002 two European Lutheran systematic theologians presented their interpretations of Luther's understanding of justification in the context of contemporary discussions of its significance. Simo Peura of Helsinki presented the interpretation of Luther's soteriology for which he,[1] his mentor Tuoma Mannermaa,[2] and others of Mannermaa's students[3] have argued over the past twenty years, with support from such leading North American theologians as Robert Jenson and Carl Braaten.[4] In the midst of ecumenical dialogues

---

[1]Simo Peura, *Mehr als ein Mensch? Die Vergöttlichung als Thema der Theologie Martin Luthers von 1513 bis 1519* (Mainz: von Zabern, 1994). The English abstract of the work (p. 303) states, "The deification of a human being [according to Luther] is realized ontologically, when Christ inhabits him. The real presence of Christ causes the union with the believer. A Christian participates in the divine nature, sharing all saving properties or goods (e.g., *iustitia*) of Christ. The participation effects a partial renovation and transformation of man. The deification is real but not perceptible. The contrast in the ontologically renewed person is apparent. He realizes the remnants of sin in himself and is willing to bear his cross and lovingly serve God and suffering neighbours. The deification shows that Luther in fact understood the effective justification ontologically, although his concepts differed from those of the metaphysics of scholasticism."
[2]See, e.g., Tuoma Mannermaa, *Der im Glauben gegenwärtige Christus, Rechtfertigung und Vergottung: Zum ökumenischen Dialog* (Hannover: Lutherisches Verlagshaus, 1989).
[3]E.g., in Simo Peura and Antti Raunio, eds., *Luther und Theosis: Vergöttlichung als Thema der abendländischen Theologie* (Helsinki and Erlangen: Luther-Agricola-Gesellschaft and Martin-Luther-Verlag, 1990).
[4]Carl E. Braaten and Robert W. Jenson, eds., *Union with Christ, the New Finnish Interpretation of Luther* (Grand Rapids: Eerdmans, 1998).

with representatives of the Russian Orthodox tradition, Mannermaa developed the contention that Luther expressed his soteriology above all in the concept of the divinization of the believer through the faith that God gives in his grace. In the distributed English abstract of his paper Peura concluded that "*theosis*" is "a logical conclusion when the Reformer wants to express the effective aspect of justification."[5]

Wilfried Härle of Heidelberg represented a quite different approach to Luther's teaching on justification in his paper, "The Exposition of Luther's Doctrine of Justification in the Disputations of 1536." His mining of these texts also engaged the twenty-first century application of Luther's concept of justification to contemporary problems. This approach focuses on Luther's concept of the justifying Word of God and his reinterpretation of what it means to be human in terms of two kinds of righteousness; such a focus, its adherents contend, delivers the most historically faithful and pastorally applicable understanding and use of the reformer's "evangelical breakthrough." Härle explored in depth the anthropology which Luther's teaching on justification postulated; he examined the contrast between sin and, for Luther, its opposite, faith, and he set forth the reformer's distinction of two kinds of righteousness, two spheres of being human.[6]

These two presentations represented two streams of current Luther interpretation, one guided and driven above all by an ecumenical agenda, the other a more traditional, historical approach to the contemporary application of the reformer's insights. Among countless approaches to the interpretation and application of the Lutheran understanding of the justification of the sinner proposed and propagated in the twentieth century, one or the other of these two reflects the ideas of many, but certainly not all, Lutherans today. In the body of biblical teaching, as the Wittenberg theologians sometimes called the *analogia fidei*, the article on justification serves as the heart, pumping the lifeblood of Christ's love into the whole body of doctrine. The richness of this teaching within the Lutheran tradition and the great variety of interpretations and applications, of misinterpretations and misapplications of that richness make the treatment of this topic a subject for volumes, not a single essay. Therefore, these two speakers give us but a glimpse of the broad spectrum of positions regarding the meaning and use of Luther's doctrine of justifica-

---

[5]Simo Peura, "Iustitia christiana in Luthers späterer Auslegung des Galaterbriefs (1531/1535)," English abstract, p. 3, distributed to participants in the Congress and scheduled for publication in *Lutherjahrbuch*, along with Wilfried Härle's and other plenary papers delivered at the Congress.

[6]Wilfried Härle, "Die Entfaltung der Rechtfertigungslehre Luthers in den Disputationen von 1536," distributed to participants in the Congress.

tion by faith among Lutheran theologians in the twentieth century.

In his study of Lutheran debate over the justification of the sinner, Gottfried Martens noted a decade ago that "the secondary literature on the subject has virtually no limits,"[7] and he also concluded that in the context of ecumenical discussions, as well as scholarly pursuit, of the contemporary significance of God's justification of sinners through Christ, Lutherans had divided into two camps regarding what their tradition regards as the critical center of biblical teaching. Some continued to define justification as God's fundamental action in reclaiming and restoring human beings fallen into sin, that is, rebellion against their Creator, through the benefits of the crucified and risen Christ, delivered in God's word of absolution. Others viewed justification as but one historical interpretation of biblical soteriology, one doctrine or doctrinal topic among others, important for Lutherans but not absolutely necessary for proclaiming the gospel of Christ.[8] The range of arguments and interpretations of Luther's proclamation regarding the justification of the sinner remains as broad and the differences as intense eleven years after the publication of Marten's work, and this brief focus on one group of scholars does not do justice to the entire ongoing discussion.

As important as the *theosis* approach to Luther's teaching is, it will not be the subject of my comments. Mannermaa's and Peura's interpretation has encountered not only support but also sharp critique. The Göttingen systematic theologian Klaus Schwarzwäller summarized that critique in a paper given in Mannermaa's seminar at the 1993 Luther Congress. For five reasons he found questionable the thesis that Luther's doctrine of justification can best be understood through the occasional passages which speak of *Vergottung*—divinization—and those more numerous which treat the biblical expression of believers being "in Christ" and Christ being "in us." First, Schwarzwäller challenged Mannermaa's method and hermeneutic of seeking a single "structuring idea" for organizing Luther's thought in view of the absence of evidence for the use of divinization in this manner in the primary sources. Luther's few uses of the term *Vergottung* are occasional and do not expressly regard this concept as such an organizing center for his way of thinking. Collateral evidence, such as his use of "Christ in us" language, does not in all likelihood refer to a process of divinization. Second, historically, Schwarzwäller argued, the reader of the texts must go against the grain of Luther's own presentation of his biblical understanding to maintain that the "real-ontic" participation of believers in

---

[7] Gottfried Martens, *Die Rechtfertigung des Sünders – Rettungshandeln Gottes oder historisches Interpretament?* (Göttingen: Vandenhoeck & Ruprecht, 1992), p. 19.

[8] Martens, *Rechtfertigung*, passim, see particularly pp. 322-44.

Christ's divinity represents the intention of the reformer's proclamation of salvation in Christ. It must also be noted that among Luther's own students this idea did not surface.[9] Third, on logical grounds, the Göttingen theologian challenged the equation of "God's being," "God's righteousness," "Jesus Christ," "the being of faith," "real participation" and "the divine being of faith" as univocal terms, observing rather that this logic ignores Luther's rhetorical way of expressing kerygmatically and doxologically the reaction of his faith to God's Word. It also ignores the Wittenberg understanding of God's Word and its pronouncement as the creative agent that produces reality for the biblical writers. Linguistically, Schwarzwäller states, the use of certain of Luther's expressions ignores his fashioning of metaphors and confuses levels of his speech. Finally, theologically, the Mannermaa school's use of the concept of ontology ignores Luther's way of conceiving of reality and drifts into a kind of abstraction while failing to consider how the Reformer treated the human being's encounter with the person of the Creator, who speaks reality into existence through his Word.[10]

Although I shall not tarry there, any treatment of late twentieth-century Lutheran formulations on justification by faith cannot ignore the long efforts that bore fruit in the Joint Declaration and its "Annex," expressions of a consensus on the lifting of mutual condemnations regarding the doctrine of justification between Roman Catholics and Lutherans. Representatives of the Lutheran World Federation and the Pontifical Council for Promoting Christian Unity of the Roman Catholic Church subscribed to this agreement on October 31, 1999, in Augsburg. The Joint Declaration states that the intention of the document—

---

[9]In fact, the doctrine of justification by the indwelling divine nature of Christ taught by Andreas Osiander has certain parallels with the *theosis* position. From his training in the Kabbala, Osiander acquired neoplatonic presuppositions similar to the metaphysical foundation that appears to lie behind Peura's and Mannermaa's position. Osiander never came to Wittenberg but supported Luther actively from his post as pastor in Nuremberg after 1525. When he openly began to teach his own doctrine of justification, however, after Luther's death, the Wittenberg circle without exception recognized that he had departed seriously from Luther (in spite of what some modern scholars, such as Emanuel Hirsch, *Die Theologie des Andreas Osiander und ihre geschichtlichen Voraussetzungen* [Göttingen: Vandenhoeck & Ruprecht, 1919] have argued). On Osiander, see also the interpretation of Simo Peura, "Gott und Mensch in der Unio: Die Unterschiede im Rechtfertigungsverständnis bei Osiander und Luther," in *Unio: Gott und Mensch in der nachreformatorischen Theologie*, ed. Matti Repo and Rainer Vinke (Helsinki: Luther-Agricola-Gesellschaft, 1996), pp. 33-61.
[10]Klaus Schwarzwäller, "Verantwortung des Glaubens. Freiheit und Liebe nach der Dekalogauslegung Martin Luthers," in *Freiheit als Liebe bei/Freedom as love in Martin Luther*, ed. Dennis D. Bielfeldt and Schwarzwäller (Frankfurt am Main: P. Lang, 1995), pp. 146-48.

more modest than is sometimes recognized—was

> to show that on the basis of their dialogue the subscribing Lutheran churches and the
> Roman Catholic church are now able to articulate a common understanding of our
> justification by God's grace through faith in Christ. It does not cover all that either
> church teaches about justification; it does encompass a consensus on basic truths of
> the doctrine of justification and shows that the remaining differences in its explication
> are no longer the occasion for doctrinal condemnations. . . . [T]his *Joint Declaration* rests
> on the conviction that in overcoming the earlier controversial questions and doctrinal
> condemnations, the churches neither take the condemnations lightly nor do they dis-
> avow their own past. On the contrary, this *Declaration* is shaped by the conviction that
> in their respective histories our churches have come to new insights. Developments
> have taken place that not only make possible but also require the churches to examine
> the divisive questions and condemnations and see them in a new light.[11]

In spite of widespread approval of the Joint Declaration in both churches,[12] individual Roman Catholic theologians have expressed a variety of reservations to the
Declaration, including its definition of grace,[13] and many Lutherans viewed the papal declaration "Dominus Jesus" issued by the Congregation for Propagation of
the Faith as an official effort to limit and hedge the significance and impact of the
Joint Declaration.[14] Furthermore, Lutheran theologians have also registered objec-

---

[11]*Joint Declaration on the Doctrine of Justification: The Lutheran World Federation and The Roman Catholic Church*
(Grand Rapids: Eerdmans, 2000), pp. 10-11 (translated from the original German, *Gemeinsame Erklärung zur Rechtfertigungslehre* [Frankfurt am Main: Lembeck, and Paderborn: Bonifatius-Verlag,
1999]).

[12]It is too early to expect an overall assessment of the Joint Declaration, but it has provided occasion
for a variety of expressions regarding the doctrine of justification as well as the document and the
process of acceptance of the document. See the brief orientation of Ted M. Dorman, "The Joint
Declaration on the Doctrine of Justification: Retropect and Prospects," *JETS* 44 (2001): 421-34.
See also "A Symposium on the Vatican's Official Response to the Joint Declaration on Justification,"
in *Pro Ecclesia* 7 (1998), pp. 398-470; *Ecumenical Trends* 28, no. 5 (May 1999), pp. 65-80, *Ecumenical
Trends* 29, §5 (May 2000), pp. 65-80, no. 8 (September 2000), p. 117, and Ernest Falardeau, "The
Lutheran-Roman Catholic Joint Declaration: Pastoral and Catechetical Implications," *Ecumenical
Trends* 30, no. 2 (February 2001), pp. 28-32.

[13]Christopher J. Malloy, "The Nature of Justifying Grace: a Lacuna in the *Joint Declaration*," *The Thomist*
65 (2001): 93-120; cf. Avery Dulles, "Two Languages of Salvation: The Lutheran-Catholic Joint
Declaration," *First Things* 98 (1999): 25-30.

[14]*Declaration Dominus Jesus on the Unicity and Salvific Universality of Jesus Christ and the Church* (Vatican City:
Liberia Editione Vaticana, 2000). See Christine van Wijnbergen, "Reactions to *Dominus Jesus* in the
German-Speaking Word," in *The Ecumenical Constitution of Churches*, ed. José Oscar Beozzo and
Giuseppe Ruggieri (London: SCM Press, 2001), pp. 147-52 for a good bibliographical introduc-
tion to the topic.

tions. The developing rapprochement between the evangelical churches of Germany, ever more beleaguered in their situation within a rapidly secularizing society, and Roman Catholic theologians had aroused expressions of reservation from evangelical theological faculties during the process of dialogue that led to the Joint Declaration,[15] and a petition signed by more than two hundred members of these faculties protested the proposal to sign the document in January 1998 under the leadership of Albrecht Beutel, Karin Bornkamm, Gerhard Ebeling, Reinhard Schwarz, Johannes Wallmann and others.[16] Wilfried Härle and six other theologians, along with the Danish church historian Leif Grane, discussed elements of the debate in a special issue of the *Zeitschrift für Theologie und Kirche* in late 1998,[17] and individual theologians issued their own critiques.[18] When the "Annex" to the "Declaration" was formulated,[19] some of the protest diminished, but it did not disappear.[20] The chief concerns of these evangelical critics included the document's failure to treat the nature of repentance, the assurance that faith has because of God's word of forgiveness, and the nature of that word as God's justifying instrument in the "means of grace." They also criticized the document's ambiguity on the definition of sin and on the relationship of God's condemning word of law and his life-giving word of gospel.[21] To this list must be added its failure to take Luther's distinction between two kinds of righteousness into account.

These ecumenical discussions of justification are obviously a significant and

---

[15]See, on the earlier ecumenical discussions of the Lutheran doctrine of justification, Nestor Beck, *The Doctrine of Faith, a Study of the Augsburg Confession and Contemporary Ecumenical Documents* (St. Louis: Concordia, 1987). See also "An Opinion on *The Condemnations of the Reformation Era.* . . ., The Theological Faculty, Georgia August University, Göttingen," "Part One: Justification," in *Lutheran Quarterly* 5 (1991): 1-62; "Part Two: The Holy Communion," ibid., 337-71. This opinion was a reaction to *Lehrverurteilungen—kirchentrennend?* 4 vols., ed. Karl Lehmann, Wolfhart Pannenberg and Theodor Schneider (Freiburg/Breisgau: Herder, and Göttingen: Vandenhoeck & Ruprecht, 1986-1994), trans. and abridged by Margaret Kohl as *The Condemnations of the Reformation Era. Do They Still Divide?* ed. Karl Lehmann and Wolfhart Pannenberg (Minneapolis: Fortress, 1990).

[16]See their statement in translation from the *Frankfurter Allgemeine Zeitung*, January 29, 1998, in *Lutheran Quarterly* 12 (1998): 193-96, and in *Dialog* 38 (1999): 71-72, with comment by Gerhard Forde.

[17]*Zeitschrift für Theologie und Kirche, Beiheft 10, Zur Rechtfertigungslehre* (December 1998).

[18]See, e.g., Jörg Baur, *Einig in Sachen Rechtfertigung? Zur Prüfung des Rechtfertigungskapitels der Studie des Ökumenischen Arbeitskreises evangelischer und katholischer Theologen: "Lehrverurtelungen—kirchentrennend?"* (Tübingen: Mohr Siebeck, 1989), and *Frei durch Rechtfertigung, Vorträge anlässlich der römisch-katholisch/lutherischen "Gemeinsamen Erklärung"* (Tübingen: Mohr Siebeck, 1999).

[19]*Joint Declaration*, pp. 43-47.

[20]Härle was among those leading this protest. For a theological critique see, e.g., Irene Dingel, "The Debate Over Justification in Ecumenical Dialogue," *Lutheran Quarterly* 15 (2001): 293-316.

[21]*Lutheran Quarterly* 12 (1998): 194-95.

critical part of Lutheran witness to the tradition's heritage, but the second line of interpretation presented at the Copenhagen conference also has ecumenical significance. It seeks to share for the benefit of the whole household of faith those insights that brought Luther to his own "breakthrough to the gospel" and that have guided Lutheran proclamation and pastoral care in one form or another for nearly five hundred years. European and North American Lutheran theologians have represented this line of interpretation with a variety of perspectives throughout the closing years of the twentieth century. These perspectives have based their interpretations of the doctrine of justification in the reformer's writings on his presuppositions regarding the Word of God as the instrument of his creation of reality and his anthropological assessment of human righteousness as twofold, "passive" and "active." Härle,[22] Schwarzwäller, Oswald Bayer of Tübingen, Jörg Baur of Göttingen and many other colleagues have pursued this line of presentation with a good many variations in their specific accents. The leading advocate of this view in North America has been Gerhard Forde of Luther Seminary in St. Paul, whose call for a "radical Lutheran" proclamation of the gospel at the end of the twentieth century has woven together elements of Luther's theology for application to modern life in ways similar to Härle and Bayer. These theologians and their colleagues have striven to demonstrate that Luther's proclamation of the God who justifies is not trapped inside sixteenth-century thought forms but is relevant and applicable to the dilemmas and distresses at the turn of the twenty-first century.[23]

In 1987, Forde called for a "radical Lutheran" proclamation of the gospel of

---

[22]I am using Wilfreid Härle, "Zur Gegenwartsbedeutung der 'Rechtfertigungs'-Lehre, Eine Problem-skizze," *Zeitschrift für Theologie und Kirche, Beiheft 10, Zur Rechtfertigungslehre* (December 1998): 101-39, "Luthers reformatorische Entdeckung—damals und heute," *Zeitschrift für Theologie und Kirche* 99 (2002): 278-295, and his *Dogmatik* 2nd ed. (Berlin: de Gruyter, 1995).

[23]See Härle, "Luthers reformatorische Entdeckung," pp. 290-95; Gerhard Forde, *Justification by Faith, a Matter of Death and Life* (1982; reprint, Mifflintown, Penn.: Sigler, 1991), vii; Oswald Bayer, *Aus dem Glauben leben, Über Rechtfertigung und Heiligung* (Stuttgart: Calwer Verlag, 1984), pp. 7-8 (ET *Living by Faith: Justification and Sanctification,* Lutheran Quarterly Books [Grand Rapids: Eerdmans, 2003]); and Bayer, *Rechtfertigung* (Neuendettelsau: Freimund, 1991), pp. 7-8. A number of Bayer's essays have appeared in English: "God as the Author of My Life-History," *Lutheran Quarterly* 2 (1988): 437-56; "Twenty-Four Theses on the Renewal of Lutheranism by Concentrating on the Doctrine of Justification," *Lutheran Quarterly* 5 (1991): 73-75; "I Believe That God Has Created Me with All That Exists: An Example of Catechetical-Systematics," *Lutheran Quarterly* 8 (1994): 129-61; "The Word of the Cross," *Lutheran Quarterly* 9 (1995): 47-55; "The Being of Christ in Faith," *Lutheran Quarterly* 10 (1996): 135-50; "Rupture of Times: Luther's Relevance for Today," *Lutheran Quarterly* 13 (1999): 35-50; and "Justification as the Basis and Boundary of Theology," *Lutheran Quarterly* 15 (2001): 273-92.

justification by faith as the defining element of the Lutheran church. In the midst of the effort to define Lutheran identity that accompanied the organization of the Evangelical Lutheran Church in America, Forde asserted that "what is at stake is the radical gospel, radical grace, the eschatological nature of the gospel of Jesus Christ crucified and risen as put in its most uncompromising and unconditional form by St. Paul." In an article that served as a kind of programmatic statement for the revived *Lutheran Quarterly* but gave no more than hints of his own carefully sculpted formulation of "the proclamation of justification by faith," as he would express it, Forde focused on theological anthropology as the locus for contemporary discussion of the "radix," the root of the Lutheran preaching of the gospel of justification by faith in Christ.

> The fact is that the radical Pauline gospel of justification by faith without the deeds of the law calls for a fundamentally different anthropology and with it a different theological "system" . . . from that to which the world is *necessarily* committed. The radical gospel of justification by faith alone simply does not fit, cannot be accepted by, and will not work with an anthropology which sees the human being as a continuously existing subject possessing "free choice of will" over against God and/or other religious goals. The radical gospel is the *end* of that being and the beginning of a new being in faith and hope.[24]

Coupled with this vantage point on justification from the perspective of the biblical teaching on what it means to be human, Forde focused on the Word of God that delivers the benefits of Christ to sinners. He commented, "We do not adequately gauge the depth of the problem unless we see that it is ultimately a problem for the *proclamation* (Word and Sacrament) of the church." Theological reflection is vital, he insisted, but "justification by faith alone or the bondage of the will and such doctrines" are presuppositions for preaching, and preaching is where God's action is. "It is the *proclamation* that makes new beings, not theology or even ethics."[25] This article projects echoes of his previously published *Justification by Faith, a Matter of Death and Life*[26] and intimations of his then forthcoming *Theology Is for Proclamation*.[27] In these works and selected writings of Bayer and Härle are found eight basic theses regarding the use of Luther's concept of justification by faith in the contemporary world.

---

[24]Gerhard O. Forde, "Radical Lutheranism," *Lutheran Quarterly* N.S. I (1987): 9-10.
[25]Ibid., p. 14.
[26]See note 23.
[27]Gerhard O. Forde, *Theology is for Proclamation* (Minneapolis: Fortress, 1990).

These theologians consciously incorporate the historical basis of the Lutheran tradition in Luther's own thought into their address of the challenges for biblical proclamation at the beginning of the twenty-first century. Therefore, a study of their writings involves looking back to their foundations in the reformer's writings. Although their accents and foci differ, Forde, Bayer and Härle agree in a number of areas (even though Härle would not label himself a "radical Lutheran"). First, Luther's distinction of two kinds of righteousness lies at the root of their expositions of justification even when this distinction is not explicitly discussed. Second, they agree that justification cannot be merely a dogmatic statement on a page: justification is something God does to sinners through those who speak this word of forgiveness and life that God has wrought through the incarnation of Jesus Christ, through his death and resurrection. God's Word is not merely information about God's gracious disposition toward hearers of his Word. It is his instrument of re-creation through the work and benefits of the Word made flesh. Luther's strong doctrine of creation brought with it the presupposition that God continues to act through his creative Word, and that he uses that Word in its various forms, oral, written and sacramental. Third, the three theologians make specific Luther's expression of the biblical teaching of justification in terms of dying and rising, God's killing sinners and out of them bringing children of God to life. This leads to the methodological observation that, fourth, the proper distinction and application of God's condemning law and God's life-restoring gospel is key to making the doctrine of justification function as God wants it to work. Fifth, faith in Christ is to be defined as the orientation and nature of the entire human creature, not simply a set of psychological characteristics. Sixth, each of the authors interprets the life of the Christian from the standpoint of Luther's observation that believers are totally righteous in God's sight but experience life as thoroughly infected by sinfulness, his famous "*simul justus et peccator*" description of the mystery of the continuation of evil in the believer's life. Seventh, this mystery raises to a greater or lesser extent for each of these three authors the issue of theodicy, which they see implicit, though not explicit, in Luther's formulation of justification because it is implicit in biblical revelation. Finally, each author wrestles with the impact of God's act of justification for daily Christian life, in the living out of his will in new obedience, in the living out of his will in following his commands within the structures of God's callings.

TWO KINDS OF RIGHTEOUSNESS

First, Luther's distinction between two kinds of human righteousness, the often unrecognized anthropological presupposition of the Reformer's understanding of justification, is explicitly or implicitly employed by each of the theologians under discussion. The Reformer placed his understanding of the justification of the sinner within the setting of this distinction, which he labeled "our theology" in the preface of his large Galatians commentary, composed in 1535. There he wrote, "This is our theology, by which we teach a precise distinction between these two kinds of righteousness, the active and the passive, so that morality and faith, works and grace, secular society and religion may not be confused. Both are necessary, but both must be kept within their limits."[28] "Active righteousness" designates the fulfilling of all the commands to action that make up God's design for human life. "Passive righteousness" refers to the human being's being what he or she was designed by the Creator to be in relationship to God. This relationship was never constituted as a reward for performance. There was no probationary period in Eden for Adam and Eve to demonstrate worthiness to receive the award of being human, God's creature, God's child. God made them on the basis of pure grace, of unconditioned love alone, "without any merit or worthiness in us," as Luther stated in his explanation to the first article of the Apostles Creed in the Small Catechism. His expectations for their performance of his plan for their lives grew out of—but did not initiate or institute—their humanity. All depends on God's choice of his own people. No other explanation satisfies the claim that God is Creator.[29]

Luther's passive righteousness corresponds to the gift of identity psychological philosophers such as Erik Erikson assign to the core of what it means to be human. Although human identity becomes concrete at several levels, its formation rests upon the gift of being able to trust or the failure to receive that gift, the gift of finding the elements of one's environment trustworthy or the failure to apprehend such

---

[28]Martin Luther, *D. Martin Luthers Werke* (Weimar: Böhlau, 1883-) [henceforth WA] 40, I:45, 24-27; *Luther's Works*, ed. Jaroslav J. Pelikan (St. Louis: Concordia, 1958-1986) 26:7. For a summary of Luther's definition of "righteousness" and bibliography, see Bengt Hägglund, "Gerechtigkeit. VI. Reformations- und Neuzeit," *Theologische Realenzyklopädie* 12 (Berlin: de Gruyter, 1984): 432-34, 440. See also Robert Kolb, "Luther on the Two Kinds of Righteousness: Reflections on His Two-Dimensional Definition of Humanity at the Heart of His Theology," *Lutheran Quarterly* 13 (1999): 449-66, and the December 1998 *Beiheft* issue of *Zeitschrift für Theologie und Kirche* 95, on Luther's understanding of righteousness and justification, particularly as it pertains to the Joint Declaration on the Doctrine of Justification; see especially Reinhard Schwarz, "Luthers Rechtfertigungslehre als Eckstein der christlichen Theologie und Kirche," pp. 15-46.

[29]See Härle, *Dogmatik* (Berlin/New York: de Gruyter, 1995), pp. 505-10, and Forde, *Theology Is for Proclamation*, pp. 30-35. Luther's *De servo arbitrio* focused on this anthropology, with its emphasis on the bondage of the will, but his strong doctrine of election appears elsewhere in his writings.

a gift.[30] Luther contended that God's act of justification creates a chosen people, faith-filled children of God; he asserted that human righteousness, human identity, depends on the gift of that identity, the creation of the trust that centers life on the Creator and Redeemer. Luther taught that human beings are righteous by their good works, but only in their relationship to others of God's creatures. In relationship to their Creator they are righteous only because of his love and mercy, only in their clinging to him as their Father.

Bayer ties together the modern thirst for establishing a sense of personal identity with Luther's proclamation of the gift of that identity as a child of God through justification. For human beings life means and demands that one's being is taken into account and appreciated. "If no one would call me by name, greet me, if no one would spare me a glance or a word, I would not only be a social Nothing. I would be a physical Nothing. I would not be alive at all if my parents had not appreciated me even before my birth and paid attention to my living."[31] Being taken into account and appreciated is a fundamental need that in modern times is continually being put to the test by the challenges and criticism of daily life. Our contemporaries are caught between their own best efforts at effective performance and the critique of those around them as well as the scrutiny and judgment of their own standards for their own achievement. Bayer places the individual's existence within the context of this battle for recognition and appreciation in the clash of power, human rights and justice that rages within individual lives, the ongoing history of the world and the development of nature. Human beings encounter at every side the demand for accountability, the burden of responsibility.[32] In this setting Bayer presents God's gift of justification to those who realize that they do not measure up. The faith which recognizes God as gracious and the self as righteous in his sight is "passive," that is, "faith is totally God's doing. It is not in any way a human decision, a human activity of finding meaning and giving meaning to life." That is not the way sinful human beings want it in their self-centered desire to assert their independence in relationship to their Creator. That is why the experience of coming to faith in Christ is painful. It involves dying to old ways of holding life together.

---

[30]Erik Erikson has treated identity as the fundamental human question throughout his work; see, e.g., *Insight and Responsibility* (New York: Norton, 1964), esp. pp. 81-107; *Identity, Youth and Crisis* (New York: Norton, 1968), esp. pp. 91-141; *Life History and the Historical Moment* (New York: Norton, 1975).
[31]Bayer, *Aus Glauben leben*, p. 9.
[32]Ibid., pp. 10-13.

Bayer observes that Luther's talking about the death of the Old Adam is not a mere picture. Passive righteousness in this case means suffering righteousness, in which sinners find obliterated their own attempts at setting the world aright through their thinking, their metaphysics or through their actions, their moral performance. Sinners must be brought to the cross, crucified with Christ and buried in his tomb to root out what Calvin called the "idol factory" of the sinful human heart. This does not mean that the cross can be made into a principle for defining the world, as some moderns are tempted to do, comments Bayer. Luther's "theology of the cross" simply "tells it like it is," labels every break with God sin, demands the death of the sinner, and proclaims and pronounces the gift of new life in the person of faith whom God has chosen and claims as his own.[33]

Härle also ties together the passivity of the human being who receives this righteousness with God's own righteousness in giving this gift of humanity. "Luther understands the righteousness of God as both God's action through which he brings the human creature to salvation and also that which God effects through his acting on and in the human creature." As God's righteousness it is the "characteristic, activity, or power through which God pronounces us righteous or makes us righteous." At the same time it is the state and disposition in which believers find themselves when God has regarded them with his favor for Christ's sake and bestowed upon them the trust that clings to him as Savior, Lord, and Creator. In searching for a way to make this concept clear, Härle turns to Old Testament scholarship and to the recent work on the concept of righteousness in the ancient world the Hebrews inhabited. There righteousness meant "faithfulness within the community."[34] God is righteous because he is faithful to his Word of promise that creates and sustains life in community with him. Human righteousness is the faithfulness of the one God has chosen, to whom he has given this Word of life.

This passive righteousness is not only necessary in Luther's way of thinking because of the impotence imposed by sin. It also arises as a necessary consequence of the creaturely nature of the human being—and God's nature as Creator.

> We live only on the strength of the fact that the Creator breathed his Spirit into the dust and gave us life. We live on "borrowed time"—time lent us by the Creator. Yet we also see in the death of Jesus on the cross our rebellion against that life, and we note that there is absolutely no way out now except one. God vindicated the

---

[33]Ibid., 23-27. Cf. Gerhard O. Forde, *On Being a Theologian of the Cross, Reflections on Luther's Heidelberg Disputation, 1518* (Grand Rapids: Eerdmans, 1997), pp. 71-77.
[34]Härle, "Luthers reformatorische Entdeckung," pp. 284-87.

crucified Jesus by raising him from the dead.[35]

Luther maintained with all seriousness, according to Jörg Baur, that God is nothing other, in relation to his world and human beings, than "creating and giving will, to which all creatures owe their entire existence; from this creative love, from its continuous almighty torrent, creation receives its being." Sin then is the destruction of the relationship to the true God, the creature's creator, and all that flows from the failure to fear, love and trust in God above all things. Liberation from sin comes through Christ's death and resurrection, which through his substitutionary sacrifice and victorious coming to life again, is given to sinners whom God chooses as his own. In them he restores trust in himself, which is the key to true human life.[36]

From Luther's explanation of the first article of the Creed in his Small Catechism Bayer lifts his confession that human creatures stand before God as creatures "without any merit or worthiness," solely dependent as creatures upon God's mercy and grace. That is the nature of being a creature. Thus, the expression of this dependence, faith or trust in the Creator, is not something human beings have, but it is actually constitutive of human identity; it is the state of being thrown totally upon God's resources, of having no other foundation on which to rely, on which to base and ground life[37]—the very heart of what it means to be human. This means that justification is the restoration of the original righteousness in God's sight, which was the product of God's grace and favor alone, as Luther confessed in describing his breakthrough to the gospel, "I felt myself completely reborn. The gates had opened before me, and I had entered into paradise."[38] Thus he could say that the believer lives "in the dawn of the future life, for we begin to achieve the knowledge of God's creatures which we lost through Adam's fall."[39] And so it is God's way that he "rewards," in the words of the hymn writer Paul Gerhardt, "preveniently," that is, he is always coming to his human creatures with his gifts before they think or ask.[40]

Luther's distinction between two kinds of righteousness takes seriously the whole of the person but also differentiates the identity that constitutes our being from the performance that flows from that identity and being. Because of that, this definition

---

[35]Forde, *Theologian of the Cross*, p. 9.

[36]Jörg Baur, *Salus Christiana. Die Rechtfertigungslehre in der Geschichte des christlichen Heilsverständnisses, Band 1* (Gütersloh: Mohn, 1968), pp. 55-560. Cf. Härle, *Dogmatik*, pp. 456-92.

[37]Bayer, *Rechtfertigung*, pp. 8-9.

[38]WA 54:186, pp. 8-9, cited in Bayer, *Aus Glauben leben*, p. 23.

[39]WA Tischreden 1:574, pp. 8-10, cited in Bayer, *Aus Glauben leben*, p. 30, cf. pp. 34-40.

[40]Bayer, *Rechtfertigung*, p. 10, citing Gerhardt's testament to his son: see Paul Gerhardt, *Dichtungen und Schriften*, ed. E. von Cranach-Sichart (Munich: Müller, 1957), p. 493.

of our humanity speaks to those many in contemporary societies who encounter crisis in their failure either to find satisfaction in their identity or to create contentment through their performance. Justification through Christ bestows death to old, unsatisfactory identities molded by sin, and it creates a new identity as child of God. This path to the rightness or true humanness of a person's core identity casts a different light upon the questions of success or failure at performance of what God, self and others expect. The highest worth and worthiness fall to us by pure mercy and only as gift, and they are free for the trusting. Secondary meaning and worth in life remain important but not matters of our core identity when Christ comes to justify and thus place himself as the loving Lord of human lives.[41]

JUSTIFICATION IS THE ACTION OF GOD IN HIS WORD

Second, fundamental to this Lutheran view of justification is the assertion that it is not merely a doctrinal concept; it cannot be reduced to merely a dogmatic statement on a page.[42] Justification is something God does to sinners. In Genesis I he created the universe through his word; in conversion he re-creates human beings as his own children through his word of forgiveness and life. That word is not merely information about God's gracious disposition toward his people. God's Word in the mouths of his people changes the reality of the lives of its hearers when forgiveness, life and salvation in and through Christ are proclaimed and pronounced. This reflects Luther's presupposition that God acts through his word in its various forms, oral, written and sacramental. He calls these word-instruments the "means of grace"—the instruments by which God effects his gracious will toward his people. He believed that through these forms of his Word of gospel God effects his will to save sinners by creating a relationship of love and trust with those whom he has chosen to be his children.[43] Härle concludes that the "center of Scripture is a living event. Not a doctrine or a doctrinal formulation constitutes the center of Scripture, but what happens in reference to the person of Christ: what delivers Christ [was Christum treibt], through proclaiming him, through explaining his work, and through applying his work to the lives of his people."[44]

Forde formulates much the same idea as he expresses his doubt about the possibility of constructing "an 'objective' and dispassionate account of the earth-shak-

---

[41]Härle, "Luthers reformatorische Entdeckung," pp. 290-91.
[42]Martens, Die Rechtfertigung des Sünders, see esp. pp. 322-26.
[43]Härle, Dogmatik, pp. 532-69.
[44]Ibid., p. 137.

ing event" of Christ's death and resurrection. "Not just what the word *means* is important . . . but what the word *does*."[45] That becomes clear, in Forde's case particularly, through Luther's "theology of the cross." "The cross is in the first instance God's attack on human sin. Of course, in the second instance, and finally, it is also salvation from sin."[46] Thus, for Forde, God's act of justification reaches from Christ's cross and empty tomb into the delivery of the new reality God effected there today. As Christians share God's Word, which bears Christ's work of dying and rising to their contemporaries, they are indeed instruments of God's Word.

> So the hermeneutics of the Word as killing letter and life-giving Spirit impels the proclaimer to a doing of the Word to the hearer and not merely an explaining of it. . . . The move to doing the Word in that fashion involves the recognition that the proclamation must be a Word of the cross. That does not mean only that there is lots of talk about the cross. The point is that the proclamation itself ought to bear the form of the Word of the cross. It is to do the cross to the hearers. The proclamation is to kill and make alive. It purposes to make an end and a new beginning. . . . To be a Word of the cross, the proclamation must cut in upon our lives to end the old and begin the new. All this is to say, of course, that the Word is an eschatological Word, a Word that puts an end to the old and ushers in the new.[47]

Like Forde, Bayer connects God's revealed nature as a God who creates through speaking with his re-creating activity in justification. "It is God's 'nature' to create from nothing, to be a Creator who creates through his Word alone." God does not do that "straight down from heaven"—nor, it should be added, only by changing his disposition toward sinners in heaven and letting the word drift down—but "through other human beings, in a very creaturely way." Faith comes by hearing (Rom 10:17), hearing the gospel that is God's power (Rom 1:16), and God has commissioned his people to use his pronouncement of forgiveness, life and salvation as his instrument. In the mouths of believers God's Word becomes his re-creative deed.

That does not mean that his word of absolution, liberation and re-creation functions magically. Bayer reproduces Luther's understanding of God as the one who creates through communication and who has created the mystery of humanity in such a way that his human creatures are to be his conversation partners. The word of forgiveness creates, awakens and renews the community of trust and love

---

[45]Forde, *Justification by Faith*, pp. 1, 16.
[46]Forde, *Theologian of the Cross*, p. 1.
[47]Forde, *Theology*, p. 157.

between God's reborn child and himself.[48] The word of forgiveness functions as a promise, which Bayer's earliest work found as the focus of Luther's theology, a pledge from God that changes the reality of existence immediately, a guarantee of God's favor forever.[49] This gospel is God's power and his way of ruling, his kingdom. He exercises this rule or power by promising: not only as a pledge of future delivery of the Good but above all as an assurance that rests upon the word of the king. And it has immediate effect and validity.[50] That word of promise is a creative word, which establishes the new reality that this child of God belongs to him and is no longer a sinner, because God no longer regards him or her as a sinner. God's view of things, God's Word, determines reality. God stands by his word, his word of forgiveness.

JUSTIFICATION IS GOD'S KILLING AND HIS MAKING ALIVE

Third, these Lutheran expositors of justification make specific Luther's expression of the biblical teaching of justification in terms of dying and rising, God's killing and making alive or, in Härle's terminology, "breaking through the power of sin" and "constituting the person anew."[51] Werner Elert demonstrated that the term *rechtfertigen*, "to justify," had embraced a number of definitions in Luther's day, including "to do justice to," as did *dikaioō* in ancient Greek.[52] Employing Paul's baptismal terminology in Romans 6, Luther taught that the Word of the Lord brings sinners into the death and burial that sin necessitates, and then raises them up through the Word of life that comes as a gift from the cross in the sacrificed and risen Lord Jesus Christ (Rom 6:23).[53] In his *Justification by Faith* Forde called for a return to Luther's death-life language, not discarding the legal metaphor of judgment and pardon by any means, but enriching it as Luther did with the

---

[48]Bayer, *Aus Glauben leben*, pp. 41-45.

[49]Bayer, *Promssio, Geschichte der reformatorischen Wende in Luthers Theologie* (Göttingen: Vandenhoeck & Ruprecht, 1971). Bayer linked God's Word of gospel as promise with the faith that responds to and lives in the promise of God in Christ.

[50]Bayer, *Aus Glauben leben*, pp. 48-49.

[51]Härle, *Dogmatik*, pp. 500-505.

[52]Werner Elert, "Deutschrechtliche Züge in Luthers Rechtfertigungslehre," in *Ein Lehrer der Kirche, Kirchlich-theologische Aufsätze und Vorträge von Werner Elert*, ed. Max Keller-Hüschemenger (Berlin: Lutherisches Verlagshaus, 1967), pp. 23-31. Cf. Henry George Liddell and Robert Scott, *A Greek-English Lexicon*, rev. ed. (Oxford: Clarendon, 1958), p. 429.

[53]See Robert Kolb, "God Kills to Make Alive: Romans 6 and Luther's Understanding of Justification (1535)," *Lutheran Quarterly* 12, no. 1 (1998): 33-56. See also Forde, *Justification: A Matter of Death and Life*, pp. 21-38; cf. Forde, *Theology Is for Proclamation*, pp. 72-85, 119-33.

Pauline description of justification as the death of the sinner and the resurrection of the new creature in Christ, the reborn child of God.[54] Neither the dying nor the rising happens by human effort. Paul, Forde says, "doesn't argue the case. He doesn't lay on more law, insisting that we *ought* to die to sin or the law or to 'mortify' the flesh. He simply announces that we already have died," in 2 Corinthians 5:14 or in Galatians 2:19-21. This means salvation is not a repair job, not a smaller or larger alteration or improvement.[55] Justification is rebirth. Sinners disappear from God's sight, and we stand before him as his new creatures, his own children. That God's Word—as in Genesis, so in absolution—actually creates a new reality is the key to Forde's analysis. Thus, Forde breaks through the long-standing debate about whether justification is "forensic" or "effective." "The absolutely forensic character of justification renders it effective—justification actually kills and makes alive. It is, to be sure, 'not only' forensic, but that is the case only because the more forensic it is, the more effective it is!"[56] For "the death inflicted by the justifying word which reduces us to nothing is the *real* death, the true *spiritual* death, the death of sin, the death of all defiance against the God who 'will have mercy on whom he will have mercy.'" God's Word "*is* the death knell of the old and the harbinger of the absolutely new . . . the unconditional word, the promise, the declaration of justification is that which makes new, that which puts the old to rest and grants newness of life."[57] From God's execution of the sinner with Christ on the cross spring new creatures, faithful children of God, raised to new existence through their Lord's resurrection. Justification is not a fictive assertion, an "illusion of being 'as-if'" righteous. God's Word creates reality, and God's word of forgiveness creates the identity of being God's child, an identity which brings with it expectations of performance of God's will.[58]

DISTINGUISHING LAW AND GOSPEL

Fourth, Bayer, Forde and Härle also agree that the proper distinction and application of God's condemning law and God's life-restoring gospel is key to making the doctrine of justification function as God wants. That is not only a necessary corollary of understanding justification as dying as sinner and rising as new creature.

---

[54]Forde, *Justification by Faith*, pp. 3, 11-12.
[55]Ibid., pp. 11, 17.
[56]Ibid., p. 36; cf. Bayer, *Aus Glauben leben*, p. 41, and Baur, *Salus Christiana*, pp. 61-63.
[57]Forde, *Justification by Faith*, pp. 37-38.
[58]Baur, *Salus christiana*, pp. 63-65.

It also flows naturally from the distinction of two kinds of righteousness. For the performance of the law never did qualify as a way to life. The first commandment demands more than performance; it demands faithfulness to God. "The law that not only demands a new way of doing things but finally a new being in the human creature precludes the realization of its content by means of its form as law."[59] It only evaluates, and it has but two standards: kept or not kept. Not kept means sin, and sin pays its wage fairly. Sinners must die.[60]

"The proper distinction of law and gospel" may be called a hermeneutical principle to guide preachers, but on a deeper level it is a summary of God's saving action, the critical step in his application of the death and resurrection of Christ to his chosen people. Because the evil of human beings' breaking faith with God permeates all of human existence, there is no fixing, no superficial healing for the patient. Sinners must die at the hand of God's good plan for human life, his law. Noting that Luther had begun his theses on the theology of the cross, presented at Heidelberg in 1518, by calling the law of God "the most salutary doctrine of life," Forde paraphrases Luther's twenty-third thesis from those theses: "The law does not work the love of God, it works wrath; it does not give life . . . it kills; it does not bless, it curses; it does not comfort, it accuses; it does not grant mercy, it judges. In sum, it condemns everything not in Christ."[61] Proclaiming law and then proclaiming gospel is the final task of Christian preaching of God's Word. Forde comments, "The final task is to *do* the story to the hearers in such a way that they are incorporated into the story itself, killed and made alive by the hearing of it. The hearers are to be claimed by the story."[62] The story is that coincidence of opposites that constitutes the recital of God's saving act of the cross and empty tomb. "God does his alien and wrathful work before he does his proper and loving work; he makes alive by killing, brings to heaven by going through hell, brings forth mercy out of wrath."[63] It was the breakthrough to understanding that his fundamental identity, the core of his person, existed only because of God's mercy that allowed Luther to refocus his life from himself to his Lord Jesus Christ and to his neighbors and their needs. Therefore, he spoke of justification, when he came to writing his first major treatise on the subject, as the "freedom of the

[59]Härle, *Dogmatik*, p. 160.
[60]Forde, *Justification by Faith*, p. 13.
[61]WA 1:354, pp. 25-26; LW 31:41.
[62]Forde, *Theologian of the Cross*, pp. 13-14.
[63]Ibid., p. 31.

Christian." Freed from the voice of the law's condemnation and the sin upon which that condemnation was based, and liberated from the need for self-preoccupation under the gospel, he could act humanely because God had restored the heart of his humanity. Luther's discovery of the distinction of law and gospel freed him from his captivity to guilt and to his delusion of being able to justify himself and freed him for truly human living.[64] For it enabled him to distinguish God's condemnation of his failure to be all that he could be from God's creative restoration of his humanity through Christ's swallowing up of Luther's sin and condemnation into his own death and resurrection.

Luther took seriously the continuing presence of sin and evil in the world and in the lives of God's chosen and faith-filled children. Therefore, he maintained the necessity of the continuing of both the call to repentance, to dying daily to sin, and of the assurance of salvation in the promise and pronouncement of the forgiveness of sins, which he regarded as life and salvation.

BY FAITH ALONE

Fifth, this repentance centers on the return to faith, which is the orientation and nature of the entire human creature, not simply a set of psychological characteristics. Luther's "by faith alone" is not a human work or accomplishment, as if he had found in theology what he could not find in monastic exertion, a shortcut to heaven. For trusting is not an accomplishment we perform. Psychologically speaking, the trustworthy elicit our trust. They do not force or compel it. Their trustworthiness creates it. When the Creator is doing the creating, faith is beyond all our attempts at explaining how trust comes to be psychologically. The Holy Spirit moves human minds and wills in ways that we can describe partially with social-scientific vocabulary. But ultimately the mystery of the conversion of sinners defies our efforts at analysis. God creates the trust that constitutes the believer's very being by promising life in Christ, a promise unshakable and therefore trust-creating. Forde hears God answering the "age-old question, 'What shall I do to be saved?' " with "Nothing! Just be still; shut up and listen for once in your life to what God the Almighty, creator and redeemer, is saying to his world and to you in the death and resurrection of his Son! Listen and believe!" What that means is that "the faith by which one is justified is not an active verb of which the Old Adam or Eve is the subject, it is a state-of-being verb. Faith is the state of being grasped by the uncon-

---

[64]Bayer, *Rechtfertigung*, p. 17, quoting a "Table Talk," WA Tischreden #5518, 5:210, pp. 12-16.

ditional claim and promise of the God who calls into being that which is from that which is not. . . . It is death and resurrection." That, Forde comments, "dislodges everyone from the saddle."[65] And it places God's children right in the middle of life and of all the activities God designed for their lives. "The faith born of the unconditional promise finds a new world opening up—in which God's creation is given back as sheer gift—the world of the other, the world of the neighbor, where 'great and genuine' works are to be done *because it is God's will*. Once one has been cured of all heaven-storming ambitions one suddenly finds God's *creation* to care about and for."[66] Forde quotes Luther's "Preface to Romans": "Faith is a divine work in us which changes us and births us anew out of God (John I:I3) and kills the old Adam, makes us into entirely different people from the heart, soul, mind, and all powers, and brings the Holy Spirit with it. Oh, it is a living, busy, active, mighty thing, this faith, so it is impossible that it should not do good."[67]

Thus, faith makes all the difference in the world in daily life, beginning with the modern self's preoccupation with itself. Bayer finds that "faith takes place as a liberation from the compulsion to secure one's own life, and thereby it is a liberation from uncertainty. It takes place as a liberation from the compulsion to search for my own identity and to find my own identity."[68] All of life is changed when faith can direct itself to its final goal, the resurrection of the dead and eternal life, that is to say, to the risen Savior.[69]

RIGHTEOUS AND SINFUL AT THE SAME TIME

Sixth, each of the authors interprets the life of the Christian from the standpoint of Luther's observation that believers are totally righteous in God's sight but experience life as thoroughly infected by sinfulness, his famous "*simul justus et peccator*" description of the mystery of the continuation of evil in the believer's life. Härle notes that Luther's understanding of this phrase embraces two distinct points, both of which are important for understanding and living the life of Christian discipleship. Believers are totally righteous because their righteousness rests on God's perfect gift, on his Word, which does not fail. That is a confession of the gospel of Christ. At the same time they experience the imperfection and incompleteness of

---

[65]Forde, *Justifiction by Faith*, pp. 22-23. Cf. Härle, *Dogmatik*, pp. 161-62, 511-16.

[66]Ibid., p. 58. See Forde's elaboration of this in *Theology Is for Proclamation*, pp. 137-41.

[67]Forde, *Justification by Faith*, p. 55; cf. WA Deutsche Bibel 7:11, pp. 6-10, LW 35:370.

[68]Bayer, *Aus Glauben leben*, p. 28.

[69]Ibid., p. 33. Bayer developed this concept of faith in his earliest work; see his *Promissio*.

every attempt at doing good because the law assesses their performance in all its severity. Luther wished to provide the comfort and assurance of Christ's gospel when he created the paradoxical statement that believers are fully righteous by virtue of God's saying so at the same time they experience the secondary reality of their own failure to be in every regard the creature God made them to be. To be sure, believers also see themselves as partially righteous and partially sinful when they use God's plan for human life to assess how they are serving the Lord by serving their neighbors. But they are to grasp the comfort of God's word of forgiveness when they despair because of their continued struggle with sin.[70]

The believer is driven to repentance by acknowledging his or her sinfulness and continuing to struggle with the evil inside. Luther's Ninety-five Theses began with the observation that the whole life of the believer is a life of repentance.[71] He may have come to understand those words more fully later, but already here, in 1517, he recognized that the mystery of the continuation of evil in the lives of God's children necessitates a daily return to God's justifying action of putting to death sin and raising up the new creature in Christ.

GOD'S JUSTIFICATION OF SINNERS AS THEODICY

Seventh, this mystery of the continuation of evil in believers' lives, and the question regarding evil's existence behind it, raises to a greater or lesser extent for each of these three authors the issue of theodicy, which they see implicit, though not explicit, in Luther's formulation of justification because it is implicit in biblical revelation. Bayer asserts "the world is not in tune, not harmonious, but it sounds 'like a cracked bell.' . . . Therefore, the question of 'theodicy' arises, the 'legal battle over God.' " Therefore "all 'reality' is a battle of justifications."[72] God justifies himself, Bayer maintains, by restoring sinners to righteousness, returning them to paradise.[73] Luther's concept of the Hidden God prevents him from pursuing the question of evil in hopes of forging an explanation that permits the theologian to be in charge of the issue. Faith clings to the Revealed God, who has placed himself in the heart of human evil by suffering death on the cross, who has shaken the foundations of evil and announced its defeat in his resurrection. The Word from the cross, weak and foolish though it seems (1 Cor 1:18—2:16), restores the human creature

---

[70]Härle, *Dogmatik*, pp. 163-64.
[71]WA 1:233, pp. 10-11; LW 31:25.
[72]Bayer, *Aus Glauben leben*, pp. 14, 16.
[73]Ibid., p. 23.

to the relationship God designed for humanity, and in so doing God provides the only justification of himself he deems he needs. It is a justification also by the faith of the believers, for the assurance of God's saving will and action in Jesus Christ provides neither proof nor logical validation.[74] It is not an explanation that gives us mastery over the question of why evil exists if God is good and almighty. But the question that comes from the mouths of all human beings is the question that Jesus shared with us at the end, "My God, my God, why have you forsaken me?" For that question Jesus gives us himself, not an explanation, as the answer. "We can only die *with him* and await God's answer in him."[75] Härle and Bayer both resort to Luther's confession of faith at the end of *On the Bondage of the Will*, in which he reviews answers to the question of God's righteousness in the face of the human experience of evil. He finally concludes with Job (Job 38—42) and with Paul (Rom 11:33-36) that God alone is righteous. That is because he is God. That is because he has been experienced as the Creator who liberates and redeems, that is justifies. That is because he has created human beings apart from their own merit and worthiness and because he has restored them to his favor apart from their own reason and strength.[76]

LIVING BY FAITH IN LOVE FOR GOD AND THE NEIGHBOR

Finally, each author wrestles with the impact of God's act of justification for daily Christian life, in the living out of his will in new obedience. Luther believed that God's plan for his human creatures is, in Forde's words, "down to earth."[77] "Faith in life is exercised in death: faith not in some pious never-never land, the quintessence of our religious ambitions or self-preservation, but faith in God's creation, where his will is done *for his sake* until he at last brings down the curtain and perfects all things."[78] Bayer points out that the separation of justification and sanctification, as the believer's living out of the new life God has given, is foreign to Luther's thought. He regarded "sanctification" as God's doing, the work of the Holy Spirit in human lives. In his Small Catechism he placed mention of the human performance that God set into his expectation at creation and restored human creatures

---

[74]Ibid., pp. 63-68.
[75]Forde, *Theologian of the Cross*, p. 3. Cf. the wide-ranging and thorough discussion of Härle, *Dogmatik*, pp. 439-455, and the treatment in Robert Kolb, "Luther on the Theology of the Cross," *Lutheran Quarterly* 16 (2002): 443-66.
[76]WA 18:784, 1-785, p. 38; LW 33:289-92.
[77]Gerhard O. Forde, *Where God Meets Man, Luther's Down-to-Earth Approach to the Gospel* (Minneapolis: Augsburg, 1972), esp. pp. 18-31.
[78]Forde, *Justification by Faith*, p. 59. Cf. Härle, *Dogmatik*, pp. 162-63, 516-32.

to accomplish through Christ's redeeming work, into the first and second articles of the Creed, not the third. The explanation to the third article speaks of the Holy Spirit's creation and sustenance of faith that leads to the fruits of that faith in carrying out God's will and plan for human life. God's justifying word of the gospel impels believers into the performance of God's expectations for their whole lives because they find their new identity in God's gift to them of Christ's death and resurrection. They live out this identity within the structures God designed and created for human life in the fundamental form or situations of life, in family, economic activity, political and social institutions, and their religious communities.[79] The promise of God in Christ produces results that the description of God's expectations for life cannot.

> It might impel toward the works of the law, the motions of love, but in the end they will become irksome and will all too often lead to hate. If we go up to someone on the street, grab them by the lapels and say, "Look here, you're supposed to love me!" the person may grudgingly admit that we are right, but it won't work. The results will likely be just the opposite from what our "law" demands. Law is indeed right, but it simply cannot realize what it points to. So it works wrath.[80]

Recognizing that we are justified alone by God's grace puts a new perspective on all of life. Believers no longer regard themselves as "condemned to success," but rather are content to put God's world in God's hands. Freed from the burden of justifying themselves by making their own lives and the lives of others turn out right, they can devote themselves to loving their neighbors with a focus on their neighbors' needs, not on their own righteousness nor on God's approving or disapproving but ever watchful eye. That means that they need not know what God is up to in the course of the events in which he has called them to serve. They simply serve, as his faithful servants and as true, faithful companions and accompanists of those whom God has placed within their reach. For as Luther said in his 1520 treatise *On the Freedom of the Christian*, those who have been freed from all the enemies of the sinner—Satan, sin, death and condemnation of God's law—are bound to love their neighbor,[81] or in Bayer's words, they are "freed for servanthood." This servanthood is not exercised in any tension with the question of how sinners become righteous but evolves naturally out of God's justification of sinners, God's total re-

---

[79]Bayer, *Aus Glauben leben*, pp. 54-57.
[80]Forde, *Theologian of the Cross*, pp. 107-8.
[81]WA 7:20-38, pp. 49-73; LW 31:333-37.

sponsibility for their being restored to their original righteousness. Because reality proceeds from God's Word, the Old Testament tradition that defines the order of the world as faithfulness within the community is brought to its completion in the love that faith practices in fulfilling God's commands.[82]

Although any attempt to summarize the twentieth-century Lutheran understandings of the justification of the sinner will be incomplete,[83] these eight theses have posited the central elements of the "radical" Lutheran understanding of justification. Its concerns are well summarized in the concluding words of Bayer's *Aus dem Glauben leben*. Those who ask in the midst of what Bayer calls "the battle of the justifications" about the foundation of their lives hear that everything is without a reason or foundation in themselves. The justification of their existence is a freely given gift, and they do not have to provide a foundation for their own lives and justify themselves. Life is "grounded and justified by God alone in his Word of love that is free and without foundation" in human performance or achievement. This Word "promises fellowship, fellowship through death itself, without obligation and without condition. Only through this promise does creation out of nothing take place, the justification of the godless, the resurrection of the dead. God's promise enables living by faith."[84]

---

[82]Bayer, *Aus Glauben leben*, pp. 35-40. Bayer also accents the idea that justification is and produces the freedom of the Christian for love and service in *Rechtfertigung*, pp. 14-19.

[83]This summary has even failed to do justice to certain aspects of the treatment of these three authors, for instance, in its presentation of their view of sin or of the means of grace, or of the connections between justification by faith and the definition of the church, or between justification and Christian responsibility in the world, or of the eschatological setting of Luther's teaching. Each of these topics deserves treatment as well.

[84]Bayer, *Aus Glauben leben*, p. 71.

7

THE DOCTRINE OF JUSTIFICATION

Historic Wesleyan and Contemporary Understandings

KENNETH J. COLLINS

The doctrine of justification by faith is soundly rooted in Scripture, especially in the writings of the apostle Paul, and it has received considerable treatment in the works of the early church fathers.[1] During the Middle Ages, however, a number of teachings and practices of the Roman Catholic Church, in particular the well-worked penitential system, detracted from both the substance and clarity of this crucial doctrine with some very unfortunate results. Faced with this predicament, in which consciences were left in an anxious state and where the peace and assurance of the gospel were not enjoyed, Luther not only boldly restored this doctrine to its preeminence, but he also developed the implicatory relations of justification by faith with respect to other key Christian doctrines and in a way that marked one of its most significant explications.

Though the contributions of key Protestant Reformers such as Luther in Wittenberg, Calvin in Geneva and Zwingli in Zurich are well known and celebrated, what is less appreciated, perhaps, is the careful articulation of the doctrine of justification by faith that occurred at Canterbury. This other major wing of the Reformation is not only critical in coming to a carefully nuanced understanding of this doctrine, where English sensibilities and reasoning hold sway, but the exploration of this wing is also required in order to assess the thought of John Wesley who, interestingly enough, became one of the greatest champions of *sola fide* on English soil.

---

[1]See the argument developed in Thomas C. Oden, *The Justification Reader* (Grand Rapids: Eerdmans, 2002).

The Anglican Context

Thomas Cranmer, the Archbishop of Canterbury during the reigns of both Henry
VIII and Edward VI, guided the English church during its reform by composing
the *Book of Common Prayer*, based in part on the earlier Sarum Missal, by producing
the Forty-Two Articles of Religion, later reduced to Thirty-Nine during the reign
of Elizabeth I, and by writing suitable homilies. In the "Homily on Salvation," for
example, perhaps Cranmer's most famous, he considers what constitutes the substance of justification in the following way:

> In these foresaid places the apostle toucheth specially three things, which must con-
> cur and go together in our justification: upon God's part, his great mercy and grace;
> upon Christ's part, justice, that is, the satisfaction of God's justice, or price of our
> redemption, by the offering of his body and shedding of his blood, with fulfilling of
> the law perfectly and thoroughly; and upon our part, true and lively faith in the mer-
> its of Jesus Christ, which yet is not ours, but by God's working in us.[2]

Beyond this, this English leader specifically affirms the *sola fide* language of the
Continental Reformers when he observes: "What can be spoken more plainly
than to say, that freely without works, by faith *only*, we obtain remission of our
sins."[3] And again the Archbishop points out elsewhere in this same homily that
"We put our faith in Christ, that we be justified by him only . . . and by no virtue
or good work of our own that is in us . . . Christ himself only being the cause
meritorious thereof."[4] Moreover, these same emphases are succinctly expressed in
Article XI of the historic Anglican Thirty-Nine Articles in language that was
originally penned by Cranmer in its earlier formulation. Article XI, to illustrate,
reads as follows:

> We are accounted righteous before God, only for the merit of our Lord and Saviour
> Jesus Christ by Faith, and not for our own works or deservings. Wherefore, that we

---

[2] John Edmund Cox, ed., *Miscellaneous Writings and Letters of Thomas Cranmer* (Vancouver, B.C.: Regent College Publishing, n.d.), p. 129.
[3] Ibid., pp. 130-31. Emphasis added.
[4] Ibid., p. 132. Alister McGrath makes the claim that although Cranmer clearly states the doctrine of
justification *per solam fidem* in an "Orthodox Melanchthonian sense," the crucial concept of the imputed righteousness of Christ is absent. Though McGrath's judgment in this context is accurate, it
nevertheless appears that the concept of the imputation of the righteousness of Christ is implied in
this sermon especially when Cranmer states, "for man [being a sinner] cannot justify himself by his
own works neither in part, nor in the whole." See Alister McGrath, *Iustitia Dei: A History of the Christian
Doctrine of Justification from 1500 to the Present Day* (Cambridge: Cambridge University Press, 1986), p.
289; and Cox, ed., *Miscellaneous Writings*, p. 131.

are justified by Faith only, is a most wholesome Doctrine, and very full of comfort, as more largely is expressed in the Homily of Justification.[5]

Despite these common affirmations, some different emphases can be found in Cranmer's teaching, when compared, for example, to that of the Continental Reformers, simply because by the time of the writing of the "Homily on Salvation" and the Article on Justification the English Church had already become apprized of the dangers of *solafidianism*, a perversion of the doctrine of *sola fide* that could easily issue in quietism, or worse yet, in outright antinomianism. Not surprisingly, then, in this significant and often read homily Cranmer underscores the importance of having a sincere and lively faith and he accordingly celebrates both the repentance antecedent to as well as the good works which flow from such a faith. To illustrate, in terms of repentance the Archbishop exclaims, "And yet that faith doth not exclude repentance, hope, love, dread, and the fear of God, to be joined with faith in every man that is justified," but he immediately adds, clarifying his meaning, "but it excludeth them from the office of justifying."[6] And in terms of good works Cranmer observes in a way that epitomizes much of subsequent Anglican theology, "And as Christ undoubtedly affirmeth that true faith bringeth forth good works, so doth he say likewise of charity: 'Whosoever hath my commandments and keepeth them, that is he that loveth me.' "[7] For this English Reformer, then, though sinners are justified by faith alone, it is by a faith that is never alone.

Richard Hooker, Anglican divine and author of *The Laws of Ecclesiastical Polity*,[8] was one of the chief apologists of the Anglican way during the reign of Elizabeth I. Facing Rome, on the one hand, and Geneva, on the other, Hooker skillfully articulated a *via media* that was moderate in its orientation and yet very much a part of the reform of the English church. This erstwhile fellow of Corpus Christi College, Oxford, took exception to the Roman Catholic notion that justification must entail an infusion of a "habit of grace" to produce an inherent righteousness within humanity.[9] In Hooker's judgment such a view was very

---

[5]Philip Schaff, *The Creeds of Christendom* (Grand Rapids: Baker, 1983), 3:494.

[6]Ibid., p. 129. Alan Clifford points out that when Cranmer affirms that *sola fide* takes away all merit of our works, this statement must be understood as indicative not of a psychological state but of the merits of Christ. See Alan C. Clifford, "The Gospel and Justification," *The Evangelical Quarterly* 57 (1985): 247-67.

[7]Ibid., p. 139. For an excellent biography on Cranmer, which is attentive to many of his theological themes, see Diarmaid MacCulloch, *Thomas Cranmer* (New Haven, Conn.: Yale University Press, 1996).

[8]Richard Hooker, *Ecclesiastical Polity*, ed. Ronald Bayne, 5 vols. (New York: E. P. Dutton, 1922-1925).

[9]McGrath, *Iustitia Dei*, p. 290.

troubling, even confused, for it made something other than the merits of Christ the basis for justification, thereby confounding the issues of sanctification and justification.

During the seventeenth century, several of the Caroline divines such as Lancelot Andrews and Bishop Thomas Ken articulated an understanding of justification that was remarkably similar to that of later Lutheran Orthodoxy.[10] Moreover, these English divines affirmed that the principle of sinners justified by faith is fully compatible with not only a vigorous employment of the means of grace (in response, of course, to the prevenient grace of God) as conduits through which justifying grace would be received but also the necessity of works after justification as evidence of a lively faith, even a faith that works by love[11]—emphases already encountered in Cranmer. However, a difference that does indeed emerge in this seventeenth-century context is that several of the Caroline divines reversed the roles of faith and works as they pertained to the important matter of Christian assurance. For these leaders, as Chamberlain aptly points out, "works became the principal means of assurance, and the testimony of the Holy Spirit receded into the background, as a relatively minor ground for security."[12]

This emphasis on works, always a part of the Anglican witness, unfortunately lost much of its balance and nuance at the hands of John Tillotson who became the Archbishop of Canterbury in 1691. To illustrate, in his sermon "Of the Nature of Regeneration, and its Necessity, in order to Justification and Salvation," the Archbishop not only develops the notion of a final justification before the throne of Christ, but he also comes "perilously close to advocating justification by works."[13] Indeed, the writings of Tillotson, along with those of Bishop George Bull, were pointedly criticized later on by such Oxford Methodists as George Whitefield and John Wesley, who both read the Anglican Reformation heritage far differently than some of its celebrated seventeenth-century exponents.

---

[10]Ibid., p. 295.

[11]Henry R. McAdoo, *The Spirit of Anglicanism: a Survey of Anglican Theological Method in the Seventeenth Century* (London: A. & C. Black, 1965), pp. 320-36. See also P. E. More and F. L. Cross, *Anglicanism: The Thought and Practice of the Church of England, Illustrated From the Religious Literature of the Seventeenth Century* (London: SPCK, 1957).

[12]Jeffrey S. Chamberlain, "Moralism, Justification, and the Controversy over Methodism," *Journal of Ecclesiastical History* 44, no. 4 (October 1993): 668.

[13]Ibid., p. 673.

JOHN WESLEY, MORAVIANISM AND THE ANGLICAN HERITAGE

The early biographical details of John Wesley's life indicate quite clearly that he had confused the issues of justification and sanctification and had sought to make some measure of obedience or willfulness in the form of rule and resolution the basis upon which he would receive the forgiveness of sins. Looking back on this fault in his treatise *A Farther Appeal*, produced in 1744, Wesley elaborates:

> I was ordained Deacon in 1725, and Priest in the year following. But it was many years after this before I was convinced of the great truths above recited. During all that time I was utterly ignorant of the nature and condition of justification. Sometimes I confounded it with sanctification; (particularly when I was in Georgia).[14]

In a real sense, Wesley was predisposed to such thinking by the understanding and practice of his own Anglican church. For example, in 1730 Wesley wrote to his mother, Susanna, that what he had liked in Bishop Jeremy Taylor's *Rules for Holy Dying* was his "account of the pardon of sins which is the clearest I ever met with: 'Pardon of sins in the gospel *is* sanctification.' "[15] And about a year and a half after his evangelical conversion at Aldersgate, Wesley complained to his brother Samuel Jr., "I fear you *dissent* from the fundamental Articles of the Church of England. I know Bishop Bull does. I doubt you do not hold justification by faith alone."[16] In fact, a couple of years later Wesley's criticism of the teaching of Bishop Bull, culled from the latter's *Harmonica Apostolica*, was remarkably incisive: "The position which he sets out is this, 'That *all good works*, and *not faith alone*, are the necessary previous *condition of justification.*' "[17] Moreover, in a letter to William Green late in his career, in 1789 to be exact, Wesley observes that the habit of the English clergy is to place sanctification before justification with the result that the holy life becomes the basis upon which one is justified.[18]

---

[14]Gerald R. Cragg, ed., *The Works of John Wesley*, vol. 11, *The Appeals to Men of Reason and Religion* (New York: Oxford University Press, 1975), 11:176.

[15]Frank Baker, ed., *The Works of John Wesley*, vols. 25-26, *The Letters* (New York: Oxford University Press, 1982), 25:245. Emphasis added.

[16]Ibid., 25:600. Later in life John Wesley was less critical of some of the teachings of Bishop Bull. And while the Methodist leader remained firm in his conviction of justification by faith alone, he nevertheless began to appreciate, on some level, Bishop Bull's notion of a second justification. See John Telford, ed., *The Letters of John Wesley, A.M.*, 8 vols. (London: Epworth, 1931), 5:264.

[17]Reginald W. Ward, and Richard P. Heitzenrater, eds., *The Works of John Wesley*, vol. 19, *Journals and Diaries II* (Nashville: Abingdon, 1988), pp. 202-3.

[18]Telford, *Letters of John Wesley*, 8:178-79. Although at least by the mid 1740s Wesley affirmed that there are two justifications, present justification and that which is to occur at the last day, his concern in this present context is only with the former. Cf. Cragg, *Appeals*, 11:105.

By the mercy and providence of God, Wesley's introduction to the graciousness of the gospel, that justification is a sheer gift indicative of the divine favor, came at the hands of Peter Böhler, a young Moravian missionary who had
been greatly influenced by Luther. Indeed, Böhler explored the *nature* of saving
faith in greater detail with Wesley by pointing out, in a very pietistic fashion,
the two fruits which are inseparable from it, namely: holiness (freedom from
sin) and happiness (the peace and joy which emerge from a sense of forgiveness). That is, Böhler, like Arndt, Spener and Francke before him, connected
saving faith not simply with justification and juridical change, but with regeneration and participatory change as well,[19] a teaching that was consonant with
the Anglican emphasis of a lively faith. Wesley searched his Greek Testament
to see if this doctrine was of God, and by the end of April 1738, when he met
Böhler again, he had no objection to what the young Moravian said concerning the nature of saving faith, that it is "a sure trust and confidence which a
man hath in God, that through the merits of Christ *his* sins are forgiven, and
he reconciled to the favour of God."[20] But what Wesley still could not compre-
hend was how could this faith be instantaneous, given in a moment, as Böhler
had suggested. Again, Wesley consulted the Bible and to his surprise he found
"scarce any instances there of other than *instantaneous* conversions—scarce any
other so slow as that of St. Paul."[21] But it was not until after Wesley was faced
with the evidence of several living witnesses that he forthrightly confessed,
"Here ended my disputing. I could now only cry out, 'Lord, help thou my un-

---

[19]For more on the influence of Pietism on the life and thought of John Wesley, Cf. F. Ernest
Stoeffler, "Pietism, the Wesleys and Methodist Beginnings in America," in *Continental Pietism
and Early American Christianity*, ed. F. Ernest Stoeffler (Grand Rapids: Eerdmans, 1976), pp.
184-221; Kenneth J. Collins, "The Influence of Early German Pietism on John Wesley [Arndt
and Francke]," *The Covenant Quarterly* 48 (November 1990): 23-42; Dale W. Brown, "The Wesleyan Revival From a Pietist Perspective," *Wesleyan Theological Journal* 24 (1989): 7-17. Sir Percy
Scott, *John Wesleys Lehre von der Heiligung vergleichen mit einen lutherish-pietistischen Beispel* [John Wesley's
Doctrine of Salvation Compared with a Lutheran-pietistic Example] (Berlin: Alfred Topel-
man, 1939).
[20]Ward and Heitzenrater, *Journals and Diaries*, 18:233-34. On April 1, 1738, while Wesley was at Mr.
Fox's society, his heart was "so full," as he put it, that he could not "confine [himself] to the forms
of prayer, which we were accustomed to use there. Neither do I purpose to be confined to them any
more, but to pray indifferently, with a form or without, as I may find suitable to particular occa-
sions." Cf. Ward and Heitzenrater, *Journals and Diaries*, 18:233.
[21]Ibid., 18:234. Wesley heard the experiences of Mrs. Fox and Mr. Hutchins (of Pembroke College)
"two living witnesses that God can (at least, if he does not always) give that faith whereof cometh
salvation in a moment, as lightening falling from heaven." Cf. ibid., 18:235.

belief.' "[22] Southey, the great biographer of Wesley, was simply incredulous at this point. "Is it possible," he asked, "that a man of Wesley's acuteness should have studied the Scriptures as he had studied them till the age of thirty-five, without perceiving that the conversions which they record are instantaneous?"[23]

Interestingly enough, Charles Wesley, John's younger poetic brother, after reading Luther's *Commentary on Galatians* in May 1738 (having been introduced to this classic by William Holland, a member of the Church of England who was affiliated with the Moravians), confessed with some puzzlement in his journal, "Who would believe our Church had been founded on this important article of justification by faith alone? I am astonished I should ever think this a new doctrine; especially while our Articles and Homilies stand un-repealed, and the key of knowledge is not taken away."[24] In fact, though both John and Charles Wesley had come to a proper understanding of justification by faith alone through the good graces of the witness of Peter Böhler and the writings of Martin Luther (John in terms of Luther's *Preface to the Epistle of Romans*; Charles in terms of his *Commentary on Galatians*), they both nevertheless explicated this teaching using the significant resources of their own Anglican Church, especially after John had returned from the Moravian community at Herrnhut in the fall of 1738 and began "more narrowly to inquire what the doctrine of the Church of England is concerning the much controverted point of justification by faith. And the sum of what I found in the Homilies I extracted and printed for the use of others."[25]

WESLEY'S DOCTRINE OF JUSTIFICATION

When Wesley explored the nature of justification in his work *The Principles of a Methodist*, produced in 1742, he did so, once again, by quoting the resources of his own Anglican Church, in particular Cranmer's "Homily on Salvation," material cited

---

[22]Ibid. At the time Böhler wrote of Wesley, "He is a poor sinner, who has a broken heart and who hungers after a better righteousness than that which he has had up till now, namely after the righteousness which is in the blood of Jesus Christ." Cf. Martin Schmidt, *John Wesley: A Theological Biography*, 2 vols. (Nashville: Abingdon, 1962-1973), I:243.

[23]Robert Southey, *The Life of Wesley; and Rise and Progress of Methodism*, vol. I (London: Longman, Brown, Green, and Longmans, 1846), p. 134.

[24]Thomas Jackson, ed., *The Journals of Rev. Charles Wesley*, 2 vols. (London: John Mason, 1849; reprint, Grand Rapids: Baker, 1980), I:88 (May 17, 1738).

[25]Ward and Heitzenrater, *Journals and Diaries*, 19:21.

earlier but in a different context:

> I believe three things must go together in our justification: upon God's part, his great
> mercy and grace; upon Christ's part, the satisfaction of God's justice by the offering
> his body and shedding his blood, 'and fulfilling the law of God perfectly'; and upon
> our part, true and living faith in the merits of Jesus Christ.[26]

Since the notion of a twofold justification had been a part of the Anglican witness, in the writings of Bull and Tillotson, for instance, Wesley made it clear in
a letter to Thomas Church a few years later in 1745 "that the justification which
is spoken of by St. Paul to the Romans and in our Articles is *not twofold*. It is one,
and no more. It is the present remission of our sins, or our first acceptance with
God."[27] By making this distinction Wesley underscored the graciousness of God
and maintained that the forgiveness of sins received by sinners is nothing less
than a sheer, unmerited gift, and therefore could never be on the basis of their
own working in the least.

One of the best windows into Wesley's teaching on justification by faith is found
in his sermon by the same name produced the following year in 1746. In this work,
the Methodist leader makes a distinction that is not only typical of the Continental
Reformation, especially the later Lutheran tradition, but one that again maintains
the graciousness of the gospel by viewing justification as a forensic act by the Most
High. That is, sinners who have no righteousness of their own are nevertheless *declared* righteous on the basis of the atoning work of Christ. Accordingly, Wesley affirms that justification is not "the being made actually just and righteous. This is
sanctification; which is indeed in some degree the immediate fruit of justification, but
nevertheless is a distinct gift of God."[28] And Wesley keeps these doctrines separate,
conceptually if not in practice, by making a distinction between the work that God
does "for us" (justification) and the work that the Most High does "in us" (initial
sanctification) as demonstrated in his later sermon, "The New Birth." In this work
he writes:

---

[26]Rupert E. Davies, *The Works of John Wesley*, vol. 9, *The Methodist Societies: History, Nature, and Design* (Nashville: Abingdon, 1989), p. 51.

[27]Telford, *Letters*, 2:191. See also Wesley's *A Farther Appeal* in which he writes: "First: the nature of justification. It sometimes means our acquittal at the last day. But this is altogether out of the present
question—that justification whereof our Articles and Homilies speak, [means] present forgiveness,
pardon of sins, and consequently acceptance with God . . ." See Cragg, *The Appeals*, 11:105.

[28]Albert C. Outler, ed., *The Works of John Wesley*, vols. 1-4, *The Sermons* (Nashville: Abingdon, 1984),
1:186.

If any doctrines within the whole compass of Christianity may be properly termed fundamental they are doubtless these two—the doctrine of justification, and that of the new birth: the former relating to that great work which God does *for us,* in forgiving our sins; the latter to the great work which God does *in us,* in renewing our fallen nature.[29]

Elsewhere Wesley teaches that justification entails a relative change, but sanctification a real one: "The former changes our outward relation to God, so that of enemies we become children; by the latter our inmost souls are changed so that of sinners we become saints."[30] The one takes away the guilt of sin by declaring sinners to be righteous; the other removes its power.

Moreover, though justification is a forensic act, this declaration is neither a legal fiction, as some critics from the Roman Catholic Church had vainly charged, nor does it imply that God is deceived with respect to those who are justified; "that he thinks them to be what in fact they are not, that he accounts them to be otherwise than they are . . . or [that he] believes [them to be] righteous when [they] are unrighteous."[31] Put another way, God simply does not judge those who are justified contrary to the real nature of things, nor does the Most High confound them with Christ. Justification, then, is not a matter of sinners remaining in the guilt of their sins while they are considered to be righteousness. Wesley explains:

The judgment of the all-wise God is always according to truth. Neither can it ever consist with his unerring wisdom to think that I am innocent, to judge that I am righteous or holy, because another is so. He can no more in this manner confound me with Christ than with David or Abraham.[32]

For Wesley, justification means pardon, the forgiveness of past sins. "It is that act of

[29]Ibid., 2:187.

[30]Ibid., 1:431-32. For some helpful studies on Wesley's doctrine of justification, see G. Clinton Walker, "John Wesley's Doctrine of Justification in Relation to Two Classical Anglican Theologians: Richard Hooker and Lancelot Andrewes" (Ph.D. diss., Baylor University, 1993), David Lowes Watson, "Justification by Faith and Wesley's Evangelistic Message," *Wesleyan Theological Journal* 21, no. 1 and 2 (1986): 7-23; and Erich Von Eicken, "Rechtfertigung Und Heiligung Bei Wesley Dargestellt Unter Vergleichung Mit Anschauungen Luthers Und Des Luthertums" (Ph.D. diss., Heidelberg, 1934).

[31]Ibid., 1:188. Bracketed material added.

[32]Ibid. In his notes on *Romans* 4:5, Wesley indicates that God can justify the sinner and yet remain "just and true to all his attributes." That is, Christ satisfies the justice of God, sin is remitted, and the great work of inward sanctification begins. Cf. Wesley, *NT Notes 2,* p. 371 (Rom 4:5) and compare with the decree of the Council of Trent on justification found in Philip Schaff, ed., *The Creeds of Christendom,* 3 vols. (Grand Rapids: Baker, 1983), 2:94.

God the Father," he asserts, "whereby, for the sake of the propitiation made by the blood of his Son, he 'showeth forth his righteousness by the remission of sins that are past.' "[33] Observe in this definition that there are three elements of special significance. First of all, notice that justification is based on the atoning work of Christ, on the "propitiation made by the blood of his Son." Indeed, Wesley explores this sacrificial idea, in concert with other variables, in his treatise *The Principles of a Methodist*, written earlier in 1742, and concludes "that in our justification there is not only God's mercy and grace, but his justice also,"[34] a justice amply displayed in the sacrificial death of Christ. Moreover, Wesley demonstrates the importance of righteousness with respect to justification when he observes, "And so the grace of God does not shut out the righteousness of God in our justification, but only shuts out the righteousness of man, that is the righteousness of our works."[35] In fact, a few years earlier, as Wesley considered the views of those who dissented from the Church of England, he observed:

> They speak of our own holiness or good works as the *cause* of our justification, or that *for the sake of which on account of which*, we are justified before God. I believe neither our own holiness nor good works are any part of the cause of our justification; but that the death and righteousness of Christ are the whole and sole cause of it, or that *for the sake of which, on account of which* we are justified before God.[36]

This means, of course, that justification is expressive not of a direct relationship but of a mediated one, that one must have faith in the mediator, Jesus Christ, in order to be reconciled with the Father. There is, in other words, no immediate access to the Father (as some Medieval mystics seemed to imply). Instead, the sinner must approach God through faith in the person and work of Christ. This is a crucial truth that Wesley himself had failed to realize while he was in Georgia.[37]

Second, since justification entails the remission or forgiveness of sins, it results in liberation from the power of *guilt* so that one may now richly enjoy the favor and goodness of God. Again, justification restores the sinner to a right relationship with God—a relationship no longer marked by alienation and excessive fear.[38] To

---

[33]Ibid., 1:189. Cf. Leon Morris, *The Apostolic Preaching of the Cross* (Grand Rapids: Eerdmans, 1955), pp. 125ff. for an excellent treatment of the term *propitiation*.

[34]Davies, *Societies*, 9:51.

[35]Ibid. Again, in this same piece, Wesley points out that justifying faith does not "shut out repentance, hope and living faith," language that echoes the teaching of Cranmer's "Homily on Salvation."

[36]Ward and Heitzenrater, *Journals and Diaries*, 19:96.

[37]Baker, *Letters*, 25:546.

[38]Justification, however, is occasionally marked by both doubt and fear in those who are but babes in Christ. See Wesley's comments on 1 John 2:13-14 in Wesley, *NT Notes*, pp. 632-33.

be sure, a genuine healing of the soul begins to take place at this level of grace as well as a quickening of the spiritual senses so that one now sees a God of love. In his sermon "Salvation by Faith," for example, Wesley notes:

> This then is the salvation which is through faith, even in the present world: a salvation from sin and the consequences of sin, both often expressed in the word "justification," which taken in the largest sense, implies deliverance from guilt and punishment, by the atonement of Christ actually applied to the soul of the sinner now believing on him.[39]

Third, Wesley limits the forgiveness of sins to those which are *past*: "This tells me that Christ hath redeemed us (all that believe) from the curse or punishment justly due to our *past* transgressions of God's law."[40] Here the English evangelical is perhaps fearful of a libertine interpretation, one that would view justification as entailing the forgiveness of future sins with the miserable result that justification, so understood, would become license *for* sin rather than freedom *from* its guilt. To avoid this conclusion, Wesley maintained that forgiveness pertains only to those sins that are past. Therefore, if one commits open, willful sin subsequent to justification, then one must confess one's sins and seek the grace of God afresh.

There is a second major movement of Wesley's understanding of justification that goes beyond the forgiveness of sins, predicated on the atoning work of Christ, to embrace nothing less than the imputation of the righteousness of Christ to the sinner. Indeed, in his sermon "The Lord Our Righteousness," produced in 1765, Wesley contends that the righteousness of Christ is imputed to believers in the sense that they are now accepted by God not for the sake of anything that they have done, whether it be works of charity, mercy or the like, but *solely* because of what Christ has accomplished through his life and death on their behalf.[41] However, earlier during the first Methodist Conference in 1744, in response to the question,

---

[39]Outler, *Sermons*, 1:124. Though Wesley does speak of "degrees of justifying faith," this phrase must be carefully understood. First of all, it must be realized that since justification occurs at the same time as initial sanctification or the new birth, a degree of justification, in Wesley's estimation, never falls below the prerogatives of the children of God, namely, faith (which delivers from the guilt and power of sin), hope and love. Second, to suggest that justification can exist without the level or degree of sanctification just referred to is also to suggest that men and women can be justified while they remain under the dominion of sin—a clear impossibility in Wesley's reckoning.

[40]Jackson, *Wesley's Works*, 10:278. Emphasis added.

[41]Outler, *Sermons*, 1:455. Wesley contends that "All believers are forgiven and accepted not for the sake of anything in them . . . but wholly and solely for the sake of what Christ hath done and suffered for them." See again Outler, *Sermons*, 1:455.

"In what sense is the righteousness of Christ imputed to all mankind, or to believers?" it was declared: "We do not find it expressly affirmed in Scripture, that God imputes the righteousness of Christ to any; although we do find that 'faith is imputed' to us 'for righteousness.' "[42] This subtle distinction articulated by the Conference, it must be noted, does not undermine the crucial notion of the imputation of the righteousness of Christ in the least; rather such a distinction was offered by this Assembly of Methodists not only to be more scripturally accurate, but also to stay clear, once again, of the shoals of antinomianism whereby the grace of God could easily be misunderstood as *indulgence*. Moreover, this concern about libertinism in one form or other was also reflected several years later in Wesley's correspondence with James Hervey. For example, Wesley wrote to this erstwhile Oxford Methodist as follows:

> Do not dispute for that *particular phrase* "the imputed righteousness of Christ." It is not scriptural; it is not necessary. . . . But it has done immense hurt. I have had abundant proof that the frequent use of this unnecessary phrase, instead of "furthering men's progress in vital holiness," has made them satisfied without any holiness at all—yea, and encouraged them to work all uncleanness with greediness.[43]

Despite these concerns about the specter of antinomianism in the Methodist societies and elsewhere, Wesley nevertheless believed it important to affirm the theological truths implied in the notion that the righteousness of Christ is imputed to all who believe. To illustrate, a couple of years earlier Wesley had already maintained in his notes on Matthew 22:12 that the righteousness of Christ is not only imputed to believers, but that afterward, in a different work of grace, it is implanted as well,[44] the former work corresponding to justification, the latter to initial sanctification or the new birth. But Wesley's clearest affirmation of the doctrine of imputation, perhaps, is found in his sermon "The Lord Our Righteousness," noted earlier, which represents his seasoned and most articulate thoughts on the matter. In this sermon Wesley observes:

---

[42]Jackson, *Wesley's Works*, 8:277. Again, in a letter to Samuel Furly in 1757, Wesley underscores the same theme: "There is certainly no such assertion in Scripture as 'The righteousness of Christ is imputed to us.' Yet we will not deny it if men only mean thereby that 'we are accepted through His merits' or 'for the sake of what He has done and suffered for us.' " Cf. Telford, *Letters*, 3:230; and Jackson, *Wesley's Works*, 10:314-15.

[43]Telford, *Letters*, 3:372. See also Wesley's *Thoughts on the Imputed Righteousness of Christ* in Jackson, *Wesley's Works*, 10:312-15.

[44]John Wesley, *Explanatory Notes Upon the New Testament* (Salem, Ohio: Schmul Publishers, n.d.), p. 73.

The first then which admits of no dispute among reasonable men is this: to all believers the righteousness of Christ is imputed; to unbelievers it is not. "But when is it imputed?" When they believe. In that very hour the righteousness of Christ is theirs. It is imputed to every one that believes, as soon as he believes: faith and the righteousness of Christ are inseparable. For if he believes according to Scripture, he believes in the righteousness of Christ. There is no true faith, that is, justifying faith, which hath not the righteousness of Christ for its object.[45]

So then, according to Wesley, the human, external righteousness of Christ, both active and passive, is imputed to believers the moment they believe. Wesley expressed solidarity with his fellow Protestants in his belief that God justifies, not the righteous, but sinners, who can have no righteousness of their own apart from Christ. He also took exception with Roman Catholic formulations which moved in the direction not of the theology of the Cross, to employ Luther's terminology, but of the theology of glory, a theology that on some level took offense precisely at the justification of *sinners*. Accordingly, Wesley forthrightly declares in this same sermon, "The human righteousness of Christ, at least the imputation of it as the whole and sole meritorious cause of justification of a sinner before God, is likewise denied by the members of the Church of Rome."[46]

However Wesley's emphasis on the work of Christ as the sole meritorious cause of justification, rather than as its formal cause, also distinguished his theology in some important respects from that of Calvinism. The late Albert Outler observed:

> The problem in justification was how Christ's sufficient merits may be imputed to the penitent believer as the righteous ground for God's unmerited mercy (i.e., the formal cause of justification). And it was on this point of formal cause that Wesley parted from the Calvinists. They had stressed the Father's elective will, the prime link in "a golden chain" of logic which led them link by link to the famous "Five Points" of High Calvinism. Wesley tilted the balance the other way because of his sense of the importance of the Holy Spirit's prevenient initiative in all the "moments" of the *ordo salutis*.[47]

---

[45]Outler, *Sermons*, 1:454.

[46]Ibid., 1:460. Earlier, in 1739, when Wesley had been accused of being a Roman Catholic, he replied, "O ye fools, when will ye understand that the preaching of justification by faith alone, the allowing no meritorious cause of our justification but the death and righteousness of Christ, and no conditional or instrumental cause but faith, is overturning popery from the foundations." See Ward and Heitzenrater, *Journals and Diaries*, 19:89.

[47]Ibid., 1:80-81. For a discussion of the employment of the phrases "*ordo salutis*" and "*via salutis*" to describe Wesley's soteriology as well the question of order and structure in the Methodist leader's reasoned way of thinking about the processes of redemption, see Kenneth J. Collins, *The Scripture Way of Salvation: The Heart of John Wesley's Theology* (Nashville: Abingdon, 1997), pp. 185-90.

In other words, the doctrine of the formal cause implied a correlated view of pre-destination and irresistible grace. The notion of the meritorious cause, on the other hand, though still evangelical, "allowed for prevenience, free will, and universal re-demption."[48] For Wesley, the evangelical Anglican, the justifying and regenerating graces of God, though they mark the sheer gifts of the Most High, may yet be re-sisted by the stubborn sinner.[49] To be sure, though believers are powerless to save themselves, they are nevertheless in some sense responsible, or accountable, for whether or not they are redeemed as they respond to the prevenient and convincing grace of God.

THE QUESTION OF SOLA FIDE

In his piece "Justification by Faith," Wesley affirms (in a way that looks very much like Luther's doctrine) that faith *alone* is the condition of justification: "Faith there-fore is the *necessary* condition of justification. Yea, and the *only necessary* condition thereof."[50] In other words, faith is the only thing without which no one is justified; it is, to use Wesley's own language, "the only thing that is immediately, indispens-ably, absolutely requisite in order to pardon."[51] No justification, then, ever takes place without it. In addition, faith is not only *the* necessary condition of justifica-tion, but it is also a *sufficient* condition. "This [faith] alone is sufficient for justifi-cation," Wesley points out in 1765. "Everyone that believes is justified, whatever else he has or has not."[52] Does this teaching, then, contradict Wesley's earlier state-ment expressed in his *Farther Appeal to Men of Reason and Religion* that "repentance abso-lutely must go before faith"?[53] Not at all, so long as it is realized that the language

---

[48]Ibid., 1:445. For other references to the work of Christ as the meritorious cause of justification, see Outler, *Sermons*, 1:382-83; 2:157-58; and 2:342.

[49]Since Wesley held an idea of original sin similar to both Luther and Calvin, then this means that "irresistible grace" had to operate at some point in his *ordo salutis*. Indeed, for Wesley it is prevenient grace, in the sense of various gifts such as conscience, a certain measure of the restoration of free will, etc., that must be irresistibly given. See Collins, *The Scripture Way of Salvation*, pp. 38ff.

[50]Outler, *Sermons*, 1:196.

[51]Ibid., 1:196. For helpful treatments of Wesley's understanding of faith in general and of justification by faith in particular, see David Lowes Watson, "The Much-Controverted Point of Justification by Faith and the Shaping of Wesley's Evangelical Message," *Wesleyan Theological Journal* 21, no. 1 and 2 (1986): 7-23; John Lawson, "Saving Faith as Wesley Saw It," *Christianity Today* 8 (April 24 1964): 3-4; Frederick Dreyer, "Faith and Experience in the Thought of John Wesley," *The American Historical Review* 88 (Fall 1983): 12-30.

[52]Outler, *Sermons*, 2:162.

[53]Cragg, *The Appeals*, 11:106. By repentance, in this context, Wesley means a "conviction of sin pro-ducing real desires and sincere resolutions of amendment."

of "whatever else he has or has not" pertains to *what* justifies, while the language of "repentance absolutely must go before faith" pertains to the soteriological process *prior to* justification itself in terms of the ongoing prevenient grace of God. This difference, which was mediated to Wesley by his own Anglican tradition, is very important and therefore must be properly assessed in order to appreciate the subtlety of the Methodist leader's position.

According to some contemporary notions, however, John Wesley was supposed to have repudiated his earlier emphasis on *sola fide* in the face of his subsequent and increasing recognition of the place and value of works of piety and mercy and the means of grace prior to justification. While Wesley did indeed develop a greater estimate of works prior to justification, especially during the early 1740s, this by no means detracted from his claim made in 1738 and reiterated late in his career that it is faith *alone* that justifies. In fact, in 1765 Wesley wrote to John Newton, "I think on Justification just as I have done any time these seven-and-twenty years, and just as Mr. Calvin does. In this respect I do not differ from him a hair's breadth."[54] Moreover, in his summary sermon "The Scripture Way of Salvation," produced the same year, Wesley reaffirms that faith is the condition, and the only condition of justification.[55] A year later, Wesley reviews the whole affair in his *Remarks on a Defence of Aspasio Vindicated* and exclaims:

> I believe justification by faith alone, as much as I believe there is a God. I declared this in a sermon, preached before the University of Oxford, eight-and-twenty years ago. I declared it to all the world eighteen years ago, in a sermon written expressly on the subject. I have never varied from it, no, not an hair's breadth, from 1738 to this day.[56]

Furthermore, in 1783, in his "General Spread of the Gospel," the elderly Wesley points out, "We are justified by faith *alone*."[57] And in his piece "On Dissipation," produced the following year, he once again states, "It is by this faith *alone* that he is 'created anew in or through Christ Jesus.'"[58] Remarkably, this is the same doctrine

---

[54]Ibid., 4:298.

[55]Outler, *Sermons*, 2:162. In this summary sermon, Wesley maintains that faith is not only the condition of justification, but of sanctification as well: "Exactly as we are justified by faith, so are we sanctified by faith. Faith is the condition, and the only condition of sanctification, exactly as it is of justification." Cf. Outler, *Sermons*, 2:163.

[56]Jackson, *Wesley's Works*, 10:349.

[57]Outler, *Sermons*, 2:491. It is interesting to note that the exact phrase "faith alone" appears over eighty times in Wesley's writings, suggesting something of its importance in his overall theology.

[58]Ibid., 3:119.

that Wesley preached in 1738 in his sermon "Salvation by Faith."[59] The continuity is striking.

Beyond this, it is no more accurate to contend that the early Wesley was a champion of *sola fide*, but that the mature Wesley maintained that we are "predominantly" or "for the most part" justified by faith. The error here is to pit the later Wesley against the early one, to set the leader fearful of *solafidianism* against the champion of *sola fide*—and in a fashion, by the way, that belies the historical record. To be sure, Wesley's subsequent emphases do not contradict the notion of *sola fide*, properly understood, but are actually complementary to it.

WESLEY'S RHETORIC AS A KEY

The key to understanding the intricate nuances of Wesley's doctrine of justification whereby he held together a healthy notion of prevenience *and* the reality of *sola fide* can be found in his language or rhetoric, that is, in terms of a crucial distinction that he makes, often neglected by his interpreters, in his *Farther Appeal to Men of Reason and Religion* and in his sermon "The Scripture Way of Salvation." In the former work, for example, Wesley reasons:

> And yet I allow you this, that although both repentance and the fruits thereof are in *some sense* necessary before justification, yet neither the one nor the other is necessary in the *same sense* or in the *same degree* with faith. Not in the *same degree*: for in whatever moment a man believes (in the Christian sense of the Word) he is justified, his sins are blotted out, 'his faith is counted to him as righteousness' . . . faith alone therefore justifies, which repentance does not, much less any outward work. And consequently none of these are necessary to justification in the *same degree* with faith.
>
> Not in the *same sense*: for none of these has so direct, immediate a relation to justification as faith. This is *proximately* necessary thereto; repentance, *remotely*, as it is necessary to the increase or continuance of faith: and the fruits of repentance still more remotely, as they are necessary to repentance.[60]

The distinctions "not in the same sense" and "not in the same degree," noted above, carry many of the nuances utilized by Wesley to articulate, on the one hand,

---

[59]Ibid., I:118. For additional references to *sola fide* in Wesley's writings cf. Wesley, *NT Notes*, p. 484; Ward, *Journals*, 19:281; Curnock, *Journal*, 7:357; Telford, *Letters*, 3:321; and Cragg, *Appeals*, 11:417, 454.

[60]Cragg, *Appeals*, 11:117. Wesley so feared a deprecation of works suitable for repentance that he omitted Article XIII of the Anglican Thirty-Nine Articles ("Of Works before Justification") when he prepared an abridged version of this historic document for the Methodists. Cf. Paul F. Blankenship, "The Significance of John Wesley's Abridgment of the Thirty-Nine Articles as Seen from His Deletions," *Methodist History* 2, 3 (April 1964): 35-47.

the *necessity* of repentance and its fruits prior to justification—that made him look like a Roman Catholic in the eyes of some Calvinists—and, on the other hand, that repentance and its fruits do *not* justify—that made him look like the evangelical Anglican that he actually was.

Again, by the first phrase, "not in the same sense," Wesley affirms that repentance is remotely *necessary* for justification, and its fruits are even more remotely so. "I cannot therefore agree, that 'we are accepted without any terms previously performed to qualify us for acceptance,' " Wesley exclaims, "for we are not accepted, nor are we qualified for, or capable of, acceptance, without repentance and faith."[61] Elsewhere, in his *Farther Appeal*, Wesley is even more emphatic and writes, "Repentance *absolutely* must go before faith; fruits meet for it, if there be opportunity."[62] Observe that the temporal element, that is, the condition "if there be time and opportunity for them," pertains only to works meet for repentance and not to repentance itself. Repentance, though still only remotely or indirectly necessary to justifying faith, is apparently *always* necessary. In fact, when Wesley considers the case of the thief on the cross, he concludes that this abject criminal likewise came to faith in Christ through no other way than the path of grace and repentance. "Even in the thief upon the cross," Wesley observes, "faith was attended by repentance, piety, and charity . . . repentance went before his faith."[63] Thus, by designating repentance as the free gift of God, Wesley underscored human inability apart from convincing grace; by designating repentance as in some sense the condition of justification, he pointed to the responsibilities entailed in the reception of such grace.

Now if the phrase "not in the same sense" (or "in some sense") allows Wesley to affirm the *necessity* of repentance prior to justifying faith, and interestingly enough in a way remarkably similar to Cranmer, then the second phrase "not in the same degree" makes it clear that repentance and its fruits *do not justify*. To illustrate, in 1765, in his sermon "The Scripture Way of Salvation," which contains many of the same theological subtleties of the earlier *A Farther Appeal*, Wesley points out:

> But they [repentance and its fruits] are not necessary in the *same sense* with faith, nor in the *same degree*. Not in the *same degree*; for those fruits are only necessary *conditionally*, if there be time and opportunity for them. Otherwise a man may be justified without them, as was the "thief" upon the cross. . . . But he cannot be justified without faith:

[61]Jackson, *Works*, 10:309.
[62]Cragg, *Appeals*, 11:106. See also 11:116. Emphasis added.
[63]Ibid., 11:453. See also Wesley's *NT Notes* where he indicated that the thief on the cross even had time to perform works meet for repentance! Cf. Wesley, *NT Notes*, p. 205 (Lk 23:40).

this is impossible. Likewise let a man have ever so much repentance, or ever so many of the fruits meet for repentance, yet all of this does not at all avail: he is not justified till he believes. But the moment he believes, with or without those fruits, yea, with more or less repentance, he is justified.[64]

So then, with this distinction "not in the same degree," in his theological repertoire, Wesley was able to declare that repentance and its works, though now in some sense necessary to justification, *do not justify*. Faith *alone* justifies. Indeed, Wesley's claim of *sola fide* is actually a credible one, but only when it is considered not in terms of the first distinction "not in the same sense" but in terms of the second distinction "not in the same degree." Indeed, it is the confusion or the neglect of these two senses which led some to argue that Wesley had retreated from the notion of *sola fide*.

Wesley, no doubt, had compounded the problem with his Calvinistic critics, the Countess of Huntingdon[65] and Walter Shirley among them, because he had resorted to a single vocabulary (that works are in some sense necessary prior to justification) in the conference minutes of 1770 to explicate a complex theological problem. However, even in the 1770s, Wesley had another theological vocabulary available to him, namely, the language of "not in the same degree," the language of *sola fide*. Such language, perhaps, would have demonstrated to and convinced some of the Calvinist Methodists that, for Wesley, repentance and its fruits, though indirectly necessary to justification, could *never* justify. Faith *alone* justifies. But so much was lost in the heat of the polemics.

A SUMMARY OF WESLEY'S DOCTRINE OF JUSTIFICATION

In light of the preceding, Wesley's doctrine of justification can now be summarized in the following points:

1. Justification entails the forgiveness of past sins and is based upon the atoning work of Christ. In a real sense, human sin is imputed to Christ who is nothing less than the sin bearer and sacrificial lamb of God.

2. Justification includes the imputation of the righteousness of Christ to *sinners*

---

[64]Outler, *Sermons*, 2:162-63. The same distinctions of *A Farther Appeal*, though somewhat modified (Wesley uses the terms "immediately," and "directly necessary," with respect to faith as synonyms for the *Farther Appeal's* "proximately necessary"), surfaced in this present sermon, "The Scripture Way of Salvation" in 1765.

[65]After the publication of the conference minutes of 1770, Lady Huntingdon declared that "whoever did not wholly disavow the theses should quit her college." Cf. Luke L. Tyerman, *The Life and Times of the Rev. John Wesley, M.A.*, 3 vols. (New York: Burt Franklin), 3:73.

with the result that they are *declared* righteous. Imputation, however, must never be viewed as a "cloak" for ongoing unrighteousness.

3. To avoid grievous error, which detracts from the graciousness and liberty of the gospel, a logical distinction must be made between justification as the work that God does *for us* and sanctification as the work that God does *in us*. Moreover, sanctification cannot in any way, in any sense, be the basis of justification, a basis that is, once again, found *solely* in the atoning work of Christ.

4. Justification is by faith *alone*. Therefore, to balk at the term "alone" can only detract from the excellence and sufficiency of the work of Christ and make some other work, however contrived or substantiated, the foundation of justification.

5. Justification by faith does not exclude the importance of works both prior to and following justification. However, neither the former nor the latter works justify, properly speaking, and the latter, therefore, are best understood as the evidence, the lively witness, of a justification that has already occurred.

6. The atoning work of Christ is the meritorious, not the formal cause, of justification. This evangelical conception embraces the prevenient action of God through which sinners, though they clearly cannot justify themselves, are nevertheless in some sense responsible for whether or not they are justified.

THE CONTEMPORARY SETTING

In light of the contributions of both Anglicanism and historic Methodism, in particular the theological reflections of John Wesley, it will be helpful to consider recent ecumenical discussions among a diversity of churches with respect to the salient issue of justification and what contributions Methodism as a Protestant denomination, deeply rooted in the English Reformation, may have to offer.

In the spirit of ecumenism and cooperation in the wake of Vatican II, the Methodists and Roman Catholics have been meeting since 1967. At that time a Joint Commission was established which met at Ariccia in order to engage in theological dialogue and to explore some common understandings and purpose.[66] A few years later, in 1971, the Commission assembled in Denver and underscored what initial similarities existed.[67] Subsequent meetings have taken place in Nairobi in 1986 and

---

[66] Geoffrey Wainwright, *Methodists in Dialog* (Nashville: Kingswood, 1995), p. 37.

[67] Geoffrey Wainwright, "The Lutheran-Roman Catholic Agreement on Justification: Its Ecumenical Significance and Scope from a Methodist Point of View," *Journal of Ecumenical Studies* 38, no. 1 (2001): 20.

in Singapore in 1991, though no major agreement has been reached.

Such an ecumenical interest has also been amply demonstrated among American Evangelicals and Roman Catholics in an unofficial way with the promulgation of the statement "Evangelicals and Catholics Together" in 1994, produced largely through the efforts of Charles Colson and Richard John Neuhaus.[68] Three years later, the ecumenical document "The Gift of Salvation" was published, hailed as Evangelicals and Catholics Together II.[69] Both documents displayed what concerns, whether theological, social or political, Evangelicals and Roman Catholics share on an ongoing basis in the face of an increasingly secular American culture. However, since both of these documents are unofficial statements, not representative of the teaching of the Roman Catholic *magisterium*, they may actually hold far less promise than some have imagined. In light of this, a more fruitful scholarly investigation, in my estimation, can be had in examining the formal ecumenical talks between Lutheranism and Roman Catholicism that have resulted in the official statement of the Joint Declaration produced in 1999 in the historic reformation city of Augsburg.

Mindful of the importance of the Reformation, as well as of the Council of Trent, the Joint Declaration nevertheless states that there now exists a basis for a common understanding of justification by faith by Lutherans and Roman Catholics as revealed in the following:

> The present *Joint Declaration* has this intuition: namely, to show that on the basis of their dialogue the subscribing Lutheran churches and the Roman Catholic Church are now able to articulate a common understanding of our justification by God's grace through faith in Christ. It does not cover all that either church teaches about justification; it does encompass a consensus on basic truths of the doctrine of justification and shows that the remaining differences in its explication are no longer the occasion for doctrinal condemnations.[70]

The central argument of the Joint Declaration is that there now exists a consensus on some basic truths with respect to the doctrine of justification; therefore, the remaining differences between these two traditions are no longer the occasion for doctrinal condemnations. This argument is undermined, in part, by the recognition that the consensus that has been achieved is improperly being employed as a

---

[68]See Charles Colson and Richard John Neuhaus, eds., *Evangelicals and Catholics: Toward a Common Mission* (Dallas: Word, 1995).
[69]See Timothy George, "The Gift of Salvation," *Christianity Today* (December 8, 1997), p. 34.
[70]The Lutheran World Federation and the Roman Catholic Church, *Joint Declaration on the Doctrine of Justification* (Grand Rapids: Eerdmans, 1999), pp. 10-11 [par. 5].

warrant for an area where consensus has not been achieved, that is, in terms of the differences that remain, differences that may yet call for theological censure. Again, what has been accomplished in one area simply does not hold consequence for the next. Indeed, given this form of argumentation, where the areas of consensus are employed to repudiate, even obviate, any form of criticism, much less condemnation, of remaining *differences*, it becomes crucial for scholars to ascertain not only whether the consensus, so promulgated and so employed, constitutes a *sufficient* doctrine of justification by faith, one faithful to the apostolic witness revealed in Scripture, but also whether the theological differences beyond that consensus actually matter.

On the one hand, the ambiguity of this document is compounded by the assertion that the doctrinal condemnations of the sixteenth century do not apply to the teaching of the Roman Catholic Church "presented in this Declaration"[71] (that is, in terms of the "consensus"), but then, on the other hand, these same Lutheran doctrinal condemnations, which supposedly are still important, do not apply to the "remaining differences of language, theological elaboration, and emphasis"[72] in the Catholic expression of the doctrine of justification as well since such differences are now judged to be "acceptable."[73] Again, given this odd form of argumentation, the subsequent statement that "the churches neither take the condemnations [of the sixteenth century] lightly nor do they disavow their own past," has been rendered all but meaningless since such condemnations can neither apply to the consensus achieved nor to the differences that remain.[74]

Given these and other problems, upon its promulgation in 1999, the Joint Declaration was greeted with very mixed reviews. Though several church leaders in both the Lutheran World Federation and the Roman Catholic Church actually believed that something significant had been achieved, others were not so convinced. In fact, more than 165 of Germany's leading theologians and historians, such as Jürgen

---

[71]Ibid., p. 26. [par. 41].

[72]Ibid., pp. 25-26 [par. 40]. Once again, the question of the *extent* of the consensus must be forthrightly addressed. Indeed, the form of argumentation in the Joint Declaration apparently allows for a "minimalist" view of the "basic consensus" whereby vital elements pertaining to the doctrine of justification are simply not treated.

[73]Ibid.

[74]Ibid., p. 26 [par. 42]. Another statement virtually emptied of its meaning is as follows: "Nothing is thereby taken away from the seriousness of the condemnations related to the doctrine of justification. Some were not simply pointless. They remain for us 'salutary warnings' to which we must attend in our teaching and practice."

Moltmann, Gerhard Ebeling and Eberhard Jüngel, criticized the new Lutheran-Catholic statement along several lines.[75] In America, Robert Preus, a well-respected Lutheran scholar, though he had died in 1995, was nevertheless aware of the language later published in the Joint Declaration. And his largely negative judgment is revealed in the following pointed observation:

> For the Lutheran churches to accept [the] *Joint Declaration* as a consensus on the doctrine of justification will not only compromise their witness to the evangelical Lutheran doctrine on justification; but will compromise the confessional principle itself.[76]

Indeed, in his further observations Preus not only points to the different cultural, religious and intellectual climates of the sixteenth century as compared to the nineteenth and twentieth, but he also suggests that both Lutherans and Catholics, if they did not succumb to the contemporary *Zeitgeist*, were at least at times heavily influenced by it.[77] Accordingly, from the Lutheran side of the equation, it must be forthrightly asked "Are mainline theological liberals the best representatives of the tradition?" especially since during the twentieth century these same theologians and historians have often looked askance at the details of soteriology as a pious indulgence, an extravagance in the face of a hurting world, as they attempted to focus almost unswervingly on social action and political ethics. In other words, given the breadth and genius of the Lutheran theological tradition, at the historic moment during which the dialogues that led to the Joint Declaration were taking place, were the wrong people sitting at the table?

Now as a Methodist theologian, well acquainted with the Anglican Reformation, and with the theological power and cogency of John Wesley's evangelical theology, I find the Joint Declaration, from my particular social location, theologically problematic in a number of respects. That is, with its omissions as well as with its ambiguities, this document, so conceived, is apparently incapable of communicating the fullness of the *Apostolic testimony* pertaining to justification, grace and the work of Christ. Three major areas illustrate this claim.

First of all, reflecting the theological preference of Rome at the Council of Trent (Session VI, Canon 10), the Joint Declaration "says nothing about the imputation

---

[75]Richard Nyberg, "Protestant Theologians Object to Lutheran-Catholic Accord," *Christianity Today*, (June 15, 1998), p. 12.

[76]Robert Preus, *Justification and Rome* (St. Louis: Concordia, 1997), pp. 114-15.

[77]Ibid., p. 104.

of Christ's righteousness."[78] In fact, as McGrath points out, the entire post-Tridentine Catholic tradition "continued to regard justification as a *process* in which man was made righteous involving the actualization rather than the imputation of righteousness."[79] So then, perhaps out of deference to the teaching of Rome at Trent that justification is intimately associated with *infused* grace, the Lutheran representatives during the 1990s simply let the whole matter of the imputation of the righteousness of Christ drop, what Luther in several, not a few, contexts referred to as "the alien righteousness of God."[80] However, if the imputation of the righteousness of Christ is not affirmed, whereby *sinners*, not those who are already righteous, are *declared* righteous, then either some basis of justification is being offered other than the life and death of Christ or the basic Pauline truth that *sinners*, not saints ("But God demonstrates His own love toward us, in that while we were yet sinners, Christ died for us," Rom 5:8), are justified is subtly being denied in preference for the teaching that only those who have the infused grace (that makes them righteous and holy) are thereby justified. Simply put, infused grace, in a real sense, becomes the *basis* of justification in this teaching in order that this crucial doctrine may not become a supposed legal fiction.[81] R. C. Sproul expresses the remaining differences between these two traditions remarkably well: "For Rome the declaration of justice *follows* the making inwardly *just* of the regenerate sinner. For the Reformation the declaration of justice follows the imputation of Christ's righteousness to the regenerated sinner."[82] This difference is vital and cannot be ignored in the name of ecumenical interest and endeavor.

Second, failing to develop or even to acknowledge the importance of the imputation of the righteousness of Christ in its doctrine of justification, the Joint Declaration quite naturally falls into yet another difficulty, which undermines both the grace and the power of the gospel, by confounding the doctrines of justification

---

[78]Ibid., p. 77. See also Robert Preus, "Perennial Problems in the Doctrine of Justification," *Concordia Theological Quarterly* 45 (July 1981): 163-84.

[79]McGrath, *Iustitia Dei*, p. 284.

[80]For Luther's use of the phrase "alien righteousness," in his treatise "Two Kinds of Righteousness," see Harold J. Grimm, ed., *Luther's Works: Career of the Reformer: I* (Philadelphia: Fortress, 1957), 31:297, 299.

[81]On this head, Preus points out, "Rome objected strenuously to the Lutheran doctrine that justification was the forgiveness of sins and the imputation of Christ's righteousness to the believer since this doctrine made justification unreal, no more than a putative judgment, and therefore a fiction." Preus, *Justification and Rome*, p. 70.

[82]R. C. Sproul, *Faith Alone: The Evangelical Doctrine of Justification* (Grand Rapids: Baker, 1995), pp. 97-98.

and sanctification. As noted earlier, this was precisely the mistake that Wesley had made while he was in Georgia until he was disabused of this erroneous notion and practice through the good graces of Peter Böhler. Observe in the following statement, then, how the recent ecumenical document, in portraying Roman differences, confuses these two senses:

> The Catholic understanding also sees faith as fundamental in justification. For without faith, no justification can take place. Persons are justified through baptism as hearers of the word and believers in it. The justification of sinners is forgiveness of sins and *being made righteous* by justifying grace, which makes us children of God.[83]

Moreover, under the heading "Biblical Message of Justification," apparently both Lutherans and Catholics affirm that justification is "the forgiveness of sins . . . [and] liberation from the dominating power of sin and death."[84] But what is this, once again, but to confuse justification with regeneration or with what can be called initial sanctification. Contrary to this document, it must be reaffirmed for the sake of gospel clarity by both the Protestant community in general and by Evangelicals in particular, that justification is not liberation from "the dominating power of sin and death"; that is sanctification. As John Wesley so clearly taught after 1738, justification, quite simply, is the forgiveness of those sins that are past. It is that work of grace that God does for us, not in us. Therefore, to confuse these two senses, as the Joint Declaration does, is to have sanctification "bleed" into the doctrine of justification with the result that, once again, some measure of sanctification or holiness, or infusion of grace, has been made the basis of justification. But it is no one less than the apostle Paul who reminds the Church, "But to the one who does not work, but believes in Him who justifies the ungodly, his faith is credited as righteousness" (Rom 4:5).

Third, though the Annex to the Official Common Statement on justification does indicate that both Lutherans and Roman Catholics have affirmed that justification takes place "by grace alone" (Joint Declaration, nos. 15 and 16), "[and]

---

[83] *Joint Declaration*, p. 20 [par. 27]. Emphasis added. Preus contends that in the Catholic view justification actually becomes the process of sanctification and the Lutheran understanding of justification as a forensic doctrine is considered "peripheral." See Preus, *Justification and Rome*, p. 26.

[84] Ibid., p. 13 [par. 11]. Clifford indicates that the Roman Catholic misunderstanding of justification as "infused grace" harkens back to difficulties with the Latin translation of an originally Greek term. Indeed, the Latin translation implies "making righteous," when the actual sense of the term, as generally agreed by scholars today, implies "declaring righteous." See Clifford, "The Gospel and Justification," p. 254.

by faith alone";[85] the main body of the Joint Declaration itself restricts the usage of the phrase "by faith alone" simply to a Lutheran understanding of justification. For example, compare the following two excerpts from the Joint Declaration:

(1) According to Lutheran understanding, God justifies sinners in faith alone (*sola fide*).

(2) The Catholic understanding also sees faith as fundamental in justification. For without faith, no justification can take place.[86]

This omission of a key component of the doctrine of justification, by faith alone, in the Catholic statement, an element that preserves the excellence and utter sufficiency of the work of Christ on behalf of sinners, is actually not surprising given the reluctance of the Roman Catholic church even to pay much attention to the doctrine of justification prior to Vatican II. Moreover, this historic Council, which, by the way, viewed Protestants as "separated brethren," a clear advance over earlier provincial and exclusivist notions, nevertheless "[showed] little interest," as Preus contends, "in the doctrine which was so central to the Protestant Reformation."[87] In fact, in the *Catholic Catechism* that was published in 1994 the sacrament of baptism, which communicates justifying grace, is as much emphasized as faith itself, perhaps even more so. Equally disturbing, especially for American evangelicals, is that when the *Catechism* proceeds to summarize the section on justification it hardly mentions faith and only, of course, in the context of the sacrament of (infant) baptism. Observe the following language:

[2017] The grace of the Holy Spirit confers upon us the righteousness of God. Uniting us by faith and Baptism to the Passion and Resurrection of Christ, the Spirit makes us sharers in his life.

[2020] Justification has been merited for us by the Passion of Christ. It is granted us through Baptism.[88]

---

[85]Ibid., p. 45 [section C].

[86]Ibid., pp. 19-20 [pars. 26, 27]. Evangelical Christians will, no doubt, be disappointed to learn that the *Catholic Catechism* has no separate section for the doctrine of regeneration or the new birth. What discussion there is in the *Catechism* falls under the topic of baptism. See *Catechism of the Catholic Church* (Mahwah, N.J.: Paulist, 1994), p. 359 [par. 1427].

[87]Preus, *Justification and Rome*, p. 20. Moreover, McGrath observes that "the very term 'justification' itself appears to have been gradually eliminated from the homiletical and catechetical literature of Catholicism." And he adds, "The general reintroduction of the term into the vocabulary of Catholicism appears to date from the Second Vatican Council." See McGrath, *Iustitia Dei*, p. 284.

[88]*Catechism of the Catholic Church*, p. 489 [pars. 2017 and 2020].

However, the mere mention of the term *faith* in the context of justification should not be sufficient for Protestants or for Roman Catholics, for that matter, who seek to communicate the generous Pauline witness to the graciousness of the good news of the gospel. To be sure, the doctrine of faith must be affirmed, and its implicatory relations demonstrated, to illuminate this teaching as being nothing less than, as Luther reminds us, the *"Rector et judex super omnia genera doctrinarum."*[89]

In conclusion, since the Joint Declaration does not affirm the imputation of the righteousness of Christ in its common statements, since it repeatedly confuses the issues of justification and sanctification in these same statements, and since it relegates the language of *sola fide* simply to Lutheran differences and to the *Annex*, failing to include such language in terms of the Catholic articulation in particular, then surely American Evangelicals have the right to ask, first of all, do the common statements on justification actually reveal a sufficient and full bodied doctrine, one commensurate with the life and witness of the historic church, or is it a doctrine that unfortunately has been eviscerated due in some measure to the ecumenical enterprise itself? Second, should some of the differences that remain, especially the vital matter of *faith alone*, become a part of the consensus and not be relegated to the periphery, as the present declaration requires?

Even judged in a most charitable way, and with great ecumenical sensitivity, the Joint Declaration contradicts the truths clearly expressed in John Wesley's doctrine of justification in theses two, three and four enumerated earlier. Since this is the case, then, Methodists as with others must still undertake the reforming labor of an evangelical, and not be dissuaded from this vital and necessary task in the least. Empowered by grace, led by the rich ministrations of the Holy Spirit, they must, in a very prophetic way, call the broader church to a clarity and witness with respect to both grace and faith that befits the so great a salvation that we have in Jesus Christ. In an ecumenical age, nothing less is warranted; in an age that seeks for truth, nothing less will do.

---

[89] *Joint Declaration*, p. 9 [preamble, par. 1] "Ruler and judge over all other Christian doctrines."

JUSTIFICATION AND ECUMENICAL ENDEAVOR

8

TWOFOLD RIGHTEOUSNESS: A KEY TO THE DOCTRINE OF JUSTIFICATION?

Reflections on Article 5 of the Regensburg Colloquy (1541)

ANTHONY N. S. LANE

In 1541 Protestant and Catholic theologians produced an agreed statement on justification by faith, more than 450 years before the Joint Declaration signed in 1999. This paper will assess the teaching of that statement and suggest that it might have something useful to teach us today.[1]

INTRODUCTION

Luther and the Reformers presented the doctrine of justification in a new light, posing new and hitherto unanswered questions. This created a problem for their opponents as there was no consensus in the Catholic Church on the doctrine of justification and, more importantly, there had been no authoritative pronouncements.[2] That left individual Roman Catholic theologians free to develop their doctrines in different ways and these varied from uncompromising hostility to the Protestant doctrine to almost complete agreement with it.

Among those most sympathetic to Luther's doctrine in the Roman Catholic Church was an Erasmian reforming group in Italy, known as the *spirituali*, which included leading cardinals.[3] One of these, Gasparo Contarini, in 1511 under-

---

[1] This chapter develops further some of the material from my *Justification by Faith in Catholic-Protestant Dialogue: An Evangelical Assessment* (Edinburgh & New York: T & T Clark, 2002), pp. 46-60.
[2] For a brief survey of Catholic opinion in the early years of the Reformation, cf. H. Jedin, *A History of the Council of Trent*, 2 vols. (London: Thomas Nelson, 1957, 1961), 2:167-71.
[3] *Spirituali* was a contemporary term. Twentieth-century scholarship introduced the confusing term *evangelism* for this movement. E. G. Gleason, "On the Nature of Sixteenth-Century Italian Evangelism: Scholarship, 1953-1978," *Sixteenth Century Journal* 9, no. 3 (1978): 3-25.

went a conversion experience that he described in a private letter later that year that has affinities with Luther's (later) "Tower experience."[4] There are different assessments of Contarini's doctrine of justification, but I have argued elsewhere that he eventually came to accept the key points of the Protestant doctrine.[5] In Germany also there was a significant group of Catholic humanists seeking reform within the Roman Catholic system. Noteworthy among these was Johannes Gropper, who in 1538 published his highly influential *Enchiridion*, a handbook for reform of the diocese of Cologne.[6] Among such Catholic humanists there was widespread sympathy for the Protestant idea that Christ's righteousness is imputed or reckoned to us. A key motive behind this development was the belief that "the converted Christian still needs to throw himself on the mercy of God."[7] In many ways these reforming humanist Catholics shared a similar spiritual background to the Reformers.

REGENSBURG COLLOQUY AND ARTICLE 5

From 1530 there was a series of colloquies aimed at reconciling the two sides in Germany to avert civil war and to enable a common front against the Turkish threat. The greatest chance of success came in three gatherings that were held in 1540 and 1541.[8] These began with a colloquy at Hagenau in June and July 1540, but some of those expected failed to appear and the two sides could not agree on

---

[4]For the text of the letter, cf. E. G. Gleason, ed., *Reform Thought in Sixteenth-Century Italy* (Chico, Calif.: Scholars Press, 1981), pp. 24-28. On the letter and the parallels and differences between Contarini's experience and Luther's, cf. H. Jedin, "Ein 'Turmerlebnis' des jungen Contarinis" in *Kirche des Glaubens; Kirche der Geschichte* (Freiburg, Basel and Vienna: Herder, 1966), 1:167-80.

[5]"Cardinal Contarini and Article 5 of the Regensburg Colloquy (1541)," in *Grenzgänge der Theologie*, ed. O. Meuffels and J. Bründl (Münster: Lit Verlag, 2004), pp. 163-90.

[6]On Gropper's doctrine of justification, cf. R. Braunisch, *Die Theologie der Rechtfertigung im "Enchiridion" (1538) des Johannes Gropper* (Münster: Aschendorff, 1974).

[7]The different doctrines are set out by E. Yarnold, *"Duplex iustitia:* The Sixteenth Century and the Twentieth," in *Christian Authority*, ed. G. R. Evans (Oxford: Oxford University Press, 1988), pp. 207-13, quotation p. 213. Cf. also J. Rivière, "Justification," in DCT 8:2159-64; R. B. Ives, "An Early Effort Toward Protestant-Catholic Conciliation: The Doctrine of Double Justification in the Sixteenth Century," *Gordon Review* 11 (1968-1970): 99-110.

[8]On the colloquies in general, cf. Jedin, *History of the Council of Trent*, 1:372-91; C. Augustijn, *De Godsdienstgesprekken tussen Rooms-katholieken en Protestanten van 1538 tot 1541* (Haarlem: De Erven F. Bohn, 1967); C. Augustijn, "Die Religionsgespräche der vierziger Jahre," in *Die Religionsgespräche der Reformationszeit*, ed. G. Müller (Gütersloh: Gerd Mohn, 1980), pp. 43-53; V. Pfnür, "Die Einigung bei den Religionsgesprächen von Worms und Regensburg 1540/41 eine Täuschung?" in ibid., pp. 55-88; B. Hall, *Humanists and Protestants 1500-1900* (Edinburgh: T & T Clark, 1990), pp. 142-70.

how to proceed. The colloquy was adjourned to Worms, where it met in November, this time with a good line-up of theologians. After long delays, discussion of original sin began in January and agreement was reached in a few days.[9] At this point Nicholas Granvella, the imperial chancellor, adjourned the debate to the coming Diet at Regensburg.[10] Meanwhile at Worms secret discussions had been taking place between Bucer and Capito on the Protestant side and the humanist Catholics Gropper and Gerard Veltwyk (Granvella's secretary).[11] Gropper, with Bucer's cooperation, went on to draw up the *Regensburg Book*, which was to be used as a basis for further discussion.[12]

Contarini was appointed papal legate for the final colloquy, which took place at the Regensburg Diet. The diet was opened on April 5.[13] On April 21, the emperor selected as the debaters Melanchthon, Bucer and Pistorius on the Protestant side and Gropper, Pflug and Eck on the Catholic side and the colloquy was able to begin. Calvin and Pighius were also present, but not as debaters.[14] The *Regensburg Book*, whose origin was a closely guarded secret, became the basis for discussion. On April 27, the first four articles, on human innocence before the fall, free choice, the cause of sin and original sin, were quickly agreed on, building

---

[9]For the debates on original sin, cf. CR 4:33-78; H. Mackensen, "The Debate Between Eck and Melanchthon on Original Sin at the Colloquy of Worms," *Lutheran Quarterly* 11 (1959): 42-56. For the formula, CR 4:32-33.

[10]For Regensburg, cf. P. Matheson, *Cardinal Contarini at Regensburg* (Oxford: Oxford University Press, 1972); E. G. Gleason, *Gasparo Contarini* (Berkeley: University of California Press, 1993), pp. 186-256.

[11]Cf. C. Augustijn, "De Gesprekken tussen Bucer en Gropper tijdens het Godsdienstgesprek te Worms in December 1540," *Nederlands Archief voor Kerkgeschiedenis* 47 (1965-1966): 208-30.

[12]On its origins, cf. H. Eells, "The Origin of the Regensburg Book," *Princeton Theological Review* 26 (1928): 355-72; R. Stupperich, "Der Ursprung des 'Regensburger Buches' von 1541 und seine Rechtfertigungslehre," *Archiv für Reformationsgeschichte* 36 (1939): 88-116; R. Braunisch, "Die 'Artikell' der 'Wahrhaftigen Antwort' (1545) des Johannes Gropper. Zur Verfasserfrage des Worms-Regensburger Buches (1540/41)," in *Von Konstanz nach Trient*, ed. R. Bäumer (Munich, Paderborn and Vienna: Ferdinand Schöningh, 1972), pp. 519-45. For the text, cf. G. Pfeilschifter, ed., *Acta Reformationis Catholicae*, vol. 6 (Regensburg: F. Pustet, 1974), pp. 21-88. The Regensburg Book went through four drafts (not all of which survive) and Pfeilschifter gives textual critical apparatus.

[13]Various participants published the *Acts* of the colloquy. In 1541 Bucer and Melanchthon produced Latin and German editions, and Calvin produced an edition in French (CO 5:509-684). An abridged English translation of Bucer's edition is found in D. J. Ziegler, ed., *Great Debates of the Reformation* (New York: Random House, 1969), pp. 143-77.

[14]On Calvin's role in the colloquies, cf. W. H. Neuser, "Calvins Beitrag zu den Religionsgesprächen von Hagenau, Worms und Regensburg (1540/41)," in *Studien zur Geschichte und Theologie der Reformation*, ed. L. Abramowski and J. F. G. Goeters (Neukirchen: Neukirchener Verlag, 1969), pp. 213-37.

on the Worms agreement.[15] The fifth article, on justification, was discussed from April 28 to May 2.[16] Eck and Melanchthon both found it too imprecise and it was agreed that a new article should be drawn up. Gropper drew up a shorter version.[17] Draft and counter-draft were discussed until eventually, on May 2, the Protestants were allowed to amend a Catholic draft to their own satisfaction.[18] All the parties gave their consent to the final draft, a translation of which is found at the end of this paper. Granvella and Contarini were jubilant; Eck needed some persuasion to sign.

The colloquy itself failed in due course, but that was because of differences on *other* doctrines, such as the Eucharist and the underlying issue of the authority of the church,[19] not because of shortcomings in the statement on justification. On May 22 the colloquy came to a close, the article on justification being its only significant achievement. Even during the colloquy there were those on both sides who were unwilling to accept the article; after the failure of the colloquy there was even less interest in supporting it. The Regensburg Diet was not to end for another two months, on July 29.

---

[15]On the Worms and Regensburg articles on original sin, cf. A. Vanneste, "La préhistoire du décret du Concile de Trente sur le péché originel," *Nouvelle Revue Théologique* 86 (1964): 500-10. For a summary of the first four articles, cf. J. Raitt, "From Augsburg to Trent," in *Justification by Faith: Lutherans and Catholics in Dialogue VII*, ed. H. G. Anderson, T. A. Murphy and J. A. Burgess (Minneapolis: Augsburg, 1985), pp. 210-11.

[16]For the text, cf. Pfeilschifter, *Acta Reformationis Catholicae*, 6:30-44. The full title was *De restitutione regenerationis et iustificatione hominis gratia et merito, fide et operibus.*

[17]Ibid., 6:44-52.

[18]Ibid., 6:52-54. The new title was *De iustificatione hominis.* D. Hampson, *Christian Contradictions: The Structures of Lutheran and Catholic Thought* (Cambridge: Cambridge University Press, 2001), pp. 64-65, has a translation of parts of the article. She seems to have confused the opening paragraphs of article 5 with the four articles that were agreed earlier (cf. 63-64 with 291-92). On this article in particular, cf. F. Dittrich, *Gasparo Contarini 1483-1542* (Nieuwkoop: De Graaf, 1972 = *Nachdruck* of Braunsberg, 1885 ed.), pp. 651-700; W. von Loewenich, *Duplex Iustitia: Luthers Stellung zu einer Unionsformel des 16. Jahrhunderts* (Wiesbaden: Franz Steiner, 1972), pp. 34-38; Matheson, *Cardinal Contarini at Regensburg*, pp. 104-13; K. H. zur Mühlen, "Die Einigung über den Rechtfertigungsartikel auf dem Regensburger Religionsgespräch von 1541—eine verpaßte Chance?" *Zeitschrift für Theologie und Kirche* 76 (1979): 331-59; Gleason, *Gasparo Contarini*, pp. 227-35, 240-56; C. S. Smith, "Calvin's Doctrine of Justification in Relation to the Sense of Sin and the Dialogue with Rome" (M.Phil. thesis, London Bible College, 1993), pp. 128-48; A. Lexutt, *Rechtfertigung im Gespräch: Das Rechtfertigungsverständnis in den Religionsgesprächen von Hagenau, Worms und Regensburg 1540/41* (Göttingen: Vandenhoeck & Ruprecht, 1996), pp. 250-60.

[19]This was the issue on which all the colloquies failed; see H. Jedin, "An welchen Gegensätzen sind die vortridentinischen Religionsgespräche zwischen Katholiken und Protestanten gescheitert?" *Theologie und Glaube* 48 (1958): 50-55.

REACTIONS TO ARTICLE 5

Right from day one there were two contrasting Protestant reactions to the agreed article on justification. The first was that it was compatible with the Protestant position and represented a significant concession on the Catholic side. The second was that it was a compromising patchwork of two incompatible positions, blighted by ambiguity.

The first reaction is well expressed by Calvin in a letter written a few days after it was produced:

> The debate in controversy was more keen upon the doctrine of justification. At length a formula was drawn up, which, on receiving certain corrections, was accepted on both sides. You will be astonished, I am sure, that our opponents have yielded so much, when you read the extracted copy, as it stood when the last correction was made upon it, which you will find enclosed in the letter. Our friends have thus retained also the substance of the true doctrine, so that nothing can be comprehended within it which is not to be found in our writings; you will desire, I know, a more distinct explication and statement of the doctrine, and, in that respect, you shall find me in complete agreement with yourself. However, if you consider with what kind of men we have to agree upon this doctrine, you will acknowledge that much has been accomplished.[20]

The second reaction was consistently expressed by Luther, who was not himself present at the colloquy.[21] In an initial letter on May 10/11, he branded it "patched and all-embracing." He claimed that the two ideas of justification by faith alone without works and faith working through love had been "thrown together and glued together," whereas one refers to becoming righteous, the other to the life of the righteous. "So they are right, and so are we." This is like sewing a new patch onto an old garment.[22] A month later he expressed his fears that the article would be understood to teach that "faith justifies through love."[23] Some weeks later he wrote again, citing eight propositions that were being taught by Catholic theolo-

---

[20]John Calvin, letter of May 11 to Farel (SWJC 4:260; CO 11:215-16; A. L. Herminjard, *Correspondance des Réformateurs dans les pays de langue française* [Geneva: H. Georg & Paris: M. Levy, 1866-1897] 7:111); in a letter of August 3/13 to Viret, he was negative about the colloquy as a whole (SWJC 4:279; CO 11:262; Herminjard, *Correspondance des Réformateurs*, 7:218). On Calvin's view, cf. W. H. Neuser, "Calvins Urteil über den Rechtfertigungsartikel des Regensburger Buches," in *Reformation und Humanismus*, ed. M. Greschat and J. F. G. Goeters (Witten: Luther-Verlag, 1969), pp. 176-94.

[21]For Luther's view, cf. von Loewenich, *Duplex Iustitia*, pp. 29-34, 48-55 (cf. pp. 26-29), where the weakness of Luther's arguments is spelled out. Cf. also Pfnür, "Die Einigung bei den Religionsgesprächen von Worms und Regensburg 1540/41," pp. 64-68.

[22]Martin Luther, letter of May 10/11 to Johann Friedrich (WABR 9:406-9, #3616).

[23]Martin Luther, letter of June 11/12 to Princes Johann and Georg (WABR 9:438, 441, #3629).

gians and complaining that such doctrines were *not* excluded by the article.[24] It has rightly been observed that the objections of both Rome and Wittenberg concerned not so much the content of Article 5 as fear of how the other side would exploit it. Unlike the participants at Regensburg, neither Luther nor the Vatican was willing to settle for anything short of total victory.[25]

These two contrasting reactions are also found in the same author. When the article was produced Kaspar Cruciger wrote to Bugenhagen affirming that the article "does not disagree with or depart from our view" and claiming that "the theologians of our party" accepted the article, believing it to agree with "the doctrine of our churches." But at the same time he also called it a patchwork.[26] Two weeks later he was more aware of the ambiguities of the article. The other side had managed to retain some of the words of their own draft, "which either contain something disagreeable or are capable of being later distorted by their sophistries."[27] On June 24 he was no more positive, noting the Catholics' reluctance to accept the imperfection of good works. He felt that the article had been too hastily agreed upon.[28]

There is a pattern that fits much of the Protestant response to Article 5—initial enthusiasm followed by reservations. There are two prime reasons for this. The first is the failure to reach agreement on other articles. *The enthusiasm that greeted Article 5 was enthusiasm for the prospect of agreement across the board, not enthusiasm for the idea of agreeing in one point only.* Events were soon to prove how unrealistic this was. The second reason was the way in which some Catholics were interpreting the article and the awareness of its ambiguities. It should be noted that while failure to agree on other articles dramatically undermined the value of Article 5 at the time, it does not of itself indicate that the agreement on justification was not genuine. Regarding the interpretations given to the article, we must distinguish between unfounded claims made about its teaching[29] and genuine ambiguities that lie in text itself. While the former were a matter of concern for the Protestant party at the time,

---

[24]Martin Luther, letter of June 29 to Johann Friedrich (WABR 9:461-62, #3637).

[25]Gleason, *Gasparo Contarini*, p. 244.

[26]Cruciger, letter of May 5 to Bugenhagen (CR 4:252-53). Cruciger also shared Burckhard's scepticism regarding the prospects for agreement on the other articles. Cf. Cruciger, letter of May 5 to Menius (CR 4:259), where he stated that the article "quae etsi non est a nostris composita, sed utrinque consarcinata, tamen a nostra doctrina, quod discrepet, nihil habet."

[27]Cruciger, letter of May 19 to Bugenhagen (CR 4:304).

[28]Cruciger, letter of June 24 to Saxon councilors (CR 4:433-34).

[29]Here I am thinking especially of the claim that it teaches that we are accepted by God "sola dilectione," reported by both Melanchthon (CR 4:430, 485, 499) and Pistorius (CR 4:445).

only the latter need detain us as we examine its teaching today.

Regensburg did not have good press. The prevailing judgment was negative.[30] But with the shift from a polemical to an ecumenical approach in recent years this judgment has been reconsidered.[31] Also, it is important to distinguish between the colloquy in general, which clearly failed, and Article 5, which did produce agreement. Matheson's pithy (and exaggerated) judgment on the colloquy is often cited: "The dialogue between Protestantism and Catholicism at the Diet of Regensburg in 1541 did not fail. It never took place."[32] But his judgment on Article 5 is much more positive:

> The article is certainly a product of diplomacy, yet it is by no means lacking in theological substance. It is a finely balanced piece of conciliation, but it exhibits an integrity all its own. It falls outside the confessional categories certainly; its language, however, is that of conviction, not caution. It is no mere mediatorial formula, offering a crumb of theological comfort to every grouping. It takes up a clear line, and it is because of this uncomfortable clarity, not because of an alleged ambiguity, that it was later rejected by Catholic and Protestant confessionalists.[33]

Not all are convinced. McGrath concurs with Fenlon's judgment that Article 5 was a "scissors and paste job." "It is clear that Article V *de iustificatione* represented a mere juxtaposition of the Catholic and Protestant positions, with a purely superficial engagement with the serious theological issues at stake."[34] Gleason likewise states that, "both style and content make it obvious that Article 5 was the work of a committee. The modern reader will search in vain for logical consistency, since the essence of the agreed-upon text was a compromise between two basically incompatible positions."[35] The present paper will imply a more favorable assessment.[36]

---

[30]Hall, *Humanists and Protestants*, p. 143, documents this, especially on the Catholic side.

[31]Cf. *Justification by Faith*, §§45-48, which conclude that Regensburg indicates that "the two ways of explaining justification are not necessarily exclusive" (Anderson, Murphy and Burgess, *Justification by Faith*, pp. 32-33).

[32]Matheson, *Cardinal Contarini at Regensburg*, p. 181, the final words of the book.

[33]Ibid., pp. 107-8. Pfnür, "Die Einigung bei den Religionsgesprächen von Worms und Regensburg 1540/41," pp. 76-77, calls the article "nicht eine Täuschung, sondern durchaus sachgemäß."

[34]A. E. McGrath, *Iustitia Dei: A History of the Christian Doctrine of Justification*, 2 vols. (Cambridge: Cambridge University Press, 1986), 2:60-61; D. Fenlon, *Heresy and Obedience in Tridentine Italy: Cardinal Pole and Counter Reformation* (Cambridge: Cambridge University Press, 1972), p. 55.

[35]Gleason, *Gasparo Contarini*, pp. 227-28.

[36]I will be arguing this in a forthcoming book, provisionally titled *Compromising Patchwork or Ecumenical Breakthrough? The Regensburg Article on Justification (1541): Introduction, Text and Commentary.*

THE TEACHING OF ARTICLE 5

What does Article 5 actually teach? Underlying the entire article is the idea of *duplex iustitia* or twofold righteousness—that conversion brings both inherent and imputed righteousness. The term itself (*duplex iustitia*) is not found in the article, but the article is built on the idea that there are these different "righteousnesses" (inherent and imputed), which are clearly set out.

What is the significance of this idea of twofold righteousness? Catholics and Protestants were offering two contrasting models of justification. The Protestant teaching was that God accepts us as righteous (what Protestants understand by justification) because Christ's righteousness is reckoned or imputed to our account. That is, we are acceptable to God not because of anything that we have done, nor indeed because of the change that God brings about within us, but because of what Christ has done for us on the cross. We are acceptable not for what we are (which remains imperfect) but in Christ. The Catholic teaching, by contrast, was that justification is about God changing us by the Holy Spirit and thus making us acceptable to himself. At baptism/conversion we are transformed within by the grace of God, by *gratia gratum faciens*, grace that makes us pleasing or acceptable, that brings about within us an inherent righteousness. Thus we have the contrast between the Protestant view that we become acceptable on the basis of *imputed* righteousness (the righteousness of Christ reckoned to our account) and the Catholic view that we become righteous through Christ's righteousness being imparted to us or infused in us, through an inner change which gives us an *inherent* righteousness. The key contribution of Regensburg was to insist that with conversion we receive *both* of these: inherent *and* imputed righteousness.

How does Regensburg develop this idea? The teaching of the article can be summarized in a few points:

1. The term "justification" is understood in the Protestant sense of being accepted and reckoned righteous by God (§4:1, 6, 5:2) though it is noted that the fathers understood it differently to refer to inherent righteousness (§5:1).

2. This justification or reckoning righteous is on account of Christ and his merit (§4:1-2, 5:2), on the basis of imputed righteousness (§3:6, 4:4, 6). It is *not* on the basis of inherent righteousness or the righteousness of works (§4:6, 5:1-2). Protestant concerns are effectively met by the clear and unambiguous insistence that acceptance is on the basis of imputed and not inherent righteousness. But it is also true that we are called righteous because of the good

deeds that flow from inherent righteousness (§5:3).

3. While God accepts us on the basis of imputed righteousness, he also at the same time (§4:3-4) gives us his Holy Spirit (§3:6, 4:4), through which we become partakers in the divine nature (§2), are renewed (§6, 8:1), have inherent righteousness (§5:1, 3), receive the infusion of love (§4:3-4) and begin to do good works (§5:3, 8:2-3, 9, 10) and fulfill the law (§4:3). We should grow in virtues (§6) and in the renewal that we have received (§8:1). This growth comes through good works (§8:2). The Catholic concern for love and good works is clearly and unambiguously met by the insistence on the simultaneous gift of the Holy Spirit and love leading to good works. Sanctification is not presented as merely a consequence (whether desirable or inevitable) of justification, but as a parallel and inseparable gift.

4. Justification and the gift of the Spirit are received by faith (§3:6). The faith that justifies is a living faith (§4:1, 4) and it is by the Holy Spirit that we are moved to this faith (§3:5, 4:2). In particular, this faith is efficacious through love (§4:1, 5), although the function of faith is to appropriate God's gifts (§3:6, 4:2, 4, 6). Faith not only believes all that God has revealed but also in particular assents to and acquires confidence from God's promises (§3:5). It is all right to teach justification by faith alone so long as this is not to the exclusion of teaching about repentance and good works (§10:1-2).

5. Coming to faith involves hating sin in mind and will (§3:1) and repenting (§3:2-5, 4:2, 10), which occur through the prevenient movement of the Spirit (§3:1).[37] Our free choice has a role to play concurring in good works (§8:3).

6. While we are renewed by the Holy Spirit, this renewal is imperfect and it is not on this that we should rely, but only on Christ's gift of righteousness (§5:1), his role as mediator (§6) and his promises (§7).

7. Nonetheless, God has promised to reward our good works, in this life and the next (§8:2-3, 9). Eternal life is an inheritance based on promise, but works are rewarded to the extent that they are done in faith and from the Spirit (§8:3).

I have argued elsewhere that Calvin was right to claim that there is nothing here which cannot be paralleled in the writings of the Reformers (indeed, in his own

---

[37]Gleason, *Gasparo Contarini*, p. 228, observes that "the relative importance of the prevenient motion of the Holy Spirit and the response of the human intellect and will is left unclear." This is true but is a problem only if one supposes that the article has to resolve all theological issues. Article 2 has more to say on the topic.

writings) and that a great deal had been conceded by the other side.[38] He was also right to admit that it was not perhaps as clearly stated as the Reformers would have wished, but that is a very minor complaint given that this was a document which had been accepted by some of the leading Catholic theologians of the day. It is noteworthy that the evolving Protestant criticism of Article 5 complained about its ambiguities and the manner in which the "other side" was interpreting it but did not concede that it was incompatible with either the Augsburg Confession or Melanchthon's *Apology of the Augsburg Confession*.

What were these ambiguities and misinterpretations? There are two key points that recur.[39] The first concerned the status of good works. The article affirms that sin remains after conversion,[40] but it needs to teach more clearly that the regenerate can never satisfy the law of God in this life and that God is nevertheless pleased with our imperfect obedience. Clarification is also needed on the distinction between those sins that do and those that do not cause us to lose grace and the Holy Spirit.

Second, there was considerable concern about the statement that the faith that justifies is a faith that is effectual through love, *efficax per caritatem*. The article states that we are justified or accepted as righteous on the basis of a living and efficacious faith (§4:1). Again, justification does not happen without the infusion of love and the faith that justifies is effectual through love (§4:3, 5). What is the problem here? None of the Reformers wanted to state that it was possible to have saving faith without love. That saving faith is a living faith accompanied by love leading to good works was not controversial. But the (separated) statements that we are justified on the basis of *efficacious* faith and that faith is effectual through love *could* be taken to mean that justification is on the basis not of faith alone but (to use the Catholic formula) of "faith formed by love." Thus it was claimed by some Catholics at Regensburg that the article taught justification by *love* alone.[41] Such an interpretation is clearly excluded by the article itself[42]—but the fact that it could be claimed (however

[38]In "Calvin and Article 5 of the Regensburg Colloquy," in *Calvinus Praeceptor Ecclesiae*, ed. H. Selderhuis (Geneva: Droz, 2004), pp. 231-61.

[39]E.g., in Melanchthon's comments in CR 4:413-19, 419-31, 479-91.

[40]The renewal brought by the Holy Spirit is imperfect (§6) and we are therefore to depend not upon our inherent righteousness but upon Christ's righteousness given to us as a gift (§5:1).

[41]CR 4:430, 445, 485, 499.

[42]The statement that justifying faith is *efficax per caritatem* is immediately followed by the affirmation that this faith justifies by appropriating mercy and imputed righteousness, and that this righteousness is not imputed on account of any imparted worthiness or perfection (§4:5-6). Acceptance on the basis of inherent righteousness (such as love) is very carefully excluded.

unreasonably) made the Protestants suspicious of the ambiguity of the formula.

In a recent ecumenical discussion of the Augsburg Confession, the Catholic theologian Erwin Iserloh posed a question to a Protestant participant. Is not the controversy over faith and love merely verbal? If Protestants maintain that faith is not purely intellectual and is a response of the heart to God, if it is a work of the Spirit that changes the heart, then is this not what Catholics understand by "faith formed by love"?[43] There are two answers to this question. As we have seen, the Reformers did not wish to deny that the faith that justifies is in fact "faith formed by love," though that was not their preferred terminology. Any difference here is hardly worth a debate, let alone dividing the church. The crucial issue, however, concerns *the basis for our acceptance by God.* Are we accepted on the basis of the righteousness of Christ reckoned or imputed to our account and received by faith? (Together with this faith other virtues like love may be found, but it is not these that lay hold of Christ's righteousness.) Or are we accepted on the basis of the righteousness that now inheres within us and, in particular, the love bestowed by the Holy Spirit that makes us acceptable to God? (So justification may be by "faith formed by love," but it is essentially love that justifies.) Here is not a minor verbal quibble but the difference between two fundamentally irreconcilable doctrines of justification. There is no serious doubt where Article 5 stands on this. Acceptance on the basis of the imputed righteousness of Christ is taught and acceptance on the basis of inherent righteousness is denied. Contarini and Gropper understood this clearly and went on to defend it *after* the colloquy.

TWOFOLD RIGHTEOUSNESS AGAIN

Having clarified the teaching of the article, let us return again to the doctrine of twofold righteousness. Is this not evidence that the article is a mere patchwork of incompatible views? Or is it in fact a consistent statement, albeit making terminological concessions to both sides? Or could it in fact be more than this and actually serve as a key to a better understanding of the doctrine of justification?

At first sight the patchwork charge appears to be self-evidently true. Catholics spoke of an inherent, imparted righteousness, the inner transformation of sinners by the gracious act of the Holy Spirit so that they actually *become* righteous, so that God accepts them as righteous because they really are. Protestants spoke of an im-

---

[43]V. Pfnür, "Die Einigung in der Rechtfertigungslehre bei den Religionsverhandlungen auf dem Reichstag zu Augsburg 1530," in *Confessio Augustana und Confutatio,* ed. B. Hallensleben and E. Iserloh (Münster: Aschendorff, 1980), p. 375 (transcript of ensuing discussion).

puted righteousness, of Christ's righteousness being *reckoned* to our account so that, unworthy as we are, we are accepted by God on account of Christ. Regensburg links these two together and affirms that in conversion we receive *both* types of righteousness. Surely Luther was right to summarize this mockingly as the claim that "So they are right, and so are we"? Or was he? The doctrine of twofold righteousness and its origins needs to be explored a little more carefully.

The first point to note is that what Regensburg calls "inherent righteousness" corresponds to what Protestant theologians called (and call) "sanctification." The Reformers all but universally agreed that conversion brings both justification and sanctification. The only concession that Regensburg demanded of them was terminological—to use the term "inherent righteousness" of sanctification. This was not much of a concession since many of them (such as Bucer and Calvin) were already accustomed to use the word "righteousness" at least sometimes when referring to sanctification.[44] On the Catholic side a rather bigger concession was demanded. They had to admit the validity of imputed righteousness. This was a significant step. Contarini appears to have been innocent of the idea prior to Regensburg. Gropper's *Enchiridion* contains some references to imputation, but the idea is not nearly as clear as in the Regensburg article.[45] Contarini was required to accept a new idea; Gropper to develop an existing idea. They both did so wholeheartedly and went on to expound and defend the theme of imputed righteousness in their later writings.[46] Both were to attract the attention of the Inquisition as a result and they and other cardinals were suspected of Protestant tendencies because of their support for Article 5.[47]

Second, Regensburg does not simply place imputed and inherent righteousness side by side as unreconciled and conflicting concepts. The reason why the Reformers insisted on imputed righteousness was that both our own inherent righteousness and

---

[44]E.g., M. Bucer, preface to *Metaphrases et Enarrationes Perpetuae Epistolarum D. Pauli Apostoli* (Strassburg: W. Rihel, 1536), pp. 11-14; *Metaphrasis et Enarratio in Epist. D. Pauli Apostoli ad Romanos* (Basel: P. Pern, 1562), pp. 11-14; D. F. Wright, ed., *Common Places of Martin Bucer* (Appleford, Abingdon: Sutton Courtenay, 1972), pp. 160-67; Calvin *Institutio* 3:3:8-9.
[45]*Enchiridion Christianae Institutionis* (Cologne: Peter Quentel, 1538), fols. 129b, 130b, 132a-133a.
[46]Contarini, *Epistola de iustificatione*, in *Gasparo Contarini, Gegenreformatorische Schriften (1530 c.-1542)*, ed. F. Hünermann, Corpus Catholicorum 7 (Münster: W. Aschendorf, 1923), pp. 27-31; Gropper, *Antididagma, seu, Christianae et Catholicae religionis . . . Propugnatio* (Cologne: Jaspar Gennepaeus, 1544), fols. 11b, 13b, 14a.
[47]P. Simoncelli, "Vom Humanismus zur Gegenreformation. Das Schicksal des Regensburger Buches in Italien: Versuch einer Rekonstruktion," in *Pflugiana: Studien über Julius Pflug (1499-1564)*, ed. E. Neuss and J. V. Pollet (Münster: Aschendorff, 1990), pp. 111-12.

the righteousness of our works remain imperfect and it is not on that basis that we can stand before God. Instead it is on the basis of imputed righteousness, Christ's righteousness reckoned to our account, that God accepts us. Article 5 makes precisely this point. God accepts us on the basis of imputed righteousness, on account of Christ, not on the basis of "the worthiness or perfection imparted to us in Christ" (§4:5). The believer depends not on inherent righteousness but only on the gift of Christ's righteousness (§5:1). Ambiguity and patchwork are not the appropriate terms to describe this. Contarini was a good learner at this point. In a letter written to defend Article 5 he places heavy emphasis on the need to rely not on inherent but on imputed righteousness *alone*, because of the imperfection of the former.[48]

Where does this idea of twofold righteousness, this careful juxtaposition of inherent and imputed righteousness, originate? Gropper has in the past been claimed as the author of the formula, in his *Enchiridion*.[49] There are various problems with this claim, not the least being the fact that the formula is not actually found in the *Enchiridion*. Bucer has a better claim in that he frequently referred to the righteousness imparted to us by the Spirit.[50] But he did not before the colloquy, to my knowledge, explicitly set the two types of righteousness (inherent and imputed) side by side in parallel. Nor have I managed to find any other theologian who does so.[51] The Regensburg article appears to contain a small but highly significant terminological development. It was, one might say, one small step for a colloquy, one giant leap for Christian theology.

TWOFOLD RIGHTEOUSNESS TODAY

We have examined the doctrine of twofold righteousness in its mid sixteenth-century setting, but what of its relevance for today? Is it not just a footnote to history, a formulation that might have had potential but was in fact doomed to oblivion? It has been wittily stated that the doctrine of twofold righteousness in the 1540s was "a doctrine with neither a past nor a future."[52] I would like to suggest, however,

---

[48]*Epistola de iustificatione*, in Hünermann, *Gasparo Contarini, Gegenreformatorische Schriften*, pp. 29-30.

[49]Jedin, *History of the Council of Trent*, 2:257-58.

[50]As cited in n. 44, above.

[51]Some theologians (e.g., Luther) used the terminology of *duplex iustitia*, but not referring to this particular twofold righteousness (i.e., imputed and imparted); others had the *content* of the doctrine (e.g., justification and sanctification) but without the terminology of *duplex iustitia*.

[52]J. F. McCue, "Double Justification at the Council of Trent: Piety and Theology in Sixteenth Century Roman Catholicism," in *Piety, Politics and Ethics: Reformation Studies in Honor of George Wolfgang Forell*, ed. C. Lindberg (Kirksville: Sixteenth Century Journal, 1984), p. 39.

that not only was it not an inconsistent patchwork, not only was it a consistent affirmation of the Protestant doctrine of justification, but it is a formulation which could be of value to us today. On what grounds do I make that claim? To answer that, we first need to take a step back.

I have argued elsewhere[53] that to understand the doctrine of justification we need to be aware that there are two truths to be held in tension:

1. In the parable of the Pharisee and the tax collector (Lk 18:9-14) the Pharisee thanked God for all his good works and that he was better than others. The tax collector by contrast beat his breast and said, "God be merciful to me, a sinner." It was the tax collector, not the Pharisee, who was accepted by God. Here we see the grace of God shown to the worst of sinners and are reminded that this is the only ground on which we can approach God. But that is only half of the story. A few chapters earlier in the same gospel (Lk 14:25-33) the same Jesus speaks uncompromisingly of the demands of discipleship and warns that "any of you who does not give up everything that he has cannot be my disciple." The promise of acceptance to the worst sinner does not rule out the demand for total commitment from all believers.

2. Paul teaches justification by faith alone, that we are accepted by God not on the ground of our good works or merits but solely on the basis of Christ's death for us on the cross. "The foulest sinner who truly believes that moment from Jesus a pardon receives." Here again is the comforting message of grace. But the same Paul also teaches, as do other New Testament writers, that we are to be judged by our works. "For we must all appear before the judgement seat of Christ, that each one may receive what is due to him for the things done while in the body, whether good or bad" (2 Cor 5:10). He warns the Corinthian Christians that those indulging in a variety of activities, such as adultery, theft or drunkenness, will not inherit the kingdom of God (1 Cor 6:9-10). The message of free acceptance does not rule out the need for obedience.

3. A similar point was made by Dietrich Bonhoeffer, the German theologian who joined the resistance against Hitler and was hanged by the Nazis in the closing days of the war. In his *Cost of Discipleship* he talks of the distinction between cheap and costly grace. Cheap grace breaks our tension by offering forgiveness without repentance, grace without discipleship. Cheap grace proclaims the forgiveness

---

[53]"What's So Dangerous About Grace?" *Whitefield Briefing* 6, no. 4 (July 2001), from which the following paragraphs are taken; *Justification by Faith in Catholic-Protestant Dialogue*, pp. 132-35.

of sins without the resolve to forsake sin. Cheap grace interprets "grace alone" to mean that we can remain as we are without changing. Costly grace, however, calls us to follow Christ. It is costly because it cost God the life of his Son and because it costs us our life. "The only man who has the right to say that he is justified by grace alone is the man who has left all to follow Christ. . . . Those who try to use this grace as a dispensation from following Christ are simply deceiving themselves."[54]

4. It is important to maintain this tension in the overall thrust of a preaching ministry. One of my students once told me that at church he expects to hear the basic message: "You're O.K. God has accepted you in Christ." That is certainly an important part of the Gospel and in a Western world that is obsessed with the need for self-esteem it is the only message heard in many churches. But there is an equal need for another message: "You're not O.K. Your life falls short of what is expected of a Christian. Don't just relax and enjoy justification but repent and get on with sanctification." Indeed, without this second message the first ceases to be the biblical doctrine of justification by faith and becomes instead a secular message of self-esteem. As Luther pointed out, if we take away the law we lose the Gospel as well.

In each of these examples we see a similar tension. There is the good news of free grace but there is also the call to discipleship—not as an optional extra for the zealous but as part of the basic package. As someone once put it, the entrance fee for the Christian faith is nothing, but the annual subscription is everything. When we are in Christ we receive the free gift of justification but we also need to press on with the arduous task of sanctification.[55] At different times one or other side of this tension has been lost. At times the church has lapsed into preaching cheap grace, as Bonhoeffer put it, and Christians have been shamefully indistinct from the ungodly. At other times the stress has been on the moral demands of Christian faith and the radical message of forgiveness has faded into the background.

Present-day evangelicalism is not very good at maintaining this tension. Some actually deny it. There are some who deny that repentance is a necessary part of the gospel message. There are some who say that it is possible to have Christ as Savior

---

[54]Dietrich Bonhoeffer, *The Cost of Discipleship* (London: SCM Press, 1959), pp. 35-47.

[55]Justification and sanctification are held together in that we receive both in Christ. They are, as Calvin put it, like the heat and light of the sun: distinct but inseparable (*Institutes* 3.2.6). That does not in itself prevent us from falling into the trap of stressing one to the exclusion of the other.

without accepting him as Lord. The overwhelming majority of evangelicals would have no problem with rejecting these two positions, but in practice and by implication teach something similar. Having worked intensively on the doctrine of justification for some three years, my ears have become very sensitive to these issues. Listening to sermons from a wide range of sources[56] I hear a never-ending flood of references to the freeness of God's mercy, to the fact that God forgives, to the grace and favor that God is eager to lavish on all who come to him. At the same time I have heard a tiny trickle of references to the fact that the Gospel involves demands as well as benefits, to the fact that repentance is needed as well as faith, to the fact that discipleship is not an optional extra. The leading Catholic scholar Etienne Gilson fundamentally misunderstood the Reformers' doctrine of justification: "For the first time, with the Reformation, there appeared this conception of a grace that saves a man without changing him, of a justice that redeems corrupted nature without restoring it, of a Christ who pardons the sinner for self-inflicted wounds but does not heal them."[57] On the other hand, if he had been attempting to describe modern evangelical preaching would he have been so far wide of the truth?

One symptom of the problem can be seen in the way that good works are commended. I have heard a number of sermons in which Christians are taught that they *ought* to love and do good works. The Reformers would have regarded this as grossly inadequate. It is not enough to state that Christians *ought* to do good works—the truth is that Christians *will* do good works and those who do not simply demonstrate that they are not Christians. (This is so often stated in the teaching of Jesus that there is no need to give references.) The Reformers were often challenged by their Catholic opponents to state whether or not love and good works are *necessary* for salvation. Their answer was that love and good works *are* necessary for salvation in that without them one cannot be a Christian. But they do not *cause* our justification. You cannot be justified without love and good works, but it is not they that bring about justification. They are necessary as consequences or symptoms of justification, not as causes of it.[58] It is necessary to have spots in order to have chicken pox. It is not that the spots cause chicken pox, but that where there is chicken pox so there *will* be (not *ought* to be) spots. It is necessary to cough in order to have SARS (Severe Adult Respiratory [Distress] Syndrome), but coughing does not

<hr/>

[56]I would exempt from this criticism my own pastor, Roger Pearce.
[57]Etienne Gilson, *The Spirit of Medieval Philosophy* (London: Sheed & Ward, 1936), p. 421.
[58]E.g., Luther in the 1536 *Disputation on Justification* (WA 39/I:96, 102); Bucer, *De vera ecclesiarum in doctrina, ceremoniis, et disciplina reconcilatione et compositione* (Strassburg: W. Rihel, 1542), fols. 179b-180b.

cause it—at least not your own coughing! As Calvin put it, justification is not *by* works, but nor is it *without* works (*Institutes* 3:16:1).

How can this point be protected in our understanding of justification? At one level the mainstream Reformation doctrine (as expounded by Calvin for example) does protect it. By faith we are united to Christ and in him we receive justification and sanctification. It is not possible to have one without the other. If this doctrine is understood and accepted there is no danger of supposing that one can be a Christian without love or good works. But the trouble is that justification and sanctification are two very different words and it is not so hard for people to separate them in their thinking and practice. That is where the "twofold righteousness" terminology scores. It makes the same point as Calvin (and others) about the inseparability of justification and sanctification—but makes it in a more direct and forceful way that is harder to miss. The inseparability of the two is not just taught as a doctrine but is implied by the very terminology. If evangelicals were to pick up the "twofold righteousness" terminology—as a supplement to traditional talk of justification and sanctification, not to replace it—they would be in less danger of lapsing into a soft form of Antinomianism, as at present. To present the righteousness that we receive as "twofold" affirms its indivisibility more unambiguously than does talking about two different things (justification and sanctification) and then affirming (to those who are still listening) that they are inseparable.

APPENDIX
THE REGENSBURG AGREEMENT (1541), ARTICLE 5
The Justification of Man

The translation that follows is my own, based on a text reconstructed from the versions given by Bucer, Eck, Gropper and Melanchthon. A very similar translation appeared in my *Justification by Faith in Catholic-Protestant Dialogue*, pp. 233-37.

1. No Christian should doubt that after the fall of our first parent all men are, as the apostle says, born children of wrath [Eph 2:3] and enemies of God [Rom 5:10] and thereby are in death and slavery to sin [Rom 6:16-20].

2. Likewise, no Christian should question that nobody can be reconciled with God, nor set free from slavery to sin, except by Christ the one mediator between God and men [1 Tim 2:5], by whose grace, as the apostle said to the Romans, we are not only reconciled to God [Rom 5:10] and set free from slavery to sin [Rom 6:18, 22], but also made sharers in the divine nature [2 Pet 1:4] and children of God [Rom 8:14-16].

3. (1) Likewise, it is quite clear that adults do not obtain these blessings of Christ, except by the prevenient movement of the Holy Spirit, by which their mind and will are moved to hate sin. (2) For, as St. Augustine says, it is impossible to begin a new life if we do not repent of the former one. (3) Likewise, in the last chapter of Luke [Lk 24:47], Christ commands that repentance and forgiveness of sin should be preached in his name. (4) Also, John the Baptist, sent to prepare the way of the Lord, preached repentance, saying [Mt 3:2]: "Repent, for the kingdom of heaven is drawing near." (5) Next, man's mind is moved toward God by the Holy Spirit through Christ and this movement is through faith. Through this [faith] man's mind believes with certainty all that God has transmitted, and also with full certainty and without doubt assents to the promises made to us by God who, as stated in the psalm [Ps 145:13], is faithful in all his words. From there he acquires confidence on account of God's promise, by which he has pledged that he will remit sins freely and that he will adopt as children those who believe in Christ, those I say who repent of their former life. (6) By this faith, he is lifted up to God by the Holy Spirit and so he receives the Holy Spirit, remission of sins, imputation of righteousness and countless other gifts.

4. (1) So it is a reliable and sound doctrine that the sinner is justified by living and efficacious faith, for through it we are pleasing and acceptable to God on account of Christ. (2) And living faith is what we call the movement of the Holy Spirit, by which those who truly repent of their old life are lifted up to God and truly appropriate the mercy promised in Christ, so that they now truly recognize that they have received the remission of sins and reconciliation on account of the merits of Christ, through the free goodness of God, and cry out to God: "Abba Father" [Rom 8:15; Gal 4:6]. (3) But this happens to no one unless also at the same time love is infused which heals the will so that the healed will may begin to fulfil the law, just as St. Augustine said. (4) So living faith is that which both appropriates mercy in Christ, believing that the righteousness that is in Christ is freely imputed to it, and at the same time receives the promise of the Holy Spirit and love. (5) Therefore the faith that truly justifies is that faith which is effectual through love [Gal 5:6]. (6) Nevertheless it remains true that it is by this faith that we are justified (that is, accepted and reconciled to God) inasmuch as it appropriates the mercy and righteousness that is imputed to us on account of Christ and his merit, not on account of the worthiness or perfection of the righteousness imparted to us in Christ.

5. (1) Although the one who is justified receives righteousness and through Christ also has inherent [righteousness], as the apostle says: "you are washed, you are sanctified, you are justified, etc." [I Cor 6:11] (which is why the holy fathers made use of [the term] "to be justified" even to mean "to receive inherent righteousness"), nevertheless, the faithful soul depends not on this, but only on the righteousness of Christ given to us as a gift, without which there is and can be no righteousness at all. (2) And thus by faith in Christ we are justified or reckoned to be righteous, that is, we are accepted through his merits and not on account of our own worthiness or works. (3) And on account of the righteousness inherent in us we are said to be righteous, because the works which we perform are righteous, according to the saying of John: "whoever does what is right is righteous" [I Jn 3:7].

6. Although fear of God, patience, humility and other virtues ought always to grow in the regenerate, because this renewal is imperfect and enormous weakness remains in them, it should nevertheless be taught that those who truly repent may always hold with most certain faith that they are pleasing to God on account of Christ the mediator. For it is Christ who is the propitiator, the High Priest and the one who prays for us, the one the Father gave to us and with him all good things [Rom 8:32].

7. Seeing that in our weakness there is no perfect certainty and that there are many weak and fearful consciences, which often struggle against great doubt, nobody should be excluded from the grace of Christ on account of such weakness. Such people should be earnestly encouraged boldly to set the promises of Christ against these doubts and by diligent intercession to pray that their faith may be increased, according to the saying: "Lord increase our faith" [Lk 17:5].

8. (1) Likewise, every Christian should learn that this grace and this regeneration have not been given to us so that we might remain idle in that stage of our renewal which we at first obtained, but so that we may grow in everything into him who is the head [Eph 4:15]. (2) Therefore, the people must be taught to devote effort to this growth that indeed happens through good works, both internal and external, which are commanded and commended by God. To these works God has, in many passages from the Gospels, clearly and manifestly promised on account of Christ a reward—good things in this life, as much for the body as for the soul (as much as seems right to divine providence) and after this life in heaven. (3) Therefore, although the inheritance of eternal life is due

to the regenerate on account of the promise, as soon as they are reborn in Christ, nevertheless God also renders a reward to good works, not according to the substance of the works, nor because they come from us, but to the extent that they are performed in faith and proceed from the Holy Spirit, who dwells in us, free choice concurring as a partial agent.

9. The joy of those who have performed more and better works will be greater and more abundant, on account of the increase of faith and love, in which they have grown through exercises of that kind.

10. (1) Now those who say that we are justified by faith alone should at the same time teach the doctrine of repentance, of the fear of God, of the judgement of God and of good works, so that all the chief points of the preaching may remain firm, as Christ said: "preaching repentance and the remission of sins in my name" [Lk 24:47]. (2) And that is to prevent this way of speaking [that is, *sola fide*] from being understood other than has been previously mentioned.

9

THE THEOLOGY OF JUSTIFICATION IN DOGMATIC CONTEXT

PAUL D. MOLNAR

One of the breakthroughs of the Joint Declaration of 1999 was the fact that the doctrine of justification was placed securely on a scriptural foundation within the context of the doctrine of the Trinity. This is no small matter as Rahner himself observed over thirty-five years ago when he wrote his remarks on Hans Küng's book on justification: "We do share with Barth a common authority, Scripture. Why should we not feel at one, where, having accepted unreservedly the *same* testimony of Scripture, we permit ourselves to think that we have come to an agreement about its interpretation?"[1]

In paragraph 8 of the Joint Declaration it is said, "Our common way of listening to the Word of God in Scripture has led to such new insights. Together we hear the Gospel that 'God so loved the world that he gave his only Son, so that everyone who believes in him may not perish but may have eternal life' (John 3:16)." And in paragraph 15 of the Joint Declaration it is said that

> in faith we together hold the conviction that justification is the work of the triune God. The Father sent his Son into the world to save sinners. The foundation and presupposition of justification is the incarnation, death and resurrection of Christ. Justification thus means that Christ himself is our righteousness, in which we share through the Holy Spirit. . . . By grace alone, in faith in Christ's saving work and not because of any merit on our part, we are accepted by God and receive the Holy Spirit, who renews our hearts while equipping and calling us to good works.

---

[1]Karl Rahner, "Questions of Controversial Theology on Justification," in *Theological Investigations*, 23 vols. (hereafter *TI*), trans. Kevin Smyth (Baltimore: Helicon, 1966), 4:197.

Finally, in paragraph 16 it is said that, "All people are called by God to salvation in Christ. Through Christ alone are we justified, when we receive this salvation in faith." A theology of justification must allow the fact that we are saved by Christ alone (*solus Christus*), and therefore by faith alone and grace alone, to dictate its theological method and its view of God, incarnation and resurrection. One would presume that if there is a common affirmation of our justification by faith grounded in the scriptural testimony, then there should be some evidence of this in contemporary Catholic and Protestant theology, specifically their view of God, incarnation and resurrection. With that in mind I propose to compare the thought of two celebrated theologians, one Roman Catholic (Karl Rahner), the other Reformed (Karl Barth), to see how close or perhaps how distant Reformed and Roman Catholic theology are from each other today in light of the doctrine of justification.

One might wonder whether or not these are theologians whose time has passed. To anyone thinking that, I would say that there can be little doubt that even today, and perhaps especially today, Barth's theology still exercises considerable influence not only among Protestant theologians but also among Catholic theologians. There is hardly a discussion of any important theological topic that does not include Barth's thinking. And in both Catholic and Protestant circles Rahner's theology still exercises considerable influence. He is seen by many as a representative *par excellence* of Roman Catholic theology. But it is not only Roman Catholics who are interested in Rahner's theology. No less a theologian than Thomas F. Torrance saw Rahner as one with whom Reformed theology might have a serious dialogue partner in the person of Karl Barth.[2]

Karl Rahner himself wrote with amazement that Barth had apparently agreed

---

[2]See Thomas F. Torrance, *Trinitarian Perspectives: Toward Doctrinal Agreement* (Edinburgh: T & T Clark, 1994), pp. 77-78. Torrance wrote that Rahner's approach to God that claimed to begin with the economic Trinity has meant, among other things, "a rapprochement between Roman Catholic theology and Evangelical theology, especially as represented by the teaching of Karl Barth in his emphasis on the self-revelation and self-giving of God as the root of the doctrine of the Trinity" (p. 78). Of course Torrance recognized even then that there were problems with Rahner's presentation because he seemed to introduce "a moment of abstraction . . . between what God is in himself and the mode of his self-revelation and self-communication to us" (p. 79). In my judgment, if Rahner's method had been truly and consistently dictated by the economic Trinitarian self-revelation, then this rapprochement could have been enormous. But as I have suggested in my book *Divine Freedom and the Doctrine of the Immanent Trinity: In Dialogue with Karl Barth and Contemporary Theology* (New York: Continuum, 2002) it is precisely Rahner's method, which begins with transcendental experience, that compromises the fact that the sole root of our knowledge of the triune God is and remains God's self-communication in Christ. See especially chapters four, five and six.

with Hans Küng's presentation of his doctrine of justification, insisting that this was important for the future union of the church because "Barth is not just anybody in Protestant theology."[3] Rahner suggested that perhaps in other areas where Barth disagreed with the Catholic position one could "correct Barth's other positions in the light of his doctrine of justification."[4] But what if Barth's doctrine of justification cannot in fact be separated from his other positions and in reality actually shapes his other positions? Then it seems two implications would follow: (1) any agreement about justification cannot just be an agreement about justification. It must also be an agreement about theological method, knowledge of God, the incarnation and the resurrection; (2) where Barth's "other positions" stand opposed to Catholic teaching it may be assumed that they do so precisely because of Barth's understanding of, and application of, the doctrine of justification.[5] It will be my contention that these differences cannot be covered over with ambiguous language that seems to express agreement on issues over which there is still genuine disagreement.[6]

---

[3]*TI* 4:193.

[4]Ibid. Rahner notes some of what Barth himself had already indicated, namely, that Barth is still separated from Roman Catholics by his view of original sin, election, the sacraments, the Church, the papacy and Mariology. It should be mentioned, however, that Rahner correctly labeled Küng's later thinking as "liberal Protestant" theology (see Stanley J. Grenz and Roger E. Olson, *20th Century Theology: God & the World in a Transitional Age* [Carlisle, U.K.: The Paternoster Press, 1992], pp. 256, 270) even though Rahner's own affinities to Schleiermacher could suggest his work had not escaped the appearance of being "liberal Protestant" either. Barth had similar suspicions about both Küng and Rahner (see *Karl Barth Letters 1961-1968*, ed. Jürgen Fangmeier and Hinrich Stoevesandt, trans. and ed. Geoffrey W. Bromiley [Grand Rapids: Eerdmans, 1981], pp. 257, 287-88). To Küng, Barth wrote in 1967, "Unless you add solid counterpoints in the sense of thinking from above to below, you can easily be led into proximity to our (Protestant) eighteenth-century Enlightenment, or fall into the corresponding twilight." To Rahner, Barth wrote in 1968, "In the way you are speaking now, so some fifty years ago Troeltsch was speaking of the future of the church and theology . . . our Neo-Protestants were and are in their own way pious and even churchly people."

[5]See, e.g., T. F. Torrance, *Theology in Reconstruction* (London: SCM Press, 1965), p. 163. Torrance writes, "The theology of Barth can be described, then, as the application of justification to the whole realm of man's life, to the realm of his knowing as well as the realm of his doing."

[6]See, e.g., Eberhard Jüngel, *Justification: The Heart of the Christian Faith, A Theological Study with an Ecumenical Purpose*, trans. Jeffrey F. Cayzer (New York: T & T Clark, 2001), p. 207. Jüngel writes, "We must not hold any view which sees justification as a process of salvation whereby we co-operate in any way at all with God. Any notion of justification as a condition which can be kept and maintained by human achievement or good works is excluded. Also untenable is the idea that justification is a process of maturation that can be checked empirically. . . . We must further rule out the thought that we can in any way prove our righteousness before God by referring to ourselves, instead of pointing only and exclusively to Christ crucified." Jüngel is here explicitly rejecting the Tridentine ideas that "our works either entirely or in part sustain and preserve either the righteousness

Barth did indeed write to Hans Küng telling him that he had done a fine job presenting his theology of justification and he also said that if what Küng himself had presented in his book was the Catholic teaching on the subject then they did indeed agree. But while Rahner is overwhelmingly positive about their agreement, in spite of his own questions to Küng and his own critical distance from Barth, there can be little doubt that Barth's response to Küng was, to a certain extent, tongue in cheek.

> The positive conclusion of your critique is this: What I say about justification— making allowances for certain precarious yet not insupportable turns of phrase— does objectively concur on all points with the correctly understood teaching of the Roman Catholic Church. You can imagine my considerable amazement at this bit of news; and I suppose that many Roman Catholic readers will at first be no less amazed. . . . How do you explain the fact that all this could remain hidden so long, and from so many, both outside and inside the Church? . . . Did you yourself discover all this before you so carefully read my *Church Dogmatics* or was it while you were read-ing it afterward?[7]

No doubt Küng, Barth and Rahner all would agree on the authority of Scrip-ture as Küng himself explained: "Sacred Scripture has an absolute precedence which no other theological argument can whittle away. And that is why from time immemorial Scripture has been the *first* font of Catholic dogmatic theol-

---

of faith . . . or even faith itself" and that good works "cause" an increase in righteousness and stresses that disagreement about this cannot be covered over as happened at the Strasbourg Insti-tute for Ecumenical Research with "an unbelievable series of contortions." And Jüngel notes that it is scandalous that these very issues are obscured and not clarified by the Joint Declaration. T. F. Torrance's thinking about justification stresses many of the same points. He noted that any sort of co-redemption, which he believed had become "rampant" not only among Roman Catholics but among "Liberal and Evangelical Protestants" who emphasized that our existential decisions are the means whereby we make real for ourselves the "kerygma," all suggested that in the end "sal-vation depends upon our own personal or existential decision" (Torrance, *Theology in Reconstruction*, p. 162). Torrance continually stresses that we are directed away from any sort of self-justification and toward Christ alone. In this context Rahner's suggestion that the churches could achieve an "ideal" unity of faith where none of the member churches would "reject out of hand an explicit doctrine of the Catholic church" seems naïve (See Heinrich Fries and Karl Rahner, *Unity of the Churches: An Actual Possibility*, trans. Ruth C. L. Gritsch and Eric W. Gritsch [New York: Paulist Press, 1985], p. 39).

[7]Hans Küng, *Justification: The Doctrine of Karl Barth and a Catholic Reflection*, trans. by Edward Quinn (Lon-don: Burns & Oates, 1981), pp. xxxix-xli. And as mentioned in n. 4 above Barth had questions about Küng's later theological developments.

ogy."[8] Still, Barth might respond to Küng with his own question about whether or not there is a second or perhaps even a third font of Catholic dogmatic theology.[9]

It is also worth noting that, in his assessment of the Joint Declaration, Avery Dulles eschews the older method of ecumenical dialogue that sought a point by point agreement within some overall system between the Lutheran Book of Concord and various Catholic Councils and instead argues that in spite of our different "thought-forms, we can say many things—the most important things— in common. And precisely because of our different perspectives we can learn from one another."[10] Dulles therefore argues that today the Lutheran theses must be judged by "some standard other than the decrees of Trent, valid though those decrees are in Catholic dogmatic teaching."[11] In this context Dulles appeals to the Gospel, that is, to the biblical foundation to find a language that can make the doctrine of justification more meaningful to people of our own day who seem so alienated from the Gospel. And he concludes by noting that it is not enough to say Lutherans and Catholics use different frameworks for thinking about justification; rather it must be shown that Lutheran and Catholic thinking derive from the same Gospel. While the Joint Declaration is helpful, he says, it has not overcome all difficulties. Dulles suggests that in spite of theological differences, the signing of the Joint Declaration by the Pope "can be a powerful symbolic event" in the face of a world on the brink of unbelief because it says that our two churches are now united "on truths of the highest import"[12] after nearly five centuries. It expresses our joint confidence that our different expressions of the same faith can be reconciled in the end.

It is significant then that so many important Catholic and Protestant theologians agree on the authority of Scripture and would also agree, I think, with the fact that the Joint Declaration places that authority in the context of the doctrine of the Trinity. With that in mind I hope to show that, in spite of formal agreement on this matter, there is not much material evidence in the thinking of Barth

---

[8]Ibid., p. 111.

[9]It certainly appears that even Küng's belief in the absolute precedence of Scripture was obscured by other criteria. See, e.g., Grenz and Olson, *20th Century Theology*, p. 269.

[10]Avery Dulles, S.J., *Justification Today: A New Ecumenical Breakthrough*, Laurence J. McGinley Lecture, October 26, 1999, Fordham University, Bronx, New York, p. 14.

[11]Ibid., p. 15.

[12]Ibid., pp. 15-16.

and Rahner as well as a great number of contemporary theologians influenced by them, to suggest they are really speaking of the same Gospel in different thought-forms. My purpose here is not negative. It is indeed positive because my goal is to propose that if, as we all say, Scripture is authoritative and therefore the doctrine of justification is decisive, then there can be no genuine union of Reformed and Roman Catholic or Lutheran and Roman Catholic theology except insofar as both sides actually begin, continue and end their theology bound by faith to Jesus Christ himself. Such a method would have far ranging influence in all areas of theology, including ecclesiology. But we ought not to get ahead of ourselves. Let us first consider how Barth and Rahner think about knowledge of God. That will raise at once the question of method and the content of Christian knowledge of God.

JUSTIFICATION AND THE KNOWLEDGE OF GOD

It is a well-known fact that in his developed understanding of the *analogia fidei* Barth insisted that no view or concept (theological or not) was true in itself.[13] It had to become true and could become true only when God acts to enable our knowledge of him, only when God "claims" our thinking and speaking. Of course this knowledge also involved "fellowship" with God; the kind of fellowship established and effective in our justification which took place in and through Christ's death and resurrection and our sanctification which takes place now through the Holy Spirit. So, ultimately, true knowledge of God involves our behavior because it calls for the obedience of faith: "The human knowledge of God is true in so far as it does not evade this requirement [to think of God based on God's revelation and truth], but fulfills it in obedience" (*CD* 2/1, p. 212). Knowledge of God then is not a work we accomplish on our own either before or after an encounter with the Word of God. Knowledge of God instead is a work that follows the free and joyous acknowledgment that God is right to act as he has acted and does act in the history of Christ. It is a work that signs and seals one's faith in Christ. It is therefore something we ourselves are unable

---

[13]Cf. Karl Barth, *Church Dogmatics*, 4 vols. in 13 pts. (hereafter *CD* and referred to in text and notes). Vol. II, pt. I: *The Doctrine of God*, trans. by T. H. L. Parker, W. B. Johnston, Harold Knight and J. L. M. Haire (Edinburgh: T & T Clark, 1964), pp. 194, 226, 358. T. F. Torrance follows Barth in this: "theological statements are of such a kind that they do not claim to have truth in themselves for by their very nature they point away from themselves to Christ as the one Truth of God" (Torrance, *Theology in Reconstruction*, p. 163).

to do but must do when God lays claim to our views and concepts.[14]

For Barth our thinking that takes place in our views and concepts "is our responsibility to ourselves" (*CD* 2/1, p. 211) while our speech "is our responsibility to others" (*CD* 2/1, p. 211). Because God tells us that he is and who he is in his revelation in his Word and Spirit we must tell this to ourselves and to others. The veracity of what is said is of course totally dependent upon "the veracity of God in his revelation" (*CD* 2/1, p. 211). Against those who suggest that Barth does not pay attention to the human situation Barth insists that God's claim "does not annul our human situation. Nor does it ignore and eliminate the fact that apart from God many other things, conditioned by ourselves and by the world-reality around us, are the content of our two-fold responsibility and therefore of our thinking and speaking" (*CD* 2/1, p. 211). Indeed it is only through God's revelation that we know of our incapacity to know God of ourselves just as it is only through God's revelation that we know the true meaning of sin and salvation. God "puts this judgment on ourselves into our mouth" (*CD* 2/1, pp. 211-12).

Barth goes further and insists that because God's claim (command) is not ineffectual but effective he can enable us to speak truly of him to ourselves and to others precisely because

> He does not ignore or eliminate but fills up the void of our impotence to view and conceive Him. . . . What we of ourselves cannot do, He can do through us. If our views and concepts and words are of themselves too narrow to apprehend God, it does not follow that this sets a limit to God Himself, that it is impossible for God to take up His dwelling in this narrowness . . . why should our views and concepts and words be too small for God to be in them in all his glory? It is not a question of a power to receive this guest being secretly inherent in these works of ours. . . . But there is a power of the divine indwelling . . . which our works cannot withstand for all their impotence. (*CD* 2/1, p. 212)

Of course this indwelling of our views and concepts by God "does not involve a

---

[14]This is why, in his explication of justification Barth writes, "Christian faith is not in any sense a fact and phenomenon which is generally known and which can as such be explained to everybody" (*CD* 4/1, p. 741) just as the Christian religion is not in itself the Christian faith. Barth insists Christian faith knows and confesses that "it cannot think of itself as grounded in itself. . . . In no case can its knowledge and confession begin with itself" (*CD* 4/1, p. 741). That is why Barth insisted that "to have the Holy Spirit is to let God rather than our having God be our confidence" (*CD* 1/1, p. 462). Christian faith is faith in Jesus Christ: "The man who believes looks to Him, holds to Him and depends on Him. . . . In faith man ceases to be in control" (*CD* 4/1, p. 743). Because of this, genuine theology can only take place in prayer and thankfulness.

magical transformation of man, or a supernatural enlargement of his capacity, so that now he can do what before he could not do" (*CD* 2/I, p. 212). According to Barth we can neither do it before or after our encounter with the Word of God. Rather we are "taken up by the grace of God and determined to participation in the veracity of the revelation of God. In all his impotence he becomes a place where his honour dwells—not his own, but God's. As a sinner he is justified" (*CD* 2/I, p. 213).

Barth insists that this justification is no illusion or game. It is a genuine justification of what he says to himself and others because it participates in the revelation of God in Christ and the Spirit. It is because sin is pardoned in justification that we can know and speak of God in truth even today. But we only know of this pardoned sin because God himself has disclosed this to us. In our obedience to God's claim we have God's promise that he will enable us to view and conceive him according to his own good-pleasure. But this means that:

> the obedience to the grace of God in which man acknowledges that he is entirely wrong, thus acknowledging that God alone is entirely right, is the obedience which has this promise. . . . It is we who have known and spoken, but it will always be God and God alone who will have the credit for the veracity of our thinking and speaking.[15]

Barth goes on to insist that while it always remains factual that God will be true though all of us are liars, this cannot lead to resignation, which would imply that we can never truly know God. Any resignation on our part would be evidence of pride and not the required humility of one who is justified and sanctified by grace. And of course if one is truly humble one will not fall into resignation: "Humility accepts grace in judgment" (*CD* 2/I, p. 213). Thus in humility one will not exist in some final unrest but in the "saving unrest" of one who continually seeks God in his revelation. We cannot know God in truth merely by repeating our prior knowledge to ourselves because living in obedience to grace means allowing God the freedom to continually bestow his grace on our knowl-

---

[15]*CD* 2/I, p. 213. This thinking finds its exact parallel in Barth's doctrine of justification when he insists that God's righteousness, which is not subject to any law because God himself is the supreme law, means that God is in harmony with himself so that when he acts for us he does so effectively because God is just in himself (*CD* 4/I, pp. 529ff.). Therefore it is in Christ's resurrection that humanity receives its justification (*CD* 4/I, pp. 564ff.). A similar argument is also presented in Barth's discussion of "The Mercy and Righteousness of God" in *CD* 2/I: "God does not have to, but He can, take to Himself the suffering of another in such away that in doing so, in founding and accomplishing this fellowship, He does what corresponds to His worth" (p. 377).

edge. That is why we must constantly seek it in prayer.[16]

Barth's doctrine of justification then determines his view of our knowledge of God. And it is striking when reading his explicit treatment of the doctrine of justification in *CD* 4/1 how his understanding of the *simul justus et peccator* bears the mark of what he said in *CD* 2/1. For instance Barth insists that God's grace is valid and effective (*CD* 4/1, p. 593) so that it is only in light of the "yes" God says to us in Christ's resurrection from the dead that we can grasp the true meaning of sin. It is only in light of the Gospel that the Law has its meaning. Hence human defeatism and pessimism have nothing to do with submitting to God. Barth insists that in receiving God's promise of forgiveness we are already the people that we will be (*CD* 4/1, p. 595). We are not half sinners and half forgiven but both altogether. Prayer for the forgiveness of sins forces itself on the just person, Barth insists. But forgiveness is exclusively an act of God. We need it but can only receive it from God. It is because we really must rely in faith on this act of God that "if he looks behind him, or into the depth of his present as determined by his past, man can never receive or enjoy the comfort of the forgiveness of sins" (*CD* 4/1, p. 596). We are, Barth argues frequently, a riddle to ourselves and we cannot solve the riddle precisely because only God can do that in the form of a miracle; and indeed that is exactly what has happened for us in Jesus Christ.[17] Barth therefore insists we have it only as it comes to us in God's promise. But God's promise is effective; it is not

---

[16]This is why Barth insisted that it is by virtue of his resurrection that "Jesus Christ lives and acts and speaks for all ages and in eternity, and in such a way that we are promised a future and hope, a being before God in reality and truth . . . 'I live and ye shall live also' " (*CD* 4/1, p. 354). The presupposition for receiving that divine verdict is faith. But Barth insists we have no power over this presupposition because this faith "which leads into all the truth in the power and enlightenment of the Holy Spirit, is only given and will continually be given to us. Without prayer for it this presupposition cannot be had . . . in real prayer for it, the prayer which is confident that it will be heard, this presupposition, the hearing and receiving and understanding of the verdict pronounced by God [our justification], is quite possible, for as His verdict it has already been passed and is valid and divinely effective. Calling on the fact that Jesus lives—for this is the real prayer which is confident from the very first that it will be answered—can never be in vain. It lays hold of the promise: Ye shall live . . ." (*CD* 4/1, p. 355).

[18]Barth writes, "If justification is a happening which we experience in ourselves, if we can find ourselves in it, so that there is no puzzle, but it can be readily conceived, then we must have made a mistake" (*CD* 4/1, p. 546). The antithesis between our yesterday and today is absolute and qualitative because like the prodigal son we were dead and then made alive again in Christ. "No one can try to maintain that this is an expression of his self-understanding. That man is, in fact, the prodigal son is the genuine riddle before which we stand at this point. . . . [I]t is to us insoluble. . . . But it is a riddle which has been solved in quite a different way. . . . [O]ur true and actual transition from wrong to right, from death to life . . . is the to-day of Jesus Christ. . . . His history is as such our

a weak remission of sins but a restoration of the state of righteousness between
God and us. That is the transition from death to life that took place in Jesus' own
life, death and resurrection.[18] And that is what he promises us: a participation in
his new humanity and thus also a participation in God's inner life (*CD* 4/1, p.
568). Divine sonship, Barth argues, is assigned to us in Christ.

I realize that it is an unpopular thing to do today to bring up that nasty busi-
ness of the *analogia entis* that Barth was supposed to have abandoned somewhere
or modified in volume 4 of the *Church Dogmatics*. But the problem that Barth originally attacked with that category is the same problem he attacked when he rejected world-views in *CD* 4. It is the same problem he attacked earlier in the
Church Dogmatics in the form of what he labeled Protestant Modernism and Roman Catholicism; and again when in *CD* 1/2 he contrasted revelation and religion arguing that there could only be true religion based on our justification by
faith; and finally when in the same volume he expounded his understanding of
the commands to love God and love neighbor, the *analogia fidei* played a decisive
role. The problem ultimately has to do with the doctrine of justification by faith.
And that problem concerns the willingness on the part of theologians to begin
and end their theology with Jesus Christ alone *(solus Christus)* or with someone
or something other than Jesus Christ. Of course we cannot begin to know God
elsewhere because God himself has laid the foundation for our knowledge in the
fellowship he established and maintains in the death and resurrection of Jesus
himself (1 Cor 3:11). Indeed it is precisely because Jesus Christ was raised from
the dead that our human justification is a reality in him. But that means that he
is now alive and with us in the power of his Spirit as the one who maintains us

---

history. . . . Jesus Christ comes to us" (*CD* 4/1, pp. 547-48). Justification takes place "in the mystery of the *simul peccator et iustus*. The justified man exists—this is the completion of his justification—
as he hopes from day to day and hour to hour, in the hope—which we now have to write with big
letters—for a final goal of his hope, for the solution of the riddle, the removal of the contradiction"
(*CD* 4/1, p. 602). Of course for Barth our future and our hope is in Christ and from Christ because
"in Him our justification is a complete justification, fulfilled on the right hand as on the left" (*CD*
4/1, p. 557).

[18]Cf. *CD* 4/1, p. 557 where Barth writes, "In Him there takes place that transition of man from his
wrong to his right, from death to life. It would not be the act of judgment of the one God if it were
not this one complete act, beginning here and completed there, beginning in the death and completed in the resurrection of Jesus Christ." The unrighteous man is done away with in Christ and
the righteous man now exists: "Jesus Christ lives as the risen One, as the bearer of the right which
God has given to man, as the recipient of His grace, completing the justification of man by His receiving of it" (*CD* 4/1, p. 557).

in our life as joyful and obedient witnesses to what he did there and then on the cross and again on Easter. Let us now compare Rahner's method and thoughts on our knowledge of God with what Barth has had to say.

KNOWLEDGE OF GOD AND THE ROLE OF CHRIST

Karl Rahner famously begins his reflections about God by saying, "We inquire therefore into man, as the being who is orientated to the mystery as such, this orientation being a constitutive element of his being both in his natural state and in his supernatural elevation."[19] This is why, for Rahner, "At this point theology and anthropology necessarily become one"[20] and knowledge of God represents human explication in reflection of "what is already present in [our] transcendentality."[21] Rahner works out the logic of this insight in his Christology by saying that "if God himself is man and remains so for ever, if all theology is therefore eternally an an-

---

[19]Karl Rahner, "The Concept of Mystery in Catholic Theology," in *TI*, trans. Kevin Smyth (Baltimore: Helicon, 1966), 4:49. This starting point is validated for Rahner because he equates justification with divinization: "Justification, understood as God's deed, transforms man down to the deepest roots of his being; it transfigures and divinises him. For this very reason the justified man is not 'at the same time justified and a sinner'" ("Justified and Sinner at the Same Time," *TI* 6:222). Rejecting the Reformation view of the *simul justus et peccator*, Rahner offers a Catholic interpretation by stressing our need for grace and the fact that we still sin and are uncertain of our salvation. But he focuses on our experience of justification and fails to stress that justification is identical with the justification that took place in Christ himself. Hence, even his discussion of this issue centers on our experience rather than on what has been done for us in Christ and thus *extra nos*. Therefore Rahner says that of ourselves we are only sin but that any good we do comes from God's free grace apparently without realizing that even in doing good we are in fact sinners who might rely on that goodness rather than on Christ alone for our justification.

[20]Karl Rahner, *Foundations of Christian Faith: An Introduction to the Idea of Christianity*, (hereafter: *FCF*), trans. William V. Dych (New York: Seabury, 1978), p. 44.

[21]*FCF*, p. 44. This same idea is repeated frequently. See, e.g., *TI* 4:50: "All conceptual expressions about God, necessary though they are, always stem from the unobjectivated experience of transcendence as such: the concept from the pre-conception, the name from the experience of the nameless." See also *TI* 4:57 and *TI* 2:149 where Rahner writes, "The so-called proofs of God's existence . . . are possible . . . only as the outcome of an *a posteriori* process of reasoning as the conceptual objectification of what we call the experience of God, which provides the basis and origin of this process of reasoning." Thus, for Rahner, the task is to "reflect upon an experience which is present in every man" (*TI* 2:150) and "we can only point to this experience, seek to draw another's attention to it in such a way that he discovers within himself that which we only find if, and to the extent that we already possess it" (*TI* 2:154). See also *FCF*, p. 21: "The knowledge of God is always present unthematically and without name, and not just when we begin to speak of it. All talk about it, which necessarily goes on, always only points to this transcendental experience as such, an experience in which he whom we call 'God' encounters man . . . as the term of his transcendence . . ." For Rahner's explanation of his method see *FCF*, pp. 24-39.

thropology ... man is forever the articulate mystery of God."[22] And this leads him
to conclude that, "anthropology and Christology mutually determine each other
within Christian dogmatics if they are both correctly understood."[23] By contrast,
of course, anthropology and Christology for Barth do not mutually determine each
other precisely because our justification by faith is exclusively an act of God.[24]
Christology, as Barth insisted, determines the validity of anthropology but anthropology cannot have a determinative effect on Christology unless you ignore the
problem of sin and fail to see that we really are a new creation in Christ and not in
ourselves. Could it be that the radical difference between Barth and Rahner over
where to begin thinking about God reflects their different views of justification? I
think the answer is yes.[25]

    Rahner clearly thinks that in virtue of our justification we are changed inwardly
and thus he sincerely believes that he can reflect on our supposed orientation to
God (which Barth would consider ambiguous) and come to a true knowledge of
God.[26] In order to accomplish this he claims that this orientation is grace and that
this grace is revelation. Of course Rahner's thinking is not without nuance. So he
distinguishes between what is supposed to be our obediential potency and our supernatural existential. The former refers to our openness to being (as spirit in the

---

[22]Karl Rahner, "On the Theory of the Incarnation," in *TI*, trans. Kevin Smyth (Baltimore: Helicon, 1966), 4:116.

[23]Karl Rahner, "Theology and Anthropology," in *TI*, trans. Kevin Smyth (Baltimore: Helicon, 1966), 9:28.

[24]In fact Barth insisted, "There is a way from Christology to anthropology, but there is no way from anthropology to Christology" (*CD* I/1, p. 131; *CD* 3/2, p. 71).

[25]Two points must be stressed here. First, Rahner himself mistakenly thought his understanding of justification as the infusion of faith, hope and charity could be reconciled with the Reformed view of grace (see *TI* 18, "Justification and World Development from a Catholic Viewpoint," pp. 260-61). Second, it is precisely such thinking that leads Rahner to compromise the Reformed meaning of justification by ascribing it to us in our universal experience, thus undercutting the need for Christ and faith in him. Hence Rahner writes, "we may assume therefore that the possibility of justification as a permanent existential is offered to man always and everywhere and can therefore be accepted by man's freedom even outside explicit Christianity (an acceptance of course, if it actually occurs, which is itself again a grace of God)" (*TI* 18:263). For Barth the offer and realization of justification is identical with what happened in the life, death and resurrection of Jesus and thus cannot be seen or accepted apart from faith in him alone.

[26]In fact, of course, Barth argued that in light of revelation we know that we have no obediential po-tency for the true God precisely because we are disclosed as sinners in need of grace and grace cannot be detached from God's action in Christ and the Spirit. See, e.g., *CD* 2/1, p. 182. We do not know God, Barth believed, "in virtue of a potentiality of our cognition which has perhaps to be actualised by revelation."

world) and as such it refers to our openness to God's self-communication, at least as a possibility.[27] "This potency is . . . our human nature as such. If the divine self-communication did not occur, our openness toward being would still be meaningful . . . we are by nature possible recipients of God's self-communication, listeners for a possible divine word."[28] The latter refers to

> a basic structure which permeates the whole of human existence; it is not a localized part or region of our being, but a dimension pertaining to the whole. Our being in the world, or our being with others, could serve as examples. . . . this existential . . . is not given automatically with human nature, but is rather the result of a gratuitous gift of God. . . . Because of the supernatural existential, grace is always a part of our actual existence.[29]

Let us pause for a moment to observe that here on a most elementary level the disagreement between Barth and Rahner is not just a theological quibble between two great theologians of the past. It concerns, rather, how one interprets sin and grace within the context of the doctrine of justification.

Paragraph 19 of the Joint Declaration states, "We confess together that all persons depend completely on the grace of God for their salvation. . . . Justification takes place solely by God's grace." Then in paragraph 20 it is said that when Catholics say they " 'cooperate' in preparing for and accepting justification by consenting to God's justifying action, they see such personal consent as itself an effect of grace, not as an action arising from innate human abilities." And in paragraph 21 it says, "According to Lutheran teaching, human beings are incapable of cooperating in their salvation, because as sinners they actively oppose God and his saving action." I am assuming that Barth's position reflects this Lutheran view since Barth maintains that "sin is not something accidental which the man who engages in it

---

[27]Note that for Barth our openness to God is not a possibility of human nature but a possibility that must always come to us as an act of God. That is why Barth insists that we must give up all attempts to be sure of ourselves and find our security in Christ alone and therefore in faith alone (*CD* 4/1, pp. 612, 614).

[28]John P. Galvin, "The Invitation of Grace," in Leo J. O'Donovan, S.J., ed., *A World of Grace: An Introduction to the Themes and Foundations of Karl Rahner's Theology* (New York: Crossroad, 1981), p. 72.

[29]Ibid., pp. 71-73. It is significant that even in his discussion of justification in relation to Barth and Küng, Rahner insisted upon a supernatural existential, that is, "an inevitable orientation towards God's strictly supernatural grace" (*TI* 4:216). Of course Rahner wishes to distinguish nature and grace and so he writes, " 'nature' is always and irrevocably conceived by God as the presupposed condition of possibility of grace strictly speaking, nature itself cannot be entitatively supernatural grace. But it is *always* and *necessarily* endowed with a supernatural finality in its existence, in its conservation in spite of sin . . . even on the natural level. . . . It is modally supernatural" (*TI* 4:217).

can brush off again like a speck of dust from his clothes" (*CD* 4/1, p. 584).

With that in mind it is hard to see where the common agreement really is here. On the one hand, the doctrine of justification, as understood by Lutherans and by Barth, rules out an obediential potency for grace and revelation and certainly calls into question any sort of supernatural existential. On the other hand the Catholic interpretation, as represented by Rahner, apparently requires both of these concepts. Yet, it seems to me, a choice is required here. Even if one were to say that our consent to God's justification is an effect of grace but then hold that we can prepare for and accept grace in virtue of some possibility of nature (or as Barth would put it, some supernatural enlargement of our capacity), then in reality it would appear that we are not accepting our justification by faith and grace. Instead it would seem that we are assimilating grace and faith to our own nature without need for radical repentance and forgiveness that can only come from Christ himself. In fact then it is here that the Reformation emphasis on salvation by faith and therefore in Christ and only in Christ encounters the Roman Catholic emphasis on the fact that salvation is a process that takes place in human experience and can even be equated with certain experiences.[30] For all the supposed agreement of the Joint Declaration, the fact remains that Roman Catholic and Reformed theology are still separated in practice by this most basic way of thinking about our relationship with God. What would it take to move forward together? In my opinion it would take a serious return to Jesus Christ as the one in whom we learn of our sin and as the one in whom we learn of our salvation. But when that happens, it would appear that we must admit that apart from Christ and faith in him we are still the sinners we always were precisely because of our proclivity to include God's grace among the possibilities we can choose by our supposedly free decisions.

The obvious problem that Rahner has from the vantage of Barth's theology then, and it is no small problem, is that his thinking does not begin and end with Jesus Christ himself so that even his concepts of grace and revelation are to a large extent determined by his reflection on our supposed orientation to God. This thinking allows him to seek God's grace in our experience whereas for Barth our experience is always ambiguous because we don't find grace *in* our experience but in faith and therefore in Christ who alone is the grace of God. We do indeed experience God's Word but that very experience points us away from our sinful experi-

---

[30]This explains why Rahner can equate salvation with our moral behavior: "wherever there is an absolutely moral commitment of a positive kind in the world . . . there takes place also a saving event, faith, hope and charity" (*TI* 6:233, pp. 236-37, 239).

ence and toward Christ in whom we already live as forgiven sinners. But Barth insists that we really don't live as the forgiven sinners we are in Christ if we don't admit our sin in this very practical way. So if, as the New Testament insists, Jesus Christ himself is our righteousness with God, then our knowledge of God must bear the mark of that truth and reality; we must really be dependent upon the living Lord here and now to be in fellowship with God and to know him. The fact that Rahner's understanding of God will not begin with the revelation of God in Jesus Christ but instead begins with the supposed revelation of God in the depths of our transcendental experience has far reaching implications and is more than a little problematic even for his famous understanding of the Trinity, as I have pointed out in my recent book, *Divine Freedom and the Doctrine of the Immanent Trinity*. Most importantly for our purposes here, however, is the contrast between Rahner and Barth over the starting point for thinking about God.

Of course this methodological difficulty affects their ideas of God. Rahner is willing to describe God as the nameless, silent term of our experiences of self-transcendence while Barth would insist that God is the eternal Father, Son and Spirit and for that very reason cannot be described at all as the nameless term of our experience without implying that we are in control of who God is (self-justification). Even in his analysis of the doctrine of justification by faith Barth insists that

> everything depends on the fact that faith is not empty in so far as it does not look into the void, in so far as it is not directed at the formless mystery of something supernatural, but has this concrete object. Everything depends on the fact that it is being in encounter with the living Jesus Christ, a being from and to this object. That is what is meant by Christian faith. (*CD* 4/1, p. 633)

Contrast that precise understanding of faith with Rahner's view. For Rahner faith is

> a trusting and open relationship to the whole of reality. . . . Where freedom admits courageously the whole of reality . . . it has the light of its certainty in itself. . . . In reflecting on certainty in faith we have worked—and we have no wish to conceal this—with a concept of "faith" according to which faith is nothing other than the positive and unconditional acceptance of one's own existence as meaningful and open to a final fulfilment, which we call God. It must, of course, be shown later in more detail that such a belief is already the original seed of the Christian faith, and vice versa, that Christian faith is nothing but the pure and healthy development of this very seed.[31]

---

[31]Karl Rahner and Karl–Heinz Weger, *Our Christian Faith: Answers for the Future*, trans. Francis McDonagh (New York: Crossroad, 1981), pp. 24-25.

Notice the crucial difference between Barth and Rahner here. First, Rahner understands faith as a trusting relationship with the "whole of reality" and ultimately with what we call God. But in fact, in accord with Barth's thinking, God the Father of Jesus Christ is not the "whole of reality" and cannot be named by us but can only be acknowledged by us as the Lord, Reconciler and Redeemer. For Barth the *solus Christus* is determinative here: because Christ alone justifies all people to all eternity in virtue of his electing grace and the covenant established and maintained in him, faith absolutely excludes any other helpers or helps and it excludes any idea that we can bring about our own conversion.[32] Second, Rahner insists that faith has the light of certainty in itself while Barth maintains, in light of the doctrine of justification, that the very nature of faith means humility, that is, it has its certainty in Christ and only in Christ. Third, Rahner thinks faith is the seed of trust in reality already at work in people's lives, while Barth insists that faith means that our entire lives are called into question and we are called by Christ to trust only in him. Fourth, Rahner finally argues that self-acceptance is the same as accepting the God of Christian faith. But in Barth's eyes that assertion is the ultimate form of self-justification. These differences are the practical outcome of two different theological methods. But these two different methods stem from two very different interpretations of the nature of our justification by faith.

The predicament we have been considering in fact is the old problem of the *analogia entis* rearing its ugly head. I make this point here simply to indicate that while there may be formal agreement between Catholics and Protestants regarding justification, many Catholics and Protestants today have virtually ignored the implications of that doctrine when it comes to knowing God. And that has practical consequences because it leads many today to think that we can and should revise our understanding of who God is, as well as our understanding of what sin is, in light of our contemporary experiences of ourselves. My point is that any such thinking is just another example of self-justification; it represents a refusal to allow God the freedom to be for us in the cross and resurrection of Jesus Christ and through faith imparted by the Holy Spirit.

Rahner, and those many Protestants and Catholics who follow him, are willing to begin thinking about God by reflecting on our experience. Barth and those who follow him insist that it is precisely our present experience that has died with Christ and was recreated through his resurrection. But since our lives are now hidden with

---

[32]Barth, *CD* 4/I, p. 632. Our conversion is real only in Christ's representative act and always remains so.

Christ in God we cannot discover our justification or the being and action of God by looking at ourselves. We are, as Barth insisted, a riddle to ourselves and always will be because we now exist in the transition from our old existence as sinners to our new existence in Christ that will not be complete until he comes again. That is why Barth argued that our justified existence, like our knowledge of God, is a miracle. For that reason he insists that we must look away from ourselves and exclusively to God in Christ as the one who actually enables true knowledge of God and of anthropology as well. Christ himself is the only true solution to the riddle of our existence. For Barth and his followers faith means joyful and thankful obedience to the righteousness of God revealed and active in the history of Jesus Christ. And indeed for Barth that history becomes our history precisely in and through the power of the resurrection, so that the very possibility of the Christian life is tied to the power of the risen Lord; if that power is confused theoretically or practically with our own power then the comfort and truth of Christianity itself would be lost.

JUSTIFICATION AND RESURRECTION

Let me give one more example of how contemporary theology should show evidence of agreement on the doctrine of justification but does not. In his recent book on justification Eberhard Jüngel quotes an Easter hymn that he thinks summarizes Christ's importance for the world: "If he had not risen, the world would have perished. If you have grasped that," writes Jüngel, "you have grasped the doctrine of justification."[33] I agree with Jüngel and I suggest that it is precisely to the extent that contemporary theology compromises a proper view of the resurrection of Jesus Christ, along with his present activity as the risen and ascended Lord, that such theology will tend toward some form of self-justification. The problem here has its roots in different understandings of the incarnation. Jüngel and Barth agree that the unique meaning of Christ's resurrection is dictated by the unique fact that it was the Son of God incarnate who died on the cross.[34]

---

[33]Jüngel, *Justification*, p. 13.

[34]See, e.g., *CD* 2/1, pp. 398ff., where Barth traces our proper understanding of sin, our justification and sanctification as God's merciful righteousness, and the fact that Christ could take our place and "could suffer eternal death in our stead as the consequence of our sin in such a way that it was finally suffered and overcome" (*CD* 2/1, p. 403) to the fact that the man Jesus from Nazareth was "God's own eternal Son." In *CD* 4/1 Barth insists that it is the unity of God with the man Jesus that gives justification its significance (pp. 306ff). And the resurrection is the bridge between Jesus' atonement on the cross and our justification today because he not only did stand before God for us but does so now (*CD* 4/1, p. 314).

Let me begin with Rahner once again, if I may. He believes in the importance of the resurrection and of the incarnation just as much as do Jüngel and Barth. In fact Rahner wanted to incorporate fundamental theology into dogmatic theology so that the justification of our beliefs would not be detached from the material content of theology.[35] On this point Reformed and Roman Catholic theology are at one as T. F. Torrance indicated years ago.[36] But Rahner's thinking differs from Jüngel and Barth because his method, while claiming to be scripturally based in some sense, is actually shaped by his understanding of justification which, as we have just seen, influences his approach to our knowledge of God. Let me explain.

Like Barth and other Reformed theologians such as T. F. Torrance, Rahner appeals to God's self-communication in Christ to link fundamental and dogmatic theology. But unlike his Reformed colleagues, Rahner thinks that self-communication can be found "in the depths of [our] existence"[37] as well as in Jesus Christ. This double grounding of his theology is where the problems become visible. And of course it is just this double grounding that was the focus of the Reformer's attack in their stress on the *solus Christus* as Jüngel makes very clear even today.[38] Rahner argues that we must avoid "a *too narrowly Christological approach.*"[39] Hence he insists, "It is not true that one has only to preach Jesus Christ and then he has solved all problems. Today Jesus Christ is himself a problem. . . . [W]e cannot begin with Jesus Christ as the absolute and final datum, but we must begin further back than that."[40] Rahner of course begins with our common human experience. Hence Rahner believes that we must find a proper basis for Christology in our transcendental experiences with the result that he maintains that "man can only find and retain what he encounters in history if there is an *a priori* principle of expectation, seeking and hope in man's finding and retaining subjectivity."[41] This belief is in keeping with Rahner's understanding of justification as something that has taken place within human experience in virtue of Christ's

---

[35]*FCF*, p. 12.

[36]See Torrance, *Trinitarian Perspectives*, p. 78.

[37]*FCF*, p. 12.

[38]See Jüngel, *Justification*, chap. 5.

[39]*FCF*, p. 13.

[40]Ibid. This is why William V. Dych believes that neither God nor Scripture can be starting points for theology today but rather "our shared human existence" ("Theology in a New Key," in *A World of Grace*, ed. Leo J. O'Donovan [New York: Crossroad, 1981], p. 3).

[41]Karl Rahner, "Jesus' Resurrection," in *TI*, trans. Kevin Smyth (Baltimore: Helicon, 1966), 17:47.

death and resurrection. And it leads to the following conclusion:

> The transcendental experience of the expectation of one's own resurrection, an expe-
> rience man can reach by his very essence, is the horizon of understanding within
> which and within which alone something like a resurrection of Jesus can be expected
> and experienced at all. These two elements of our existence, of course, the transcen-
> dental experience of the expectation of one's own resurrection, and the experience in
> faith of the resurrection of Jesus in salvation history, mutually condition each other.[42]

The obvious question to this line of thinking of course is if our expectation of our
resurrection is the horizon for understanding Jesus' own resurrection, how necessary
is Jesus' own resurrection for what we learn about sin and salvation from such reflection? Rahner insists that none of what he says could be said without Christ's resurrection just as nothing of what he says could make sense without the incarnation. But
in fact it is precisely this thinking that allows and even requires Rahner to argue that
"wherever and whenever we experience the unshakeableness of our own hope of a final
victory of our existence, there takes place, perhaps anonymously, that is, without reference to the name of Jesus, an experience that he is risen."[43] Indeed Rahner writes:

> If one has a radical hope of attaining a definitive identity and does not believe that
> one can steal away with one's obligations into the emptiness of non-existence, one
> has already grasped and accepted the resurrection in its real content. . . . The abso-
> luteness of the radical hope in which a human being apprehends his or her total ex-
> istence as destined and empowered to reach definitive form can quite properly be
> regarded as grace, which permeates this existence always and everywhere. This grace
> is revelation in the strictest sense . . . this certainly is revelation, even if this is not
> envisaged as coming from "outside."[44]

---

[42]*FCF,* pp. 273-74. Cf. also *TI* 17:16ff. Thus, for Rahner: "we might now formulate the proposition
that the knowledge of man's resurrection given with his transcendentally necessary hope is a statement of philosophical anthropology even before any real revelation in the Word. But we should have
to counter this by saying that, at least initially, the elucidation of man's basic hope as being the hope
of resurrection was in actual fact made historically through the revelation of the Old and New Testaments" (p. 18). This last statement shows that even Rahner's understanding of the scriptural view
of revelation is largely determined by what is experienced in transcendental experience. Thus, in order to experience the fact that Jesus is alive "he (the Christian) has only to accept believingly and
trustingly his own transcendental hope of resurrection and, therefore, also be on the look out, implicitly or explicitly, for a specific event in his own history, on the basis of which his hope can be
believed in, as something that has been realised in another person" (p. 19). Indeed, "the 'facts' of
Jesus' resurrection must simply be determined in the light of what we have to understand by our
own 'resurrection' " (p. 20).
[43]Rahner and Weger, *Our Christian Faith*, p. 113.
[44]Ibid., pp. 110-11.

And this leads to the following conclusions: First, "*faith* in his [Jesus'] resurrection is an intrinsic element of this resurrection itself. Faith is not taking cognizance of a fact which by its nature could exist just as well without being taken cognizance of."[45] Second,

> Jesus is risen into the faith of his disciples. But this faith into which Jesus is risen is not really and directly faith in this resurrection, but is that faith which knows itself to be a divinely effected liberation from all the powers of finiteness, of guilt and of death, and knows itself to be empowered for this by the fact that this liberation has taken place in Jesus himself and has become manifest for us.[46]

This last point illustrates why Rahner believes he can define faith by exploring the human experience of self-transcendence. If Jesus is risen into the faith of his disciples, then the power of the resurrection is already operative wherever anyone has faith and hope in some sort of liberation from guilt and death. This may even happen anonymously. And whenever anyone has some sort of ultimate hope that person has already grasped the meaning of the resurrection even if that person has never heard the Gospel. It is hard to see how Rahner's understanding has not collapsed Jesus' Easter history into the faith of the church and then used the resulting understanding to validate his theology. Barth and Rahner could not be further apart on this issue since, in Barth's eyes, Rahner's thinking is marked once more by a kind of self-justification, that is, a use of the resurrection as a type of a priori principle by which to explain faith and hope as categories that make sense with or without any material need to rely on Jesus Christ himself at the beginning, middle and end of his reflections. And that material need was already compromised by Rahner's understanding of the incarnation.

Rahner understands the incarnation in light of his conception of our indefinable human nature. When God assumes human nature then it "simply arrived at the point to which it always strives by virtue of its essence."[47] Human nature must disappear, Rahner says, into the incomprehensible. This happens, strictly speaking,

> when the nature which surrenders itself to the mystery of the fullness belongs so little to itself that it becomes the nature of God himself. The incarnation of God is therefore the unique, *supreme*, case of the total actualization of human reality, which

---

[45]*FCF*, p. 267.
[46]Ibid., p. 268.
[47]*TI* 4:109.

consists in the fact that man *is* in so far as he gives up himself.[48]

It is difficult to avoid the conclusion that on the one hand Rahner is suggesting that the incarnation is the result of the human achievement of ultimate self-transcendence.[49] On the other hand it is hard to avoid the conclusion that Jesus is only the highest instance of this anthropological achievement.[50] The former insight is almost classically Ebionite while the latter insight is almost classically Docetic because the former suggests the apotheosis of a man while the latter suggests that it is Rahner's idea of God as the mysterious, nameless, incomprehensible Whole that determines his thought about Jesus.[51]

By contrast Barth insists:

> If the freedom of divine immanence is sought and supposedly found apart from Jesus Christ, it can signify in practice only our enslavement to a false god. . . . [T]he Church must . . . see that it expects everything from *Jesus Christ* and from Jesus Christ *everything*; that He is unceasingly recognized as the way, the truth, and the life (Jn 14:6). . . . The freedom of God must be recognised as His own freedom . . . as it consists in God and as God has exercised it. But in God it consists in His Son Jesus Christ, and it is in Him that God has exercised it. . . . If we recognise and magnify it, we cannot come from any other starting point but Him or move to any other goal. (*CD* 2/1, pp. 319-20)

Barth refuses to start his thinking about the resurrection, incarnation or any other theological question any place but with Jesus Christ himself. In fact his thinking is dictated by his understanding of the doctrine of justification. It is precisely because only God can rescue human existence from death and because he has done so in Jesus Christ that we cannot look past Jesus Christ when attempting to explain Christian faith and hope. Indeed it is just because Jesus Christ himself is the Son

---

[48]Ibid., pp. 109-10.

[49]After explaining how Rahner's theology of the symbol influences his view of the incarnation, one Rahner commentator actually writes, "In the light of Rahner's evolutionary view of Christology, this process wherein the Word becomes flesh is identical with the process wherein flesh becomes the Word of God" (William V. Dych, S.J., *Karl Rahner* [Collegeville, Minn.: Liturgical Press, 1992], p. 79).

[50]This is why Colin Gunton criticizes Rahner's Christology as a form of *degree* Christology. See Colin E. Gunton, *Yesterday and Today: A Study of Continuities in Christology* (Grand Rapids: Eerdmans, 1983), pp. 15ff. Though John Hick, *The Metaphor of God Incarnate: Christology in a Pluralistic Age* (Louisville: Westminster John Knox, 1993), differs from Rahner by explicitly rejecting Chalcedonian Christology, his is also a degree Christology: "We are not speaking of something that is in principle unique, but of an interaction of the divine and the human which occurs in many different ways and degrees in all human openness to God's presence" (p. 109).

[51]For more on the effects of Ebionite and Docetic Christology today see Molnar, *Divine Freedom*, chap. 2.

of God incarnate that he provides the justification of our existence and thought about God and us. It is just because the man Jesus was and remains the unique mediator that our existence is justified and sanctified by God himself. By contrast, it is exactly because Rahner will not start his Christology with Jesus Christ that he attempts to ground his Christology and his view of the resurrection in our experiences of hope and faith as generally understood. What difference does this make? For Barth it marks the difference between a theology that refuses to live its actual justification by faith and one that does.

Barth insists that Christian faith is marked by its relation to Jesus Christ himself. Barth maintains that Christ's resurrection took place in time and history and was not a "timeless idea, a kind of *a priori*" through which his earthly life was interpreted. The very man Jesus who died on the cross and was buried existed in this "later time" (CD 3/2, p. 442). This time of the forty days gave content to the early apostolic preaching. Here Barth's thinking differs from Rahner's. Whereas Rahner appeals to our experiences of hope and of faith to understand the meaning of the resurrection and the incarnation and then explains that meaning in terms of our *a priori* subjective transcendental horizon, Barth insists that the meaning of Christian hope and faith is determined by Jesus himself who rose from the dead and who alone is therefore capable of enabling faith and hope through the Holy Spirit even today.[52] That is why Barth insists that our justification cannot be found within our experience but must be sought and found in Jesus Christ himself as he lived the transition from death to life for us and as we participate in that new life in faith and hope.

Further, the truth of Jesus' Easter history, Barth writes, "does not depend on our acceptance or rejection of the Easter story" (CD 3/2, p. 442). Whatever we may think of this second history, Barth insists that all must agree that for the New Testament it is "essential and indispensable" (CD 3/2, p. 443). It is the starting point for the New Testament portraits of Jesus. But again Barth and Rahner are separated here by the fact that Rahner refuses to begin his thinking about the res-

---

[52]Barth writes, "By virtue of His resurrection from the dead, by virtue of the righteousness revealed in His life, in Him and from Him we have a future and hope, the door has been opened, and we cross the threshold from wrong to right, and therefore from death to life. Risen with Him from the dead, we do this, or rather it takes place for us" (CD 4/1, p. 557). The resurrection actually means that the man Jesus received and lived his eternal life on our behalf so that it is neither our faith nor our hope that provide the horizon for understanding the resurrection. Rather that understanding comes from the risen Lord himself and through faith in him. And this faith is real only as the Holy Spirit unites us to the risen Christ.

urrection and thus about faith and hope with the risen Lord himself. Instead he begins with our transcendental experiences or what he calls our common human experience. And his conclusions create uncertainty where there should be certainty. Rahner argues that the resurrection would have no objective meaning without the disciples' faith and without ours and that in his humanity Jesus is the supreme instance of human existence and so becomes the Word of God. By contrast Barth stresses that the resurrection and the incarnation have an objective meaning with or without both the faith of the disciples and ours. The risen Lord calls for and enables faith and hope but one could never say that faith and the resurrection or Christology and anthropology were mutually conditioning factors unless one had somehow confused the power of the resurrection with the faith of the disciples and our own faith once again. That is why Barth insists that for the disciples and for us the resurrection is something that goes "utterly against the grain."[53] In an actual encounter with the risen Lord the disciples were enabled by Christ to believe in him; today the same risen and ascended Christ, through the Holy Spirit, enables us to believe in him. But the movement is from unbelief to belief in Jesus Christ himself and not from belief in our experiences or ideas to Christian faith and hope. The former view reflects Barth's application of the doctrine of justification by faith while the latter view represents another form of self-justification.

CONCLUSION

What then can be learned from this dogmatic exploration? First, I would suggest that where the current Joint Declaration presents a common statement of faith and then presents the Lutheran and Catholic interpretations, it would be more helpful not to have a Lutheran and Catholic interpretation as though they were just different ways of thinking about the same Gospel. What I think can be learned from this presentation is that in fact, at least as it concerns Reformed and Roman Catholic theology in the persons of Barth and Rahner, both theologians use quite similar language with quite different meanings. Somehow that must be taken into account by not allowing the two sides to think that their different explanations are simply variations on the same theme when they clearly are describing quite different realities. Second, I think a genuine common agreement would require a common explanation that would rule out any sort of self-reliance and would illustrate how and why Jesus Christ as the grace of God revealed is necessary for that explanation. But

---

[53] *CD* 3/2, p. 449.

most importantly, any joint declaration should include a statement about theological method, our knowledge of God, the incarnation and the resurrection as starting points for that knowledge of God and therefore of our justification by faith.

What has been accomplished here then is not a negative evaluation of the Joint Declaration. Rather it is to demand that the declaration cannot stand by itself; it must be integrated with a theological method that systematically involves our knowledge of God and the Christological inferences that include the incarnation and resurrection. My ultimate concern then is not to challenge the purpose and sincerity of the Joint Declaration. Rather it is to stress that the Joint Declaration has now set the agenda for what theologians on both sides must do to reconcile what are still differing issues regarding the incarnation, resurrection, knowledge of God and Christology. Unless and until that goal is recognized and pursued, then the Joint Declaration will remain a symbol of a new moment of rapprochement without realizing its full potential that we "all may be one."

10

THE ECCLESIAL SCOPE OF JUSTIFICATION

GEOFFREY WAINWRIGHT

There is a Lutheran dictum that justification is the point at which the church stands or falls: "When this article stands, the Church stands; when it falls, the Church falls" (WA 40/3:352).[1] When Luther called the article of justification "the lord, ruler and judge of every kind of doctrine, which preserves and governs all Christian teaching" (WA 39/1:205), he naturally had in mind for this status and function his own doctrine of justification, which he considered Pauline. Clearly, there is on any reckoning a substantive connection between the doctrine of justification and the doctrine of the church—and therefore also the identification and location of the church. Without tying myself to Luther's doctrines, I wish to explore ways in which variously nuanced understandings of justification play out in ecclesiology, and how, contrariwise, different ecclesiologies affect the doctrine of justification. This exploration will be undertaken in light of modern interconfessional discussions and ecumenical procedures. My hope is to find a scripturally and systematically responsible range of interactions between justification and church that may both aid the reconciliation of historically divided Christendom and also improve our insights into the gospel. These two desired outcomes are, of course, reciprocally related.

WHERE THE CHURCH STANDS OR FALLS?

After setting out the undisputed trinitarian and christological faith in terms close to those of the ancient ecumenical creeds, Luther in the Smalcald Articles of 1537

---

[1] Citations from Luther are made according to the Weimar Edition of his Works, thus: WA volume: page.

moves into soteriology and formulates the "first and chief article" concerning "the office and work of Jesus Christ, or our redemption" thus:

> Jesus Christ, our God and Lord, "was put to death for our trespasses and raised again for our justification" (Rom 4:25). He alone is "the Lamb of God, who takes away the sin of the world" (Jn 1:29). "God has laid upon him the iniquities of us all" (Is 53:6). Moreover, "all have sinned," and "they are justified by his grace as a gift, through the redemption which is in Christ Jesus, by his blood" (Rom 3:23-25).
>
> Inasmuch as this must be believed and cannot be obtained or apprehended by any work, law, or merit, it is clear and certain that such faith alone justifies us, as St. Paul says in Romans 3, "For we hold that a person is justified by faith apart from works of the law" (Rom 3:28), and again, "that he [God] himself is righteous and that he justifies the one who has faith in Jesus" (Rom 3:26).
>
> Nothing in this article can be given up or compromised, even if heaven and earth and things temporal should be destroyed. For as St. Peter says, "There is no other name under heaven given among men by which we must be saved" (Acts 4:12). "And with his stripes we are healed" (Is 53:5).
>
> On this article rests all that we teach and practice against the pope, the devil, and the world. Therefore we must be quite certain and have no doubts about it. Otherwise all is lost, and the pope, the devil, and all our adversaries will gain the victory. (*BSELK*, pp. 415-16; Tappert, p. 292; cf. Kolb-Wengert, p. 301)[2]

Thus the gospel—its ground, its content, its proclamation and its reception—can be summed up as "*solus Christus*," "*sola gratia*," "*sola fide*." "Justification" is the favored category to describe the event in which divine action makes over the redemptive work of Christ to the believer as well as the result of that application for the believer. The Augsburg Confession of 1530 in its fourth article had already said this "concerning justification":

> It is further taught [among us] that we cannot obtain forgiveness of sin or righteousness before God by our own merits, works or satisfactions, but that we receive forgiveness of sin and become righteous before God by grace, for Christ's sake, through

---

[2] Citations from the Lutheran Confessional Documents are made according to *Die Bekenntnisschriften der evangelisch-lutherischen Kirche* (Göttingen: Vandenhoeck & Ruprecht, 1930), abbreviated as *BSELK*; English translations are provided in Theodore G. Tappert ed., *The Book of Concord: The Confessions of the Evangelical Lutheran Church* (Philadelphia: Fortress, 1959), and in Robert Kolb and Timothy J. Wengert eds., *The Book of Concord: The Confessions of the Evangelical Lutheran Church* (Minneapolis: Fortress, 2000). The translations in the text are given on my own responsibility, especially where, for the sake of conciseness, it has been a question of fusing the German and the Latin versions of the original; but I have tried not to depart unnecessarily from Tappert or Kolb-Wengert.

faith, when we believe that Christ suffered for us and that for his sake our sin is forgiven and righteousness and eternal life are given to us. For God will regard and reckon this faith as righteousness, as St. Paul says in Romans 3 and 4. (*BSELK*, p. 56; Tappert, p. 30; cf. Kolb-Wengert, pp. 39-40)

In its very next article (5: *"De ministerio ecclesiastico," "Vom Predigtamt"*), the Augsburg Confession had gone on to recognize that the attainment of such faith depended on the divine institution and efficiency of an evangelical ministry of word and sacrament:

To bring about such faith, God has instituted the office of the ministry, that is, provided the Gospel and the sacraments. Through these, as through means [*Mittel; instrumenta*], he gives the Holy Spirit, who works faith, when and where he pleases, in those who hear the Gospel. (*BSELK*, p. 58; Tappert, p. 31; cf. Kolb-Wengert, p. 40)

And the seventh article could consequently define "the one holy church which will endure for ever" as "the gathering [*congregatio; Versammlung*] of saints [*sanctorum*] or all believers [*aller Gläubigen*] in which the Gospel is purely taught [*docetur*] or preached [*gepredigt*] and the sacraments are administered rightly [*recte*] or according to the Gospel [*lauts des Evangelii*]" (*BSELK*, p. 61; Tappert, p. 33; cf. Kolb-Wengert, p. 42). There we have both the church active and the church passive: on the one hand, the church as the witness to the gospel, the administrator of the means of grace, which are the "instruments" by which the Holy Spirit effects faith; on the other hand, the church as the company of those who in faith respond to the gospel and are being thereby made righteous and holy, receiving the gift of eternal salvation. Having received the gospel, the church must pass it on.

The seventh article of the Augsburg Confession immediately goes on to speak of the unity of the church:

It is sufficient for the true unity of the Christian Church that the Gospel be preached according to a pure understanding of it and that the sacraments be administered in accordance with the divine Word [so the German; the Latin has: it is enough to agree (*consentire*) concerning the preaching of the Gospel and the administration of the sacraments]. It is not necessary for the true unity of the Christian Church that humanly instituted [Latin: traditions or rites or] ceremonies should be observed uniformly in all places. It is as St. Paul says in Ephesians 4, "There is one body and one Spirit, just as you were called to the one hope of your calling, one Lord, one faith, one baptism." (*BSELK*, p. 61; Tappert, p. 32; cf. Kolb-Wengert, p. 42)

Ironically, however, it may appear that it was precisely the question of justification that split the Western church in the sixteenth century. Or, if Luther be interpreted stringently, then the Roman Church "fell" on account of its false doctrine in the matter, and only those who followed Luther's version of the gospel "stood" as the church.

In the twentieth century, the Ecumenical Movement sought to mend the fractures among those communities which—albeit with degrees of plausibility that varied according to one's vantage point—claimed the name of Christ and of church. A leading motive came from an insight derived from the prayer of Jesus in John 17:21, that his disciples might "be one in order that the world may believe": division is not only a practical hindrance to mission but in fact an intrinsic contradiction to a gospel of reconciliation with God whose entailment is reconciliation and love among its beneficiaries. At its best, the Ecumenical Movement did not indulge in compromise over matters of evangelical truth; rather, its advocates and activists were open to the possibility that communities other than their own might have insights into the gospel that they themselves had neglected.

ECCLESIA SANCTA ET PECCATRIX?

If I may speak autobiographically, it was first from Lesslie Newbigin that I gained a sense of the potential of the doctrine of justification both to necessitate and to support the restoration of ecclesial unity. An English Presbyterian who had in 1936 been ordained by the Church of Scotland for missionary work in South India, Newbigin participated there in the final stages of negotiation that brought about, in 1947, the union of Anglicans, Methodists (in the British line), Presbyterians and Congregationalists, and he became one of the first bishops in the newly united Church of South India. The neuralgic point in the creation of the episcopally ordered CSI had to do with the ordained ministry, and Newbigin undertook the defense of the plan and its realization in the face of some on the "catholic" wing of Anglicanism, who were concerned to maintain their historic succession of bishops, as well as some on the "protestant" wing of the Reformed tradition, who were concerned to maintain their historic suspicion of bishops. In *The Reunion of the Church*, Newbigin placed the whole matter within a deeper and wider reflection on ecclesiology, in which the doctrine of justification played a crucial part.[3]

It was Newbigin's contention that the doctrine of justification by faith—"central to the teaching of St. Paul" but usually expounded in an individualistic man-

---

[3] J. E. Lesslie Newbigin, *The Reunion of the Church: A Defence of the South India Scheme* (1948; 2nd ed., London: SCM Press, 1960). Principal page references are given from the second edition.

ner—provides a way for "understanding theologically the issues involved in moving from disunity to unity" (p. xvi). For this to happen, interpretation of the apostle's thought must include his valuation of the fellowship of the church "equally fundamentally" with the faith of the individual believer (p. 97). Newbigin argued that the theological clue to reunion lies in the fact that "the Church has its being from the God who justifies the ungodly, raises the dead, and calls the things that are not as though they were" (p. xvi). The atoning sacrifice of Christ, as God and man, allows the holy and loving Father to forgive and restore sinners when, in and through Christ alone, they return with penitence, gratitude and adoration to him. Faith is "the acceptance of the grip of Christ's pierced hand upon the hand that pierced Him," it is "the soul's humbled and trembling 'Amen' to the revelation of the wrath and the love of the Lord God Omnipotent" (p. 91)—and it "involves a death and rebirth," a "new creation of the creative love of God Himself" and of "Christ's redeeming love" (pp. 91, 93). "This restoration to God *is* justification," and "good works are not its condition but its fruit," for "if God so loved us, we ought also to love one another" (p. 94). Yet this gift and this life we know at present only as a foretaste and earnest: "its power now works in us, but it is not yet fully realized"; the old self is dead and yet its works have still to be mortified; the "saints" are "yet still engaged in the struggle with sin in themselves" (ibid.). Now all this, says Newbigin, is *just as true of the Church as it is of the individual believer*, for the church is "a communion of sinful souls with the Holy God" (p. 100): "The Church is both holy and sinful, as the Christian is both holy and sinful" (p. 101).

That "it is both holy and sinful" is the "fundamental paradox of the Church's being" (p. 85). This Newbigin asserts, even while affirming that "the Gospel only comes to us through the ministries of the Church" (p. 97). Newbigin's recognition is that "we know the Gospel of God's redeeming grace through the fellowship of redeemed men and women" (ibid.), whose "mutual service and mutual dependence" remain in fact spoiled by "faction and division" springing from "carnality, from relying upon man rather than upon God" (p. 100). The "denominational" pride that springs from whatever combination of "historical correctness, evangelistic zeal or ethical achievement" (p. 101) can only be subdued "by the word of the Cross, before which no flesh can glory": "The word of the Cross to the Church is a summons to return in penitence and faith to Him in whom alone is our righteousness, to abandon confidence in everything save His mercy, and to accept and embody in our institutional life that unity with one another which is given to us in Him" (p. 103).

Concretely, Newbigin rejects certain views of the church, its unity and its continuity, and then composes from the valid elements in each rejected position an account that he argues is more faithful to the Scriptures. Admitting the caricatural quality of each description, Newbigin designates one mistaken position Catholic and the other Protestant; their failure—and it is sinful—consists in driving apart what the New Testament correlates, the spiritual and corporeal nature of the church. The "Catholic" position resembles that of St. Paul's opponents in the letter to the Galatians, the "Protestant" that of the Corinthians whom the apostle redresses.

On the one side, "the Epistle to the Galatians was addressed to people who were seeking in the outward rite of incorporation into the Israel of God an additional assurance of their salvation" (p. 44), but "to insist on outward and institutional continuity with 'Israel after the flesh' is to contradict the Church's nature" (p. 39). This occurs when, characteristically, Roman Catholicism has held that belonging to the church entails the acceptance of additional elements that do not belong to the essence of the gospel but rather have accumulated in the course of a corporate history that has known its share of sin. It is impossible to ignore, Newbigin says, that "the Church as a society within history is made up of a multitude of human and sinful wills, and that the fact of incorporation in the Church does not here—*in via*—remove this sinful element" (p. 62), and "when [a church] seeks to find the criterion of its status as a Church in the fact of its continuous institutional existence, it has abandoned the one standing ground that sinners have before God" (p. 66).

On the other side, "the First Epistle to the Corinthians was written to people whose confidence in their own possession of the Spirit was destroying the unity of the Body": it

> was leading them into factions and jealousy, into extreme laxity on moral questions, into abuse of the Lord's Supper, and into the perversion of Christian liberty into a self-destructive anarchy. Factions had developed, each boasting the name of some revered leader and each—apparently—glorying in the possession of particular gifts. They were destroying the temple of God, the Church. They were denying the unity of the Body of Christ. They were misusing the Spirit's greatest gift, which is a love that never boasts, never envies, never seeks its own. The apostle uses of them a word that must have surprised and shocked them. He calls them "carnal." (p. 44)

It is difficult not to see adumbrated there the fissiparity of Protestantism. Each type—the Catholic and the Protestant—"does justice," says Newbigin,

to one aspect of the New Testament teaching about the Church: the first to the fact
that the Church in the New Testament is one visible society, the new Israel, the holy
temple in the Lord, in whom Christians are builded together for a habitation of God
in the Spirit; the second to the fact that the Church in the New Testament is Israel
after the Spirit, created and constituted by the union of its members through the
Spirit in the ascended life of the Lord. Both fail, as it seems, to do justice to the effect
of sin in severing the two things that God has joined, and both, therefore, in fact
deny the existence of the real problem. (p. 25)

An accurate and responsible account of the church—its given unity, its actual
dividedness, and its ecumenical vocation—depends on the proper correlation of
body and Spirit:

When St. Paul calls the Corinthians carnal, his meaning is that they have fallen
away from dependence solely on God and his grace and have begun to depend on
possessions of their own, upon human leaders and the particular spiritual gifts
which each has. Dependence upon the one Holy Spirit would have produced the
visible unity of the one body. Their divisions are the outward sign of their carnality, of the fact that they have fallen back on man. "After the flesh" and "after the
Spirit" are contraries for St. Paul, but the Spirit and the body are correlates. "In
one Spirit were we all baptized into one body," he says (1 Cor 12:13), and when
he urges the Ephesians to guard the unity which they have in the Spirit (Eph 4:3),
he is not (as the following verse so clearly shows) speaking of a spiritual unity
which is distinct from a bodily unity, but precisely of their unity in one visible fellowship which is the gift to them of the one Spirit. . . . The one body is the counterpart of the one Spirit. . . . If the body is divided, it is because Christians are not
spiritual but carnal, not walking after the Spirit, but after the flesh. (pp. 49-50,
51, 54)

That "sin still works in the Church" (p. 48) is a function of the fact that "the
Eschaton has entered history" (p. 73), "yet the end is not yet" (p. 76). As long
as "the mystery of sin" lasts, the historical church is affected by it (p. 96) and,
even as "a colony of heaven," remains under God's judgment until his eternal
purpose is accomplished at Christ's final appearing (cf. pp. 74-77). "If there were
no sin in the Church, there would be perfect congruity between the outward and
the inward" (p. 81). The church comes closer to its proper nature and calling
when, in penitence and faith, its divided parts make a common return to the
Christ who has not ceased to hold them in his grace and when they accordingly
let their broken unity be visibly and tangibly restored (cf. pp. 105, 123). Toward
the end of his life, Newbigin expressed the matter in popular vein in a magazine

article.[4] The church is "a company of forgiven sinners," even "a bunch of escaped convicts"; it is maintained only by "the paradox of grace." Christians "confess belief in 'one holy catholic and apostolic Church.' But the Church is divided, sinful, sectarian, and lazy about its mission. We can only continue to confess this faith because God is mighty and merciful and is able to raise the dead and 'call into existence things that do not exist' (Romans 4:17)." Yet "it is a terrible thing to abuse God's mercy and think we can get away with it"; in particular, a claim to "spiritual" unity must not be used as "an escape from actually sharing a common life." Rather, the pentecostal Spirit is given us "in order that we may be in active truth one, holy, catholic, and apostolic."

It seems that Newbigin's application of the Luther-inspired "*simul iustus et peccator*" to the life and structures of the church was little remarked on at the time he wrote *The Reunion of the Church* in 1947-1948. According to the author's introduction to the book's second edition of 1960 (p. xvi), the one reviewer of the first edition who had mentioned it—perhaps from the "catholic" side of Anglicanism—judged that the argument from justification was "out of place in a book on the Church." Certainly there would be a problem with viewing the church simply as the individual believer writ large, or merely an aggregation of individual believers: such a view would leave out of account all that is traditionally meant by the church as "mother" of our salvation; the church is the locus of salvation, not only in the passive sense as the result of God's saving action, but also in the active sense of bringing faith to birth and nurturing it.

Mitigating the danger of such an omission are some features in Newbigin's ecclesiology that are not necessarily lacking in Luther and Lutheran confessional documents but have surely not figured prominently over certain stretches of later Lutheranism. These features may derive from Newbigin's Reformed background (John Calvin was prepared to cite St. Cyprian's dictum that one cannot have God for one's Father without having the church for one's mother),[5] and perhaps even from his engagement with Anglicanism in the formation of the Church of South

---

[4] Newbigin published a series of short articles on dogmatic topics in *Reform*, the magazine of the United Reformed Church in the United Kingdom. "The Church: A Bunch of Escaped Convicts" appeared in the issue of June 1990.

[5] For Calvin on the Church as mother, see *Institutes* 3.1.1, cited by Newbigin, *Reunion of the Church*, p. 29. Even Luther, in the Large Catechism, can call the church "the mother that begets and bears every Christian through the Word of God" (*BSELK*, p. 655; Tappert, p. 416). See also Carl E. Braaten, *Mother Church: Ecclesiology and Ecumenism* (Minneapolis: Fortress, 1998).

India (he himself acknowledged the influence upon him of A. M. Ramsey's *The Gospel and the Catholic Church*). Thus Newbigin holds a stronger doctrine of sanctification than is characteristic of Lutheranism, and an ecclesiological application might be made of his affirmation that "faith places men in that relation with God for which men were created, and inasmuch as it becomes *the settled direction of their wills* it issues in *the remoulding of their whole lives* in conformity to the holy love of their Creator" (p. 86, emphasis added). Moreover, Newbigin could draw from Calvin and the Reformed confessions a stronger insistence on the importance of order and discipline in the church, and hence the need for a permanent office of pastoral oversight. In Michael Ramsey's book he found "a doctrine of the ministry which did not contravene but rested upon the biblical doctrine of justification by grace through faith": "I saw that the historic episcopate could be gladly accepted as something given by the grace of God to be the means of unity"—provided that it "not be made a *conditio sine qua non* of the fullness of grace."[6]

From his book *The Household of God* (1953) onward, the triad that constantly recurs in encapsulating Newbigin's ecclesiology is that of the church as firstfruits or foretaste, as sign and as instrument of salvation or God's kingdom. Precisely because the church is, by the sheer gift of grace, the *firstfruits*, it can be the *sign* pointing beyond itself to its source (passively by its very existence, and actively by its witness), and an *instrument*, in God's hands, toward the realization of God's purposes. It is possible that such an ecclesiological framework would, in turn, bring fresh insights into the doctrine of justification. Such an exploration was in fact undertaken by the Second Anglican-Roman Catholic International Commission in its "agreed statement" titled *Salvation and the Church* (1986-1987).[7]

SALVATION AND THE CHURCH

The Second Anglican-Roman Catholic International Commission (ARCIC-II) recognized that the historically contentious issue of justification could be "properly treated only within the wider context of the doctrine of salvation as a whole," which in turn necessitated discussion of "the role of the Church in Christ's saving

---

[6] Lesslie Newbigin, *Unfinished Agenda: An Autobiography* (London: SPCK, 1985), p. 75.

[7] *Salvation and the Church: An Agreed Statement by the Second Anglican-Roman Catholic International Commission* (London: Church House Publishing, and Catholic Truth Society, 1987); reprinted in *Growth in Agreement II: Reports and Agreed Statements of Ecumenical Conversations on a World Level 1982-1998*, eds. Jeffrey Gros, Harding Meyer and William G. Rusch (Geneva: WCC Publications; Grand Rapids: Eerdmans, 2000). Cited here by paragraph numbers.

work" (co-chairmen's preface). On the basis of a strongly trinitarian account of God's will and work for human salvation (paragraph 1), the statement offered resolution of such disputed matters as the nature of faith, the place of good works, and the believer's assurance concerning salvation. It ascribed the differences—indeed the confusion—between Anglicans and Roman Catholics on the doctrine of justification to the fact that "the theologians of the Reformation tended to follow the predominant usage of the New Testament, in which the verb *dikaioun* usually means 'to pronounce righteous,' " while "the Catholic theologians, and notably the Council of Trent, tended to follow the usage of patristic and Medieval Latin writers, for whom *iustificare* (the traditional translation of *dikaioun*) signifies 'to make righteous' " (14). With appeal to 1 Corinthians 6:11, the Commission determined that "justification and sanctification are two aspects of the same divine act": "God's grace effects what he declares: his creative word imparts what it imputes. By pronouncing us righteous, God also makes us righteous. He imparts a righteousness which is his and becomes ours" (15). "God's declaration of forgiveness and reconciliation does not leave repentant believers unchanged but establishes with them an intimate and personal relationship. The remission of sins is accompanied by a present renewal, the rebirth to newness of life" (18). "God's declaration that we are accepted because of Christ together with his gift of continual renewal by the indwelling Spirit is the pledge and first installment of the final consummation and the ground of the believer's hope" (16).

Justification and sanctification thrust the believer towards an ecclesial life: "We are freed and enabled to keep the commandments of God by the power of the Holy Spirit, to live faithfully as God's people and to grow in love within the discipline of the community, bringing forth the fruits of the Spirit" (19). "Our liberation commits us to an order of social existence in which the individual finds fulfilment in relationship with others. Thus freedom in Christ does not imply an isolated life, but rather one lived in a community governed by mutual obligations" (20). Mutual obligations both demand and supply mutual support:

> The believer's pilgrimage of faith is lived out with the mutual support of all the people of God. In Christ all the faithful, both living and departed, are bound together in a communion of prayer. The Church is entrusted by the Lord with authority to pronounce forgiveness in his name to those who have fallen into sin and repent. The Church may also help them to a deeper realisation of the mercy of God by asking for practical amends for what has been done amiss. Such penitential disciplines, and other devotional practices, are not in any way intended to put God under obligation.

Rather, they provide a form in which one may more fully embrace the free mercy of God." (22)

Where does that leave us with regard to the "sixteenth-century disagreements" that included "the role of the Church in the process of salvation": "Protestants felt that Catholic teaching and practice had interpreted the mediatorial role of the Church in such a way as to derogate from the place of Christ as 'sole mediator between God and man' (I Tim 2:5). Catholics believed that Protestants were abandoning or at least devaluing the Church's ministry and sacraments" (7). As a "foretaste of God's Kingdom," the church "is itself a *sign* of the Gospel": "In its life the Church signifies God's gracious purpose for his creation and his power to realise this purpose for sinful humanity" (26). "Servant and not master of what it has received," the church is "entrusted with a responsibility of *stewardship*" in respect of the mystery of "the free gift of God"; entirely empowered by the Holy Spirit, the church exercises this responsibility "by proclaiming the Gospel and by its sacramental and pastoral life" (27). As "an *instrument* for the realisation of God's eternal design, the salvation of humanity," the church "is called to be a living expression of the Gospel, evangelised and evangelising, reconciled and reconciling, gathered together and gathering others. In its ministry to the world the church seeks to share with all people the grace by which its own life is created and sustained" (28). As "*sign, steward* and *instrument* of God's design," the church "can be described as *sacrament* of God's saving work"(29).[8]

With regard to justification: the church is a fellowship "where all, because of their equal standing before the Lord, must equally be accepted by one another; a fellowship where, since all are justified by the grace of God, all must learn to do justice to one another (Gal 3:28)" (30). "Those who are justified by grace, and who are sustained in the life of Christ through Word and Sacrament, are liberated from self-centredness and thus empowered to act freely and live at peace with God and one another. The Church, as the community of the justified, is called to embody the good news that forgiveness is a gift to be received from God and shared with others (Matt 6:14-15)" (ibid.).

---

[8]"Foretaste," "sign," "instrument": it may be worth noting that, in the immediately preceding dialogue between the Anglican Communion and the World Alliance of Reformed Churches, the final report *God's Reign and Our Unity* (1984) had been largely drafted by Lesslie Newbigin from the Reformed side. Newbigin's triad had in fact become an ecumenical commonplace by then, and his ecclesiology may even have had some influence on the Second Vatican Council. See Geoffrey Wainwright, *Lesslie Newbigin: A Theological Life* (New York: Oxford University Press, 2000), pp. 123-26, 395, and many indexed entries under "Church, as sign, instrument and first fruits of the Kingdom."

Clearly, there are implications in face of ecclesiastical divisions: "The credibility of the Church's witness is undermined by the sins of its members, the shortcomings of its human institutions, and not least by the scandal of division. The Church is in constant need of repentance and renewal so that it can be more clearly seen for what it is: the one, holy body of Christ" (29). "Only a reconciled and reconciling community, faithful to its Lord, can speak with full integrity to an alienated, divided world, and so be a credible witness to God's saving action in Christ and a foretaste of God's Kingdom" (30). "Nevertheless the Gospel contains the promise that despite all failures the Church will be used by God in the achievement of his purpose: to draw humanity into communion with himself and with one another, so as to share his life, the life of the Holy Trinity" (29). The comfort and confidence that may be drawn from that last affirmation of God's grace are clearly not intended to signal acquiescence in division: "We are agreed," concluded the Commission, that the Christian doctrine of salvation "is not an area where any remaining differences of theological interpretation or ecclesiological emphasis, either within or between our Communions, can justify our continuing separation" (32). It appears, then, that the doctrine of justification, where sufficient agreement exists, should itself constitute an impulse to churchly unity.

Sufficient agreement? The terminology of sign, instrument and firstfruits or foretaste belongs historically in the area of sacramental theology, and its application to the church itself is not likely to pass unnoticed among self-conscious Protestants, particularly when it occurs in a document that avers that, in speaking of salvation, the language of the New Testament knows "no controlling term or concept" (13): "The juridical aspect of justification, while expressing an important facet of the truth, is not the exclusive notion in the light of which all other biblical ideas and images of salvation must be interpreted" (18). It was further noted that "*simul iustus et peccator* is a Lutheran, not a characteristically Anglican, expression. It does not appear in Trent's Decree on Justification" (21, footnote).

Might a Lutheran charge that, if not Lesslie Newbigin coming from the Reformed tradition, then at least the Anglican partners in dialogue with Roman Catholics had betrayed the Reformation doctrine of justification? Eberhard Jüngel probably would. In face of the "catholicizing" implications that he finds in the Joint Declaration on the Doctrine of Justification signed in 1998-1999 between the Lutheran World Federation and the Roman Catholic Church, the Tübingen theologian has made himself the chief defender of the doctrine of justification as it has been held among German Lutherans in the line of Gerhard Ebeling in the second half of the twentieth century. In 1998-1999, Jüngel wrote a long and rapidly composed book, *Justification: The Heart of the Christian Faith* (English translation, 2001; originally *Das Evangelium von der Rechtfertigung des Gottlosen als Zentrum des christlichen Glaubens*). Before that, however, he had in the quincentennial Luther year of 1983 delivered an address to a Spanish conference on "questions in Luther's theology and ecclesiology" under the fiercely interrogative title "The Church as Sacrament?" It is an important piece for our exploration of interactions between justification and ecclesiology.[9]

THE CHURCH AS SACRAMENT?

According to Jüngel, justification by faith is a criterion that must be applied to any and every matter of Christian doctrine and practice. The Pauline teaching, as Jüngel understands it, recognizes, depends on and assures the proper distinction between man and God. It allows God to be God, and man to be man. It is a soteriological criterion, discerned *a posteriori* from the saving work of God and its proclamation in the gospel: God alone acts for our salvation, and we neither need nor can be saved by our works. Human beings may simply receive in faith what God graciously gives them on account of the merits of Christ: forgiveness of sin and eternal life. All this has consequences for the church and its worship. The church is first a *hearing* church, which then preaches what it has heard. Whether by sermon or by baptism or by the supper, the church "portrays" the Word or gospel it receives. The function of the church is to "display" salvation *(Darstellung)*; it cannot in any way "mediate" it as its subject *(representatio)*: Christ alone makes himself present in the creative power of his promissory word to provoke and strengthen faith.

We may wonder whether Jüngel, in his affirmation that God has done *all* for our salvation, recognizes *all* that God has done for our salvation. There is a noticeable pneumatological deficit in Jüngel's soteriology, which ignores what might be drawn in the way of sanctification from such (Pauline) passages as 1 Corinthians 6:19-20 and Galatians 5:22-25. When, in the final pages of his Salamanca lecture, Jüngel transposes the *simul iustus et peccator* into an ecclesiological key, it is again unrelieved by any notion of the indwelling and transforming Holy Spirit (2 Cor 6:16-7:1). Quoting Luther's *"non est tam magna peccatrix ut Christiana ecclesia"* (WA 34/I:276), Jüngel will have nothing of "holy Church" as the source of holiness for her members; rather she is the one who needs continually to pray for her own forgiveness

---

[9]Eberhard Jüngel, "Die Kirche als Sakrament?" in *Zeitschrift für Theologie und Kirche* 80 (1983): 432-57.

and not merely for that of her members who might somehow be distinguished from her. Soteriologically, the church, according to Jüngel, is always "passive," can only "receive"; and if, in its proclamatory witness to salvation, the church "acts," it does so in a *purely* human way—and therefore not in a way that is constitutive to salvation, or even its mediation. But the New Testament warrants our asking: How far may, and indeed must, the church be viewed as the continuing body of Christ in which the Holy Spirit dwells transformatively in such a way that in its very being, as well as in its words and in its gestures, the church becomes an *active bearer* of the gospel by which it is itself constituted?

For Jüngel in 1983, Reformation and Catholic teachings on justification remained so far apart as to be unbridgeable in ecclesiological theory or ecclesial practice. If agreement on justification *could* be attained, however, then on Lutheran terms (and those would presumably, for Jüngel, be the terms of such an agreement) the *immediate* consequence should be ecclesial fellowship, since the church, in both its Lutheran and Catholic forms, would ecclesiologically be "standing" rather than "falling."

Ecumenically, things between Lutherans and Catholics were perhaps not quite as frozen as Jüngel perceived. On the ecclesiological plane, the Second Vatican Council had been prepared to view the church as "*sancta simul et semper purificanda*" (*Lumen Gentium*, 8). That might indicate an openness to considering her as *simul sancta et peccatrix*, at least in the sense in which, soteriologically, even Luther had been willing, in his writing *Against Latomus*, to contemplate a continuing "sanation" of the believer (WA 8:107); and some were beginning to call attention to Luther's late text *On Councils and the Church*, in which a stronger doctrine of progressive sanctification appeared, Luther there speaks not only of Christ's work of "*redemptio*" but also of the Holy Spirit's daily work of "*vivificatio*" and "*sanctificatio*" until "one day we shall become perfectly holy and need no forgiveness" (WA 50:599, 625, 627, 642-43). Quietly, too, a new interpretation of Luther's soteriology was developing among Finnish scholars, in dialogue with Orthodox partners, whereby the notion of "participation" or "union with Christ" was starting to challenge the exclusive dominance of the forensic account engraved in German Lutheranism.[10]

Meanwhile developments were taking place, particularly between Lutherans and Catholics, on the official plane of interconfessional dialogues and ecumenical procedures. In 1994, the international Roman Catholic-Lutheran Joint Commission, in

---

[10]See Carl E. Braaten and Robert W. Jenson, eds., *Union with Christ: The New Finnish Interpretation of Luther* (Grand Rapids: Eerdmans, 1998).

existence since 1967, published a lengthy, and biblically rich, report on "Church and Justification." On October 31, 1999, authoritative representatives of the Lutheran World Federation and the Roman Catholic Church signed a Joint Declaration on the Doctrine of Justification, based on theological studies undertaken by official national commissions of the churches in Germany and the United States as well as on the work of the international commission. The Joint Declaration did not address the ecclesiological theme directly, but it bears considerable ecclesial significance, for in their "official common statement" the signatories affirmed that the mutual anathemas issued on the two sides in the sixteenth century against the assumed positions of the other in respect of the doctrine of justification did not strike the current teaching on the subject as jointly and respectively set out in the Joint Declaration.

CHURCH AND JUSTIFICATION

The 1994 report *Church and Justification*[11] begins with the statement that "Catholics and Lutherans in common believe in the triune God who for Christ's sake justifies sinners by grace through faith and makes them members of the Church in baptism. Thus faith and baptism link justification and the Church; the justified sinner is incorporated into the community of the faithful, the Church, and becomes a member of it. Justification and the Church thus stand in a vital relationship and are fruits of the saving activity of God" (paragraph 1). All teaching concerning justification and the church must therefore respect that "vital relationship" between them and their joint origin in "the saving activity of God"; and the connection between them will be bi-directional: "Everything which is believed and taught regarding the nature of the Church, the means of grace, and the ordained ecclesial ministry must be grounded in the salvation event itself and bear the mark of justification-faith as reception and appropriation of that event. Correspondingly, all that is believed and taught regarding the nature and effects of justification must be understood in the total context of assertions about the Church, the means of grace, and the Church's ordained ministry" (paragraph 168, as a variant formulation of paragraph 2).

The historic controversies between Lutherans and Catholics are summarized thus: "Catholics ask whether the Lutheran understanding of justification does not diminish the reality of the Church; Lutherans ask whether the Catholic understanding of Church does not obscure the Gospel as the doctrine of justification explicates it" (paragraph 166). The church's "indestructible" holiness is "rooted in

---

[11]Reprinted in Gros et al., *Growth in Agreement II*, pp. 485-565. Cited here by paragraph number.

the holiness of the Triune God" (paragraphs 148-49), but both sides see the church also as "standing under God's judgment for the duration of its earthly pilgrimage and depending upon God's daily renewal of grace and fidelity" (paragraph 51), needing to "confess the sin" which is "present in the Church" (ibid., and 147): "The confession of the Church's holiness has always gone hand in hand with the knowledge that the power of evil and sin, although it will not overcome the Church, is nevertheless at work in it" (paragraph 153). Differences between Lutherans and Catholics "emerge in answering the question: Where does the idea of the Church's need for renewal or of its sinfulness find its necessary limit, by reason of the divine pledge that the Church abides in the truth and that error and sin will not overcome it?" (paragraph 157): "From the Lutheran standpoint, serious questions to the Catholic view first present themselves where the God-given indestructible holiness of the Church and God's promise that the Church will abide in the truth are so objectivized in specific ecclesial components that they appear to be exempt from critical questioning. Above all, this Lutheran query is directed at ecclesial offices and decisions that serve people's salvation and sanctification. The question arises when the Holy Spirit's aid is attributed to them in such a way that as such they appear to be immune from the human capacity for error and sinfulness and therefore from needing to be examined" (paragraph 160); contrariwise, "Catholic thinking finds it hard to see why the effects of divine decisiveness should be intrinsically open to criticism and why it is not enough to distinguish between human sinfulness and the divine saving activity in such a way that, although they remain exposed to human inadequacy and sinfulness, God's works are inherently good and cannot be rendered ineffectual" (paragraph 164). The nub of the matter appears to reside in the *simul iustus et peccator*—at least when a Lutheran understanding of it is applied to the church as *simul sancta et peccatrix*.

The matter comes most concretely to a head in questions of church order, both diachronic and synchronic, particularly in so far as agreement on them in theory and in practice is considered necessary for unity. Both sides agree that a divinely instituted, appointed, sustained, and empowered "ministry of reconciliation" (2 Cor 5:18), by its continuity, "effect[s] and testif[ies] to the permanence of the Church" (paragraph 178). On the one side, however, Lutherans are unwilling to allow a particular form of such ministry that may have legitimately emerged in ecclesiastical history but was not directly given by Jesus Christ himself—say "episcopacy"—to "endanger the unconditional nature of the gift of salvation and its reception" (paragraph 192). On the Catholic side, by differentiating between "the subjective and personal consideration of human salvation by reason of God's grace and the objective and ecclesiological view of the Church as recipient and mediator of salvation," Catholics believe they can hold to "the ecclesial necessity of the episcopal office in apostolic succession" without making it "necessary for the salvation of individual persons" and thus without "contradicting the doctrine of justification" (paragraphs 201-2). From a Lutheran viewpoint, lack of an intrinsic connection between (the doctrine of) justification and *a particular form* of doctrinal and disciplinary oversight would make the adoption by Lutherans of that particular form both unnecessary and, therefore, possible; it could even be "important," "profitable" and "desirable" (paragraphs 197, 200)—provided that the Catholic Church "does not contest the point that the Lutheran churches are Church" (paragraph 204). In those conditions, it becomes "possible to advocate theologically the regaining of full communion in the episcopate" (paragraph 204), with both sides agreeing in principle that the understanding and practice of this ministry be subject to the truth of the gospel (paragraphs 205-22) and aimed at the salvation of souls (paragraphs 223-42). One may wonder whether what thus applies to "an episcopate in a historic succession" could also be applied to a universal ministry of unity (cf. paragraph 106 on the claimed and offered primacy of the see of Rome as a task for further dialogue).

Throughout *Church and Justification* the thought moves mainly in the direction of how doctrine on the justification of the individual believer may and should affect ecclesiology. But we were led from the start to also expect feedback from teaching concerning the church in the area of individual soteriology. At one point indeed it is hinted that "the self-understanding of the Roman Catholic Church," dependent on its belief that "God's activity in this world—in its decisive and definitive quality—is incarnational and anticipates the eschaton," is at stake in "the institution of the canonization of saints" which Lutherans question: "The saints perfected by God are not all anonymous but are named by canonization as those who may be addressed as the perfected of God" (paragraphs 160, 163-64). At the very end of the text, Lutherans and Catholics are able to agree, with regard to the final kingdom of God, that "the assembly of the faithful as a community of the perfected is the consummation of the Church in the unveiled, pure presence and reign of God who is love, with whom and in whom all those made perfect have community and are in constant touch with each other [cf. I Cor 15:24-28; Rev 21:3-5]" (paragraph 308); but paragaphs 291-96, on "the communion of saints," venture nothing direct concerning the precise question of justification and its relation to sanctification.[12]

In *Church and Justification* paragraph 167 it is claimed that in the question of the relationship between justification and church, the argument between Lutherans and Catholics "is not primarily a matter of how the saving event can rightly be described and how God communicates his righteousness to the sinner." Somewhat surprisingly, this latter is said to have "no immediate critical implications for ecclesiology": "these emerge only when . . . justification is seen as both centre and criterion of all theology."[13] But *if* (as both sides say) justification is rooted in the salvation event, then surely it *must* at least rank among the criteria of ecclesiality— and it becomes necessary to find *sufficient* agreement on justification to allow it to function as such. Paragraph 2 of *Church and Justification* hints that a modulated agreement may suffice: "A consensus in the doctrine of justification—even if it is nuanced—must prove itself ecclesiologically." The need for an agreement on justification is what led to the elaboration of the Lutheran-Catholic Joint Declaration on

---

[12]These matters have been further discussed more recently in the document of the working group between the German Catholic Bishops' Conference and the authorities of the Evangelical Lutheran Church in Germany, *Communio Sanctorum: Die Kirche als Gemeinschaft der Heiligen* (Paderborn: Bonifatius, and Frankfurt am Main: Lembeck, 2000). "Saints" in the special sense are there defined as "those members of the Church who, by grace and by faith alone, have lived a life of Christian love and the other virtues in exemplary fashion, and whose life-witness has found recognition in the Church after their death" (para. 229). It is said that "Christians turn to God and, in God, to *all* the saints, when they honor one such man or woman among them" (para. 246). We may, I think, suppose that informal recognition of saints across historic confessional boundaries advances the cause of Christian unity, and one might suggest that *official* recognition, from whichever side, would to some degree constitute ecclesial recognition of the "other" communities in which those saints had lived, been nourished and borne their witness.

[13]When justification is made the sole point at which the church stands or falls, it may be that too much weight is being placed on one spot. If justification does not imply classic trinitiarian and christological doctrine (Father, Son and Holy Spirit, one God; the Son, one person known in two natures), it is inadequate for ecclesial recognition; if it does, then let that be made explicit, as in fact *Church and Justification* does (paragraphs 4-7). Or take the Lord's Supper: Faith and Order's Lima text, *Baptism, Eucharist and Ministry*, declared that "the eucharist is essentially the sacrament of the gift which God makes to us in Christ through the power of the Holy Spirit. Every Christian receives this gift of salvation through communion in the body and blood of Christ" (E2). When the text further stated that "the Church confesses Christ's real, living and active presence in the eucharist" (E13), that statement was almost universally welcomed by the churches, but many of them nevertheless responded that such a statement failed to "accommodate" differences among them on the relation between the signs of bread and wine and Christ's presence; and the churches, including Lutherans and Catholics respectively, have often considered a false or inadequate faith concerning that matter a reason for refusal of communion with another community and to the members of that community. What then, more precisely, is the relation between the doctrine of justification and eucharistic belief and practice?

the Doctrine of Justification (1998-1999).[14] This document registers "a consensus on basic truths of the doctrine of justification" (paragraphs 5, 13 and 40), while recognizing that "the remaining differences of language, theological elaboration and emphasis" are "acceptable" (40; cf. 14) and "no longer the occasion for doctrinal condemnations" (5; cf. 13 and 41). The achievement has subsequently been described as a "differentiated consensus."

JOINT DECLARATION ON JUSTIFICATION

Against an Old Testament background, the Catholic-Lutheran Joint Declaration on the Doctrine of Justification sets out the "biblical message of justification" (paragraphs 8-12) in strongly Pauline terms, while recognizing both the presence of "righteousness" and "justification" in other New Testament writings (Mt 5:10; 6:33; 21:32; Lk 18:10-14; Jn 16:8-11; Acts 13:39; Heb 5:3; 10:37-38; Jas 2:14-26; 1 Jn 1:8-10) and the fact that Paul himself uses other language also to describe the gift of salvation, such as "for freedom Christ has set us free" (Gal 5:1-13; cf. Rom 6:7), "reconciled to God" (2 Cor 5:18-21; cf. Rom 5:11), "peace with God" (Rom 5:1), "new creation" (2 Cor 5:17), "alive to God in Christ Jesus" (Rom 6:11, 23), "sanctified in Christ Jesus" (1 Cor 1:2, 30; 2 Cor 1:1). The Pauline teaching on justification is expounded chiefly on the basis of Romans, Galatians, and 1 and 2 Corinthians. Philippians 2:12-13 on "working out your own salvation" receives a mention; but, given our interests, it is noteworthy—and disappointing—that the soteriologically and ecclesiologically important letters to the Colossians and to the Ephesians are nowhere cited.

Its framers having "together listened to the good news proclaimed in holy scripture" (14), the Joint Declaration in paragraphs 15-17 formulates "the common understanding of justification" thus:

15. In faith we together hold the conviction that justification is the work of the triune God. The Father sent his Son into the world to save sinners. The foundation and presupposition of justification is the incarnation, death, and resurrection of Christ. Justification thus means that Christ himself is our righteousness, in which we share through the Holy Spirit in accord with the will of the Father. Together we confess: By grace alone, in faith in Christ's saving work and not because of any merit on our part, we are accepted by God and receive the Holy Spirit, who renews our hearts while equipping and calling us to good works.

---

[14] Reprinted in Gros et al., *Growth in Agreement II,* pp. 566-82.

16. All people are called by God to salvation in Christ. Through Christ alone are we justified, when we receive this salvation in faith. Faith is itself God's gift through the Holy Spirit who works through word and sacrament in the community of believers and who, at the same time, leads believers into that renewal of life which God will bring to completion in eternal life.

17. We also share the conviction that the message of justification directs us in a special way towards the heart of the New Testament witness to God's saving action in Christ: it tells us that as sinners our new life is solely due to the forgiving and renewing mercy that God imparts as a gift and we receive in faith, and never can merit in any way.

The Joint Declaration then "explicates" the "common understanding of justification" with reference to seven implicates or aspects of the doctrine that have historically been controversial between Lutherans and Catholics: "human powerlessness and sin in relation to justification"; "justification as forgiveness of sins and making righteous"; "justification by faith and through grace"; "the justified as sinner"; "law and gospel"; "assurance of salvation"; "the good works of the justified." In each case a "common confession" is followed by distinct paragraphs in which Lutherans and Catholics respectively restate their characteristic positions in such ways as to meet the doubts or fears of their partners concerning them and be recognized as "compatible" with the "consensus in the basic truths" concerning the doctrine of justification (14).

The Catholic and Lutheran signatories of the Joint Declaration recognize that the consensus must now "prove itself" in the "life and teachings of our churches." Ecclesiology in its various aspects figures prominently among the topics in need of "further clarification" in order to prolong "this decisive step forward on the way to overcome the division of the Church" and attain the "visible unity which is Christ's will" (44), namely: "the relationship between the word of God and church doctrine," "ecclesial authority, church unity, ministry, the sacraments, and the relation between justification and social ethics" (43).

Clearly, much remains to be done, and Catholics and Lutherans are ready to have others join them. In response to a congratulatory message from the World Methodist Council, the Lutheran World Federation and the Pontifical Council for Promoting Christian Unity invited Methodists to explore a process by which they, too, could become associated with the achievement so far and the work still to be accomplished. A consultation in 2001 led to the idea of a Methodist Statement by which the Methodists would endorse the consensus and enter into the commitment to further clarification and practical results. Such a statement is being drafted, with the aim of its adoption in 2006. Methodists would affirm the basic agreement on justification and regard the specific characteristics of Catholics and Lutherans on the question as insufficient grounds for continuing division, while having the characteristic "profile" of their own soteriology similarly recognized by Lutherans and Catholics in regard to the seven historically contentious points.[15]

A METHODIST CONTRIBUTION?

In my estimation as a Methodist, the following four features of Methodist soteriology could be particularly relevant to the connections between justification and Church:

I. *Prevenient and cooperating grace.* According to John Wesley's Sermon 85 on Philippians 2:12-13, "On Working Out Our Own Salvation," the destructive effects of the Fall are countered by the universal availability of prevenient grace, which is responsible for even the first "motion" toward "deliverance from a blind, unfeeling heart, quite insensible of God and the things of God" (2.1; 3.3-4);[16] and the sanctifying work of God in the believer, once a person has come to faith, enables and requires the believer's continuing cooperation with God: "First, God works; therefore you *can* work. Second, God works; therefore you *must* work" (3.2, and 5-8).[17] Now Wesley also held that "the end [purpose] of all ecclesiastical order" is "to

---

[15]I should reveal that I have been commissioned by the World Methodist Council, together with Bishop Walter Klaiber of Germany, as chief drafters on the Methodist side. There is a background in Methodist discussions on justification with Lutherans and with Catholics respectively. In 1984, the dialogue between the World Methodist Council and the Lutheran World Federation produced the report, "The Church: Community of Grace" (see Gros et al., *Growth in Agreement II*, pp. 200-218), which supplied the framework for official action in 1987 by the Lutheran and Methodist Churches in Germany to enter into fellowship of word and table (see *Vom Dialog zur Kanzel- und Abendmahlsgemeinschaft* [Hannover: Lutherisches Verlagshaus, and Stuttgart: Christliches Verlagshaus, 1987]), and later in Austria, Sweden and Norway. In 1988, the English Roman Catholic-Methodist Committee issued "Justification—A Consensus Statement," which was revised and expanded in 1991; see *One in Christ* 24 (1988): 270-73, and 28 (1992): 87-91. These latter texts have not been officially adopted by the respective churches, and indeed a later paper recognizes that there is a long way to go before a positive answer can be returned to the question "Can the Roman Catholic and Methodist Churches be reconciled?"; see *One in Christ* 29 (1993): 165-69.

[16]John Wesley, *Works of John Wesley*, vol. 3, ed. Albert C. Outler (Nashville: Abingdon, 1986), pp. 203-4, 207.

[17]Ibid., pp. 206, 207-9.

bring souls from the power of Satan to God, and to build them up in His fear and love."[18] It seems, then, that the church is not only the gathered *result* of God's grace, nor even also the *witness* to God's grace, but indeed by its grace-enabled ministries a grace-conveying *channel* of salvation from its first appropriation to its final consummation. The existence and presence of the church before and around believers thus safeguards against any pelagian or even semi-pelagian understanding of faith as an unaided work. The more the church is, by the Holy Spirit, transparent to Christ in its unity and holiness, the more clearly and effectively it will bear that testimony and function as that conduit.[19]

   2. *The nature of faith.* Lutheran expositions of justification have sometimes so exclusively stressed divine grace as apparently to turn the "*sola fide*" into "*sine fide*," "without faith altogether" rather than "by faith alone"; happily, that view is repudiated in Joint Declaration, no. 21, where Lutherans "do not deny that believers are fully involved personally in their faith." Wesley teaches that the grace of God "assists" but does not "force" the human response, the "happy choice" (Sermon 63, "The General Spread of the Gospel," 2).[20] He speaks often of "living faith," which is always a "faith that works by love" (cf. Gal 5:6); Catholics and Lutherans are able to say together that "justifying faith . . . includes . . . love" and is "active" in it (Joint Declaration, no. 25). It is noteworthy that in its Decree on Justification, the Council of Trent has in view, explicitly from chapter 5, the case of "adults," who "freely *(libere)*" turn to God in penitence, hope and trust (chapter 6), and "willingly accept the grace *(per voluntariam susceptionem gratiae)*" (chapter 7); this seems to be what John Wesley also has in mind in his principal sermons on "Justification by Faith" (Sermon 5) and "The Scripture Way of Salvation" (Sermon 43).

   Ecclesiologically, Wesley's understanding of justification tends to favor a "free

---

[18]Letter of June 25, 1746, to "John Smith," in *Works of John Wesley*, vol. 26, ed. Frank Baker (Oxford: Clarendon, 1981), p. 206; see Geoffrey Wainwright, *Methodists in Dialogue* (Nashville: Abingdon, 1995), pp. 73-87, 299-301 ("The End of All Ecclesiastical Order"), reprinted from *One in Christ* 27 (1991): 33-48.

[19]The British Methodist Conference's 1937 official statement on *The Nature of the Christian Church according to the Teaching of the Methodists* declares, "The Church today is gathered for the most part in certain denominations or 'churches.' These form but a partial and imperfect embodiment of the New Testament ideal. . . . It is their duty to make common cause in the search for the perfect expression of that unity and holiness which in Christ are already theirs" (London: Methodist Publishing House, 1937, p. 39).

[20]John Wesley, *Works of John Wesley*, vol. 2, ed. Albert C. Outler (Nashville: Abingdon, 1985), p. 489.

church" concept of the church, which the Methodist *Neutestamentler* Walter Klaiber sees as one of the two poles in a Pauline vision of the matter: "That justification of the godless is justification of the believer marks the poles of the tension in which the Church must take shape. This must prevent the folk church from appealing to the *justificatio impii* in order to justify a 'religion without decision'; it must also warn the free church against allowing the congregation of believers to become an 'association of the religiously qualified.' "[21] It may well be that Methodism, by its "free church" understanding and experience, can help to maintain the Pauline dialectic in a way that neither Lutherans nor (for different reasons) Catholics alone have been able to do in their historically dominant forms as "folk church."[22]

3. Assurance of faith and salvation. John Wesley held that it was the "common privilege" of believers to be given a divine assurance of present salvation; it was not an unconditional guarantee but lasted only as long as the divine promises continued to be freely received in faith. In the context of the international Methodist-Roman Catholic dialogue, I suggested what might result from the transposition of this individual assurance to the faith of the church as corporately believed and taught.[23] In Wesleyan categories, the assurance of ecclesial faith:

(i) would be a gift from God by the Holy Spirit;

(ii) would express a lived and living experience of the redeeming work of God in Christ;

(iii) would result in a confession of faith in which the *fides quâ creditur* corresponded to the *fides quae creditur*, and vice versa;

(iv) would focus on truths "of the last [ultimate] importance," entering "into the very heart of Christianity";

(v) would be the "common privilege" of the Church in its everyday living, teaching, preaching and mission;

---

[21] Walter Klaiber, *Rechtfertigung und Gemeinde: Eine Untersuchung zum paulinischen Kirchenverständnis* (Göttingen: Vandenhoeck & Ruprecht, 1982), p. 265. In a brief closure (pp. 265-68), Klaiber draws some contemporary conclusions from his exegetical study.

[22] See Geoffrey Wainwright, *Methodists in Dialogue*, pp. 109-14, 306-11 ("Ecclesiological Tendencies in Luther and Wesley"), translated from "Ekklesiologische Ansätze bei Luther und bei Wesley," in *Ökumenische Erschliessung Martin Luthers*, eds. P. Manns and H. Meyer (Paderborn: Bonifatius, and Frankfurt am Main: Otto Lembeck, 1983), pp. 173-83.

[23] Geoffrey Wainwright, *Methodists in Dialogue*, pp. 57-71, 295-99 ("The Assurance of Faith: Methodists and Infallibility"). My membership of the Joint Commission for Dialogue between the Roman Catholic Church and the World Methodist Council dates from 1983; since 1986 I have been its co-chairman on the Methodist side.

(vi) would concern the rightness of the Church's present faith and proclamation at a given time (there would be no guarantee in face of a loss of living relationship to God, whether past or future).[24]

The Methodist-Catholic joint commission, in its Nairobi Report of 1986, *Towards a Statement on the Church,* considered this suggestion worth exploring:

74. An approach towards convergence in thinking about infallibility may perhaps be reached by considering the Methodist doctrine of assurance. It is the typical Methodist teaching that believers can receive from the Holy Spirit an assurance of their redemption through the atoning death of Christ and can be guided by the Spirit who enables them to cry "Abba, Father" in the way of holiness to future glory.

75. Starting from Wesley's claim that the evidence for what God has done and is doing for our salvation, as described above, can be "heightened to exclude all doubt," Methodists might ask whether the Church, like individuals, might by the working of the Holy Spirit receive as a gift from God in its living, teaching, preaching and mission, an assurance concerning its grasp of the fundamental doctrines of the faith such as to exclude all doubt, and whether the teaching ministry of the Church has a special and divinely guided part to play in this. In any case, Catholics and Methodists are agreed on the need for an authoritative way of being sure, beyond doubt, concerning God's action insofar as it is crucial for our salvation.[25]

On the neuralgic question of "papal primacy" and a "universal ministry of unity" in the doctrinal and pastoral spheres, the language of the Methodists in the Nairobi Report floats between necessity, possibility and suitability:

58. Methodists accept that whatever is properly required for the unity of the whole of Christ's Church must by that very fact be God's will for his Church. A universal primacy might well serve as focus of, and ministry for, the unity of the whole Church.

62. It would not be inconceivable that at some future date in a restored unity, Roman Catholic and Methodist bishops might be linked in one episcopal college, and that the whole body would recognize some kind of effective leadership in the bishop of Rome. In that case Methodists might justify such an acceptance on different grounds from those that now prevail in the Roman Catholic Church.

---

[24]Wainwright, *Methodists in Dialogue,* pp. 62-63.
[25]Gros et al., *Growth in Agreement II,* p. 596.

72. Methodists always accept what can be clearly shown to be in agreement with the scriptures. The final judge of this agreement must be the assent of the whole people of God.[26]

In response to Pope John Paul II's invitation, made in his 1995 encyclical *Ut Unum Sint*, to a "patient and fraternal dialogue" on this matter, I proposed the following practical exploration:

> My respectful suggestion is that the Pope should invite those Christian communities which he regards as being in real, if imperfect, communion with the Roman Catholic Church to appoint representatives to cooperate with him and his appointees in formulating a statement expressive of the Gospel to be preached to the world today. Thus the theme of the "fraternal dialogue" which John Paul II envisaged would shift from the *theory* of the pastoral and doctrinal office to the *substance* of what is believed and preached. And the very *exercise* of elaborating a statement of faith might—by the process of its launching, its execution, its resultant form, its publication, and its reception—illuminate the question of "a ministry that presides in truth and love." *Solvitur ambulando.*[27]

4. Sanctification and perfection. Wesley taught that sanctification, as the work that God does *in* us, begins simultaneously with the work that God does *for* us in forgiving us; the relational change entails a real change.[28] Sanctification presses towards the completion of "entire sanctification" or "perfection" (Phil 3:12-14); grace left idle may become forfeit (Mt 13:12).[29] Christian perfection is not the absolute perfection that belongs to God alone, nor does it, in this life, exclude the frailty and ignorance that linger from the Fall; positively, it consists in the single-

---

[26]Ibid., pp. 593, 594, 595.

[27]The suggestion was first made at a consultation in Rome in 1997; see Geoffrey Wainwright, " 'The Gift Which He on One Bestows, We All Delight to Prove': A Possible Methodist Approach to a Ministry of Primacy in the Circulation of Truth and Love" in *Petrine Ministry and the Unity of the Church*, ed. James F. Puglisi (Collegeville, Minn.: Liturgical Press, 1999), pp. 59-82; here p. 82.

[28]John Wesley, Sermon 43, "The Scripture Way of Salvation," I.3-4, in *Works*, vol. 2, ed. Albert C. Outler (Nashville: Abingdon, 1985), pp. 157-58; Sermon 85, "On Working out Our Own Salvation," II.1, in *Works*, vol. 3, ed. Albert C. Outler (Nashville: Abingdon, 1986), pp. 202-3. Wesleyan eyes might view the Joint Declaration as bringing together the respective strengths of Lutherans and Catholics and correcting their respective weaknesses; see Wesley's Sermon 107, "On God's Vineyard," I.5, in *Works*, vol. 3, ed. Albert C. Outler (Nashville: Abingdon, 1986), pp. 505-6.

[29]See Wesley's Sermon 85, "On Working Out Our Own Salvation," III.7, in *Works*, vol. 3, ed. Albert C. Outler (Nashville: Abingdon, 1986), pp. 208-9.

hearted love of God and neighbor (Mt 5:43-48; 22:34-40).[30] Such love clearly has ecclesial resonances: it builds up the unity of the body of Christ. Jesus prayed that his disciples and followers might be "perfected into one" (Jn 17:23).[31] Their unity will be a unity in the truth (Jn 17:17-19), into whose fullness the Holy Spirit leads (Jn 16:13). The more that happens, and the more visible the fruits that grow from God's love outpoured by the Holy Spirit into believers' hearts (Rom 5:5; Gal 5:22-25), the more credible will be the witness of Christians and the church to Christ and his divine mission: *ut unum sint, ut mundus credat!*

CONCLUSION

In summary and conclusion: Reflection on the ecclesial scope of justification reveals a series of controversial tensions which, if ecumenically accepted and contained, could make for an understanding of the gospel that was both sharper and more comprehensive, and this in turn could open the way to greater unity among Christians and their communities. Three such polarities may be highlighted.

The first concerns the question of the priority between the individual believer and the church. When, with the Protestant tendency, the believer as *simul iustus et peccator* is taken as the starting point, the ecclesiological application of the doctrine of justification allows sin to be honestly recognized in the church, though not acquiesced in. The move in this direction serves to stimulate ecclesial repentance and renewal, two features of the gospel that are needed for the overcoming of divisions and the attainment of unity. When, with the Catholic tendency, the church is taken as the starting point, the ecclesial framework of justification actually helps to make apparent the encompassing character of divine grace which, through the instrumentality of word and sacrament, arouses and sustains faith;

---

[30]See Wesley's Sermon 40, "Christian Perfection," in *Works*, ed. Outler, 2:96-124. For a retrospective compendium of Wesley's teaching, see "A Plain Account of Christian Perfection" (1767), in *Works of John Wesley*, ed. Thomas Jackson, 3rd ed. (London: Wesleyan Methodist Conference Office, 1872), 2:366-446.

[31]The nineteenth-century Wesleyan ecclesiologist Benjamin Gregory, in his study of *The Holy Catholic Church, the Communion of Saints* (London: Wesleyan Methodist Conference Office, 1873), made the most of this text and of Ephesians 4:11-16 to emphasize the dynamic connection between the unity and the sanctity of the *"una sancta"* in the truth. "The unity of the Church and the spirituality of the Church must progress [together] equably," he wrote, "and the consummation of the one is the consummation of the other" (p. 187). Further, "To despair of the holiness of the Church is to despair of the outward unification of the Church; and to despair of the holiness and unification of the Church is to despair of the regeneration and reconciliation of the human race. The maintenance of a discipline maternal yet effective is the direct way to the ultimate union and universal inclusiveness of the Church, and the accomplishment of its benign and holy mission in the world" (ibid.).

and it is only by faithful attendance on God's grace that the reconciliation of divided Christians in the truth of the gospel will take place.

Second, all agree that the gospel must first be received, but there are historic tensions over the sense in which that initial "passivity" is to be accompanied or followed by activity on the part of the believer and the church. Ecclesiologically transposed, the "differentiated consensus" achieved between Lutherans and Catholics in the Joint Declaration on the Doctrine of Justification would allow for differences of emphasis in ecclesial understanding and practice within a common recognition that none of the church's "activity"—whether as witness or as mediator of salvation—was meritorious but, positively put, a grace-enabled service of God and the human neighbor, aimed at "bringing souls from the power of Satan to God, and building them up in His fear and love."

Third, historic tensions over the relation between imputed and imparted righteousness, or between justification and sanctification, reflect the character of the church on pilgrimage between what Christ has achieved once and for all for our salvation and what we shall fully and finally enjoy in the kingdom of God. Holiness is both a gift and a task; as a gift, it is to be both received thankfully and prayed for, and as a task it is to be striven after. Similarly with unity among Christians. Indeed there is an intrinsic connection between unity and holiness, for both are the work of the Holy Spirit, whose firstfruits we have and are, and the first of whose fruit is love. And so we may heed a couple of verses from the twelfth chapter of Romans, into which the apostle packs much good ecumenical advice: "Let your love be genuine; hate what is evil, hold fast to what is good; love one another with brotherly affection; outdo one another in showing honor" (Rom 12:9-10).

It may be that the subtext underlying all these reflections has been the challenge resident in Schleiermacher's perception, in section 24 of the *Glaubenslehre*, that "Protestantism makes the individual's relation to the Church dependent on his relation to Christ, while Catholicism contrariwise makes the individual's relation to Christ dependent on his relation to the Church."[32] To my mind, however, Schleiermacher's stark "antithesis" is simplistic, and the real interest lies in the nuances of the matter. It is these that permit the hope for an ecumenical accommodation that embraces tensions without acquiescing in a disjunction that would necessitate a permanent division.

---

[32]F. D. E. Schleiermacher, *The Christian Faith*, ed. and trans. H. R. Mackintosh and J. S. Stewart (Edinburgh: T & T Clark, 1928), p. 103.

CONTRIBUTORS

D. A. Carson is Research Professor of New Testament at Trinity Evangelical Divinity School. Among the more than forty books he has written or edited, two editorial projects are especially relevant to this book. *Right with God: Justification in the Bible and the World* contains essays prepared in a consultation for the World Evangelical Fellowship. Most recently, he has coedited the two-volume *Justification and Variegated Nomism: A Fresh Appraisal of Paul and Second Temple Judaism.*

Kenneth J. Collins is Professor of Historical Theology and Wesley Studies at Asbury Theological Seminary in Kentucky. He has published multiple books on John Wesley, including *The Scripture Way of Salvation: The Heart of John Wesley's Theology* and *John Wesley: A Theological Journey.* He is currently working on a book in the area of American evangelism.

Robert H. Gundry is Scholar in Residence at Westmont College. He has written significant commentaries on Matthew and Mark, plus the recent *Jesus the Word According to John the Sectarian.* On justification he penned a conversation-starting essay in *Books & Culture* titled "Why I Didn't Endorse 'The Gospel of Jesus Christ: An Evangelical Celebration' ... Even Though I Wasn't Asked To."

Robert Kolb is Mission Professor of Systematic Theology and Director of the Institute for Mission Studies at Concordia Seminary in St. Louis. He has written numerous works on Luther and Lutherans, and helped to edit *The Book of Concord: The Confessions of the Evangelical Lutheran Church* in its new edition.

Anthony N. S. Lane is Director of Research and Professor of Historical Theology at London School of Theology (formerly the London Bible College). He has published significant work on John Calvin, while his recent book on justification is entitled *Justification by Faith in Catholic-Protestant Dialogue.*

Bruce L. McCormack is the Frederick and Margaret L. Weyerhaeuser Professor of Systematic Theology at Princeton Theological Seminary and author of the revolutionary *Karl Barth's Critically Realistic Dialectical Theology,* in addition to significant journal articles on the Reformed doctrine of salvation.

Paul D. Molnar is Professor of Systematic Theology at St. John's University. He is the author of a major new contribution to Trinitarian theology, *Divine Freedom and the Doctrine of the Immanent Trinity*. He is currently working on a monograph concerning the relationship of the resurrection and the incarnation in contemporary theology.

Mark A. Seifrid is Professor of New Testament Interpretation at The Southern Baptist Theological Seminary and has written extensively on righteousness in biblical theology, notably the volumes *Christ Our Righteousness* and *Justification by Faith*, and has coedited (with D. A. Carson and Peter O'Brien) the two-volume *Justification and Variegated Nomism: A Fresh Appraisal of Paul and Second Temple Judaism*.

Geoffrey Wainwright is Cushman Chair of Christian Theology at the Divinity School of Duke University. His own systematic theology is entitled *Doxology*. He has also written a biography of Lesslie Newbigin and has long been active in ecumenical theological dialogue with a robust commitment to trinitarian orthodoxy.

Philip G. Ziegler is Assistant Professor of Theology at the Atlantic School of Theology in Halifax, Nova Scotia. He is noted for introducing the work of the East German theologian Wolf Krötke to the English-speaking world.